Diary of a
Foreign Minister

BOB CARR

Diary of a
Foreign
Minister

NEWSOUTH

John,
all my
best
Bob
Carr

April
2014

As always, to H, my co-conspirator.

A NewSouth book

Published by
NewSouth Publishing
University of New South Wales Press Ltd
University of New South Wales
Sydney NSW 2052
AUSTRALIA
newsouthpublishing.com

© Bob Carr 2014
First published 2014

10 9 8 7 6 5 4 3 2 1

National Library of Australia Cataloguing-in-Publication entry
Author: Carr, Bob, 1947– author.
Title: Diary of a foreign minister/Bob Carr.
ISBN: 9781742234175(hardback)
       9781742241708(ePub)
       9781742246741(ePDF)
Subjects: Carr, Bob, 1947 – Diaries.
       Foreign ministers – Australia – Biography.
       Politicians – Australia – Biography.
       Australia – Politics and government.
       Australia – Foreign relations.
Dewey Number: 327.940092

Design Josephine Pajor-Markus
Cover design Xou Creative
Front cover image Photograph by Lisa Maree Williams, Getty Images
Back cover images Photographs by Mark Graham, Trevor Collens and Yuri Gripas;
<www.dfat.gov.au>
Printer Griffin Press

There comes a time when you

realise that everything is a dream,

and only those things preserved in writing

have any possibility of being real.

– James Salter, *All That Is* (2013)

PREFACE

It's the end of the drama. The results are in.

There's a single character standing on the stage.

It's 1993, Helena and I are in London at a performance by the National Theatre of David Hare's *The Absence of War*. Watching, spellbound. After all, I'm Opposition Leader in the New South Wales parliament and this is a play about a Labour opposition leader in the UK, based on Neil Kinnock. And his fate.

He's lost the election. He gives up the leadership and now he speaks direct to the audience, reflecting on the bruising experience:

> I found myself asking a question which will always haunt us
> and to which no easy answer appears.
>
> Is this history? Is everything history? Could we have done
> more? Was it possible? And how shall we know?

The stage directions require the company to remain frozen as the lights fade and the music swells.

These are questions anyone can ask, at the end.

Was it history?

Is everything?

Could we have done more?

***

Six years after I retired as Premier of New South Wales, Sam Dastyari, then secretary of the New South Wales branch of the Australian Labor Party, and his assistant secretary, Chris Minns, came into my office and said, 'We have an idea.' It was an idea suggested by a new planetary alignment, something unusual: a vacancy for Foreign Minister *and* a vacancy for Labor senator from

New South Wales. Here was a possibility I could return to politics as Australia's Foreign Minister, although with the high likelihood I would hold the job for a mere eighteen months. Another Prime Minister might have shrunk from inviting a former Premier aboard. Julia Gillard did not.

I see life as a learning experience and it would be hard – very hard – to deny oneself this. I got on board, signing up for the duration.

Six months later, in September 2012 during Leaders Week at the United Nations, advisers and I walked up First Avenue towards the UN headquarters at One United Nations Plaza. Autumn was settling. There were scudding clouds, wind in the air. Facing the UN, blocked off behind a massive police presence, was a big demonstration chanting under the direction of a leader with a megaphone.

His voice was high-pitched, the crowd's response in rhythm, the total effect mesmeric:

Shame, shame, Ban Ki-moon.
Shame on the nations of the world.

The phrase 'the nations of the world' lodged in my prefrontal cortex like a shard of glass. The peoples of our battered planet are organised into nations. Foreign policy is to see that these – 'the nations of the world' – avoid going to war and manage some level of cooperation.

'The nations of the world.'

What's foreign policy, if not the conduct of all this?

In meetings at the UN I will seek the support of a majority of the nations of the world to place Australia on the Security Council for a two-year term. I will talk to them all: the old friends and our obvious partners as well as the small island states, the nations of the Caribbean, the nations of the Pacific and of the African world. Their response will be shaped by how they see Australia's international personality.

There is a catastrophic descent into civil war in Syria and many of its twenty-two million people are suffering. Yet there seems no available mechanism for giving expression to the principle of Responsibility to Protect, endorsed here at the UN General Assembly in 2005.

Beyond the UN agenda – the multilateral arena – there is a debate within Australia's leadership about our approaches to China and the United States. Three former Australian prime ministers – Fraser, Hawke and Keating – and some business figures and academic commentators say that in 2011 Australia tilted away from China. This is part of a wider discussion among nations in the region about how we will adjust to the phenomenon of the age: the re-emergence of China. And this re-emergence of China is part of a larger narrative about the shift of economic clout and strategic weight to Asia.

In Canberra the supporters of Kevin Rudd are unlikely to accept his departure from the cabinet that resulted in me taking his post and becoming Foreign Minister. Behind the tensions between him and Julia Gillard there lies a larger anxiety about the competence of a government lacking a majority in the House of Representatives. To me, party ethos and leadership quality are at the core. Beyond this sits an even more fundamental question: whether the Australian Labor Party, like other social democratic parties, is in long-term structural decline.

We enter the foyer of the General Assembly. Foreign ministers followed by flocks of self-important officials, cutting across the public space like migratory waterfowl, as we convene – the nations of the world. Due to a political fluke I'm now part of this fraternity, the Foreign Ministers' Club, which consumes such time and energy and may sometimes yield results.

In total it will be eighteen months to test what propositions hold, what fall by the wayside.

And to decide whether it was history.

MONDAY, APRIL 9, 2012
Sydney to New York

Okay, in my next life I return as a bon vivant, gourmet and imbiber.

Breakfast of croissants lathered with tangy French butter and bitter marmalade; outsize cups of caramel-coloured black coffee; fried eggs and burnt-to-a-crisp bacon. Buoyed through the day with heavily watered whisky and a pint of champagne, in the Churchillian manner. Getting off a train or plane, exhaling fumes of Pol Roger, waving around a cigar dunked in cognac. A bowler hat held aloft a silver-topped cane. Flushed and merry.

A pre-lunch gin while a bottle from Côte de Nuits breathes on a table, and the crisp tablecloth being set with asparagus in hollandaise sauce and snails with garlic and butter; the beef bourguignon whirled in potatoes sautéed in duck fat; even a plate of snout, udders, brains and tongue.

Followed by profiteroles.

Bismarck ate and drank like this.

A flamboyant cholesterol level. Rolls of blubber stretching my belt. My cardiac apparatus straining.

Dead at seventy. Big deal.

This is my fantasy, slumped on the plane flying QF107 Sydney to New York.

A tediously long journey, first, to campaign in the UN for a seat on the Security Council. Then fly to Brussels for a conference of coalition partners in Afghanistan. After that divert to Malta to clinch their vote in that UN ballot and return to Washington for my first meeting with Secretary of State Clinton. The distance cruel, the jetlag manic.

I decline bread, alcohol, desserts; half doze over volumes of briefing notes.

In my next life ...

TUESDAY, APRIL 10, 2012
New York

At our first meeting – departmental head and new minister –
Dennis Richardson's advice had been unequivocal: my first overseas trip as Foreign Minister could not be China; it had to be the
US. 'Going to China first is just not worth the fuss.' I presume he
meant it would require too much explanation, too much messaging, even pressure for overcompensation down the track.

I was happy to accept his advice, apart from a trip to New Zea-
land, which I visited even before I was sworn in, and a visit to the
ASEAN world – Cambodia, Vietnam and Singapore – between
March 24 and March 31.

Now in New York we stay with our Permanent Representative – that is, our UN Ambassador – Gary Quinlan, at the Beekman Place apartment that has been residence for our ambassadors
since the early 1950s. Beekman Place comprises two blocks of
townhouses and apartment buildings. Tree-shaded and secluded,
it could be a stage set for a comedy about upper-class life in Manhattan. The swanky 16-storey building was completed in 1930
in the same era as the Pierre Hotel and the Empire State Building, a brick building from the grand era of Manhattan construction. It has a platoon of doormen on duty whenever we host a
cocktail party. Prehistoric Rockefellers are said to be stranded on
some of the upper floors. It overlooks the East River – Roosevelt
Island in full view – and is a block from the UN. It's a two-floor
apartment, gracious and roomy, but, in our corner room upstairs,
it is marred by nagging traffic noise. Just the thing to really agi-
tate jetlagged nerves, and no species of jetlag competes with that
engendered by a 21-hour trip from Australia to the American east
coast. Medical journals should chronicle it. I slept last night after
a melatonin tablet, and when I snapped awake – wide awake,

stubbornly awake, ready for battle – at midnight, *two* Normison.

Last night, having just arrived from Sydney, I had gone straight into a video conference with Canberra, at the mission's Midtown offices. The subject was my budget, the prospect of cuts in the rate of growth in spending on overseas aid. A week ago there was a hint from the Prime Minister's foreign policy adviser, Richard Maude, that the Prime Minister might be open to revisiting this. Reversing the decision to cut growth and settling on a softer option previously considered and rejected. So I took this up over the conference line. Penny Wong (Finance) was in the chair. She and the others listened. After ten-and-a-half years running my own government, with the final say on money, here I am cast as a mendicant minister. Wong may have been receptive. No decision taken. A relief if the Prime Minister sides with me. I'm booked in to talk to her by phone on Friday.

Today started with briefings in the Beekman Place apartment. I countered the jetlag – sleep deprivation, melatonin, Normison – with a strong coffee followed by cups of hot water with lemon. I took up the cause – politely, tentatively (I'm a neophyte minister) – of getting more personality into the department's briefing notes. 'It's dead prose,' I told them. 'Please, some journalistic colour.' Quinlan agreed; he's worked for Kevin Rudd as Prime Minister; it'd been fought over before. I was doing a lunchtime address to the American Australian Association. Still not getting decent prepared speeches from my department or my staff so I cobbled together notes, added anecdotes, inserted jokes. A lunchtime address. You don't need much. A joke, an anecdote, a bit of praise for the Yanks. For what? American creativity. American resilience. That *always* works. Plus eye contact with the audience – don't clutch a script. In the end, it ended up a lively speech. Years of practice sometimes works.

I texted Indonesian Foreign Minister Marty Natalegawa, spoke by phone to British Foreign Secretary William Hague. Saw my op-ed on our bid for a Security Council seat published back home in *The Australian*.

I'm absorbing all the diplomatic trivia I can. Will I soon begin to be a Foreign Minister?

Every fibre of my being tells me, 'It's 3 am at home! Get some sleep!'

I stare down jetlag, defy it.

WEDNESDAY, APRIL 11, 2012
New York

Formal meeting with UN Secretary-General Ban Ki-moon in his small conference room on the third floor of the famous UN building overlooking the East River. A largely scripted meeting. Opening remarks from both of us. Then I raised a point; he responded. Pessimism on Syria, Iran, North Korea. I have to remember what former Secretary-General Dag Hammarskjöld said in 1954, a quote Quinlan is always ready with: 'The United Nations was not created in order to bring us to heaven, but in order to save us from hell.'

Then I met Michelle Bachelet, Under-Secretary-General and Executive Director of UN Women. A former centre-left President of Chile (2006–2010) and likely to run again, her family a victim of the blood-spattered Pinochet and his torturers. She likes Australia, lived with us as an exile from Pinochet and had been involved in Third Way Blair–Clinton initiatives and politics. I said our AusAID program had lifted the number of women who serve as PNG village magistrates from ten to 700 over the last ten years. The Pacific region is the worst for women's participation in politics. She acknowledged this. She is just back from Libya. Democracy in the Arab world – the Arab Spring – means nothing for gender, she said. Women in Egypt will go backwards.

At 3 pm I gave a speech to the Permanent Representatives – that is, ambassadors – from nations belonging to the Organisation of Islamic Cooperation. A decent departmental speech and I stuck to it. Full turnout of the fifty-seven members; even Syria and Iran represented. I acknowledged the Syrian and expressed a hope for peace in his battered country. I was happy with this effort. No neuralgic issues. But my little triumph was a 6.30 pm speech to a reception at the Ambassador's for the representatives from the Asia–Pacific – Mongolia to Palau, Japan to Pakistan. Threw away the boring text. Lifted the atmosphere with humour and person-ality. If this activity and goodwill amounts to anything (it may not, of course), well, we couldn't be cramming more in to harvest votes for October's ballot for the Security Council.

Back home, the Israel lobby complains at my statement expressing concern at settlements. So, we can't even 'express con-cern' without complaint. This lobby must fight every inch. The old story. What *do* they want? That Australia declares its full sup-port for Israeli colonisation of the Palestinian Territories? Urge that settlement numbers be lifted beyond half a million? Dou-bled? Bruce Wolpe, on the Prime Minister's staff, has suggested I do a teleconference with 'the community'. My response: no.

Slept okay with one melatonin tablet, one Normison. Worked out in the building's gym – intervals on the cross-trainer and sumo squats with forty-five kilos. The kitchen staff – the chef, Ian White; the butler, Danny Espinola; and the housemaid, Teresa Guerrero – know that for breakfast it's got to be (1) organic steel-cut oats (2) lots of berries, every kind (3) two poached eggs. Fight jetlag with fibre and protein ricocheting with antioxidants.

THURSDAY, APRIL 12, 2012
New York

Today I spoke in the 'high-level debate on disaster risk reduction' convened by the President of the General Assembly. Later I was briefed on our relations with the twenty-one Arab nations prior to hosting a lunch with their Permanent Representatives at our Ambassador's residence. In the evening I hosted a reception on disaster risk reduction in the marquee in the grounds of the UN.

Then a five-minute trip to 52nd Street.

A sea of emerald gladioli; potted orchids; spot-lit paintings in gold frames; Nancy Kissinger tall and lean and welcoming in a dress that trails, and Henry deliberate at eighty-eight, same stubborn wavy hair, outsize square-frame glasses and alert, humorous eyes – Henry Kissinger, just as in all the documentaries about foreign policy and US politics in the '70s. My favourite world-historical figure. We were first at the dinner he was hosting in my honour in his apartment in River House on 52nd Street, Midtown East, the 26-storey tower of limestone and grey brick right on the East River. The building was thrown up in 1931 – again, from that enchanting period of Manhattan construction: an Art Deco block looking over the East River. Enter by a landscaped courtyard and the foyer is a long gallery reception hall. In fact, until the construction of FDR Drive in the 1940s there was a private mooring for the yachts of the residence. It's a symbol of the WASP-moneyed America of the 1930s. The place is said to be so exclusive the board rejected Gloria Vanderbilt, Diane Keaton and Richard Nixon.

'The celebration in the Kissinger family on the news of your appointment was indecent,' he said – so generous, so gracious – at the circular table in the wood-panelled dining room, Dutch flower painting on the wall behind him, and Rupert Murdoch, Mayor Michael Bloomberg, the historian Margaret MacMillan, the Indian UN Ambassador Hardeep Singh Puri, and the head of Alcoa, Klaus Kleinfeld, at the table – me by Nancy's side, Helena with Henry. And Susan Rice, Obama's Ambassador to the UN, was present, even though this was the day the North Korean missile was fired and expired a minute into the air and the day a fragile ceasefire was settled in Syria.

Henry asked me to talk to the table and I told – with reference to Bloomberg and Murdoch's presences – an old story that Ed Koch had told me about Murdoch ringing him to endorse him for Mayor in 1978. Koch had told me, 'I was in my Greenwich Village apartment and a caller on the phone said he was Rupert. Rupert? I didn't know any Rupert. It is not a Jewish name. Then I recognised the accent. Oh … Ruuuuupert! He asked if I would be embarrassed if his paper endorsed me. I said no.'

I praised Bloomberg to the skies – for insisting on calorie counts on menus in fast-food restaurants, for backing the supporters of a Muslim Centre near the World Towers, for city-based greenhouse initiatives. No response. Perhaps the old rule applied: you never flatter a healthy ego, the egoist sees it as the bald truth. But it doesn't matter: Bloomberg is a great public servant. I mentioned Australia's balancing act: China and the US – we don't have to choose. Told them the US was one budget deal away from reversing decline. They *always* warm to that. Americans love hearing that.

Henry said the Chinese bonding to North Korea goes back to the Korean War. I said China had put serious pressure on them this time round. I said this based on a cable reporting an exchange between Kim Beazley, our Ambassador to the US, and Kurt Campbell, Assistant Secretary of State for East Asian and Pacific Affairs, but Rice said their pressure had amounted to 'pretty please', nothing more. Later I cornered her and said I hadn't wanted to sound gullible about Beijing but my views reflected what our Ambassador had heard from Kurt Campbell, namely that this time China had been twice as strong as 2009 in pressuring the North Koreans. The last thing I wanted was for her to say somewhere the new Australian Foreign Minister was soft-headed on China, naïve about this latest threat.

'Bob, I don't believe you are naïve.'

Okay, fine, made that clear.

Margaret MacMillan is now writing a book on the causes of World War I (Henry, in introducing her, had said her book on Richard Nixon and China was ninety-six per cent accurate). She asked me what I thought had caused the breakdown of 1914. The Kaiser's hatred of his English mother, I said. That plus his withered arm. I said I hated the lies we were told at school about the war having neat, compartmentalised 'causes'. That it had 'economic causes'. Completely bogus.

After dinner, back to One Beekman Place to do radio interviews for Australia on Syria and North Korea. Combined with the glittering dinner this left me too upbeat to sink into the deep sleep I craved.

To sleep, perchance to dream.

FRIDAY, APRIL 13, 2012
New York

Started at 9 am, meeting Burundi Foreign Minister Laurent Kavakure in his mission's modest office, off one of the streets in the vicinity of the UN headquarters. We're funding one simple project in Burundi: edible mushrooms. And we think they will vote for us for the Security Council. Then a walk – thank God: air, light, sun, ambulation – in New York spring weather to buy protein powder at a GNC store ('My God, you're skinny,' Nancy Kissinger had said – blast! Seven years' weight training burnt off in the three-week adrenalin flow of the job) and I bought books at Argosy: a box set of Herzen's memoirs, a limited edition of D. H. Lawrence's *Women in Love* and a boxed limited edition of Irving Stone's *The Agony and the Ecstasy* (out of curiosity for how a popular novelist shapes the paltry material on the life of a genius, and out of a love for the look of this special edition). None of which I will read while I am Foreign Minister. Anyway, you own a book and absorb its contents by osmosis.

Then the car whisked us from the bookshop to Beekman Place for morning tea with ten Permanent Representatives of the Pacific states. We talked climate change, oceans, Arms Trade Treaty, the approaching Rio+20 conference that we will fund them to attend. I'm seized by this notion: Australia as the champion of the world's SIDS (Small Island Developing States). Then lunch with fifteen sub-Saharan African ambassadors. Kevin Rudd had visited the Organisation of African Unity and told them, 'We are Australia. We are not Europe, we are not America; we are Australia, and we look across the Indian Ocean to the African world.' I will repeat this. And repeat this. I use it at this lunch. Then afternoon tea with CARICOM, the fourteen Caribbean representatives whose votes we are confident of. They like Australia – like our position on climate change, marine environment, small arms treaty. Our diligent, infinitely patient UN Ambassador, Gary Quinlan, is fundamental to all of these relationships. He's a soft-footed, low-key, unthreatening omnipresence on Australia's behalf. It's the Permanent Representatives – the ambassadors to the UN – who do the voting and they can ignore their ministers' instructions. Gary cultivates the Permanent Representatives: he joined an ambassadors' cigar club; he joined a fraternity of Catholic ambassadors; he assuages, soothes, assures. I'm a professional politician – I live in a world of handshakes and ballots – and I haven't the patience to do what he has to.

Tonight H and I walked into the 18-room apartment of Mercedes Bass, on East 66th Street near the Pierre Hotel, for Nancy Kissinger's birthday party. It was like one of the palatial apartments in Proust: gilt panelling, museum-quality French antiques, ranks of footmen. I counted ten Picassos in the dining room. A commanding Matisse in one of the drawing rooms, Degas statues on side tables. 'Her husband's just divorced,' Barbara Walters said, sitting next to me. 'He took all the Monets.' Mercedes, born in Iran and educated in England and Switzerland, is an entrepreneur and patron of the arts. Her other guests: Robert Hormats, the Under Secretary of State for Economic Growth, Energy and the Environment; columnist Peggy Noonan; Don Graham, the son of Katharine of the *Washington Post*; Joel Klein, the former Chancellor of the New York City Department of Education; and his wife, Nicole Seligman, who chairs Sony America; TV host Charlie Rose and Happy Rockefeller, widow of Nelson.

Kissinger lauded me, again proving my greatest friend and supporter. He told the table I was an historian who knew all about American presidents and their history and Rome. He said he and Nancy had stayed in touch since I had looked after them during the Sydney Olympics, we'd stayed friends even out of office … and he asked me to address the table as he had last night. I spoke about the US–China balance, repeating some of the things I had learnt in Southeast Asia. I quoted George Yeo, former Singapore Foreign Minister: 'We want the US … but just over the horizon … under the radar.' Bob Hormats then said the Singaporeans had *asked* the US to increase ship deployments. Henry said he had quoted an Indonesian official in his March/April 2012 *Foreign Affairs* article 'The Future of US–Chinese Relations': 'Don't leave us, but don't make us choose.'

Henry's tribute to Nancy was touching. They had met at the Republican Convention of 1964. He said he had been in three (Rockefeller) presidential campaigns with Happy Rockefeller and they 'lost each of them by a different method. We did not repeat ourselves.' This was typical of his understatement, his irony.

A lot of talk across the table about the Bo Xilai affair – the arrest of the Chongqing Municipality Communist Party secretary and his wife – which is discussed obsessively in the US, almost with relief that China's vulnerabilities are emerging, its leaders caught out. Henry told Helena he could tell more if he could speak privately. Last night he had said China was 'traumatised' by this drama.

Anti-Chinese rhetoric runs through this election year. Romney, now the presumptive candidate, says on day one of his presidency he'll declare China 'a currency manipulator'. Peggy Noonan, Reagan's speechwriter interjects, 'He can do nothing on day one!'

I told her that her book on Reagan was a delight. And asked her – an adviser to *The West Wing* – what her favourite episode was. She said the episode where President Jed Bartlet's secretary, Mrs Landingham, dies in a car accident and he stands alone, as President, in Washington's national cathedral and lights a cigarette and stubs it out and curses God. Yeah, I remember *that*. She thought the program as a whole had kept Democrats' dreams alive in the Bush years and today lifts youngsters' commitment to the public service.

Henry took me aside and asked whether I knew about what I thought he said was 'The Bohemian Girl'. I thought it must be a revival of an operetta. Then it clicked: 'Bohemian Grove'. The exclusive retreat for business–political leaders in the redwoods north of San Francisco. Again, so thoughtful, so generous, he was asking me to be there as his guest. *As his guest*.

Back to Beekman Place. Popped two Normison to smother the excitement.

SATURDAY, APRIL 14, 2012
New York

Got up around six for half an hour of high-intensity exercise on the cross-trainer in the basement gym. H and I had breakfast next door with the Consul General in New York, Phil Scanlan, and his wife, Julie.

A magic spring day in New York. A *Saturday*! No meetings.

By 9.30 am, with the Scanlans, we were in the new Islamic wing of the Metropolitan Museum of Art, part of their permanent collection: the cultures of Timur, the Umayyads, Abbasids, Ottomans. A handful of objects to illustrate a culture, the half-satisfactory experience of any art history museum. Yet there's the re-assembled reception room of an eighteenth-century Damascus courtyard house and it gives the illusion we long for, that of walking into a different world.

Then across Central Park, thinking of F. Scott Fitzgerald, who wrote about travelling in a cab through the park – the lights of the buildings through the leaves and the mauve and rosy sky – tempted to cry because he had everything he wanted and could never be this happy again. Central Park West is the most beautiful street in the world: buildings from the magic era of Manhattan architectural creativity, a wall of apartments – the New York of Mayor Jimmy Walker and Al Smith – facing the spring colours of the park. Here we find the building of the New York Historical Society. Its current exhibition is 'Revolution! The Atlantic World Reborn', which boldly plants the American Revolution in the context of Atlantic history – rendering it not an exclusive, special North American eruption of liberty but one part of an anti-colonialist movement in the Americas – and measures the Haitian Revolution of 1791 to 1803 against it. Bold! The American Revolution on the examination table with the Haitian

Revolution! Now this is a serious historiographical enterprise and it stretches my grasp of American history, as has everything I've seen here, at this museum, in its exhibitions over the last ten years.

Stunning spring day – the leaves in the park have been out for two weeks – and I have one more exhibition in me: on Kazakhstan, at a little place on the Upper West Side. I had promised their Ambassador I would go. I want their vote, after all. I told the desk to let her know the Australian Foreign Minister had turned up and *loved* the archaeological treasures of nomad culture. Glad I did: there was a catalogue waiting for me. Their Ambassador had told the museum to expect the Australian Foreign Minister. If we can clinch her vote ...

Flying to London on BA184 at 6.25 tonight for a meeting of the Commonwealth Ministerial Action Group.

MONDAY, APRIL 16 –
TUESDAY, APRIL 17, 2012
London

A crisp, clear spring day in the heart of imperial London: Buckingham Palace, Lancaster House, Clarence House, St James. My jetlagged Normison-induced dullness evaporated as I got out of the Jaguar and strode from the Mall into the courtyard of Marlborough House for the thirty-seventh meeting of the Commonwealth Ministerial Action Group, a nine-member 'spearhead' (or executive) of the 54-member Commonwealth. That's us, Canada, Bangladesh, Jamaica, Sierra Leone, Tanzania, Vanuatu, Trinidad and Tobago.

I grabbed the Tanzanian Foreign Minister, Bernard Membe,

and steered him into the garden so I could talk while I soaked up a ration of Vitamin D. He is considered a post-2015 President of Tanzania. He's been to Australia and likes Kevin Rudd and Stephen Smith. Indicated support for Australia in our UNSC bid. Said we are really liked in Africa. 'Why?' I asked as we crunched the ground around the lawn. He quoted Rudd standing up and telling the African Union 'We are not America. We are not Europe. We are Australia.' Said there was applause from the delegates. He quoted our aid, specifically the bridge built over a gorge – I think near where he lives. He said it was practical, small, specific. It helped farmers get to their fields and saved children from being taken by crocodiles. Saves kids from crocodiles – I'll use that. I'll use that in a thousand speeches.

I rang the PM and left a message quoting this and saying it was proof positive that we needed to maintain our support for Africa in the aid budget and that meant we must veer to my favoured option in the treatment of aid in the May budget. I've already – from New York – made this bid with her.

Then, before our meeting started, I also grabbed Alfred Carlot, Foreign Minister of Vanuatu, and coaxed him into the garden sunshine. Yesterday, in our bilateral meeting at Stoke Lodge, he had been somewhat reticent and shy. To help, I had switched to Melanesian mode, been hesitant and low key, not my bossy self, as I moved through our agenda with them (a return to democracy in Fiji, a human-rights commissioner for the Commonwealth, our United Nations Security Council bid). Today I got him talking about Vanuatu's volcano and tourism. Later he talks about Fiji: on the border of the Micronesian, Polynesian and Melanesian worlds, with a Polynesian chieftain culture, addicted to African-style coups. He's studied coups himself, at university. Interesting.

Anyway, I want to build a relationship with him, not hectoring or lecturing in the Australian style.

Then the Commonwealth meeting started – my first international conference – under pompous portraits of the Hanoverian dynasty.

The white-haired Foreign Minister of Jamaica, a descendant of slaves, spoke in his rolling basso profondo (a truly operatic voice, the best in world politics, could topple governments with that voice), a portrait of Queen Charlotte, 1744–1818, on the yellow, white-bordered wall behind him. He had told me at dinner last night he had won an election in central Kingston as a supporter of Michael Marley back in the '80s when Jamaica had been on the verge of civil war. Now he made the case for immediate elections in the Maldives, the item we got on to after a discussion of Fiji's move towards democratic norms.

We heard from reps from both sides of the Maldives dispute: the former High Commissioner in London putting the case for former President Nasheed; the current Attorney General for the incumbent Waheed. Coup or not? Suspend them from Commonwealth councils? Call for an immediate election? 'We in Africa have had eight military coups,' declared Foreign Minister Membe of Tanzania. 'This was a coup.' But Bangladesh waded in to weaken it. We got into a communiqué-drafting squabble. Just like COAG.

After lunch the 'Anglosphere' partners, Canada and Australia, pressed hard to get a Commonwealth Commissioner for Human Rights and Rule of Law. It was a proposal drafted by former High Court judge Michael Kirby as part of an Eminent Persons' Group. But emphatically, sincerely, viscerally, the voices of Africa, the Caribbean and South Asia declared against the notion of a Commonwealth person devoted to rights. I spoke for a commissioner, offered a softer version of Canada's, but the Anglosphere went down to defeat. Or defeat for now; it got referred to all Commonwealth foreign ministers. I have rapport with John Baird, the Canadian Foreign Minister, a right winger wielding his 'values-based' foreign policy. (Echoes of Alexander Downer's advice about the reality of an Anglosphere conveyed when I took him to dinner in Sydney to get him to download.)

I loved the Commonwealth meeting. I now appreciate this multilateral organisation.

Other meetings in London were good too. One was with the man who should lead British Labour, David Miliband, forty-six, energetic, bright, athletic and stranded on their backbench. I met him when, as a Blair adviser, he came to Sydney as a DFAT special visitor and spent some time in the Premier's Department. After Gordon Brown's defeat, his brother Ed beat him to the leadership. In his office today he dispenses advice for a Foreign Minister: (1) it is an advantage to be a politician – like Hillary (2) relationships count (that is, the Foreign Ministers' Club counts) (3) use ideas; they matter too (4) seize opportunities as well as solve problems.

He says: 'I failed to see opportunity in Australia and Brazil but did in Turkey. I tried to solve problems in Afghanistan, Pakistan and the Balkans.'

He is as passionately pessimistic about Afghanistan. He thinks it will all end up a messy, tribal, regional chequerboard, whatever is done. He is as pessimistic about British Labour being led by 'brother Ed'. Doesn't sound like he thinks he can ever become party leader. I tell him to read biographies of Gladstone and Disraeli and be patient: 'Anything can happen in politics. Stay in.' He needs the patience of politics. The capacity to bide one's time, to survive a decade in the wilderness.

Another meeting with William Hague – someone who did indeed bide his time, after serving as Leader of the Opposition – inhabits the roomy expanse of the Foreign Secretary's office. He allows me to flatter by proffering him an as-yet-unread copy of his biography of Pitt the Younger for autographing. He says he never gets time to read in his job, maybe three books a year. This is going to be my experience too. So far I've found no time.

Sanctions on Iran now serious, not much hope on Syria,

sanctions coming off Burma – we tick off the agenda. I ask how far he goes in criticising the settlement policy of the Israelis. I made a statement expressing 'concern' about them from New York; he says the UK openly 'condemns'. 'How do you get by with their gloomy, taciturn, Russian-born Foreign Minister Avigdor Lieberman?' He says by bypassing him; going to Dan Meridor, Deputy Prime Minister, or Ehud Barak, Defence Minister.

Other good meetings in London too: UK Shadow Foreign Secretary Douglas Alexander, UK Shadow Minister for Foreign and Commonwealth Affairs John Spellar, Commonwealth Secretary-General Kamalesh Sharma, Tanzanian Foreign Minister Bernard Membe and other Commonwealth foreign ministers.

A boring National Theatre production of *She Stoops to Conquer* seen through drooping eyelids (why revive that creaky old thing at all?) and a snatched one-hour visit to the Lucian Freud exhibition at the National Portrait Gallery (enough time to sicken of the acres of belly and parted groins) on the way to the Eurostar.

WEDNESDAY, APRIL 18, 2012 – THURSDAY, APRIL 19, 2012
Brussels

Yesterday, April 17, took the Eurostar 9148 from London to Brussels.

Did not know what to expect, coming to the big NATO conference on Afghanistan – fifty nations represented by foreign and defence ministers. I am lucky Stephen Smith, who knows the country like inner-city Perth, is with me. There will be twenty or so bilateral meetings with foreign ministers on the side.

I am a convert. I like NATO. I like the fact it has mobilised its twenty-eight members to fight the jihadists. Okay, something I have learnt: the Afghanistan operation is not just the US, UK, us. It's the twenty-eight NATO nations, plus another twenty-two partners in ISAF. As General John Allen, commander of the International Security Assistance Force (ISAF) – successor to David Petraeus – says on Wednesday morning, 'The greatest coalition of modern times.' In fact, there'd be something wrong if our civilisation can't defeat the terrorists and allied insurgents.

Allen talks about 'fissures' in a Taliban that is subject to 'slices and slivers'. This time last year only 600 of the Taliban had 'gone home' or 'reintegrated' (Pashtun warriors never surrender); this year there have been 4000. As in Iraq, when an insurgency decomposes from the bottom up, 'the leadership listens'. And chatter – collected from surveillance – confirms Taliban leadership is surprised at Afghan National Security Forces (ANSF) successes. An insurgency must be defeated by indigenous forces. The locals are now performing night raids, an essential part of the counter insurgency; they will start leading the raids. These night raids are the reason insurgents are retiring from battle.

Later James Stavridis, the NATO Supreme Allied Commander, tells us that fifty per cent of operations are now under Afghan security. It will rise to seventy-five per cent in the fighting season. The weekend attacks from suicide bombers had been ludicrously compared with the Tet offensive; ludicrous because the North Vietnamese assault in early 1968 involved 100,000 troops and produced 80,000 deaths.

I liked Afghan Defence Minister Abdul Wardak saying: 'Success is not final, failure is not fatal,' I think quoting Churchill. He pleaded for us to support his war-weary country. These brave, decent Afghans, audacious enough to believe in rights for women and girls, a political system separate from religion, mullahs confined to mosques. And I like America's scholar–warriors like

Admiral Jim Stavridis and General Allen, rewriting the texts as they garner war experience. Some have said Allen is superior to David Petraeus.

Of course, I may be mad. 'Drinking the Kool-Aid' as Americans say.

Still, we've got a relationship here. Our Prime Minister had given a speech back in Canberra on Tuesday on progress towards transition in Afghanistan and a reference had her misinterpreted as Australia now supporting an expedited pull-out from Afghanistan. It had gone right round the world. In my raft of bilateral meetings, the Germans, the Czechs and the Norwegian foreign ministers were disturbed at reports that we were pulling out a year early. Smith and I had to correct it. I told Stavridis that I had seen Australia grouped in a TV graphic with Spain, Holland and Canada. I joked: 'We're not that kind of ally.' He laughed. He had read Gillard's speech instead of reports of the speech and needed no persuasion.

Speaking at the forum on Afghanistan after Hillary Clinton, I sent the message that we will be with Afghanistan *beyond* 2014, with training, and advice and occasional special force operations. There is a transition: we are loading more fighting on to the local Afghan forces, teaching them to run armies and operations, to do the fighting themselves. After 2014, a new NATO mission; with us as partners.

***

I like the Americans. But I'm still worried about American judgment, about their capacity to be driven by anxiety and paranoia into producing a Cold War with China, studded with incidents at sea. And their record of walking breezily into two wars since September 11 – that's a worry too.

Iran? A third war? Catherine Ashton is the EU High

Representative for Foreign Affairs and Security Policy (or Foreign Minister of the EU) and our meeting was one of the best. She's a politician (according to David Miliband, politicians make good foreign ministers) from Blair's government. She's engaging, effective and pro-Australian. We focused on Iran and she spoke about the EU talks with Ali Akbar Velayati, Iran's Supreme Leader's Adviser on International Affairs, a close devotee of the Supreme Leader, which seemed positive. He said to her that the Supreme Leader thinks nuclear weapons are un-Islamic, and will issue a fatwa against them. He sticks with this across two sets of talks, or two days of talks. Sanctions *are* hurting. Maybe they are searching for a way out and the Israelis are just keeping up the pressure.

While in Brussels I enjoyed one-on-one meetings with the foreign ministers from the Czech Republic, Slovakia, Norway, Sweden, Germany, Afghanistan, Denmark, Bulgaria, Macedonia, Turkey and the European Union. 'Speed dating' it's called.

In fact, on one level this job is a club of foreign ministers talking to one another. I mean … that's one way of understanding this job. It's not the only interpretation. It's not the most important role: that's avoiding war and loss of national sovereignty. Having rapport with colleagues – for the day when that phone call has to be made – is one part of it.

After Brussels, I visited Waterloo with the two-star Australian General stationed here. Then to the airport for an Air Malta flight to Malta.

Brussels to Frankfurt to Malta. On the flight I read *The Economist* April 7 cover story on China's military rise, an Office of National Assessments (ONA) report on China's foreign policy-makers, an embassy cable from Tehran on the P5+1 talks with the Iranians and an embassy cable from Beijing on the Bo Xilai affair.

Global trivia. Glorious. My life for eighteen months. Soak it up.

Arrived in Valletta, the capital, at 10.30 pm. Checked into the Phoenicia Hotel. Art Deco, highly polished, very Somerset Maugham. Sad I am here for less than a day. There's only one reason to come: the department insists a visit is necessary to clinch a vote for the Security Council. The Luxembourg Foreign Minister and the Finnish Foreign Minister have been going *everywhere*. Panic subsumes the department and the mission at the UN. So, all this way to Malta, then back to the US to finish business. Insane.

FRIDAY, APRIL 20, 2012
Malta

No time for exercise in the morning; straight into a breakfast briefing with the High Commissioner. We then met the young Opposition Labour leader, Joe Muscat, who could be Prime Minister shortly – within months, as the government hangs on, kept in power with the support of a grumpy independent. Then, in their offices, the Prime Minister; and the Deputy Prime Minister and Foreign Minister. Then, at a photographic exhibition on the Maltese immigration to Australia, the Culture Minister. But the guts of it was my meeting the Maltese Foreign Minister, Tonio Borg: will you support our bid for the Security Council given that you have committed yourself to the two Europeans, Finland and Luxembourg? Yes, he says – on the quiet. Or, more precisely, he says, 'Of course I cannot say. But *the wind is blowing in the right direction.*' Of course, I assure him, I'd say nothing. Later I and the staff relish his 'the wind is blowing in the right direction'.

Try that with caucus colleagues.

'Will you back me in the ballot?'

'Ohh … can't say. But … the wind is blowing in the right direction.'

How would you ever know how his Permanent Representative in New York will deliver in October? How could you know? And the department's taskforce on the Security Council vote sent me all the way here for this ambiguous response? 'The wind is blowing in the right direction.'

We get an hour to walk through streets of bleached honey-coloured limestone in spring sunshine to St John's Co-Cathedral and see the two Caravaggios, the huge 'Beheading of Saint John the Baptist' and the 'Saint Jerome Writing', before heading for the Lufthansa flight to Frankfurt and the United flight to Washington. After London, Brussels and Malta, across the Atlantic again, back to the US. My body clock is busted.

Business class. No edible food. No airline pyjamas. I lie in my tailored suit; I'll be as crumpled as Dr Evatt, who, according to Paul Hasluck's memoirs, would wear suits at the 1945 San Francisco Conference that had been rumpled up and strewn on the end of his bed overnight. Or strung from the bedhead. In this tradition I will arrive, sleepless, dishevelled, in Washington for my meeting with Hillary.

Our cornerstone relationship. Our most important bilateral one. The bottom-line guarantor of our security. And yet …

FRIDAY, APRIL 20, 2012
Washington

The wars in Afghanistan and Iraq have been bankrupting disasters for America, both unnecessary. All nations suffer pathologies, the great republic being no exception. Even before September 11, influential Americans were working themselves up into a frenzy about China. Bill Clinton said it well when I chatted to him in Sydney a few days before September 11: 'Some people in my country believe America must always have enemies.' Norman Mailer told me when Helena and I visited him at Provincetown in 1995 that the end of the Cold War had left the air full of iron filings, America had to have *new* enemies to replace the unifying, energising hatred they'd been able to direct at the Soviet Union. Then there's Gore Vidal's radical thesis: nothing short of an attack on America justifies the loss of a single American life in a war. Speaking for a strain of American isolationism, he believed interventions by America *always* leave things worse. These themes resonate. I wrote on my blog (last year, in retirement) of pathologies at work in America's view of the world. Watching this empire get into trouble and fail to learn lessons from Vietnam tempers my fondness with caution.

My first visit to the imperial capital was in 1972, arriving on a flight from Los Angeles, weary but galvanised. I was on a study tour, thrown my way by the US Consul General in Sydney. I was President of Young Labor and had had one year's experience as Education Officer of the Labor Council of New South Wales and had impressed Frances Cook, the Consulate's Cultural Affairs Officer. There I was, given a ticket on Pan Am and a per diem allowance – $35 a day, I think – to travel with a group from East Asian countries to observe the contest between the incumbent Republican Richard Nixon and his Democrat challenger George McGovern. It was midnight in Washington and from my room I could see the spire of the Washington Monument. It thrilled me just to be there. Actually, I was to find Washington and most of America pretty tawdry. I had followed Senator George McGovern's primary campaign reading Hunter S. Thompson's articles in *Rolling Stone* but in this last month of electioneering I was to see his position dwindle. Nixon's 'Southern strategy' in once-Democrat strongholds like Georgia and Mississippi and statesmanship in opening up to China were impossible to beat. Watergate was a sidebar story I read about in the *New York Times*, over a motel breakfast in Tennessee. Not even US campaign techniques impressed.

Forty years on, I'm in the city – the art collections and historic sites and surrounding battlefields I now know like the back of my hand – as Foreign Minister, this time in the Willard Hotel, where in 1861 Lincoln checked in, described so brilliantly in the opening chapter of Vidal's *Lincoln*. (The rest of the novel never quite fulfils the promise of this vivid, unforgettable opening.)

As Foreign Minister, I'd been describing the US alliance as a 'cornerstone'. That's our liturgy. All Australian foreign ministers say that. Simple truth is, I haven't got a mandate to change it, or a burning conviction about doing so. No mission to tilt us to armed neutrality, which is the only alternative to a treaty relationship with the world's, the region's, dominant maritime power. In eighteen months, moreover, I can't do anything that generates a misunderstanding, that puts the relationship at risk. I would like to make us a little less craven, to correct the recent tilt away from China and the too-desperate embrace of the US, symbolised in last year's announcement of a rotating marine presence in Darwin and Obama's criticism of China in our parliament. I would like to capture some of the instincts on this of Paul Keating, Malcolm Fraser and even Alexander Downer; and I value the words of Gareth Evans – that we should not approach the Americans 'happy to lie on our backs like puppy dogs with four paws waving and pink tummies exposed'.

On the other hand, there's ANU's Hugh White's advice (quoted by Malcolm Fraser in conversation with me in my early days as Minister) that this recent tightening of the alliance might have proceeded *too far to be reversed*. Think of the troop presence in northern Australia and speculation about militarising Cocos Islands.

In New York I had read a short article by Peter Leahy in *The Australian*. Leahy, a former Australian army chief, argues that Australia should practise caution in broadening military ties with the US to ensure that they do not lead to tension, or even conflict, with China. He says:

> As a sovereign nation Australia should maintain the ability to say no to the US and separate itself from its actions. This will require careful thought and deft diplomacy ...

> Future Australian agreements with the US will no doubt involve greater access for air and naval forces to ports, training areas, mounting bases, and repair and sustainment facilities in and across Australia.

> These are momentous decisions with far-reaching consequences. They potentially implicate Australia in a series of actions that could lead to increased tension and even conflict with China. War is improbable but not impossible ... Australia needs to be careful that it does not make inevitable the future that it should fear the most.

This seems sensible.

I sent an email to Beazley saying that I thought the article captured a lot of current sentiment in Australia. Perhaps I enjoyed being provocative. His reply only confirmed the sensitive nature of this terrain. His reply ran for three-and-a-half pages; I certainly felt I got my money's worth.

Email from Kim Beazley

Dear Bob,

Thank you for your email. I am looking forward to seeing you in DC this weekend. I am, as they say, at your disposal. The matters you raise are serious, involving as they do the long-term security and happiness of the country. Can I make a few points early.

Whatever the content, I find Peter Leahy's article infuriating. This is personal. In the 1980s we refashioned Australian defence policy from a focus on forward defence with an expeditionary force structure assuming regular association with allies, to a stance based on self-reliance, defence of Australia's approaches, with allied relationships used to enhance our intelligence and weapons capabilities. Our stance had the added advantage, without offending our allies, of freeing our hands diplomatically. I was heavily identified with this approach. John Howard always sat uneasily with it but recognised the political potency of an argument that said you assigned priority to defending the country.

When the Liberals came to office with me as Opposition Leader, the government sought to amend our self-reliant approach. In force structure terms, it came down to an argument on where you prioritise spending. Our approach heavily focused on maritime defence; obviously, our approaches are maritime. The Liberals assigned priority to the Army, particularly its capacity to interact with US ground forces and fight expeditionary wars. The principal agent for this in the government was Max Moore-Wilton. I suspect his passion was somewhat spurred on by having a son in the

Army. Air Force and Navy were to have a focus on transporting troops, not defending the country.

Within Army the principal instigator of a change of doctrine, based on the assumption that we would largely engage in the future alongside a forward-leaning expeditionary United States, was Peter Leahy. He served two terms as Chief of Army. You can understand how infuriating I find his stance now. However if you look at the subtleties of it, it nevertheless rings true. He supports the Darwin move. Why not? The marines will be useful partners in joint expeditionary training. The next foreshadowed moves, which he questions, would improve maritime surveillance capabilities in Australia's approaches, a focus he despises.

Can I respectfully disagree on the novelty of the backlash on cooperation with the US? The sentiment is always there and always has to be carefully thought through. From the time I became Opposition Leader through to taking up this post, I have been routinely advised by four former prime ministers and numerous former diplomats that we are too aligned with the Americans. Malcolm Fraser always enjoyed his tease of me at the annual AFL grand final breakfast, that I was still struggling to get to the left of him.

Difference then was they had something to complain about. It was the era of the appallingly misjudged Iraq War. Even more problematic in our region was our basking in the title of Deputy Sheriff in Southeast Asia, backing up George W. Bush's doctrine of extended deterrence. If I am a bit phlegmatic about current Southeast Asian responses, it is because I remember the vehemence of their criticism then. Then, they meant it. Now, by comparison, they are much more nuanced.

Criticism of proximity to the US is a continued theme in Australian politics. Thirty per cent of the country is regularly identified in the polls as against it. When the commentariat and foreign policy cognoscenti are considered, the percentage rises. Nothing contemporary compares with the battering I used to get as Defence Minister when I lost a perfectly good suit to a can of red paint at the ANU and was shouted down at most university campuses.

Nothing to do with above miscreants, but there is a pattern among former politicians, diplomats and military leaders to abandon their handiwork when going into print. That is not to say their views should not be taken into account. One of the side consequences here, however, is that we can be seen as a bit shifty. We say one thing in office, another out.

The difference in your situation since you assumed the Foreign Ministry is that you are the lightning rod now. As Defence Minister, Security Committee Member, Party Leader and now Ambassador, I used to be a lightning rod too. The conversations you are having now are the same conversations I have had for years. You are going to get it with both barrels because you are new and in the most powerful position.

As you know, you cannot conduct foreign policy without criticism. Criticism in Australia perforce must focus on our principal alliance. The answer is that we leverage this relationship, based on our security needs, to advance our own independently arrived at conclusions on what global and regional politics should look like. This government has used all our strengths to pursue successfully a variety of initiatives. These include creation of the G20, advancing the non-proliferation agenda, advancing global responses to climate change, and reorienting US policy away from an unproductive focus on the Middle East to deeper engagement in the Asia–Pacific for economic, political and security purposes (p.100 of Jeff Bader's book refers).

When I came here the US was vigorously urging me to urge Kevin Rudd to back away from his interest in creating an Asian regional cooperation entity not unlike the EU. The view they expressed to us was that we were talking above ourselves and infuriating our neighbours. Gradually they came to see that we were pushing them into greater engagement. Now they are engaged, they all believe they are in part responding to our pressure. They would be rightly aggrieved if all of a sudden we were perceived to be backing away now. Actually we would look a bunch of dilettantes. That is not to say we need to do much more immediately. What we have done takes a bit of absorbing and with budget and election issues here, things are a bit on hold. US participation in EAS and the opening to Burma, things we urged on them much against their will, are going pretty well.

You and we do have a growing problem with China. This tends to come in waves and new ministers, and definitely new governments, get tested. They are building up a list as they did in 2009. Then a defence matter was on the list, the White Paper. Now Darwin. What really gets them however is something that impacts their national unity or commercial interest. Then Muslim advocates in China visiting Australia and the Stern Hu case. Now apparently Tibet and our action on their communications company. The latter by the way is a big deal. We are not alone in our actions but we are very prominent. Rudd was pretty good at sitting it out. We recognised then that their trade with us was not done as a favour. Whether we are a satrap or an echidna for them, they will seek to diversify whatever they might say. Their relationship with the US will always take more of their time and routinely engage more of their senior figures than theirs with us.

DC now is consumed with Iran, Korea and Afghanistan. They will want to engage you on those topics and probably hear from you in your speech. I sent a few suggestions to [senior adviser] Graeme Wedderburn and the department's speechwriters but I recognise we are pretty small potatoes on that matter. If you wanted to break new ground you might find something interesting in pushing out the agenda on natural disaster responses and oceans environment.

At home with the critics I would push back vehemently on our record of independent action. On Darwin itself I would push back on how ludicrous the assumption is that it is a threat to China. I would also go, as I do in the notes I sent your speechwriters, to using American words on their purposes which do not include 'containing' China, no matter what a few senators might say. Give Obama his due for a subtle and pretty effective foreign policy. On Cocos, two things: one, it has for decades supported Australian surveillance flights; and two, there are no decisions.

Welcome to the wilderness of lightning rods. Love to Helena.

I will reflect.
I will test all theses.
I will watch where events take me.

SATURDAY, APRIL 21 –
WEDNESDAY, APRIL 25, 2012
Washington

In the suite at the Willard Hotel, I had about ten departmental people and staffers at the table. Jetlagged and edgy, I was getting panicky. The bland briefing notes were the problem. BORING! How am I supposed to engage the interest and attention of a Hillary Clinton or a James Clapper with comments like: 'The bilateral relationship is in good order' or 'Intelligence cooperation is at a high level'?

'How am I to get them interested with observations as dull as these?' I asked. Ambassador Beazley calmly replied, 'Mate, they just want to meet you. They see you as a heavy, they want to know where you stand, they want to know there's continuity.'

'Yes, but we've got to do better … '

One idea I had was that we try to engage them on the need to think together about the future of Indonesian leadership. President Susilo Bambang Yudhoyono's term expires in 2014. Nobody thinks his successor will be anywhere near as internationalist as he has been. There are elements in the country that are nationalistic, paranoid about their two Papuan provinces. They believe the marine presence in northern Australia is a threat. They may see us as the Christian West wanting to dismember the Islamic Indonesian republic as – in their view – we did over East Timor.

So this is something to talk to the Americans about, to enliven the exchanges.

I ended up raising it – the uncertainties in Indonesia after Yudhoyono – with Director of National Intelligence James Clapper, National Security Adviser Tom Donilon, Petraeus and Hillary herself. They took it seriously. Their interest level lifted. Better than the bland stuff. 'Our bilateral relationship is in good working order.'

31

Intelligence types are abidingly grateful to Australia; a level of cooperation is real. We may be the most useful of 'the four eyes', as America's Commonwealth intelligence partners are known – the UK, Canada, Australia and New Zealand – although perhaps that is far-fetched. Indeed one of the first intelligence matters I had been asked to approve as minister would certainly confirm this. But intelligence figures larger in the job than I would have imagined.

James Clapper has had a career in the business. He had us sit down in his dining room with top analysts and we went through the agenda: Afghanistan, Iran, China and, at my suggestion, Indonesia. Perhaps the most positive news was that Pakistan appears to be moving to support a broad political consensus in Afghanistan that includes the Taliban but was not dominated by pro-India factions. One of Clapper's senior staffers said there were other 'small rays of light'. This included modest progress in India–Pakistan rapprochement and the Pakistan's Inter-Services Intelligence (ISI) Director appearing more temperate than his predecessor. But Pakistan still shows no indication it was reconsidering its strategy of using militant Islamic groups to build strategic depth against India. Clapper himself said on Iran that Israel was underplaying the severity of Iran's likely response to a strike. He also said the US assessed Iran as viewing the US as complicit in any Israeli action and would likely retaliate against US forces in the region.

Clapper's China specialist said there were divisions in the Chinese leadership about how assertive and reactive their foreign policy should be. This was apparent in the debate over the South China Sea. Beijing civilian leaders wanted no international fights that might disrupt this year's leadership transition or divert resources from Beijing's development priorities. But the Central Military Commission believed that China must respond to the territorial provocations of its neighbours. This internal debate explains the occasional inconsistency in Beijing's foreign policy.

As we parted, Clapper said there were things in Australia that were important to him. One was Pine Gap. My reply was when I was in my twenties, speaking to state ALP conferences as chairman of the Foreign Affairs Committee, I was familiar with the arguments for justifying the presence on Australian soil of this spy facility or one of the 'joint facilities' as they came to be called. I used to argue, I told him, that the information from them sustains the nuclear balance of power. That the material drawn down from US satellites gives America accurate information on whether the Soviets might be launching a missile against them. Forty-five minutes' notice of a missile going up. But *reliable* information, eliminating the guesswork, and reducing the chance of a war starting by accident.

In those old days, the Left might casually throw the insult that we on the Right were CIA agents. If the loudspeaker system failed at one of our tedious meetings, the inevitable mirthless jest was a CIA plot. The so-called 'leader grants' dispensed by the US Consulate to enable study tours of America by trade unionists or Labor MPs – like the one that had brought me to Washington for the first time in 1972 – were casually referred to by all of us as 'CIA trips'. They were, in fact, from the State Department but who cared? Just grab the per diem and the fascinating itinerary and get to the Pan Am check-in. I formed a view after reading Tim Weiner's *Legacy of Ashes: The History of the CIA* that the CIA's blunders as a spy agency and intelligence gatherer vastly outweighed its successes. Actually, the author claimed he couldn't identify *any* successes from the agency's 60-year history.

And here I am visiting 'the Company'.

On Tuesday, April 24, I crossed the marble foyer of the agency headquarters in Langley, Virginia, past a statue of Wild Bill Donovan, a monument '[i]n honor of those members of the Office of Strategic Services who gave their lives in the service of their country' and another memorial to the dead of the CIA. Lost in action, tunnelling under East Berlin? In the highlands of Vietnam? In the alleyways of Peshawar? In the Labor Party Right the view was that, up against the Soviet empire, we were more or less on the same side. More or less. This was when 'the Goths were at the gate'. Why shouldn't Radio Free Europe broadcast to the oppressed populations under Marxist dictatorship? Which is not to forgive them for the coups in Guatemala and Iran or the ill judgment of the Bay of Pigs.

In David Petraeus's outer office, there is a framed photograph of Soviet missile sites in Cuba around 1962 and a picture of a famous Soviet spy, Oleg Penkovsky, with a quote attributed to Napoleon, 'One spy in the right place is worth 20,000 men in the field.' Penkovsky was executed by the Russians, but in his two years as an American mole he'd secreted rich material behind loose bricks or heaters in Moscow apartment blocks, including a tip-off that the Soviets were installing missiles in Cuba.

We were ushered in to see Petraeus, who I'd been reading about in a book called *The Gamble*. His hip had been shattered by a grenade during a training exercise he had been inspecting. His lung had been punctured as well. But he has a maniacal insistence on exercise each day. He is in that elite of Americans: the lean Americans. Outside a circle of the ruling elite, nobody in America is lean anymore. 'Did you run today?' I asked him. No, he said, he'd done the exercise bike. 'Intervals – good,' I said. We talked – an agenda like that with Clapper – for half an hour.

Petraeus expressed his appreciation for the intelligence relationship. He described the relationship as 'a model'. He, too, said that China will become more assertive/adventurous in the future. But they were being challenged by corruption, environmental problems, the disparity between urban and rural areas and the real-estate bubble. They would continue to focus on regime stability, especially in the wake of the Bo Xilai eruption.

On Iran and Israel he believed there was internal debate in Tehran and intelligence was inconclusive about it. Israel had not yet made a decision whether to launch a strike, but it appeared the Israeli Prime Minister believed he was facing a 'Holocaust moment'. And if a strike did take place, Iran's response would be proportionate and aim mostly at Israeli strategic targets. When I raised Indonesia, Director Petraeus admitted that Indonesia didn't make the top-ten foreign-policy issues of concern to the administration. But given the 'pivot', the US needed to focus more.

After this meeting Beazley, ASIS Director-General Nick Warner and I left the Director and sat down in a boardroom with some CIA staffers. Over sandwiches and chilli beans we started with Afghanistan. One officer said that the Taliban believed it had time on its side and it faced an incompetent opponent in the government in Kabul and continued to enjoy safe haven in Pakistan. For their part, Pakistan was willing to live with a higher level of violence in Afghanistan and even within its own borders if it hurt India. Pakistan–Taliban relations are not good but they have worked. Safe haven was a critical element. We were told that no Afghan government since the 1840s has survived without significant international backing. For Kabul to retain broad control of Afghan territory with security forces backed by the West was still possible, but nearly everything would have to go right for that to occur. Strategic stalemate, warlordism and civil war or an outright return to the Taliban rule were the alternative trajectories in the absence of strong international support.

On Iran they believed the sanctions were hurting. There was a debate in the Iranian leadership about the need to make concessions to mitigate this pressure. But the threat of an Israeli military response was not a factor in their calculations. The rulers in Tehran thought the nuclear program could withstand an Israeli attack.

On China the analysts said that Deng Xiaoping's 'hide and

bide' policy – the framework that had governed China's foreign policy so successfully since the 1980s – was still the dominant driver of China's strategic thinking. The CIA sensed that Beijing would stick with the policy until at least 2020, which it considered a period of strategic opportunity. China didn't want expensive wars. But there are worrying signs, particularly that the internationalist school in Beijing is outnumbered by the nationalists with an abiding resentment towards the West for holding China back. Chinese leaders recognised that China's neighbours were nervous about uncontested Chinese hegemony in the region but thought Asian nations would be reluctant to pick sides, probably because they doubted the US commitment to balancing China in Asia and believed Washington was hampered by political gridlock and economic decline. For this reason China calculates some Asians aren't persuaded that the US pivot would last. According to the Americans, China tells Southeast Asia this: 'Alliances with the West come with criticisms about human rights and interference in internal politics.'

We also spoke about North Korea and the Asia–Pacific.

All this was solid but unexciting. Where were the revelations? Was there anything here one would not pick up from *The Economist*, let alone cables? This thought stirred my instinctive scepticism about intelligence. How often do we get to relish the knockout revelation that we can wholeheartedly believe and on which we can base policy, taking our rivals altogether by surprise?

I began to get somewhat tired of this bland terrain and switched the topic.

'Do you read spy fiction?' I put to the officer closest to me, whom I had met once in Canberra.

Got the conversation on to John le Carré and Alan Furst.

The President's National Security Adviser, Tom Donilon, is a professional politician rather than a foreign-policy specialist but sits in the office once occupied, I guess, by Condoleezza

Rice, Zbigniew Brzezinski, Henry Kissinger. If I was going to get rebuked for my old blog opinions, it was going to be here. But there was only the gentlest hint when, at the end of our friendly exchange, he made reference to the President's speech in Australia – that is, his speech to the Australian parliament where he attacked China, something I had criticised on my blog. And something that Paul Keating had explicitly attacked. In a *Lateline* interview Keating had said, 'Well here we are in our parliament – not in the American parliament, our parliament. The American President gets up and says, "The Chinese model will fail. It is bound to fail." And then all the speech's basically hard rhetoric against China.'

So at the end of our meeting Donilon said of Obama's speech, 'It was a great speech, a clarion call for freedom.' I guess he'd been primed to serve me up a little rebuke. After all, Kurt Campbell had reportedly told people he'd come to Sydney to set Bob Carr straight. He'd taken me aside after our March 23 meeting in the Park Hyatt Hotel to say, 'About your blog, those fellows in the White House are a tough Chicago bunch of politicians ...' At the time I'd replied, 'Well, you better look at what I've actually been saying since I've got the job.' Later, however, I had thought of a better riposte – what the French call '*l'esprit de l'escalier*', a reply you think of going down the stairs, too late: 'I come from a tough political school too, the New South Wales Labor Right.'

Anyway, that's not the way you talk to the Foreign Minister of a friendly country, delivering a childlike pat-on-the-head rebuke. Gareth Evans later told me he thought Kurt Campbell was a bully. He'd certainly given me little time to respond at our meeting in Sydney, although several of the things he said were designed to persuade me that this year America was taking a more cadenced approach to China. Which was – is – extremely interesting, and welcome.

My department's view, by the way, is that I should not be transacting business with Campbell. 'The Americans have every-one coming after them. If they thought they could deal with you through the janitor they would,' says Dennis Richardson. Camp-bell takes infinite care of Australia and its interests; when he visits he sees everyone; he has a supple intelligence and acute memory. He believes in the reality of anthropogenic climate change, which, of course, separates decent humanity from the indecent these days. He was irritated, as I was, when nutty climate-change deniers ran wild at meetings of the Australian American Leadership Dia-logue. But Richardson's role as departmental head to a minister is to enforce the proper protocol for a middle power – namely, that I must pick up the phone to the Secretary of State, not to her assistant for East Asian and Pacific Affairs. I got the impression that this is the department's standard view. Yet Kim Beazley seems to be very close to him. Kim suggested that on the Sunday night I have dinner at his home with Kurt Campbell to prepare me for the meeting with Hillary. 'No,' I said, recalling that Richardson admonition. 'I don't think that will be necessary.'

Yet in this I could be wrong. Surely when it's the US – the superpower – you make an exception and settle for number two.

Let it pass.

***

In my first days in the job, as the adrenalin was stripping kilos off my weight and the excitement made sleep elusive, I had somewhat nervously placed the obligatory call to Hillary Clinton. It was late at night, in the Realm Hotel, Canberra. I reminded her that as Premier of New South Wales I had welcomed her just after her husband's triumphant re-election in 1996 and that we had hosted Chelsea during the Sydney 2000 Olympic Games. She claimed to recall both. I said something about Papua New Guinea and Fiji but didn't feel comfortable talking China, ASEAN, grand strategy. I certainly did not make any bid for new architecture. I am opposed to new architecture. We've got enough architecture. Officials at the ASEAN countries criss-cross the region all the time having meetings. We have the East Asia Summit, APEC and the G20. My instincts are *to make existing architecture work*. In retrospect, this might have left her bemused, especially after the conceptual grandeur of my predecessor. Later there was a bit of tentative feedback that this may indeed have been the case.

I have long admired the Clintons' dedication to our common craft, to career politics. I understood their rage with the White House media during the beat-ups over Whitewater and the failure of the media to report a single positive achievement and to focus on process over substance. I could understand their anger and bewilderment – captured when Bill lashed out at the media during the North Carolina primary – that the media was buying Obama's candidacy uncritically: 'Give me a break. This whole thing is the biggest fairy tale I've ever seen.' I loved her fight back during the Texas primary when she elevated her defence and security credentials. At the end of that irresistible book *Game Change: Obama and the Clintons, McCain and Palin, and the Race of a Lifetime*, the authors, John Heilemann and Mark Halperin, described her shell-shocked in her office, analysing her own failure. 'We had the entire press corps against us which usually Bill and I could care less, but this was above and beyond anything that had ever happened. I mean, it was just relentless, total hit job, day in and day out.'

Know the feeling.

She has been involved in election campaigns since 1970. She has contributed one way or another in public office for decades. Here she is – at my age – in the final stretch of a term as Secretary of State. And now here I was in the waiting room in the State Department with Ambassador Beazley, my advisers James

Larsen and Graeme Wedderburn, and some of our embassy team waiting to see her. A room with a panelled interior based, apparently, on that of a Georgian plantation house on the James River in Virginia. A cut-glass chandelier hangs from the 13-foot ceiling; a Tabriz rug smothers the mahogany floor. Eighteenth-century American furniture – a bombe desk, a secretary desk – present themselves as in a museum.

I was somewhat nervous, aware of my threadbare credentials, about to see 'a world-historical figure' *with no obvious or specific or urgent mission*. That's what made me anxious. Where was the beef? Nothing, I feared, to render us interesting.

We sat down at the boardroom table, one side facing the other. Referring to the deadly prose of my notes, I began by congratulating Secretary Clinton on her leadership at State and the historic rebalancing of American foreign policy towards Asia. I said that rebalancing was strongly supported in Australia. We were keen for AUSMIN – the annual talks between our foreign and defence ministers – to be held, dates to be settled. I referred to the apprehension in Indonesia about the 'force posture initiatives', that is, the location of marines in northern Australia. I suggested Australia and the US needed to start thinking about Indonesian leadership after the 2014 presidential elections.

Secretary Clinton – making reference to *her* notes, to my relief – recalled Australia's encouragement for the US to engage more in Southeast Asia. They'd worked hard on Indonesia, she said. She had visited it on her first overseas trip, but it had taken three meetings to create some trust. It was 'a true crossroads country' and a challenging partner. President Yudhoyono's leadership in the region had been very helpful, including his role in encouraging the Burmese military regime to open up. Kurt Campbell spoke up. He said that the overall story of Yudhoyono's leadership had been very positive and that the US had decided to treat Indonesia as a global player and that was central to the US engagement.

But it would take a serious effort over several administrations to deepen the relationship.

Secretary Clinton added that the US was concerned with the spread of Iranian or Saudi-style Islam but counter-terrorism cooperation with the Indonesians had been very good. Middle East issues were now always raised by the Indonesians in their bilateral discussions. She mentioned that the US was concerned that sections of the Australian press continued to portray the US marines initiative as an 'anti-China one'. It was not meant to be. She said she was travelling to China for the US–China strategic and economic dialogue next week and would take up the Democratic People's Republic of Korea (DPRK) satellite launch and possibility of a nuclear test. And Australia needed to help keep South and Southeast Asia united on the DPRK threat.

We discussed the need for progress on a code of conduct for the South China Sea given the ever-present possibility of 'accidents waiting to happen'. I mentioned that I was going to China in a fortnight. I said there may be complaints about the force posture initiatives – that is, the marines – but this rated as a secondary issue for the Chinese. I said I would be alert to Chinese sensitivities but would stand firm. The deployment was in Australia's interests. I said I expected the Chinese to complain about the Australian decision taken in 2011 on blocking Huawei from supplying the National Broadband Network (NBN). She said China, of course, would not allow Western investment in its telecommunications sector. She added, 'The Chinese practise gamesmanship in seeking advantage, but we would not let that change our own national interests.'

I explained our position on Fiji, firm on sanctions, edging them to a decent constitution and fair election. She said she appreciated our diplomacy. Kurt said the US would follow our lead and be supportive. On Papua New Guinea, she said the political deadlock was worrying and the government was missing economic opportunities. I said it was now a day-to-day proposition, outlining recent events. I said we were worried about the prospect that elections might be cancelled. She expressed appreciation for Australia's role in Myanmar and wanted to continue to press for the release of political prisoners, a halt to the ethnic conflicts and severing military ties to the DPRK. She said the US made the normalisation of its relations with Myanmar dependent on the last. I said we would raise the DPRK issue with Myanmar.

And that was it, moving briskly down our checklist of concerns, a touch of clarification here and there.

According to ritual, she then departed to work on lines for our joint press conference, and my team and I sat in the conference room doing the same thing. She returned, refreshed and primed. The two of us stood facing the double doors. They opened as if by magic and we strode into a splendid room with gold-fringed flags and Federal-era mirrors with eagles and paintings of former Secretaries of State. Cameras flashed. We stood at our lecterns. The press party looked expectant. They were allowed questions, one for the American media, one for the Australian media. Secretary Clinton made a statement that touched on Syria, Afghanistan, the defeat of al-Qaeda leadership, our support for the marines presence in Darwin and the reform process in Myanmar. I said our relationship rested on a broad and enduring community of common values and shared interests and that's why we were 'such comfortable allies'. An Australian asked her what it was like to deal with me after dealing with Kevin Rudd. She said she was picking up right where we'd left off with Rudd.

You are allowed a bit of self-indulgence on occasions like this, standing side by side with an American Secretary of State, especially one who may be President. For me, it was a moment – just a fleeting moment – of nostalgic regard, for the fifteen-year-old kid who walked from his family's fibro house in Oxley Street, Matraville, in 1963 down to a monthly meeting of the Malabar–

South Matraville branch of the ALP. The branch met in a classroom at Malabar Primary School, so the twenty or twenty-five members sat at little school desks on little chairs. The members were men in blue-collar jobs for the most part; I had joined them, the only youngster, with the intention of being one day a Labor Member of Parliament.

Today the jobs these men had in breweries, power plants, print works and factories have all been globalised out of existence, and the grand old party is wobbling on its feet. But that old party and those workers – all of them, I think, passed on – elevated me into public life to do things on their behalf: right now to represent our country in this imperial capital. And, as Mrs Loman said in Arthur Miller's *Death of a Salesman*, 'Attention must be paid.' To those workers, who believed in the idea of an Australian labour party and gave a kid from their neighbourhood the chance to be one of its leaders.

Attention must be paid.

The US–Australia media conference was then over and I was off to meet with Senator Harry Reid and Senator John Kerry. The notion I entertain as a result of the Washington trip is that when America has first-class public-policy people, they are simply the world's best. There was Senator John Kerry engaging with me on oceans policy and climate change and Burma. There was understated Senator Roy Blunt of Missouri, a Republican, talking knowledgably on defence and foreign policy. He told a story of an encounter with Lee Kuan Yew in which the founding statesman of Singapore had said that the future belongs in Asia. Blunt had asked whether this was a good or a bad thing. Lee Kuan Yew replied, 'Whether it's good or bad, it's going to happen.'

And all the others. The internationalism runs deep. The charm of liberal internationalism. The charm of US values at their best.

THURSDAY, APRIL 26, 2012
Washington

John McCain is younger and more sparkle-eyed than I might have expected. Plastic surgery? Two days earlier I noticed something about the skin under John Kerry's eyes, smooth and slightly discoloured. Today at lunch retired US Ambassador Frances Cook, who we knew in 1972 when she served in the consulate in Sydney, apologised for slight bruises under *her* eyes: she and everyone in politics, she explains, have plastic surgery – navy secretaries, congressmen, senators take cosmetic-surgery holidays in Thailand or South Africa.

So much for trivia.

McCain is confirmation of my notion that when America produces a public-policy athlete he or she is first class. He knows the global terrain. He asked me about the absence of democracy in 'that beautiful country, Fiji'. He spoke knowledgably about Myanmar where on a recent trip he found among the ministers who had queued to meet him several trained in US military schools. He liked the idea of sanctions only being suspended. He and his buddy Senator Joe Lieberman had visited a camp of Syrian refugees in Turkey. He thinks the US should intervene. 'How?' I asked. 'Well, if Ronald Reagan were President – we keep saying that – we'd get involved. I'd declare sanctuaries. I'd supply the opposition with anti-tank weapons. We've got the Saudis *wanting* to get involved.'

I explained that on Afghanistan we will be there for the transition and beyond, contrary to the misinterpretation placed on our Prime Minister's recent speech. He said Barack Obama was going around saying he was ending the war. McCain thinks that's shameful.

We spoke about the vulnerability of the Chinese system after the Bo Xilai affair.

He said he had loved his R and R in Australia. 'Yes, I would fly in and spend my time in the library stacks … at Kings Cross.' He showed me the memorabilia on the walls of his office, once Barry Goldwater's, who he succeeded as senator from Arizona. 'They let us nominate for President from Arizona but always defeat us.' There were photos of his military-men father and grandfather; and of his two soldier sons. There was a cablegram from diplomat Averell Harriman in Paris about conversations with Vietnamese negotiators monitoring Admiral McCain's POW son. He told me how his son had been offered early release but refused.

Leon Panetta, Secretary of Defense, was out of town so at the Pentagon I met Dr Ashton Carter, Deputy Secretary for Defense. I mentioned the Chinese propaganda line that America would not be able to sustain its newly announced commitment to Asia. Dr Carter was keen to emphasise that US defence budget cuts would not affect the refocus of US 'strategic weight' to the Asia–Pacific region for three reasons: the drawdowns in Iraq and Afghanistan presented an opportunity for the US to do more in Asia; budget cuts in a range of lower priority areas would allow more resources for military activity in the region, particularly through new means such as cyber; and the key investments in the region would be protected from the budget cuts that Carter said that he would be pursuing in other areas to get better value for money. He said that his role was to 'teach the department' the art of getting full value for the taxpayer's dollar.

MONDAY, APRIL 30, 2012 –
TUESDAY, MAY 1, 2012
Fiji

Back in Sydney for two days and now to the Pacific.

The VIP jet lowered itself over Suva. I was struck by the verdant beauty of Fiji, such an unlikely presence only 4666 kilometres from Australia. First time I'd been here since the stopover from the US in January 1971 when I got to know a Malaysian girl who had been visiting her sister in LA and worked for CSR in Sydney. The Pacific is a nice corrective to talking Afghanistan in Brussels, or Syria in London, or Iran in Washington. I was here with the foreign ministers of New Zealand, Samoa, Papua New Guinea, Vanuatu and Tuvalu, a Ministerial Contact Group to probe and press the interim government (or 'regime', which I'm told I am entitled to call it) to hold elections in 2014, as they'd been promising and lift restraints on freedom of assembly and freedom of the press.

That night the government hosted a big outdoor reception in a colonial-era building overlooking the coast. Businessmen came up to me and gently put the view that Fiji was doing well under the military and implied that we should go easy on them. With one who pushed a bit harder than the others, I gave him the response: 'In the end dictatorships only become lazy, corrupt and brutal. Think of Zimbabwe. You've got to remember that the Commonwealth is a community of democracies. The Pacific island nations are a community of democracies. There's just no respectable future for a country where military officers rule by decree.'

After a few hours' jetlagged sleep at the Holiday Inn, I did a one-hour walk in the fresh, tropical morning with my adviser Ed Vrkic around Suva Bay. Glorious highlands: I'd love to drive into them and spend days hiking the rainforests. For the rest of the day, we drove in a caravan with motorcycle escorts between government offices to speak to heads of departments, other public servants and ministers. Aiyaz Sayed-Khaiyum, the Attorney-General, was prickly, offensive. He started the 8.30 am meeting after we introduced ourselves by saying 'I used to live in New South Wales when you were Premier. I used to admire you ...' He's the hard-liner of the regime. The department says his influence on the Prime Minister of Fiji, Frank Bainimarama, is negative.

I hit him with questions about freedom of assembly, freedom of the media and asked him whether he had plans to reserve seats in the legislature for representatives of the army, as in Myanmar or Suharto-era Indonesia. There's no real basis for this; I had heard it somewhere and perhaps I was being provocative. At the end of the day, in the headquarters of the Pacific Island Forum, our group of foreign ministers worked on our communiqué. I was able to tighten it up. I eliminated expressions of thanks to the government for agreeing to see us – craven. I inserted an insistence that we make further relations dependent on government reforms allowing freedom so that, for example, the Methodist church can hold its conference and discuss politics if it wants to and New Zealand TV crews don't get kicked out for negative reporting. All credit belongs to Murray McCully, the New Zealand Foreign Minister, who's worked away at this and produced this exercise in engagement. I enjoyed it, especially the relationship with the ministers from the small states and the opportunity to meet Papua New Guinea Foreign Minister Ano Pala.

This is my real introduction to the world of the Pacific Islands and I can understand the appeal. Imagine seeing some of those hundreds of islands around Fiji and getting into the highlands.

On the jet headed home, I was asked whether I wanted curried chicken or salmon. I said, 'Both.' My weight is slowly edging up again, the anaemic descent to twelve stone within days of me taking the job now behind me. Drained with jet fatigue, I slept in the plane on the four-and-a-half hour flight to Sydney. I plan to hijack this VIP jet and grab Parliamentary Secretary Richard Marles and hit four or five of the Pacific Island states at the first opportunity: the allure of the Pacific, of the Melanesian and Polynesian states – make sure we can never be accused of taking this world for granted.

THURSDAY, MAY 3, 2012
Sydney

Woke up to hear my Indonesian mate Foreign Minister Marty Natalegawa running on *ABC News* using meticulously chosen words to describe a visit by Julie Bishop, Shadow Minister for Foreign Affairs. She had been excoriated by an Indonesian parliamentarian for the Abbott policy of sending back the boats. Marty, however, carefully withheld judgment. So I texted him: 'Your neutral diplomatic comments just broadcast. Well done.'

His reply invoked the catchphrase of Indonesian diplomacy: 'Dynamic equilibrium!'

That is a term the Indonesians use to describe the regional balance of power. The Americans don't like it because they think it smacks of the non-aligned movement and would exclude their presence from the region. But I enjoy Marty invoking it to describe his choice of words as he ventured on to the margin of Australian politics. And I replied: 'Love the notion! Don't understand it but wish I had thought of it!'

And then he replied: 'Ha ha. Take care!'

Consummate diplomat.

SUNDAY, MAY 20, 2012
Sydney

Got back home from my trips to China and Japan yesterday with an overnight flight from Tokyo and spent the day recovering. I started today with a workout at the gym and catching up with paperwork in the office.

A great relief to get through my first China trip without one of those mistakes the media loves trapping foreign ministers in making. Verbal slip-ups. All those potentially neuralgic issues: Tibet, Taiwan, Xinjiang, human rights, the consular cases. I had rehearsed my first press conference in Shanghai – the Australian reporters had come down from Beijing – and had the advantage of good, tight briefing notes. I had stuck to them. I was not going to be caught out like Alexander Downer on his first China visit, trapped into speculating on ANZUS and the Taiwan Straits.

On Huawei:

China should understand that it is normal for any country
to look carefully at resilience and security issues when
developing core items of national infrastructure like the
NBN. China does no less.

Why does our Ambassador want to visit Tibet?

The Ambassador would use the visit to become better
acquainted with the situation there, including through
meetings with local leaders and officials. He would also visit
Australian aid projects.

On consular cases: did you raise these cases during your visit to China?

Yes. I won't go into details, but suffice to say will continue to raise our concerns about consular cases as appropriate.

Are the trials of Charlotte Chou, Matthew Ng and Stern Hu fair?

We are obliged to acknowledge China's judicial sovereignty as with any other country. The government is, of course, very mindful that these cases are being watched closely by the Australian business community and do affect perceptions of the commercial environment in China.

Yes, the lines were watertight. I got Graeme Wedderburn and an embassy official to rehearse me. And I stuck to the script. Painstakingly.

In Shanghai, a meeting with Deputy Mayor Tu Guangshao and dinner with Australian businesses who gave me a reasonable understanding of the economic reform process, which is continuing despite leadership instability, and the continuing restraints on Australians doing business, especially in the services sector.

Travelled by train to Beijing, nearly empty because high-speed rail is expensive. It provided good pictures for the media party. Fitted in a visit to the National Museum in Tiananmen, captivated by the great scroll paintings of the Qianlong Emperor's Southern Inspection Tour. Painted by royal court painter Xu Yang, the scrolls depict scenes of the Emperor's visit to South China to inspect the water systems, military arrangements and social conditions. Those three great Qing Dynasty emperors – Kangxi, Yongzheng and Qianlong, who ruled from 1662 to 1795 – provided a kind of golden age. One of my favourite periods in China's dynastic history.

On Monday, serious meetings started. First with Lieutenant General Wei Fenghe at PLA headquarters. A polite exchange – I didn't know what to expect – although he referred to closer security ties between Australia and the United States. I gave him my standard response. But the substantial exchange was the 11 am meeting with Foreign Minister Yang Jiechi at the MFA building.

It was livelier.

I said I was honoured to be undertaking my first visit to China as Foreign Minister and mentioned who I had met in Shanghai and told him I would visit Shenyang, the largest city in northeast China. Mr Yang noted that in the past four decades, Australia–China relations have tended to forge ahead. They've been in close contact at top levels. A secure bilateral relationship provided tangible benefits for both countries. I said that I was deeply committed to the Australia–China relationship. I said my political mentor Gough Whitlam had established diplomatic relations forty years ago. I said that it was a key relationship for Australia and that we were opening a Consulate General in Chengdu. I raised the question of advancing bilateral relations with a senior working-level dialogue and engagement, and said DFAT Secretary Dennis Richardson would come to discuss it further. Mr Yang said he was studying seriously this Australian proposal and he appreciated Australia's assistance in the lead-up to the visit to Australia of Guangdong Party Secretary Wang Yang, the head of China's most economically strong province. He said his side would stay in close touch on a possible visit to Australia this year by a senior Chinese party leader.

Then Mr Yang emphasised the importance of 'strategic mutual trust'. He said that 'all sides needed to break free of the shackles of outdated Cold War thinking and respect each other's development models'. He said that several issues have impacted negatively on the degree of strategic mutual trust between Australia and China. These were first, actions between Australia and the US in the military field, and two, discrimination against Chinese companies investing in Australian infrastructure. He said most alliance relationships in the Asia–Pacific had been formed during the Cold War era and recently some sides had taken steps to upgrade their military activities. It was not clear whom they were targeting with such steps. Then he moved on to the South China Sea and said 'some countries' deliberately and falsely used the so-called freedom-of-navigation issue in relation to the South China Sea. But this was already guaranteed. And he said the sea lines of communication in the South China Sea were also lifelines for China. He said that it was not clear why Australia had stressed the freedom of navigation and 'fanned the issue'. Both sides ought to put themselves in each other's shoes. One could, for example, talk about the need for freedom of navigation in the South Pacific.

He then attacked the Philippines for tension over the Scarborough Shoal. I replied that Australia had been very careful not to take a position on competing claims in the South China Sea. Australia supported a binding code of conduct for the South China Sea. Australia had a big stake in seeing the peaceful resolution of all issues.

He then moved on to Huawei, blocked by the cabinet from selling its equipment to our NBN on security grounds. He noted that over the next five years China would invest $500 billion in foreign countries, and the Chinese government would not dictate where the money went. He personally hoped much of the money would be invested in Australia. But the recent decision by the Australian government 'not to grant an infrastructure project to a certain Chinese company on security grounds had raised concerns on the part of the Chinese people'. It had caused a noticeable drop in the degree of strategic mutual trust the Chinese public felt towards Australia. He warned this would inevitably impact on the decisions the Chinese government made, as governments need to reflect the wishes of their people.

I replied that since 2007 the Australian government approved 380 proposals involving Chinese investment in Australia. None had been refused. There had been a twenty-fold increase in

Chinese investment over the past five years. I mentioned some of them: the Channar joint-venture iron-ore project between Rio Tinto and Sinosteel; Minmetals investments, including recent acquisitions in OZ Minerals; and in agriculture, Bright Food and Tully Sugar. I said it was perfectly normal to take security considerations into account when evaluating projects involving core items of national infrastructure. It was important to remember it was Huawei that had publicised the decision.

Mr Yang said that among his colleagues, he was a champion of the free trade agreement with Australia; I said it was important the FTA be comprehensive and not just cover agriculture, that removing barriers to investment and trade should be an important element. Mr Yang said he had high hopes for the bilateral relationships but 'speaking frankly, he was not happy with the status quo'. The relationship could be far better than it was today. On a professional and a personal level, Mr Yang had invested much in the relationship. It was not overall that things were bad, but some issues were unsatisfactory. Both sides needed to put aside the Cold War mentality and establish a new security concept based on mutual trust, mutual benefit and mutual equality.

Then he said that he hoped Australia would handle issues in relation to Taiwan and Tibet appropriately by continuing to adhere to the One China policy and continuing to recognise Tibet as part of Chinese territory. He was concerned by reports that Lobsang Sangay (who I'm told is Prime Minister-equivalent of the Tibetan government-in-exile) wanted to visit Australia in July and was 'plotting' to seek meetings with Australian government ministers, including me. To this I said that Australia's position regarding Tibet and Taiwan remained unchanged, and in respect of the possible Sangay visit, I said no one had sought a meeting with me and I acknowledged China's sensitivity on the issue and would make a decision on any meeting in due course.

We then had an exchange on human rights where I said to him

that the bilateral human-rights dialogue was a very good forum for frank and constructive discussion on issues of concern, including Tibet. He said he hoped the human-rights dialogue would resume soon, and that China stood ready to continue the dialogue on human rights on the basis of mutual respect and equality.

We then passed on to areas of agreement – the East Asia Summit, the ASEAN Regional Forum – and I had an opportunity to mention our concern with the three consular cases and request an early release for Stern Hu, which I said would be 'helpful to the bilateral relationship'. After saying that all individual cases would be treated in accordance with international and Chinese law, he said he would pass on our concern to the judicial authorities.

We had more discussions over lunch.

A meeting with Li Keqiang, Vice Premier and future Premier, in Zhongnanhai, the leadership compound. The exchange was mainly at the stratospheric level without any opportunities for abrasion. That is, he did not touch on the marines or Huawei.

Next – to Japan. While in Tokyo I had a meeting with Deputy Prime Minister Katsuya Okada and had been warned that visiting Australia he had encountered a full-bodied assault from Prime Minister Rudd on the question of whaling. Really adamant, with emphatic body language to match. Certainly in our meeting, which stuck very much to talking points, I found him somewhat, yes, nervous. Might it be he expected me at any minute to vault the table, grab him by the lapels and, with a finger thrust in his face, demand an immediate cessation? I avoided the subject. As I said, it's in a box, set to one side, while our bilateral relationship proceeds on all other fronts.

It makes me think of my first meeting with Foreign Minister Shanmugam of Singapore on my trip to visit three ASEAN nations in my first month as Foreign Minister. On the way to the meeting our High Commissioner had warned me that Kevin had come close to roughing him up at his last meeting or, at any rate, had

been very forceful as he pressed the case for Singapore supporting the inclusion of Timor-Leste in ASEAN. 'The body language
was very strong,' our head of mission had told me. I had resolved
to not even raise this with the Singaporean Foreign Minister and
indeed it wasn't in my speaking points anyway. I was determined
to avoid any hint of the hectoring or lecturing Australian-style in
which Kevin – along with his better qualities – may have been a
specialist.

Also in Japan we had meetings with representatives of think-
tanks. China dominated the discussion. One of them told us that
an academic contact in Beijing had said there's more pessimism
in China than ever before. The pessimism is based on corruption,
nepotism, demographic trends and the difficulty of finding a new
economic growth model.

And the booming social media? He said there were two views:
one, that it is a challenge to the party; and two, that it gives the
party an advantage, a new means to control opinion.

The phenomenon of 'princelings' is entrenched and widespread. All of the sons and daughters of the top party people are
roaring ahead in business. Jiang Zemin's son is wrapping up a
deal with – wait for it – Walt Disney. The army of graduates each
year sees the connected people getting the best jobs. And there is
Bo Xilai, once seen as a hero in a country where there is a hunger
for heroes and now discredited.

A retired Japanese ambassador said simply, 'We have a liberal
economic and political system. They don't.' By which he meant
they'll never succeed in getting close to them. Yet Japan's economic dependence on China is growing. Foreign direct investment in China is growing.

And how does Japan feel about America rebalancing towards
the Asia–Pacific? The Japanese foreign-policy community wel-
comes it, with one qualification: its sustainability. This focus on
the Pacific – where will it stand in Obama's second administration?

When the Asia hands like Kurt Campbell are gone? Or under a Republican administration? Funding for the relocation of marines to Guam has already been suspended by the Senate. In the American system, Congress can block the administration.

How does China see the world? They are focused on SLOC (sea lines of communication) from Africa to China. They see the West occupying Diego Garcia and the American troop presence on Okinawa and Guam. These are roadblocks in their precious sea lines of communication. And now there's a new one: Darwin! And there's another loss of strategic positioning in Myanmar.

I asked the think-tankers about China's military modernisation. When do we get to the point where China has three aircraft carrier groups? A very long time was the consensus. 'Many pilots will drown' to get to that point. On North Korea – well, nobody, not even the Japanese, knows very much. We could only speculate how change might come to the hermit kingdom. It could be a power struggle inside the ruling circle. But in the meantime, China's policy may in fact be prolonging the regime's life. But no one knows. Living standards there are better than in the mid-'90s. Meanwhile, they are deadly serious about creating nuclear weapons. They are not using this as a bargaining chip. As a result of North Korea there is a convergence of security policy between the Japanese major parties.

My time in Japan – excellent access right up to the Deputy Prime Minister, a relaxed dinner with Foreign Minister Koichiro Gemba, meetings with friends of Australia in the parliament. All comfortable and easy, and I loved my exposure to the civilisation about which I know so little. Its great achievement is its urbanism: the workability of its cities, or at least its capital.

***

My principal adviser, James Larsen, says with America and China out of the way, the hard ones are done. I rang our Ambassador in Beijing last night. She said it is a 'highly functioning relationship and our metrics are as good as anyone else's'. There is nothing wrong with saying to the Australian media, as I had, that the Chinese had invited me to talk about the US alliance. She reminded me that other countries are going through worse patches: the Chinese are threatening retaliation against Britain because David Cameron met the Dalai Lama at a religious service at St Paul's. Filipino bananas are rotting in Chinese ports.

FRIDAY, MAY 25, 2012
Sydney

What would Rudd do if he came back? He would ditch the carbon tax and institute a floating price, an emissions trading scheme – which I, from retirement, had recommended to them. He could disown Craig Thomson. Go to the people, still lose. 'He's saying he'll at least have been Prime Minister twice. Only the fourth,' says Jason Clare, talking about Rudd's motivation.

Oh, to be Foreign Minister in a normal government, with a floor majority, and an interesting, authoritative Prime Minister with a routine lead in all the polls and a forty-four per cent primary vote; to be Foreign Minister with five years in the job stretching ahead.

I'm dragged down by the circumstances.

SATURDAY, MAY 26, 2012
Sydney

It gets worse. Chris Bowen and Martin Ferguson announce a Labor scheme that reportedly benefits Gina Rinehart and her iron ore mine – 1000 foreign workers allowed in – after a week in which jobs have gone in aluminium and Qantas. News of this scheme breaks, and Gillard, stuck in a conference with unionists, says she was not consulted and that she's furious. Abbott says the government is dysfunctional. The *Sunday Telegraph* rings to ask whether it's true I'm 'not opposed' to Rudd's return. How do they divine these things? I deny everything and despair. I can feel another leadership change closing in. As the great charmer Iago said, 'There are many events in the womb of time which will be deliver'd.'

Today I did a workout in the park at Maroubra with trainer Ralf and saw my physio about a sore shoulder produced by heavy bench-pressing. Windy, sunny, cold: before long I will have days like this to roam my books, the light pouring in the lounge room and a view of the sea through the windows. But … the agony, not to have this job longer, not even the minimum eighteen months.

Fly to Canberra and back for a reception for ASIS staff. My own little CIA, my own spies.

SUNDAY, MAY 27, 2012
Sydney

Disastrous leadership speculation in the papers again, the party determined on self-destruction. I get caught, as I appear live on Channel 10's *Meet the Press*, and swear that there is one leader and one alone. I also talk on Papua New Guinea. Later, I catch an ABC TV crew to talk about a massacre of 108 people in Syria where the Assad regime is fighting for its life. Do an hour in the gym at Bond Street where a new recorded message warns that 'inappropriate' behaviour on the floor or in the change room or steam room will result in suspension of membership. Cold enough in Sydney but we fly to Canberra at 6 pm, a gloomy Canberra by every test. It's a death-haunted govenment.

MONDAY, MAY 28, 2012
Canberra

Speaking from Washington, Beazley says, 'Keep your powder dry.' He says Rudd is unable to get more than forty-five votes in the caucus. He adds, 'I've pointed out to a few people that the constitution does not even mention the Prime Minister, let alone what house he serves in. Rudd is damaged. He will be wounded by another challenge. You are now a viable alternative.'

This is fantasy, a bit of flattery. And who would want it, in these circumstances?

Placed a call to Gareth Evans to tick off advice on Syria, PNG, Fiji, China. He said, 'I see you've been endorsed by Greg

Sheridan. That should last five weeks.' Gareth advises I keep out of domestic politics. Must steel myself against the temptation to be colourful.

SATURDAY, JUNE 2, 2012
Sydney

Everything happens in a welter of contradictory, paradoxical, overlapping developments. Last week, I sold the public the Schapelle Corby clemency decision by President Yudhoyono. I explained how it wasn't a deal. This week, the good President – proven friend of Australia's – started taking heat because of this decision that will carve five years off her sentence. Marty phoned me to say 'We are being criticised', and this was confirmed by very depressing cables from our mission in Jakarta: our friends there are taking a pounding; Yudhoyono is being savaged.

There is a wave of nationalist sentiment in Indonesia, a view that their country always gets cheated in deals with foreign powers. This seems linked with a strong anti-narcotics movement that wants drug dealers in jail for life. Probably some residual anti-Yudhoyono, anti-Western feeling mixed up in this as well. The result is that the President is attacked in the *Jakarta Post* and *Kompas*. Some opposition MPs threaten to haul him before parliament to justify his use of the presidential prerogative. All because he listened to our representations on behalf of an Australian convicted of importing marijuana – representations made by three Australian prime ministers and as many Australian foreign ministers, a matter of routine in meetings with the Indonesians.

We feel very sorry for him.

I take a call from Marty asking about the Indonesians in captivity here, mainly the minors picked up on fishing boats being run in people-smuggling operations. I raise it with Nicola Roxon, the Attorney-General: how can we expedite their release, the President is being pounded, he needs some relief on this question of Indonesian minors? I speak about it at the end of a National Security Committee meeting devoted to the antics in the PNG parliament that threaten to remove their Prime Minister and perhaps derail the forthcoming elections there. Throughout the week I work at squeezing a decision out of the Attorney-General's Department that would see more Indonesian minors handed back to Indonesia, and keep in touch with Marty about it. By the end of the week I think that over the next seven days we could probably offer up nine and beyond that we need to work on a proper prisoner transfer agreement, something that has never been progressed with Indonesia because of difficulties at the Indonesian end.

Meanwhile, a massacre is revealed in Syria and slated home to the Assad regime. On Tuesday I get departmental advice that we have an opportunity to be the first to dismiss our Syrian diplomats and I seize it. Throughout this I've got to explain to the Australian people why no simple solution to Syria can work. First, Russian and Chinese opposition prevents a decision of the Security Council. Second, America has no appetite for another Middle Eastern war. Third, the Syrians have a formidable army and thousands of missiles ready to be launched against any foreign air force.

Another consular issue rears its head: Julian Assange. And I decide to take this one head-on. Fed up with complaints from his family suggesting he hasn't been supported by Australia and the opposition spokesperson saying the same thing, I stride out of an Estimates Committee in the morning-tea break to do a press conference and point out that he has had more consular support in a comparable time than any other Australian. Strictly speaking, I don't know whether this is the case. But it is a broad, healthy truth that I don't think anyone could disprove. I do it to needle his self-righteousness. Let him go to Sweden and face questioning for sexual assault and rape. He's no more likely to be extradited by the Americans from there than from the United Kingdom. The British court decision he has fled has nothing to do with Australia and we have no standing in it. Sure enough, my needling has an effect. His mother is sounding off on *AM* the next morning claiming we should be defending him in Sweden – as if it's our job to fight the court cases of Australians in trouble overseas. In fact we have already made representations to Sweden that he be treated with due process; that is, treated in the way any Swede would be treated.

Syria exposes the limitations of the noble principle of Responsibility to Protect and I work at explaining these limitations in an op-ed for the *Daily Telegraph* and interviews on *Lateline* and the *7.30 Report*. Breakfast this morning with Paul O'Sullivan, former head of ASIO and just retired as High Commissioner in New Zealand. He does not echo the line that we are too close to America. The reverse. He thinks we should aspire to be in a different class of ally, not an ally like Holland or Canada but a country that can be relied on pretty well all the time. This is novel. The first time I've encountered this notion on the alliance, at least explicitly expressed. He asked, 'Do we want to live in a world dominated by Chinese values, or American values?'

On the front page of *The Australian* there was a revelation about an explicit discussion of the Chinese military threat and an Australian strategy to respond to it based on an unpublished chapter of the 2009 Defence Review: missile strikes, port blockades, submarine warfare … my God! I have no idea why the Defence bureaucracy insisted on this mental exercise. All it can do is feed Chinese paranoia. I wonder if anyone in Canberra imagined the effect it would have on us if the Chinese had worked on a document with a mirror image of these games? Paul said he, as head of ASIO, and Peter Varghese, then head of ONA, had opposed an inclusion of this sort of material in the discussions at the time; the then head of DFAT, Michael L'Estrange, had wobbled. But Kevin Rudd had swung behind it.

His judgment again.

'The Chinese won't mention it to you. But they'll file it away,' Paul said.

I spent two days facing questions in Senate Estimates. The Greens asked about Tibet and I was able to put on record that I would not meet the leader of the Tibetan government-in-exile when he comes to Australia. I justified not meeting him in terms of Australia's consistent position that Tibet was part of China. I had been asked about it by Chinese Foreign Minister Yang Jiechi in Beijing and had said I would make a decision on a meeting when I was asked about it but 'I understood Chinese sensitivities'.

Back in Australia, having thought some more, I'd told their Ambassador that I had no intention of meeting the Prime Minister of the Tibetan government-in-exile. Now at Estimates, here was a chance to get it out publicly. One for the Chinese. I will see that the Ambassador gets a copy as soon as the Hansard of the Estimates is available. A modest reassurance for them after they had been forced to read blood-curdling war plans.

We treat the Chinese to a vision of our submarines attacking their sea lanes and we coax the Indonesians to reducing the sentence on an Australian convicted of drug dealing and see their President get mauled as a result. And we have the temerity to puff our chest out and point to a forthcoming paper on 'Australia in the Asian Century'.

SUNDAY, JUNE 3, 2012
Sydney

Publicity is the lifeblood of politics. No use doing good policy and people not knowing. Peter van Onselen wrote a dismissive piece about me in *The Australian*, taking up every nit-picking critique of Carr available to him.

Since then I pulled off the interview with Greg Sheridan, shaped the news on Schapelle Corby's clemency, kicked out Syrian diplomats and delineated our position on Assange. Big op-ed in the *Daily Telegraph*. More media monitor mentions than other ministers.

Mounting credibility in the job, the gaffe on Papua New Guinea – when in March I had speculated about sanctions on PNG if they did not hold elections – well behind me. In and out of the TV studios in Parliament House, like a fiddler's elbow. Peter Crawford, an old mate, jokes I'm a self-generating publicity machine. Another old friend acclaimed the blue tie I sported as I made the announcement on Syrian expulsion. Bulgari or Hermès. You can't go wrong.

I need the publicity to ensure that Rudd can't dump me if he takes over. A Simon Benson piece in the *Daily Telegraph* had him campaigning in the Hunter with Joel Fitzgibbon and dining two nights in a row with a dozen supporters in Parliament House. Wayne Swan rang to chat with me yesterday; he was obviously 'ringing around' – that is, to shore up Julia's support. Has he heard that I listened as Dastyari put to me the inevitability of Rudd coming back? That I did not repel it? This place is porous. Last week the *Sunday Telegraph* put to me that I 'wasn't opposed' to Rudd returning. 'No!' I exploded. 'I'm not talking to anybody … I'm too busy with my job … you can't write me into the story …' Fortunately I wasn't written into it.

Meanwhile, I love being back. I love the contact with the people, like the airport security guard who told me I explain foreign affairs so people like him can understand it. Or the old Carr supporters who stop me in the street to say it's great to see me back.

Went to my old office today, now my senatorial outfit. Read cables and briefing notes.

Did half-an-hour interval training on the bike this morning, a legs workout at Bond Street this afternoon. An hour-and-a-half's exercise. Chicken and beans for lunch, protein shake in the afternoon. Setting myself up for the next trip.

MONDAY, JUNE 4, 2012
Sydney

Nielsen poll puts us at twenty-six per cent, only a quarter of Australians support the ALP. If we can get that low we can get to twenty. Surely it means a Rudd comeback. But today I was with Gillard at two meetings – people-smuggling; uranium sales to India – and she's fresh-faced and focused. Remarkably.

With ministers, in the corridors or at the airport, I don't talk about the catastrophic polls or the simmering inevitable leadership challenge. I levitate above it, determined to squeeze this job for all it's worth. For Australia. For me.

Malcolm Fraser, who I consulted in March, phoned to say that in China the Foreign Minister told him Australia is not worth talking to because we go along with the US all the time. He said Panetta (the US Secretary of Defense) told the Shangri-La Dialogue in Singapore the US is shifting sixty per cent of its ships to the Pacific and planning port visits to Cam Ranh Bay in Vietnam. Legislation currently before the US Congress facilitates missile deployments in Asia. 'If it means war, that may be a good thing,' one Republican has declared. Malcolm said if my people in Washington – he meant Beazley, 'who thinks he *is* an American' – haven't reported that legislation to me they 'bloody well should have'.

He continued, 'They *always* think war. Never a diplomatic accommodation. The Chinese say they see two Americas. One is Hillary – her visit went well. But the other is the military build-up.'

'What did they complain about with us? The marines in the Northern Territory?'

'Yes.'

'Well, we just persuaded Gillard not to visit the marines. If she'd gone up, that would have rubbed it in.'

He said he told them they should find me sympathetic.

Yes, I thought, but the thing's gone so far to be reversed, to be nuanced. There used to be differences between the US and us (dipped into Bill Hayden's memoirs and confirmed that); now there are none. None. The Prime Minister, for example, gave them the $100 million a year for Afghanistan they asked for. The Japanese Foreign Minister, talking to me, was surprised that we gave them what they asked for. Even Smith thought that contribution was disproportionate. It helped the Yanks leverage more from the others.

There are *no* differences now.

It's Paul O'Sullivan's point – that we are in a different category of ally. For better or worse.

TUESDAY, JUNE 5, 2012
Canberra to Rangoon (Yangon)

I'm on board Boeing Business Jet 737, standard seating for thirty passengers with a Canberra to Honolulu or Hong Kong range. It's the bigger of the VIP planes, with two pilots and three flight attendants. First time I've travelled in it. Sunshine pours in as I read Margaret MacMillan's *Nixon and Mao: The Week That Changed the World* (sat next to the author at Kissinger's apartment when he hosted dinner in April).

Also read about the Panetta speech that so irritated Malcolm. Christ! It's in the context of 'a closer military partnership with Vietnam' and publicity about sixty per cent of the US fleet being stationed in the Pacific. That includes six aircraft carriers, radar-evading fighter jets and anti-submarine planes. Cam Ranh Bay is to be used, Panetta said, 'as we move our ships from our ports on the west coast to our stations here in the Pacific'.

Where does this leave Kurt Campbell's strong hint, when he delivered his lecture to me at our meeting in Sydney in March, that the Chinese had drawn 'a red line' across Vietnam and the US would not cross it? His promise that this year the US–China tension would go off the boil?

Helena and I sit in our own compartment. Just a hint of Air Force One. I'm benign: did three ABC radio interviews on Myanmar before 10 am and have three reporters on board (the *Sydney Morning Herald*, *The Australian*, SBS) with ABC TV to fly in from Bangkok. I get them around the table and give them a briefing, highly classified cables in my hands.

Later as we fly over the South China Sea, I listen to a lecture by Hugh White on my iPod. The familiar themes: can Australia live happily in an Asia–Pacific where there's no Western maritime dominance? Already America has lost its capacity to jam the

Seventh Fleet into the Taiwan Straits. America with its aircraft carriers; China with long-range attack submarines. Do we resist the emergence of China maritime power, organising peripheral states to line up with us, or accommodate it?

FRIDAY, JUNE 8, 2012
Yangon

The Strand Hotel in Yangon is stylish – an echo of the late British Empire – but it's got no gym and I get restless. The food is inadequate by my standards, the helpings derisory – the daily battle for enough protein to stop getting gaunt again.

Walked through downtown Yangon inspecting the historic-building stock and talking with Thant Myint-U, historian and grandson of the first Asian Secretary-General of the United Nations, who runs the Yangon Heritage Trust. In Yangon the most spectacular building is the sprawling and labyrinthine Secretariat, a red-brick fortress of the imperial bureaucracy where in 1947 General Aung San was assassinated. Thank God they rejected a plan to restructure this as a hotel but – the perpetual problem of adaptive reuse – God only knows what they can do with it. Whatever, we will be there to help. We will provide aid to restore these buildings and protect Yangon's heritage. My instincts as a former Minister for Planning and Environment come to the fore.

The embassy organised talks with all shades of political opinion here: non-government organisations working in civil society; advisers to the President; and someone jailed since 1988 for his work for the opposition. I asked him how he survived being in a tiny cell all those years. 'Buddhism,' was the answer. We met

Daw Aung San Suu Kyi, Chairperson of the National League for Democracy, at her residence, made familiar in the movie *The Lady*.

Out of all these meetings I formulated what I think is a credible Myanmar policy. One, we will lift, and not suspend, our sanctions. When I told this to the President and the Foreign Minister I could see them light up. So we have edged ourselves gently ahead of Aung San Suu Kyi's position although other opposition figures did not seem to care. Second, at the suggestion of one of the President's advisers, we will lobby other nations in the UN to change the language of the annual resolution in the General Assembly that ignores progress under President Thein Sein and beats Myanmar up every year. Third, we will lobby European foreign ministers to have them lift, and not simply suspend, their sanctions on Myanmar because their current position is making it harder for European firms to invest – they lack any certainty. Four, we'll not only increase our aid but talk it up. We will become the biggest provider of aid to Myanmar, and our aid will flow overwhelmingly to education.

So I've crafted us a Myanmar policy. Using the new nomenclature – dropping 'Burma' – fits in with this.

This is one of the best days of my life, being driven on a narrow road through the delta country, past the simple farmers' homes to inspect a school and a pre-school. Australia is funding these institutions, and mums and dads had turned out to see their little youngsters, in crisp uniforms and their hair plastered down, on the occasion of the Australian politician's visit. As I left the school an embassy official pointed out that one of the proud dads was wearing a T-shirt that identified him as a supporter of the National League for Democracy. 'Tell him that yesterday I met The Lady,' I said to the embassy official. Back came the reply, 'Yes, I know ... I saw it on television.' The country has changed: a visiting foreign minister meets the chairman of the major opposition party and it now gets reported on television. The change is irreversible. Off to Oman.

SUNDAY, JUNE 10, 2012
Muscat

In his book *Monsoon*, Robert Kaplan invokes the 'eerie affection' of Oman. He said it's curiously aided by its Ibadi form of Islam, which is neither Sunni nor Shi'ite and which stresses conciliation, the avoidance of conflict and the importance of saving face. He says:

> There is a calming common Buddhist aspect to Ibadism. It represents the opposite of jihadism. Here the few dissidents have been co-opted and work for the government.

Oman is ruled by a sultan who is unmarried. All attention focuses on the succession. He may leave a name in a box to settle it. Right now he is on his yacht off Croatia, a summer retreat. Their politics is the politics of a court, with the prospect of an Arab Spring uprising simmering in the background, warded off for now by a raft of reforms and new members in the cabinet.

The Sultan has been compared to Singapore's Lee Kuan Yew except that he is a quasi-recluse. He rules over a country that has been subjected to a chaotic hinterland spilling over with lawlessness and tribalism – hence the 500 forts littered across the landscape. On the other hand, it has been shaped by the liberalising effect of the ocean carrying Omani traders with the monsoon winds to the Indian subcontinent and to Zanzibar.

The grey-brown mountains run right down the coast to Yemen with its al-Qaeda precinct, but here in Oman the US Ambassador, alone of his colleagues in the Middle East, drives around unguarded. The government spends twenty per cent of its income on defence and security. Seventy-five per cent of the population are Ibadis, with twenty per cent Sunnis, five per cent Shi'ite. The government is wary of the Wahhabis in Saudi Arabia. There is less of a chasm between rulers and workers than in the UAE. They are tolerant, they allow churches.

Another strand: the country has enjoyed good relations with Iran since the Shah sent troops to put down a communist revolt against the Sultan in the 1970s. Yet Oman had an Israeli trade office until October 2000 and sent their foreign minister to Prime Minister Yitzhak Rabin's funeral.

Muscat is low-rise, with Islamic architectural touches, against the tawny sides of the mountain chain.

All in all, fascinating.

I had drinks with a small group of Australian businessmen here in the Hyatt last night.

This morning, I sat down with one of the Sultan's new ministers, Minister of Agriculture and Fisheries Dr Fuad bin Ja'afar al Sajwani, and spoke about cooperation on fisheries, agriculture and food security. But the department failed to put specifics in front of me – I'll challenge them about this, another somewhat unimaginative briefing note – and the opportunity of fully engaging this fluent English speaker and former central banker was probably lost.

On the steps coming down to the car I asked him about the crisis in Syria. He said Assad should be encouraged to leave and an acceptable interim figure put at the head of a government with a mandate to plan elections in a year's time. My Ambassador says that was the solution in Yemen – the interim ruler, the Vice President, was approved by referendum and former President

Saleh went off with immunity from prosecution in Yemen and, reportedly, a bulging seven-figure bank account with Saudi cash. But he cautions me that Syria is different. In Yemen all sides wanted a solution, even the demonstrators, and could agree on the figure to head an interim regime.

Still, a better plan than sectarian civil war spreading across the region.

I'll make it my peace plan. Go away and flesh it out, I tell my people.

The Omani Foreign Minister has held his job for thirty years. Only his Saudi counterpart beats that record.

Over lunch I talk to Dr Salem Ben Nasser Al Ismaily, the senior trade official in the country, about the overlap of cultures. He told me that before Muhammad had taken Mecca, his people had got as far as Addis Ababa. Muhammad had told his followers that there was a Christian king in Abyssinia, he believed in the same god and he would protect them. This is the dream that must sustain us, that the Abrahamic faiths can rediscover commonalities.

MONDAY, JUNE 11, 2012
Muscat to Jeddah

I'm writing this on a flight from Muscat to Jeddah.

A devilishly tricky consular issue has descended on us, one to give the Schapelle Corby issue a run for its money. Melinda Taylor, an Australian lawyer with the International Criminal Court (the ICC), has been in Libya, as part of the defence team for members of the Gaddafi regime overthrown in last year's revolution. Suddenly she and the three other members of her ICC team – Helene Assaf,

Alexander Khodakov and Esteban Peralta Losilla – are detained in the mountainous town of Zintan, charged with grave offences against Libyan national security. Specifically, they say Taylor was handing over documentation to Saif al-Islam Gaddafi, the dictator's son, who the ICC and the Libyans both want to put on trial.

In a burst of phone calls, I've asked the Deputy Foreign Minister of Libya, Mohammed Abdel Aziz, to treat her humanely. I've made contact with her husband in The Hague and parents in Brisbane; spoken to the head of the ICC, Judge Sang-Hyun Song; and coordinated our Ambassador in Italy, accredited to Libya, in getting to Tripoli. We got a TV team to the hotel in Muscat last night and again this morning to force me into the Australian TV news on the issue. I've done ABC current affairs interviews.

Libyan public opinion is agitated. The Libyan Foreign Minister, while friendly, talks darkly of threats to security – threats that have been documented. On the other hand, he assures me she is not being held by militia but by the government. And as we boarded this flight we heard of a BBC report that she had been shifted to a prison and I rang Aziz again to press him on this.

High-risk conversations, all of them. Picking one's way over land mines.

Because I found Salem so interesting on Oman and Islam, I had him to the hotel for coffee and another discussion today before my flight. He says he negotiated with Iran's Supreme Leader to get American hikers out of jail. Says he learnt everything he could about Ali Khamenei and cultivated him after meeting him at a service in the mosque. I assume he was running a mission between Iran and the US, and is more than Oman's trade adviser, his putative role. When I asked him if he could help in the Taylor case he said they have people 'on the ground' in Libya and referred to our liaison officer in the UAE who could be brought into this. Liaison officer? Our Ambassador said to me, 'That would be the other agency you're responsible for.' Right.

Salem gave me drafts of two of his books. One was a history of Zanzibar, between the eighteenth and nineteenth centuries, when it was part of the Omani empire. The other was a Socratic dialogue between a Jew, a Christian and a Muslim teasing out the overlap and differences in the three Abrahamic faiths.

Graeme got woken last night by a call from the Prime Minister's office asking me to take a flight from Sydney to Canberra in the VIP aircraft. He explained we were overseas. 'She's locking you in,' he said. Shoring up support. A report by Phil Coorey in the *Sydney Morning Herald* picks up a Sunday newspaper story that Labor Senators Bishop, Stephens and Farrell are worried about losing their seats if Julia stays leader with the polling as wretched as it is. Coorey speculated that the parliamentary sitting in the last week of June is her danger zone, with Rudd circling.

Has someone told Julia I've got to be watched? Let's rehearse this: Dastyari told me Gillard could not last if terrible polling showed, for example, we would lose everything in Queensland under her but save eight seats under Kevin. I said, well, if the transfer back to Rudd happens, make sure the New South Wales branch insists I stay Foreign Minister. Did Dastyari pass this on to someone – Joel Fitzgibbon, perhaps (bad judgment if he did) – and say that 'Carr would not oppose Rudd's return'? (The story I heard from the Sunday paper.) And did the journalist present this rumour to someone in the Prime Minister's staff or to Wayne Swan? The place *is* porous.

On the plane I read a batch of recent articles on Saudi Arabia, provided by the Ambassador. David Ignatius from the *Washington Post* on how the Arab people are writing their own narrative. An *Economist* report on the pressures for reform in Saudi, buffeted by unemployment (10.6 per cent concentrated among young males) and inflation. Religious police probe into private lives. The country is doubling its armed forces over the next ten years: 'a bonanza for European and US arms merchants'.

TUESDAY, JUNE 12, 2012
Jeddah, Riyadh

Melinda Taylor is shifted from guest house to prison in Zintan but our Ambassador has arrived in Tripoli to visit her, along with ICC staff and other ambassadors concerned about their nationals in the four-person ICC team. She could be given forty-five days, plus another forty-five. The Libyans accuse her of handing over documents, one in code, to Saif Gaddafi, and of having spy equipment.

This one, I think, is going to be tough. And she's got a two-year-old in The Hague waiting for her mummy to come home and worried parents in Brisbane.

Somewhere in this city, Graeme found a TV studio to set me up for an ABC *7.30 Report* interview about the case. New Bulgari tie, purchased at Abu Dhabi Airport, won the case for me; along with my Sydney tailor's latest suit: costume perfect for my current role. Then to a meeting with His Royal Highness Prince Saud al-Faisal, a Princeton graduate who has been the kingdom's Foreign Minister since 1975, the world's longest serving: thirty-seven years to my three months! Somewhat frail, and slow in his speech, walking with a stick, his brown eyes flashed and his pronouncements cut through. Especially when, after briskly despatching the bilateral questions, we went into lunch in the official dining room.

What did he think of the tension between the Supreme Leader and the President in Iran? 'It's open warfare,' was his reading. He had visited Khamenei once, after they met at a conference in Africa in the '80s. In the salon the mullah had taken off his head-dress and produced a pipe and tobacco. 'I love music and poetry,' he'd said, and talked nothing else the whole meeting.

HRH said the world didn't know the difference between Shi'a and Sunni before Iran unleashed it. 'If we wanted to play the same game we could unleash it against them. Because of how they treat their Sunnis. They have no amenities or facilities. They are poor. They cannot get jobs. The only minority they don't persecute is their Jews because of the effect in America.'

On Egypt he said there was talk of a coup – presumably following a victory in the presidential elections of the Muslim Brotherhood – that he implied would be catastrophic. The US, he said, had announced that Hosni Mubarak should go before the Egyptian people had reached that point.

On Israel–Palestine he said it was just like they say happens in long wars: the enemies become like each other. He said Israeli Prime Minister Benjamin Netanyahu should act like Moses – by creating a Palestinian state (or, I guess, he means like the Pharaoh). In general he said that Jews in the Diaspora 'out-Herod Herod'. Although he later praised American Jews. He said Israel was at the acme of its influence. Now was the time to make peace.

I agreed. Told him I had told a Jewish delegation that without a Palestinian state they would see Israel bursting with an Arab population; and in twenty years' time it would be young Jews in America leading a campaign to brand Israel an apartheid state and boycott and isolate it.

He expatiated on the Saudi peace plan that encompassed all the difficult issues like right of return.

Jeddah resembles Los Angeles: totally car dependent, decentralised without a city centre, dispersed commercial buildings. A boom town. H off at a meeting with progressive businesswomen pushing the boundaries of women's rights. Who could have predicted four months ago I would be here, whizzing through this Arab city with a police escort, having recruited Graeme back to the staff, assigned to the best job in public life?

WEDNESDAY, JUNE 13, 2012
Riyadh to London

Flying British Airways Riyadh to London, eating plastic – no, ceramic – food, passengers lying in cribs, packed in business class, a design that owes a lot to transatlantic slave traders, looking down on Turkey. Sunny, clear – I've been watching the olive-green landscape pass under since we flew over the Syrian border. I'm profoundly sleep-deprived. When we arrived in the Ritz-Carlton in Riyadh last night at 9.30 pm I had ordered curries from room service and had gone into overdrive with Australian media on Melinda Taylor. Armed with the latest information from our Ambassador to Libya, David Ritchie, who got to see her for ninety minutes, I rang ABC *News 24* and *AM*, 2UE, 2GB, Radio National; then, wiping chicken curry from my chin, a stand-up with a crew Graeme recruited to send back a few grabs for TV news. It was midnight before we got to bed and we woke at four. In our suite – *at four in the morning* – I ripped into six sets of four body-weight exercises one of my personal trainers taught me, wolfed down a room-service breakfast and polished off five more drive-time radio interviews (Brisbane, Melbourne, Perth and two more in Sydney) while I packed. Got driven to Riyadh Airport and sat in the VIP room. On my mobile I was wrapping up Howard Sattler of Perth as I went through security.

I could be a young minister – say, a Minister for Planning and Environment circa 1984 – making a name for himself all over again. I don't know any other way of doing public life. Sell yourself and your cause hard, carry the electorate with you, explain your policies, be the huckster.

Crossing the Black Sea now, but missed a view of Istanbul.

Must get some sleep, even in these slave-quarters confines.

THURSDAY, JUNE 14, 2012
London

Staying at Stoke Lodge, the High Commissioner's residence in London. No sleep, blinding headache from looking out the plane window at Turkey. But I summon up the energy to speak by phone to the UAE Foreign Minister Abdullah bin Zayed Al Nahyan, to press another consular case – that of two Australians, Matthew Joyce and Marcus Lee, before their courts in a commercial matter. They face long prison sentences. I tell His Highness a case in Melbourne confirms the validity of Joyce's position and the error of their accusers. Can the UAE court take this into account? He's helpful. It may work. And I ask him to help with Libya.

Groggy with fatigue, I sit in Stoke Lodge, this dowdy residence that needs an upgrade but which no government is game enough to do, and struggle to master the thick brief for the Commonwealth Ministerial Task Force: a meeting of twelve foreign ministers (India, Malaysia, Belize, the Solomon Islands, Seychelles, Nigeria, Rwanda, South Africa, UK, Barbados, Canada and us). The meeting has to endorse a Commonwealth charter and settle about fifty recommendations of the Eminent Persons Group on Commonwealth reform left over from CHOGM in Perth last October.

These things reek of COAG, with all the frustration of moving people to a common goal (you get Western Australia and – oops – there goes Tasmania), fussing over words with people who don't use simple declarative sentences, being patient with people who lose their way in the text – but, this time, with the burden of being catastrophically wrung-out with fatigue. Will my temper hold? *I've got to chair the thing. With no sleep.*

FRIDAY, JUNE 15, 2012
London

Well, it ended very happily, this meeting in Marlborough House, next to St James Palace with its walled garden fronting the Mall. I was drawing on those years of chairing meetings of Young Labor, Kingsford Smith Federal Electoral Council, shadow cabinet and, between 1995 and 2005, on a weekly basis, meetings of state cabinet. Actually I'm the best chairperson I know – well, Gillard is pretty good – and suffer a lot when trapped at meetings with slow-moving and uncertain people in the chair. We got the charter adopted in an hour – particularly deft on my part, this – even with a strong human-rights section opposing discrimination on any grounds (a win for Michael Kirby, who was part of the Eminent Persons Group that worked on this).

And then I ended the meeting with half an hour to spare, which people joked was the first time ever in Commonwealth history. The Assistant General Secretary, Stephen Cutts, claims he had been savaged by Rudd at CHOGM in October ('When I want your views, I'll ask for them,' he claims Rudd had snapped in his face) and said he liked the humour I had been using that helped feed the general goodwill. In fact it was a delight to work with them all, to hear the Nigerian Foreign Minister Olugbenga Ashiru talk about freer tourist travel in the Commonwealth; the Seychelles Foreign Minister Jean-Paul Adam say we're the only body that amplifies the voice of small island states; to hear Kamalesh Sharma, the somewhat ponderous Indian bureaucrat who acts as Secretary-General, talk of the Commonwealth as having 'no centre and no peripheries'; and others talk with respect of its peacekeeping.

Hey, I think we can elevate this drowsy old outfit into a community of democracies based on rule of law, separation of powers and respect for human rights. That old notion of Community of Democracies that John Wheeldon, my friend the maverick Labor Senator, used to talk about in the early '80s – we've sort of got it now, in the Commonwealth.

I coaxed them along, sensed the parts where we could get an easy consensus, disposed of sections that did not ring true or upset too many, gently suggested at times we quicken the pace, then allowed them to talk out other propositions that needed to be aired to exhaustion.

I'm the best chairman I know.

Hell, I thought, I'm in the role – Australian Foreign Minister. Over morning tea telling the Malaysians we've got to work together to help Myanmar: 'ASEAN was right. You guys said we're better off engaging with them and we are.' With the Indians: 'I can't wait to get there in August … you've got the best cuisine and the best conversationalists … Have you read *The Argumentative Indian?*' I encouraged shy Polynesian Clay Forau Solaui, Foreign Minister of the Solomon Islands, who visits the five islands that make up his electorate in a small outrigger, and confirmed Seychelles Foreign Minister Jean-Paul Adam as a friend of Australia's. He's an Olympian who swims the ocean towing his young daughter or, at least, used to do until bull sharks took a few tourists. They'll vote for us for the Security Council. He told me how pirates commandeered a ship with six months of the Seychelles' energy supplies. Over lunch I spoke to the Foreign Minister of Belize about his country's slave history.

Just like working Young Labor or a branch or caucus.

Once or twice I saw faces looking my way for guidance, say the foreign ministers of the Seychelles and the Solomons sitting together. Me? Hell, I'm new to this myself. Just making it up as I go along. As I told them when we opened, 'I'm the least experienced and most jetlagged among you.'

I would count the day one of the best in my life.

Today I called Laurent Fabius, the new French Foreign Minister who I had met in Sydney in 1999 when I hosted him to a one-on-one lunch in my office in Parliament House. Enlisted his help on Melinda Taylor and Libya. Discussed Syria.

SATURDAY, JUNE 16, 2012
Istanbul

Out of London, to Turkey.

Sitting in a conference on the Non-Proliferation and Disarmament Initiative, chaired by the professor Turkey recruited in 2009 to be Foreign Minister in the government of the AK Party, Ahmet Davutoğlu. My embassy brief describes him as 'hyperactive, enthusiastic, unflagging, optimistic activist – an academic who finds himself in his dream job at the time of Turkey's rise'.

> Like most senior AK Party figures, he is genuinely pious,
> without any hint of intolerance or extremism. He never
> comments on domestic politics, and almost never debates or
> criticises other Turkish politicians, but is fascinated by, and
> opinionated about every foreign-policy issue.

Now that's an interesting model – never comments on domestic politics. As Gillard fails to lift her government's ratings, as we edge closer to Götterdämmerung, I'm inclined to think that's what I must now do. Mark Aarons, a former staffer in the state Labor government, said to me, 'Don't be part of the fetid politics of the Gillard government.' Sheridan said the same in his generous piece in *The Australian*. And as diplomacy absorbs me, and I gain confidence in the job – sitting here with my Turkish, Japanese and Dutch counterparts after the Commonwealth meeting in London – I think I've settled on it: levitating above the domestic.

In any case, the travel schedule puts me overseas most of July, and at least two weeks of every subsequent month.

I resolve not to be tainted by the sickness around the parliament. I could be one Minister who emerges enhanced.

Back home I led the news all day, with the Security Council issuing a statement supporting release of the detained staff of the International Criminal Court. Gradually the idea has grown on me: rearrange the schedule and charter a plane to get to Libya – only Tripoli, of course – in and out in a day, grab an armoured vehicle from the UK Embassy.

Outrageous.

Doable.

SUNDAY, JUNE 17, 2012
Istanbul

I now feel a little queasy about the above. And Helena presses me. How safe is the charter plane? What if we're forced to sit around in Tripoli all day? How safe is the city? God, I think, why take any risks? This week the British Ambassador's convoy in Benghazi was hit with a rocket-propelled grenade, although the Canadian Ambassador – here for the conference – told me the capital is safe. Graeme has got the Prime Minister's approval and organised the charter and visas.

MONDAY, JUNE 18, 2012
Libya

Took off from Istanbul at 8 am on a chartered jet like our smaller VIP aircraft and right now flying over the Sea of Marmara, in beautiful weather, headed for Tripoli. In the airport lounge spoke to Melinda's husband, Geoff, in The Hague and her mum and dad, Janelle and John, in Brisbane. Said to them – and in a release, tweet and radio grabs back home – that my expectations are modest because the Libyans are focused on a full investigatory process. But I said we can send a strong message her case is the highest priority for Australia and we want her treated humanely and released as soon as possible.

I am in the region so how could I not give it a try? At least go through the motions? It's the right thing to do and back home it creates a storyline and plants me in it, pursuing the release of a young mother, to reunite her with her husband and two-year-old.

Looking down on the Aegean and the mountains and plains of northern Greece – we will pass over the Peloponnese – I think again on the priceless satisfaction of public life and the need to revel in it, in the time I have left, making personal linkages that could last, loading up memories for life.

Three peninsulas below, and the northernmost, and most rugged, Mount Athos with its 1000-year-old monasteries. Must see that sometime.

In that idle, self-indulgent holiday last Christmas – Venice, London – I could never have believed I'd have another cycle of public life given me, that I'd be doing these things now. Then – in a puff of smoke – in August next year it'll be gone. Chairman Mao wrote in a poem quoted by Nixon, 'Seize the day, seize the hour.'

It is 9.30 am. To the right, Sicily: tawny, mottled green, distant Mount Etna. Beautiful weather over the Mediterranean. I read the

briefings on the Libyan revolution – set off on February 16, 2011;
a declaration in October in Benghazi by Libyan National Transitional Council chair Mustafa Abdul Jalil; an interim government
made up of technocrats. Then I look down on Malta, Valletta Harbour in perfect view. Back in the cables I learn that Libya is run
by representatives of tribes and factions. The Zintan militia in the
Nafusa Mountains see themselves as more nationalist, revolutionary and trustworthy than their rivals and won't disarm yet. Libya's next step is the election of a 200-member body to draft a new
constitution and, six months on, the election of a new legislature.
There is no unified Islamist grouping as in Egypt or Tunisia.

Land at just about empty Tripoli International Airport, dusty
and somnolent, to be greeted by Deputy Foreign Minister Aziz,
whom I'd lobbied by phone on the Taylor affair. He's urbane,
helpful.

We're also met by David Ritchie, our Rome-based Ambassador, and we follow motorcycle escorts to the Prime Minister, Dr
Abdurrahim El-Keib. There is only one block of devastation – a
flattened palace – but the city is in reasonable shape, not especially
impoverished. People at outdoor cafés, under trees. Dr El-Keib is
a quietly spoken electrical engineer who left the country in 1976
and spent time in Alabama. He is a Sunni Muslim from a prestig-
ious family in Sabratha, seventy kilometres west of Tripoli.

He tells me he'll talk to his Attorney-General and prosecutor to have the prisoners allowed home calls and visits. He would
like – he says this very politely – to have the ICC express regret
and state its friendship with Libyans and to disassociate itself with
... well, with what exactly? The Libyans believe that trust had
been breached. I pick over a form of words ... what if we can say
the ICC should have worked on 'protocols and procedures' before
sending its people in? This view forms when, after another trip
behind motorcycle escorts, we visit Deputy Foreign Minister Aziz
in his office. He says there are opponents of the regime still in

Egypt and Tunisia with money and weaponry; there are Gaddafi supporters south, in Chad and Mali; they have 4000 kilometres of land borders. It seems they believe Melinda Taylor did something that was risky: passing over a document to Gaddafi Junior, having some sort of spy pen in her possession. The charge is irrelevant; I just want her out. I talked to the ICC team and the four affected ambassadors in the Corinthia Hotel. The ICC counsel is of the view our side needs the ICC to offer up an apology. Flying out in the chartered jet to Algeria we work on the words and I end up dictating a plan, *a peace plan*:

» early completion of the investigation by the judicial prosecutor who has completed interviews with all four ICC detainees in Zintan in the presence of the ICC's legal counsel

» the Libyan government allowing visits by ambassadors to those detained, full consular access and phone contact for the detainees with their families

» the release of the four detainees

» Australia facilitating discussions between the Libyan government and the ICC to ensure Libyan concerns and perspectives are heard in respect of the criminal proceedings against Saif al-Islam Gaddafi

» the ICC issuing a statement which addresses the concerns of Libyan authorities and extends an apology for inadequate consultation on protocol and procedures.

After we arrive in Algeria I have it released.

Dennis Richardson, travelling with Prime Minister Gillard, explodes. And really savages James over the phone for allowing me to make this statement; he presumably considers it high-risk for us to urge an apology on the ICC.

The publicity plan for the day: interviews at 9 pm from an

Algiers studio for ABC TV; a radio interview with Fran Kelly (so any listener would hear me leading the ABC radio news then interviewed as a lead item on *AM* and talking to Fran); other TV programs with audio only. Later I learn this blanket-bombing gets a little push-back from the Prime Minister's party, now in Mexico, for the G20. For their part, typically, they have struck the wrong note: Gillard 'lecturing' the Europeans on fiscal management. This didn't impress anyone, not even the Australian media. They use Dennis to send back some message of irritation at the campaign I'm running. Think I'm taking some risk. Nothing *they* do ever comes off. The old problem: a leader who, despite fine qualities, falls a little short in authority. It is the old challenge: the journalists basically want a leader more knowledgeable, urbane, clever and verbally adroit than themselves. If the leader falls short – as with John Gorton or William McMahon – they let it be known. Respect evaporates and they close in for the kill, like sharks gaining courage at the flailing of their victim.

TUESDAY, JUNE 19, 2012
Algeria

His Excellency Abdelaziz Bouteflika is the President of Algeria. He is small, bald, moustached. Seventy-five years old. He wears a three-piece suit. He *looks* Francophone. In the palace, at our audience, he barely looks at me, instead peering at the coffee table – intently, concentratedly – until an observation occurs. His arms expand, his little body inflates, his eyes widen; and he delivers some wisdom on Syria, on Indonesia, on terrorism and drugs in the Sahel, on potent war in Nigeria. Rising up in his chair like a clairvoyant summoning some spirit. He is a revered hero of their civil war that claimed a million lives.

After our talk, our Air Algérie flight is boarding and their friendly Foreign Minister has been assigned to escort us to it. The airline is state-owned and it waits on the tarmac until our police escort whisks us through freeway traffic; we pass housing blocks with patchwork washing hanging out the windows.

Dennis Richardson has been trying to reach us to object to my reflections on the ICC in the Carr peace plan. But James shows me a secret cable from a source reporting a Libyan contact in Zintan saying they have completed their investigations and the release of detainees is up to their political masters. They have no objection to personal contact.

Great if it happens.

We are about to land in Casablanca.

Getting Melinda released would be delicious. A public win, the icing on the cake, topping my serious work chairing the Commonwealth meeting and enriching our ties with Myanmar.

THURSDAY, JUNE 21, 2012
Casablanca

Finished our visit to Rabat, the capital of Morocco, and flying out – to Dubai and home. Yesterday we drove from Casablanca to the Sofitel in Rabat. Night to ourselves. I phoned Judge Song, head of the ICC, from our room and, to my relief, he's already talking about an ICC apology over the affair despite, he said, vigorous opposition from 'hard-liners' in the Court. Good – that vindicates my own hard line about an apology being required by the

Court. But the prospect of a release is disturbingly far off, it seems. Deputy Foreign Minister Aziz just told me, in effect, he cannot even deliver approval for another visit by our Ambassador to see if Melinda Taylor is alright. I virtually begged for a telephone call from her to her husband and child. But he can't deliver. Talks tomorrow in The Hague between the Libyan Attorney-General – at least it's at the political level – and the ICC. But, in the car from Rabat to here, James shows me a cable based on CIA sources about the Zintan militia: they are fierce, independent and may only hand over Saif Gaddafi to the Transitional National Council – that is, the interim government – if they get paid to do it. They may take the same view with the detainees. Oh God, a hostage crisis and a mother separated from her two-year-old.

Pressed some Australian business interests in meetings – mining and agriculture – with three ministers and got the Foreign Minister to confirm support for us in the Security Council ballot. Fair going. But if there's a second ballot? Vague answer. All this way and I don't even get the now infamous Maltese Foreign Minister's 'the wind is blowing in the right direction', which has become an office joke. In turn I get lectured on the Western Sahara and reply lamely I'll talk to our UN Permanent Representative. But the atmosphere at the Foreign Ministry lunch is good and later, meeting the Speaker of the Parliament, we see the core of the city with Art Deco buildings above gracious colonnades as fine as those in Turin. And earlier, between appointments, we did a short walk in an old-town area above the beach and the river. And the country has Fez and Tangier as well. Must pay a private visit.

With its Arab Spring reforms from last year, this country can claim to be like Turkey and Indonesia – a model of multiparty politics in an Islamic country.

Plane taking off. And it's seven hours in the air before Abu Dhabi and the 14-hour journey home. How did I allow this? This journey alone will carve a week off my life, and I want to live to be 102 (2050). Anyway, I did a Lateline interview on Assange and Melinda and Syria from a little studio and pre-recorded an AM piece.

Later

Seven hours from Casablanca to Abu Dhabi; fourteen hours from there to Sydney. They upgraded Helena and me to first class – pathetic that the public service rules reduce me to that, an upgrade for a middle power's Foreign Minister – so I got some scraps of sleep without Normison. I have a few hours at home in Maroubra before flying to Melbourne at 4 pm – this, the coup de grâce – to do a party fundraiser.

SATURDAY, JUNE 23, 2012
Melbourne to Sydney

Victorian Labor Senator David Feeney told me last night at the fundraiser – fifteen or so lobbyists and defence industry types in an Italian restaurant – that Rudd has lifted his caucus support from the low thirties to low forties and has been circling to strike this week. I note Fitzgibbon is in the diary to see me. This will be to push Rudd. I settle on a plan to handle this. Put the onus back on him. What would Rudd do about carbon tax? About boats? Who would he make head of PMO? His chief of staff? How would he construct a cabinet? 'We're brilliant at sacking leaders,' I had told Dastyari. 'Bloody hopeless at the follow-through.'

At breakfast in Melbourne this morning saw Steve and Terry

Bracks and reported my lament that I need five years in the job and would love to be Foreign Minister in a *normal* government: majority in the parliament, authoritative Prime Minister, fighting chance of re-election. Time to roll out big plans.

The Libyans and the ICC have wrapped up talks in The Hague with a statement that says what I argued for: a virtual apology. To make the deal stick with the local boys in Zintan is the thing.

In the Sofitel I slept last night between 11 pm and 1.30 am and again for an hour or two after 5 am. Will do an ALP Indian Sub Continent Party function in western Sydney tonight.

WEDNESDAY, JUNE 27, 2012
Canberra

At last, the Libyans allowed Melinda Taylor to phone her husband. This followed a visit by our Ambassador to the Zintan prison, where she's been held now for over a week. I spoke to her parents, John and Janelle, who are extremely relieved that the Libyans seem to be moving down that roadmap. I was out of bed in the hotel room before six o'clock ringing radio stations.

An awful week in Canberra, the last sitting week before a two-month winter adjournment. Today my diary is filled with these sorts of meetings: with the Australia–Papua New Guinea Business Council, the Australian American Association, the Maritime Union of Australia, the ALP International Secretary – it goes on, having begun at 8.15 am with me addressing the Joint Standing Committee of Foreign Affairs, Defence and Trade. Among other things, I told them about my meetings with Myanmar. My plans to befriend the government and assist it with that annual UN

Resolution that condemns them are now well advanced. Yesterday I spoke to Gary Quinlan, our UN Ambassador, steering him towards engaging with the Myanmar representative and working to get the European-sponsored resolution condemning Myanmar reworded, or reshaped, or replaced. I told Greg Sheridan of *The Australian* – his article should appear tomorrow – that we could give ourselves a stock of goodwill in the country by taking up this cause when they are still so vulnerable. We will work with Malaysia and Thailand in doing this. No real resistance to this from the Parliamentary Committee, although Melissa Parke, Labor Member for Fremantle, did raise the condition of Kachin State and the allegation of atrocities.

I simply told the Committee that there's more to be gained by engaging with them and the reforms did appear irreversible, as ASEAN nations have been arguing. Janelle Saffin, Labor Member for Page, cautioned, 'On the cusp of being irreversible.' That's probably a fair point, a cautionary warning.

I've got to appear at the US Embassy for a Declaration of Independence event. There is nothing – repeat, nothing – that can be said about July 4 that is fresh or interesting and I won't even attempt it.

I am currently proving that one can operate with barely any sleep if the job's interesting enough, if you don't drink and if you do a lot of exercise. I am managing workouts in the parliament gym, big focus on abs. My current crusade is to live without eating sugar and not to have coffee at breakfast. Sugar-sweetened food and drink upsets the blood-sugar balance in the body and increases fatigue in the long-term. It results in deeper fatigue after the initial energy boost. I accept all this. Perfection, however, is hard. This side of the grave, as Alan Reid used to say in my *Bulletin* days, does not exist.

Feeney told me yesterday that the Rudd forces were ten short of the numbers they need to replace the leader. This has been simmering away for weeks. It looks, however, like they are finishing the parliament without the challenge. The Prime Minister's office remains edgy; Rudd sits in caucus by himself, making no eye contact, buried in his papers.

Joel Fitzgibbon came to see me – an advocate of the Rudd cause – on Monday. Before he could start his presentation I simply asked him, as planned: 'What's the plan, Joel? What's the plan? Your plan for getting rid of the carbon tax, getting an emissions trading scheme through the Senate, reopening Nauru for people-smuggling? Who would be the chief of staff, Joel? Who would be the head of the Prime Minister's Department? What would be the timetable for an election? We are the world's experts at replacing leaders, but we are the world's experts at never following through …' He said he'd raise this with Rudd. He suspects there's more of a plan than he knows about.

I let him have some more. 'Don't forget that Rudd's support – if he suddenly got the job – would slump back to Gillard's levels if he starts getting these things wrong. Why doesn't he go to KPMG and get a detailed paper on how you turn a carbon tax into an emissions trading scheme? And then think about how you would get that through the Senate, where it would be opposed by the Coalition and the Greens. And what's his plan for returning to a budget surplus given recent events in Europe?'

The best way of handling Fitzgibbon's approach.

Don't get drawn into half-baked conspiracy.

Put the onus back on the corridor plotters.

Letter from Bill Clinton

Wednesday, June 20, 2012

Dear Bob,

I was happy to learn of your return to politics as Senator and Australia's Foreign Minister – both Canberra and Washington are lucky to have you back!

Congratulations, and I hope this means that Hillary and I will see you soon.

Sincerely,
Bill

Letter to Bill Clinton

Wednesday, June 27, 2012

Dear Bill,

I'm honoured to receive your congratulations on my return to politics and to the job of Foreign Minister.

A photo in my office records your visit with Hillary in 1996 when I had the pleasure of welcoming you by Sydney Harbour. I also recall your address to a fundraising dinner here in Sydney two nights before the September 11 attack when you mentioned the globalisation of terror. You referred to al-Qaeda's operations in East Africa, its funding from Saudi Arabia and its training camps in Afghanistan. You urged progressive parties to be alert to globalised terror. And two days later, you were being flown back to the USA in the wake of the Twin Towers tragedy.

It is a great pleasure to work with Hillary whose energy and intelligence is plain inspiring, so good for the world and reflecting such credit on your side of politics in the US. I hope to see the two of you soon.

With best wishes,
Bob Carr

THURSDAY, JUNE 28, 2012
Canberra

I briefed Greg Sheridan on my strategy for Myanmar and he's devoted his column to it in *The Australian* today. A big spread, a cartoon of me in Burmese national dress (inevitably), an accurate and supportive exposition of how we will take the initiative in the UN in redrafting their annual motion on condemning Myanmar.

Specifically, Canberra will campaign to change the language of the UN General Assembly's annual resolution on Burma.

This is part of a considered Australian push to reinforce the moves towards political and economic liberalisation in Burma. It is also designed to give Australia a much higher profile there …

It was a big investment of time and represents a serious effort by Australia to exercise influence, establish a profile and make a difference …

Carr has made a strategic decision to take Burma's democratic opening as genuine and to support it.

I engaged in another bit of diplomacy. To win the vote in October for the Security Council we can't afford to have a vote on some irritating Middle East issue that sees us put our hand up for Israel and lose the support we've carefully cultivated among Arabs and Africans. One vote coming up at the UN is on a motion that criticises Israel for the conditions of Arabs in the occupied territories and I want to support it but I need to manage the local Israel lobby and its faction – 'the falafel faction' as they self-mockingly call themselves – in caucus. I saw Yuval Rotem, the Israeli Ambassador, and asked him to cut us some slack, to watch us vote for the motion without a fuss. I told him we could do some good for Israel as a member of the Security Council for two years. On Tuesday he said he'd take advice on it and today he was back in my office saying he'd cleared it with Jerusalem. Smart politician, he even told me he'd seen Liberal Senator Glenn Sterle from Western Australia who, with Labor Melbourne MP Michael Danby, heads the pro-Israel faction.

I want to meet a Palestinian or Arab delegation for every Jewish or Israeli delegation. So I ticked off a meeting with the Australia Palestine Advocacy Network, whose president, Reverend James Barr, is said to be a political realist, but some of their affiliates may lean in a militant direction. It was a mirror image of my discussion with the Jewish community. I tell them we oppose settlements, but I said as long as rockets are launched from Gaza at Israeli towns, support in Israel for a peace settlement will shrink. 'Will you condemn the dividing wall?' they asked. I said if bombs had been going off in central Sydney while I'd been Premier, I would have built a dividing wall. As I said when I welcomed Palestinian scholar and activist Hanan Ashrawi when she came to Australia to be awarded the Sydney Peace Prize in 2003, Israel will not be bombed towards a peace agreement. Yet, I told them with more settlement activity a two-state solution would become difficult, if not impossible. I told them I told this to the Jewish community as well. And I said without a two-state solution, Israel will face a burgeoning Arab population denied civic rights and an insurgency and international boycott and isolation activity. I quoted the line from *The West Wing*, 'Revolutionaries will outlast and out-die occupiers every time.'

Back on the UN.

I'm beginning to delude myself that we can win this ballot.

I am locked up in this loathsome mausoleum of a parliament as the House of Representatives clears Rob Oakeshott's people-smuggling legislation and it arrives in the Senate where the Greens and the Coalition will defeat it. The Greens again, as on climate change, are adopting a purist position that is entirely counter-productive. They blocked climate change in 2009 when we could have secured it and locked it in place from a position of political strength; by delaying it they produced the outcome we're struggling with now where the carbon tax is paving the way for an Abbott government with a massive majority. And on people-smuggling they refuse to contemplate offshore processing so they vote with the Coalition to block legislation that secures the borders by instituting the Malaysia Solution as a disincentive to people-smuggling. More people will die at sea as a result. And Tony Abbott will get more wind in his sails on the issue.

As Whitlam said, 'Only the impotent are pure,' and this indictment that the great Gough deployed against the Labor Left now indicts their successors, the Australian Greens.

At the Press Gallery Ball last night, Greg Turnbull, former Channel 10 reporter, and before that Labor Press Secretary, said,

'You've got the perfect Foreign Minister's voice.' Well, on a good day perhaps. David Marr said my appointment was just terrific. 'But it's only eighteen months,' I replied. 'It doesn't matter,' he said. 'You are the only one in the government to speak as if they're in charge.' Well, as long as it works, that's fine. I talked Myanmar with the new editor of the *Sydney Morning Herald*. Spoke with others.

FRIDAY, JUNE 29, 2012
Sydney

This last sitting of federal parliament was dominated by the dead-lock over people-smuggling – the Oakeshott legislation, which the government supported, defeated in the Senate. I spoke. It was only a workmanlike text. But with the crisp acoustics of an empty Senate chamber, I was able to make it sonorous. I urged the Malaysia Solution because you need offshore processing to deter people smugglers; I said we want a policy that does that but does it humanely. My parliamentary office's switchboard lit up with callers supporting this common sense.

Graeme and I were hoping to return to Sydney in a Commonwealth car, leaving parliament at nine or 10 pm after the last flight had taken off, getting to sleep in our own beds even if it took a two-and-a-half hour drive. Sick of staying at the Realm Hotel; sick of hotels in general. But nothing doing. The Greens kept moving amendments to legislation and we were still going after 2 am, with me trudging every half-hour the interplanetary distance from my ministerial office to the Senate chamber. I grew to hate the place. Graeme and I got back to the Realm Hotel at 3 am and I got a couple of hours' sleep before catching the 9.15 am flight to Sydney, my head slumped all the way. Then did a one-hour chest and back workout with my personal trainer Arryn Ottley at Fitness First. An hour in the Bligh Street office and then I returned to Fitness First to do an abs routine – all this to make up for the forced inactivity of parliament, although even in that prison I hit the gym four days in a row. Tonight a fundraiser for Michael Daley, my successor as State member of Maroubra.

In today's *Sydney Morning Herald*, Linda Jakobson of the Lowy Institute attacks Australian leadership on China, which she says must move beyond 'mouthing platitudes that no one believes' – like saying that Washington's military rebalancing is not aimed at China, or that we can have America as an ally and China as a friend. The trouble with this thesis is that, as Nick Moore of Macquarie Bank put to me, Australia is always going to want to choose the United States. Or as Paul O'Sullivan, retired Ambassador and ASIO head, put it to me, it's American values versus Chinese values and we'll go with American values if we've got to choose. The other thing wrong with her thesis is the differences between the Chinese and us right now – now, at this moment – are substantive, not amenable to rhetorical adjustment. We have decided to rotate 2500 marines through the Northern Territory. We have blocked a Chinese company with military links from buying into our National Broadband Network. These decisions, once taken, can't really be talked away. Naturally they are of concern to the Chinese.

Only time can fix it, this irritation the Chinese evince to us.

SUNDAY, JULY 1, 2012
Sydney to New York

I don't mind doing fundraisers for the party. I consider it a duty. Any place, any time – but it helps if they're worthwhile. Last night they had me entertain a dinner with a handful of people. Doubt if they got more than $5000 from it and the irritation and overstimulation stopped me sleeping until I swallowed one Normison. Then we got to the airport at 8.30 am and in the Qantas first-class lounge – best breakfast in Sydney – I stoked the fire of my restless energy with a coffee – failed again to beat this addiction – and mobilised my staff. I laid down an op-ed on the issue of controlling small arms for the *Sydney Morning Herald* and *The Age*; I rang James to explore whether having AusAID commit to building a school in Zintan might get Melinda Taylor released; I retreated to a private room and called radio stations on Syria and the six Australians being accused of murdering a hotel employee in Lima.

I told my staff to do me a Foreign Minister's diary we could flog to, say, the *West Australian*, and another paper, say, the *Daily Telegraph*. No use doing good things unless the mob knows about it. But my new discipline is to ignore domestic politics, attacks on the opposition, doorstop observations and the like. Defending Australians abroad will give me my populist edge and the policy slog on Myanmar and other areas of policy will give me substance.

Before boarding I ring Ben Hubbard, chief of staff to the Prime Minister, to say I favour the government undertaking constant movement on asylum-seeker policy. Just do what Abbott proposes. 'Better than sitting still,' I say.

Then, on the way to the plane, I ring Melinda's parents in Brisbane. Mention the possibility of a school – but not, I said, if I was advised it could be counter-productive. They are very appreciative, poor anxious folk. Messages from Libya are ambiguous. I get told that the Zintan militia are ferocious and running their own agenda and could conceivably be holding out for a ransom. On the other hand, there are suggestions they will help the government in Tripoli on this issue.

When we stop in LA I will tell our embassy at the UN not to adhere to that steamed-fish policy. Every meal the Foreign Minister is served bland steamed white fish. This apparently reflects a Führer-directive that I had the department send out about my diet. But whoever drafted it overshot the mark. We are sick of steamed fish. As a result, my weight is still down, face gaunt, seven years of weight training melting away. I want turkey, I want grass-fed beef, the table in Beekman Place groaning with fibre, protein. This is the new Führer-directive.

Ah! Then – on the ground in New York – my phone lights up: they've released Melinda Taylor and she's headed home to her husband and two-year-old. I'd love to witness that reunion!

MONDAY, JULY 2, 2012
New York

The entrance to the UN building is makeshift. Exposed piping, industrial lamps, concrete flooring and improvised artwork from member states – all of it bad. We're stuck here waiting for the deadlock to be resolved on discussion of an Arms Trade Treaty. The sticking point? Palestinian status. One proposal is that the seven nations that have sponsored the treaty – that includes us – all agree to abstain on the issue of whether the Palestinian delegation is admitted.

TUESDAY, JULY 3, 2012
New York

Ambassador Susan Rice came alive when I put to her it was time to move on Myanmar. I told her Thein Sein's reforms were irreversible and that ASEAN was right all along. She asked me why I'd reached this conclusion. 'Well, the growth of civil society ... all those youngsters with their Facebook campaigns ... then there's the attitude of the parliament. I spoke to the Speaker in detail about the value of Estimates Committees and daily Question Time and he's in the ruling party ... the President and his team know that any backsliding will see an enormous loss of international credibility ... there's the aid that's now flowing into the country and the investment that will follow it ...'

She looked a bit quizzical. Still, my campaign on Myanmar is gathering momentum. The Myanmar Ambassador seemed aware of it when I bumped into him in the street outside the UN. Our mission seems to be taking it seriously.

I tested Gary Quinlan on whether Susan Rice would be the lead choice for Secretary of State should Obama be re-elected. He thought Senator John Kerry, who I met in April, would be more likely. Probably ahead of her in gravitas and experience. Susan Rice would perhaps be National Security Adviser.

The overriding impression I got back in April in Washington has been confirmed again: when America breeds public-policy racehorses, it breeds the world's best. McCain, able to talk about democracy in Fiji and the Burmese generals he met who had gone to US military colleges or the refugee camps he visited with Lieberman in Syria. Or the formidable Bob Zoellick who, running the World Bank, can find time to launch a campaign to save the world's oceans and protect threatened tiger species. So too with Rice – an easy familiarity with all the matters we canvassed.

I walk back in baking New York heat to the residence to host lunch for seventeen ambassadors from small island states, including Vanuatu, Seychelles, Fiji, Barbados and Cuba. It turns into a seminar on fishing rights, coral reefs, rising sea levels and ocean quality. On these issues they see Australia as their friend.

As Ronny Jumeau, the Seychellois Ambassador, put it, 'We're small island states but we have big ocean territories.' I referred to the contents of the ocean being 'vacuumed up' in areas beyond national jurisdictions, 'the mining of the oceans beyond exclusive economic zones'. This partnership with the small island world reflects creative Australian diplomacy, the fact that we have Joseph Goddard, Ambassador of Barbados, and Dessima Williams, Ambassador of Grenada, coming under the Australian umbrella to talk about these things.

Later we had half-a-dozen ambassadors for drinks. They were being invited to Australia under our special visits program, unabashedly a bid for their votes. Luxembourg and Finland have seen us doing this over the last couple of years and they've now copied us, thus producing a bonanza of overseas travel for people lucky enough to represent third-world countries in the UN. I tried to put on all the charm but they must be seriously inured, knowing that this is all directed at nailing down their nation's vote.

Suddenly a message: a compromise over the Palestinians means our conference on arms control can begin. I race back to the General Assembly just in time to follow the Assistant Foreign Minister from Japan, and speak for Australia, loud and clear, I hope.

That night, satisfied at edging forward a global good, despite the roar of the air-conditioning and traffic and the jetlag, I again slept like the dead.

WEDNESDAY, JULY 4, 2012
New York

The pressure's off: America's great birthday. A holiday for all. A little work, however. I rang Aurelia Frick, Foreign Minister of Liechtenstein, and congratulated her on the birth of her son. I had an excellent briefing note that told me that plucky little Liechtenstein had been running campaigns to promote the ratification of the 2010 amendments to the Rome Statute declaring aggression a crime; was pursuing women's rights; and had organised a group dedicated as Friends of the International Criminal Court. This gave us some substance to our conversation. And I moved on to a fourth issue she'd committed to, which was more transparency and accountability in the work of the Security Council and, of course, this enabled me to ease into some lobbying to secure Liechtenstein's vote. She was receptive. She said she would need to take it to the government as a whole but implied that generally they accept her advice. That's worth a tick in the FOR column.

We might be tracking well on this but there could also always be a Palestinian status vote. That would blow the campaign to bits.

Gary Quinlan and Caroline Millar from DFAT's UN Security Council team brief me. They highlight the inherent difficulty with our campaign, which is that we entered it late. Luxembourg and Finland were in the race from 2001 and 2002 respectively; Kevin committed us in 2008. As a result, there are over thirty nations that have stated a simple 'no' to Australia with the perfect justification they'd given a commitment elsewhere already. Malaysia and Indonesia are in this category, even Canada. If we lose, this will be the reason.

But this was July 4.

We took a van up to West Point for a tour of the military

academy established by Thomas Jefferson in 1802 because of his deep suspicions of Alexander Hamilton's militia who were all linked with the Federalist Party, which Jefferson opposed and hated. Hence the President who loathed a standing army made the decision that had America train officers on this site, the site, incidentally, that George Washington had occupied as his nearest fort to Manhattan.

Life is a war against boredom and I counted the tour moderately interesting and our guide was lively. I asked him about counter-insurgency and he admitted candidly that military opinion is divided over COIN – the acronym it's known by. Some want to make it the centre of everything, some make it one tactic among many. 'We have a consistent record of predicting where we will fight the next war,' he said. 'And we are always wrong.'

When Nixon came here in '71, he saw the monument to West Point graduates killed in the Civil War and gave a directive that West Point must build one to the Confederate dead. He had Alexander Haig follow through. It was all about the Southern strategy: Nixon's bid to get the South to vote for him in the wake of the Democrats making themselves a party of desegregation. But the small number of black cadets heard about this and staged a revolt. They put the argument that if they had joined the Black Panthers, a revolutionary movement, they could hardly expect to be commemorated. They said the Southern Confederacy was nothing more than a revolutionary movement against America, as indeed it was. They threatened the administration that if the plans for the memorial proceeded, they would object every way they could. And the administration – that of West Point and that of Washington – backed down. America at its best.

I would have liked to press on and pay my third visit to the Roosevelt home at Hyde Park but that would have made it a long day. As it was, a Fourth of July parade with fire trucks slowed down our return.

FRIDAY, JULY 6, 2012
New York, Paris

Still jetlagged – I had woken up at 2 am – we drove to JFK for a
five o'clock departure to Paris. This was another bit of exquisite
torture: the flight to Paris was too short to take a Normison and
get five or six hours' sleep. H, the staff and I drove from Charles
de Gaulle to the Hotel Raphael on the Right Bank near the Arc
de Triomphe, showered, gobbled down some breakfast, hurtled
off to the Friends of Syria Conference, arriving at 8.30 am, and
tried to function with two layers of jetlag on top of grotesque sleep
deprivation.

Ministers of over fifty countries sit facing one another. There
are officials from another fifty countries behind them. President
François Hollande opens with a speech in which he refers to 'an
escalation of massacres' in Syria. He says the role of the meeting is
to encourage the UN and to encourage the Syrian people. He says,
'I would like to tell people who are not here that the crisis in Syria
is a threat to peace and security.' This is the big threat to Russia
and China, conspicuous in their absence and conspicuous in their
support of the Assad regime. Statements from the Syrian opposition and Laurent Fabius, the new Foreign Minister of France,
refer to the need to have a reconstruction plan. The real fighting
campaigning speech is that of Hillary Clinton – Hillary at her
best, Hillary of the Texas primary – who sails right in. You can see
why she is so good on the stump, fighting Obama every inch of
the way in those 2008 primaries. She lays it on the line: we must
all make Russia and China pay for their support for the Assad
government. I have a statement supplied by the department and I
use that as the basis for my contribution. With no sleep, it's a challenge to listen to three-minute contribution after three-minute
contribution from members of the Foreign Ministers' Club – fifty

such speeches – but a consensus congeals that there should be no impunity for Assad, that there must be real and effective sanctions applied (that means UN sanctions), there must be more support for the democratic opposition and a lift in humanitarian aid and – beyond that – a pledge to rebuild the country when the fighting is over.

The meeting breaks up at around 2 pm and we get in buses to take us along the Seine to the Quai d'Orsay where foreign ministers gather in the splendid dining room for a lunch hosted by Fabius. I have a lively conversation with Canadian Foreign Minister John Baird who is fascinated by Rudd. He can't believe that Rudd is again contemplating a return to the prime ministership. He says it just couldn't happen under the Canadian system. He can't believe the audacity of it even though he knows Rudd well and likes him. I do my best to explain it all.

Back to the Hotel Raphael and a half-hour walk around the adjoining streets with our Ambassador, Ric Wells, talking about books and then to Charles de Gaulle Airport with another acrobatic motorcycle escort, sirens sounding, cars being brushed aside for the All Nippon Airways flight to Tokyo. Fabius is up there in first class with me but we all have our little compartments and I opt not to go over and harass him.

MONDAY, JULY 9, 2012
Tokyo

I arrived at Narita International Airport at three in the afternoon on Saturday after an all-night flight and went into a reception hosted by Koichiro Gemba, the Japanese Foreign Minister, with an opportunity for a 'pull aside' with Guido Westerwelle, the German Foreign Minister, who had come here on his own jet, lucky fella.

Yesterday morning a briefing with the whole delegation before we convened for the opening session of the Tokyo Conference on Afghanistan, where half the world will pledge support for building Afghanistan. I had a pleasant exchange with Hillary and got her a coffee from the machine in the corridor. I spoke third and read out Australia's statement, making a declaration of aid support of $250 million a year over four years from 2015–16. We will deliver on education, rural development and the provision of training for Afghan government officials in financial and electoral management. Then I'm free for 'pull asides' with the Deputy Foreign Minister of Kazakhstan, Kairat Sarybay, the Deputy Foreign Minister of Tajikistan, Nizomiddin Zohidov, and the Deputy Foreign Minister of Uzbekistan, Usmanov Oybek Arifbekovich. In the afternoon bilateral meetings with Foreign Minister of Pakistan Hina Rabbani Khar, French Foreign Minister Laurent Fabius and the Deputy Prime Minister of Croatia, Neven Mimica. Then more 'pull asides' with UK Secretary of State for International Development Andrew Mitchell and UAE Assistant Minister for Security and Military Affairs Faris Al Mazrouei.

Today my advisers and I got some fresh air and a walk at Hakone before a meeting with Foreign Minister Gemba at the Ministry of Foreign Affairs.

TUESDAY, JULY 10, 2012
Tokyo to Phnom Penh

Travel devastates my diet. The Palace Hotel in Tokyo served no oatmeal, no muesli. None of the official meals have serious protein content. Miserable tokenistic shreds of chicken or beef. I used to live on slabs of kangaroo, salmon and lean grass-fed beef, cooked by Helena for dinner and packaged for lunch. Right now I'm spending a day eating Thai airline food. I've got to order two main courses to come close to my protein targets. I've been wolfing down whey protein powder ('cross-flow, micro-filtered and hydro-lysed') and branched-chain amino acid tablets. At least there's a bountiful buffet at the Raffles in Phnom Penh – which I visited in April – that allows you to load up. They even have *unprocessed* rice. Now that – like having blueberries and organic steel-cut oats – is the sign of a serious hotel.

WEDNESDAY, JULY 11, 2012
Phnom Penh

At the Asian Regional Forum, Hillary dozes. Why not? She's travelled like me to Paris for Friends of Syria, then to Tokyo to discuss Afghanistan aid. Then she had several stops in Indo-China before arriving here in Phnom Penh. Ministers sit in a horseshoe, each with a little table in front with our country's flag, bottled water and box of sweets. One by one, the ministers read solemn set-piece speeches. The South Korean minister wins my award for best tie: a lime-green Hermès for which I would ransack any

airport store. Idly, I tick off the women foreign ministers: Pakistan
– the deep-voiced Minister Hina Rabbani Khar, a fierce defender
of her somewhat isolated country; Bangladesh – Minister Dipu
Moni, my old friend from Commonwealth meetings, tentative but
now growing in confidence; EU High Representative Catherine
Ashton – an alert, energetic UK politician who likes Australia.
And of course, the US Secretary of State, my heroine. How she
must sometimes savour having stared down that 'vast right-wing
conspiracy' to triumph in election to the Senate, come close to the
2008 nomination, and get appointed Secretary of State.

Play the game: you win.

Play the game: you lose.

Play the game.

Later there's a lunch for the foreign ministers of ASEAN
nations and their dialogue partners in the Peace Palace. Here the
Foreign Minister of Cambodia, Hor Namhong, a veteran survivor
of Cambodian politics, presides over the grilled fish and Australian tenderloin. I order both, two mains, winning for one meal at
least the quest for protein. But he doesn't speak a lot of English,
our conversation is limited and he seems happy to stare out ami-
ably at his guests.

Around the table I see foreign ministers checking their telephone messages. S.M. Krishna from India, an elderly figure from
Karnataka state with what looks like a grey hairpiece, seems
happy to simply look ahead of him. John Baird, the bluff conservative from Canada, with whom I now have a joking, familiar
relationship, works hard. 'How's Indonesia going?' And, 'How's
Brunei going?' He gets a response from the super-urbane Foreign
Minister Marty Natalegawa who, Julia Gillard says, reminds her
of Johnny Depp. Brunei has less to say.

Most of the exchanges are pretty formal. The Foreign Minister sitting opposite me I couldn't place and he didn't seem to
speak English or be interested in conversation in any case. North

Korea? Down the table, conversation looked desultory, between, for example, Vietnam and the Philippines.

I reflect on how wrong I was to assume that foreign ministers were a lot full of lively interest in the cultures and civilisations of the planet, scholars of statecraft, apostles of diplomacy. Krishna and I settled down at the end of the table for a bilateral meeting, still chewing our tenderloin. He was a seasoned state-level politician who had been elevated by Congress Party politics. He served first under Indira Gandhi, then under Rajiv Gandhi before becoming Chief Minister of Karnataka and later the Governor of Maharastra. He would have been lost without his briefing notes, which were bustled onto the table by his chief of staff who dragged up a seat and sat between us to check on what his minister might be up to. The minister did seem to recall that there'd be trouble with Indian students in Australia and was happy to note that was behind us. He searched for his paper for the next subject. We moved down our respective list of talking points.

Then out of the banquet room and upstairs for what was to be a bilateral meeting with the Philippines Foreign Minister Albert del Rosario, but he was delayed in an emergency meeting of ASEAN ministers, torn apart by a difference over the language that should be used on the South China Sea. At the Tokyo Conference on Afghanistan I had had a bilateral meeting with Japanese Foreign Minister Gemba, who, not to be distracted with any other subjects, sailed straight in to the South China Sea. Specifically, he wanted all of us speaking at the East Asia Summit, to specifically nominate Scarborough Shoal as a concrete example of a dispute in the South China Sea – as it happens, between China and the Philippines – and then go on to state the need for disputes to be settled according to the UN Convention on the Law of the Sea etc. That last bit is the Australian position anyway. But he wanted specific mention of Scarborough Shoal, contested between the Philippines and China, something the Chinese would bristle at and I thought would not serve Australia's interests. Why be specific about one dispute? I was non-committal, somewhat anxious about yet another issue opening between China and us.

After arriving in Phnom Penh last night, I indicated to advisers a preference for leaving a little daylight between us and this Japanese position, supported as it is by America and, of course, the Philippines. Now today the issue has really opened up. In a rare display of differences among the consensus-minded ASEANs, the Cambodians, close to the Chinese, have put out a statement, strongly rejecting the Philippines' approach. Meanwhile, the Philippines have reiterated their strident disagreement with China.

So right now, I'm back at the Raffles Hotel, not at the bilateral meeting with del Rosario while he's holed up sorting out the mess.

WEDNESDAY, JULY 18 – FRIDAY, JULY 20, 2012
Palo Alto, Bohemian Grove

Left Phnom Penh for Indonesia on Saturday, July 13, for my bilateral visit. We started in Yogyakarta to view Australian aid projects – a needle-and-syringe program and methadone-maintenance treatment for heroin addicts, plus a bridge construction and microfinance activities at Umbulharjo Village. This makes the point that our aid for Indonesia is flexible. We're able to tailor support for a community group that backs President Yudhoyono's own programs and plans for alleviation of poverty at the village level.

In Jakarta a Foreign Ministers' meeting with Marty Natalegawa that canvassed the bilateral issues, meetings on development assistance and an official dinner hosted by the Natalegawas.

Departed Jakarta for San Francisco on Tuesday, July 17. Spent a night at a hotel at Stanford, jetlag bubbling in my system at carcinogenic levels.

On Wednesday, July 18, to the university.

Beazley set up a meeting with Condoleezza Rice, making use of the time I've got here before I head over the Golden Gate Bridge north to Bohemian Grove.

This is the way a career as Secretary of State for a disastrous president ends up: in a room filled with memorabilia, including signed photos of your boss, George W. Bush. Rice hosted a lunch for me and Beazley – sandwiches (can't avoid them in this country but when the others aren't looking I extract the protein and leave the bread on the side) – in this office and I briefed her on the recent Friends of Syria meeting in Paris. She said that the failure of both Russia and China to force an outcome from Assad was indicative of 'a new binary divide in international politics'. Russia under Vladimir Putin was showing 'nationalism and recidivism'.

Rice said that the clock was ticking on Iran's nuclear program. She thought that the United States would be prepared to use military force against the nuclear sites in Iran, if sanctions and other measures failed. It would be better for the United States to act, rather than allow Israel to conduct military operations, which 'would significantly degrade the regional security outlook'. Rice expected that Iran would retaliate by closing the Strait of Hormuz and by using its proxy Hezbollah to attack Western and Israeli targets in the region.

I asked if a military strike on Iran's nuclear facilities would, in fact, be sufficient to end the nuclear program. Rice said a military strike would delay, not end, Iran's nuclear ambitions but would be useful in buying more time for diplomacy.

Condoleezza Rice has been named by some US media outlets as a possible vice-presidential running mate for Governor Mitt Romney. She has denied the speculation. Beazley says she was advising the Romney campaign on foreign policy.

My brain is stuck to the top of my head, glued up with jetlag. Where is my body clock located? In what continent? All I want to do is get back to the little hotel and press a pillow to my head and go to sleep. What time is it in Sydney? Jakarta?

But reflecting on the meeting with this former Secretary of State I try to sort myself through the facts. In 2001 a band of terrorists out of the mountains in Afghanistan pulled off the attack on the World Trade Center. Then America, with all its capacity to make calibrated decisions and tease out diplomatic nuance and take a strategic view, allowed itself to be taken over by its pure blood-in-the-eye instincts. A coalition of ultra-nationalists and neo-cons clawed their way into the ascendancy and quickly set off two wars. One in Afghanistan and another in Iraq. They bankrupted the country and drained its military strength. One's got to ponder how America got it so wrong and wonder about accountability for this damage.

No one is being held accountable. Yet I can't think of more horrendous errors of judgment since Washington decided to dig in rather than exit Vietnam.

Our closest friend, our ally, our partnership of interests and values cemented by its liberal internationalism: all true.

And yet ...

Before we leave the campus the Ambassador steers me to its bookshop – a vast book emporium – and insists on buying me Allen Guelzo's *Fateful Lightning*, the latest work on the Civil War.

In the hotel I press a pillow over my face but sleep eludes me.

In the evening Beazley drops me at a spacious, classic American home on the Stanford campus, one of the several residences of former Secretary of State, George Shultz. He served Reagan between 1982 and 1989 and he was a great friend of Bob Hawke's. In fact, he had known Hawke from his time as a Bechtel representative making visits to Australia and rubbing up against Hawke as ACTU President. There's a party in his back garden with an Italian theme, which I join. Soon, we're sitting down to dinner outdoors. I have Henry Kissinger on one side and across the table Condoleezza Rice, two former Secretaries of State to Republican Presidents. She repeats her argument from our earlier meeting in her office that it would be better for the US to bomb Iran; that is, better than leaving it to Israel. Kissinger's line, however, is different. He believes Obama does not want to take military action. And he believes that the military does not want another war. If they are ordered to plan one, someone will leak it to the media to render it controversial and force the government to back down.

I spend the night as a guest and the next morning enjoy breakfast with the Shultzes, Kissinger, and their other house guest, Andrew Knight, a member of Murdoch's board and a former editor of UK paper the *Daily Telegraph*. We start happily enough with a big bowl of berries but the next course is a knockout: sumptuous flapjacks with maple syrup extracted from the trees in their Massachusetts home, the ultimate in organic. Also, sausages. I passed up the burnt-to-a-crisp bacon on which, I noticed, the others munched away.

An embassy car drove me the two hours to Bohemian Grove and I did a few interviews with Australian radio on the Syrian crisis. Russia has just vetoed a British motion in the Security Council that would have invoked Chapter VII of the UN Charter against Assad. This leaves the world nowhere to go. It is a tragic end for the principle of Responsibility to Protect, accepted by all UN Member States at the 2005 UN World Summit. Under this doctrine, if a nation fails to protect its own people, the nations of the world have a responsibility to take up protection. But they must have UN authority to intervene and UN decision-making is subject to a veto by any permanent member of the Security

Council. But, with this Syrian deadlock, the noble goal of humanitarian intervention dies.

The Bohemian Grove is a narrow valley between steep inclines covered with towering redwoods, the tallest trees in the world, I think. Encampments run up the sides of both gully walls. They are picturesque, like something designed in the Disney studios in the 1930s or '40s. Each camp has a captain, a business figure. The captain of Mandalay, where Kissinger and I are to stay, is David O'Reilly, former chairman of Chevron. The camp comprises businesspeople and a smattering of artists, in our case at our camp, an American popular singer whose name, of course, I didn't recognise and can't remember. The other businesspeople include Steve Wynn, who owns casinos in America and China, and Bob Joss, who used to head Westpac and now teaches at Stanford. I share my spartan bedroom with 87-year-old Steve Bechtel, the owner of the vast engineering, procurement and construction company.

The people who attend – there are about 118 camps and I guess a few thousand campers – are the millionaire class. They are the men – no women, not one – who own America. I could hear the donations to the Romney campaign being sucked skyward. Many conversations confirm Obama is seen as a socialist transforming – no, perverting – the American system.

So our camp comprises cabins on the hillside, linked by tracks to a shower block, and to a platform with a dining room and kitchen running off it. Walking with toothbrush or towel to a communal shower block had me thinking of the Sunday school camp at Otford when I was eleven or twelve. The good news – the unexpectedly sensational news: the food was excellent, with a team of five or so turning out big bountiful breakfasts, lunches and dinners. Slabs of protein, mountains of vegetables.

And of course, every opportunity to listen to Henry. Here I conflate what I heard him say when he dazzled several breakfast

meetings with formal talks and informally chatted over a couple
of lunches.

We're living through the first time that events that occur within
countries have global impact in international affairs, he said. In
China, there are 500 million people being moved from the countryside to cities. He asked, 'What values will they bring with them,
and how will they change once they are transplanted to an urban
environment?' China's leaders don't even talk about communism
'liturgically' these days. Useful adjective, that. The policy of one-
child families means each child has four grandparents 'beating
up on him': producing kids who are egotistical, anxious, compul-
sive, competitive. He referred to a recent conversation with Lee
Kuan Yew, the former Singaporean Prime Minister, who said he
hadn't the faintest idea what political system could take the place
of the current one in China. Here Henry offered up what I think
is a strikingly original observation: at present the party is carefully
managing – as carefully as it can, given the Bo Xilai affair – the
replacement of the Party Secretary (in October) and President (in
March) and Chairman of the Central Military Commission (sometime later). But everyone knows that in ten years' time they cannot
manage the next leadership transition the same way. As a result,
there is bound to be a debate about process. But Kissinger's view is
the next leadership transition will have to be a different one.

All the time there's the ever-present danger that the Chinese
use nationalism as a replacement for communism. This was
something I picked up at a conversation with Fu Ying, their Assistant Foreign Minister and former Ambassador to Australia, when
we were in Phnom Penh. She told me that eighty per cent of the
online commentary in China questions why China even negoti-
ates with Southeast Asian countries on what they see as justified
territorial claims in Chinese seas. Fu Ying spoke about the impact
of the internet on Chinese politics. She said that local government
now has a three-hour turnaround – that is, faced with criticism of

their performance, a local government entity has to have a reply out on the internet within three hours. She had later told Helena – this was our encounter in Phnom Penh – she remembers being humiliated by Kevin Rudd in their encounter in a TV studio in London when she was Chinese Ambassador to the UK. Rudd deliberately got up and moved from the seat next to her to sit next to David Miliband. Apparently he was anxious about being seen as too close to the Chinese (given taunts about 'the Manchurian candidate' that I seem to recall from his early days). All these years later she still remembers this and expressed her hurt in a conversation with Helena.

Back to Henry. On Europe, he says we are witnessing a loss of capacity of governments to demand sacrifices of their people. There is no vision of Europe other than a technical one. Then, returning to the US, he says, bluntly, it has to rethink its military strategy. There have been three wars that have ended up in debate about withdrawal. He said the US needs a peripheral base strategy. It needs to intervene but not for protracted conflicts. America's strength lies in mobility, technology and firepower. He said America has ten years to work on a relationship with China that makes them part of an international system. In the meantime – in the disputes over maritime territory – the world has a nightmarish echo of how World War I arrived. It was a slide into a conflict from which Europe never recovered. No leaders who had made the decision to go to war in 1914 would have done it if they'd known what was going to happen.

He talks about the Middle East with the same realism. America, he says, will always favour democratic values as a matter of instinct and national character. But in regions with no history of democracy and where the most organised groups reject pluralism, it is a mistake to treat countries' immediate willingness to adopt Western-style political institutions as the sole criterion for foreign policy. Not every group capable of winning an election is democratic. An allowance for particularities of history and culture is needed.

'We shouldn't have to apologise for having a national interest,' he says. 'We are a nation, not a foundation.' A neat point too. (I feel sometimes I've got to explain I'm running a foreign policy for Australia, not for Human Rights Watch or the Tamil National Alliance.) On Egypt, he said people who make revolution rarely survive it. This has happened to the people who made the revolution in Tahrir Square. Revolution wipes out existing institutions. In the end, one of the old pre-revolutionary institutions has to move in and provide authority.

The Israelis, he said, see their position with Iran as approaching the last moment when they can act against the nuclear program. They watch as Iran moves its nuclear facilities underground. He agrees that nuclear weapons in Iran would be extremely unsettling. He seems to subscribe to the notion expressed by Condoleezza Rice that it would be better for America, and not Israel, to bomb them. 'But I want to know what happens day by day for the three weeks after. All the cables, all the foreign leaders, all the resolutions, all the top-flight journalists ... all this has to be attended to. Whoever wins in November should assign a taskforce straightaway. We need a 72-hour schedule spelling out who does what and when.'

He said: 'I oscillate. I've been 50–50 on whether there'll be an Israeli attack. Now it's down to thirty per cent likelihood because of Netanyahu's majority being reduced to six with the withdrawal of the Kadima coalition partner.'

On Russia, Henry says there's no point continuing to present a resolution on Syria to the UN. It won't affect Putin. Putin sees the West wanting to intervene wherever there is an insurgency against a regime.

Throughout my time at Bohemian Grove, Kissinger returned to his observation that the Russians, staring at demographic decline, face one billion Chinese. The Russians can't get their own people to live in Siberia and they won't allow Chinese or other Asians to work there. Their border with China runs for 3000 miles. And then Russia faces borders with Islamic states. Ten per cent of its own population is Muslim. They have a border with Europe that involves an independent Ukraine. It's very hard for Russia to accept an independent Ukraine because Russia is programmed to think of itself as an empire; they did for 300 years. Russia sees itself as threatened on all sides.

Out of this Kissinger argues that in the longer term, the foreign-policy challenge is to bring Russia into the international system. As a country it faces a middle-class starting to ask hard questions about governance. He argues that if the US has a proper relationship with Russia it makes Russia's internal evolution more likely.

Kissinger says, 'If a Chinese leader says to his people, "Work hard and you will become the greatest people in the world," they believe him. If a Russian leader said it, the Russian people would not believe it. The greatest quality of their people is endurance.' Again, he says the argument with Russia on Syria is not just about their stake in Damascus. The Russians think one day the West will apply the same sort of intervention we're proposing in Syria to them, to Russia itself.

We think of countries as coherent cultural units, says Henry. But Pakistan is nothing like that at all. It is simply that part of British India that didn't want to be Hindu. No civilian government there has ever served its full term. It's unified by Islam and fear of India. And they see Afghanistan as part of their war with India. They have 100 nuclear weapons. If we pull out of Afghanistan, we could leave a hole there, he says. He urges a conference of surrounding countries to do what was done with Belgium in the nineteenth century. And work towards a free trade agreement with India and Pakistan. Give the Pakistanis something to do apart from fighting India.

Later, in a quiet chat with Henry, sitting on the balcony, I asked him whether he thought Reagan was a great President. He said that Reagan's qualities were perfectly suited to his time – facing a Soviet Union whose material and psychological foundations were starting to crumble – but rejected the idea that being 'Reaganesque' was the key to American presidential greatness. This attitude, of course, would separate Henry – realist, geostrategist, diplomatist – from the others milling around this campsite. This is confirmed when he said to me we can no longer solve problems from a position of predominance. And in foreign policy, we shouldn't be scoring every quarter. A longer-term view is required. Our problems, however, are easier to solve than those of other powers. One would rather be the President of the US than the new President of China. Kissinger made this point in all of his presentations at Bohemian Grove.

By contrast, old George Shultz remains a Reagan devotee. But sitting next to him at one of the breakfasts, I asked him about another Republican President. I said I was becoming increasingly interested in Dwight Eisenhower, rising in estimation in most of the recent assessments. He recalled an encounter with Eisenhower. He visited the old man in hospital when he was serving as Secretary of Labor under Nixon. Eisenhower advised him to play golf. 'You're probably intent on working fourteen hours a day, seven days a week while you're in Washington,' he said. But he told Shultz he would perform better if he took time off at the golf course. Shultz said that Eisenhower was seen as a vague figure floating above his cabinet but he had a detailed knowledge of the work of government. Shultz found that he knew all about the Labor Department and knew it in detail.

Then there was an exchange I had with another former Secretary of State, James Baker, whom I sat next to at another breakfast. He said unless one party controls the House, the Senate and the presidency, then each party is going to continue to have a veto over budget reform – and debt to GDP is already 100 per cent. And here's the frightening thing, he added: 'If we didn't have dollars as a de facto world currency, we'd be Greeks.' He said America's sliding into inflating its way out of the debt problem.

A Navy SEAL addressed a gathering at our camp, a member of this elite special force. He came up with an expression I liked. He said the problem of terrorism was now so widespread – Mali, Somalia, Yemen, Afghanistan, Pakistan – that we need to 'triage' world terrorist problems. Work out what we can afford and what we can't afford. Again, the tone of a sober American realism is surfacing.

And George Shultz said it as well: 'Future actions against terrorists should be surgical strikes, not ten-year-long wars.' There was a Bush – Jeb Bush, as it happens – somewhere in the encampment. I didn't beat a path to the presentation he was giving. Shouldn't judge him by his brother. Still …

This is all good. All educational, all astute. But it was spread pretty thin. Bohemian Grove doesn't offer the intense lecture-on-lecture, panel-on-panel that you get at Davos or Aspen. It was time for a walk and there was a lot of entertainment.

One night, before a concert performance of American songs, a big brassy orchestra played 'The Stars and Stripes Forever'. This business audience of one to two thousand rose as one and belted out 'The Star-Spangled Banner'. Sung it with passion, the passion of people extolling the country they own. They were a very decent lot. But after four nights here, I'd had enough of American charm and I was happy to be picked up at the entrance – like a prisoner being released from the gates and being driven away – for the drive south to San Francisco and a meeting with the man everyone at the Grove will vote for: Mitt Romney.

SUNDAY, JULY 22, 2012
Bohemian Grove to San Francisco to Sydney

We drove down to San Francisco in summer weather and dropped in to see book dealer Robert Dagg, who I've known for thirty years. He lives in a weatherboard house in The Mission and I poked around his small collection of modern first editions. Bought a 1941 Thomas Mann published by Knopf and an old-fashioned biography of William Jennings Bryan, the Bible-quoting populist who the Democrats nominated for President in 1896, 1900 and 1908. Then to the Fairmont Hotel up on Nob Hill where the embassy had set me up for the afternoon in a room with a view from the Bay Bridge to the Golden Gate Bridge: a blue sky with scudding clouds, the sun-bleached hill-hugging buildings, the islands of the bay. But I didn't leave the hotel: ordered grilled salmon from room service, did a workout in the gym, and at 5.30 pm went downstairs for, astonishingly, a one-on-one meeting secured by the embassy with Mitt Romney.

I had resolved to respect his time and not risk boring him. Instead of the allotted twenty minutes I would take ten. He walked in, tall, trim, the finest-looking specimen of a presidential candidate since Warren G. Harding, another candidate from central casting. I told him we'd both had the experience of running Olympics and got him talking about how he salvaged the Winter Games in Salt Lake City. We discussed ticketing policy, of all things. Then I said I wanted to give him some information about Australia and the alliance and watched as he rearranged his face, moving from relaxed, friendly mode to 'I'm listening, serious and intent' mode. I said that Australia was a firm friend of the US; I said we had 1550 troops in Afghanistan, the largest non-NATO contributor, and we were committing $250 million in aid per year for the four years after 2014. I said we would have special forces in there beyond transition. He acknowledged all of this.

Then I gave him the line I used with Bob Zoellick to such effect: America is one budget deal away from banishing talk of American decline. I wished him well at this task were he to be elected President. 'Can I use that?' he asked, meaning the line about the country being one budget deal away from banishing talk of decline. Recollecting how Bob Zoellick had used the same line when I served it up to him, I said, 'Yes. Sure.' He went off to two fundraising receptions. Henry had told me at the Grove he'd be addressing a $50,000-a-head fundraising dinner for Romney, but doing it without any clear idea of where the candidate was going on foreign policy. Henry had said he had to tell the organisers he could not take questions about what Romney would do in foreign policy because he had no idea.

To San Francisco Airport where I bought myself a quarter of a chicken from a new farmer's market store – healthy food in airports, what a breakthrough! – because US airlines do not serve nutritious food on domestic flights. Ate it in the first-class lounge, and bought from the airport bookshop the latest Alan Furst spy story, Jean Edward Smith's new book on Eisenhower and – of more practical relevance – James Mann's *The Obamians*, about the struggle inside the White House over foreign policy. To Los Angeles and home by Qantas.

WEDNESDAY, JULY 25, 2012
Sydney

Can't believe it! Romney took my reference on American power and gave it his own crude spin. He told the media that foreign leaders were *alarmed* at American economic policy and quoted the Australian Foreign Minister as his source. This really took me by surprise but served a larger purpose of reminding the public I'd scored a coup with our embassy getting me in to see the presumptive Republican nominee. And it gave me fodder for a burst of media. The US Embassy in Canberra is smart enough to know what I actually said and how Romney twisted it. They relayed a message from the White House that they knew what Romney had done.

THURSDAY, JULY 26, 2012
Sydney

Crippled with jetlag I got up early, invited myself on to Fran Kelly's *AM* to talk about the Romney statement and other things. Then busy appointments in the office and a Graham Richardson interview for *Sky News*. More appointments in the office – a lunch with Dennis Richardson, a meeting with the Friends of Bethlehem, a pro-Palestinian group, a phone call from Malcolm Fraser, a meeting with Sub Continent Friends of Labor, and I pre-recorded a *Lateline* interview with Tony Jones on the way home. I don't know where I get this energy. All psychology, all motivation. Underlying anxiety and pessimism is the best fuel. Also the stuff is so interesting.

Letter from Singapore Airlines Regional Vice President

Tuesday, July 31, 2012

Dear Senator Carr,

I am writing to you following feedback I received this week from our Cabin Crew Division after your recent journey onboard flight SQ002 from Hong Kong to San Francisco on 17 July.

At the outset, please accept my sincere apology if any part of our First Class inflight offering fell below your expectations. Your feedback will ensure that we do better next time.

Specifically, I have taken note of the lack of English subtitles for the Wagner Opera 'Siegfried'.

I do agree with you that our KrisWorld Entertainment System should display such programs with several subtitle options, including English, in order to make the viewing experience more meaningful to our global customers.

In addition, I am very sorry to hear that the breakfast meal you requested, including scrambled eggs in oil, wholemeal toast and muesli, was not available.

The meal service is a very important part of our First Class product offering and we must ensure that sufficient quantities of the meal choices are available.

I look forward to the opportunity to welcome you onboard our services in the future and to serve you better.

Yours sincerely,

Subhas Menon
Regional Vice President
South West Pacific

WEDNESDAY, AUGUST 1, 2012
Abu Dhabi

Set up here in the Etihad Towers Hotel in Abu Dhabi at the start of my Middle East trip: UAE–Jordan–Israel–Ramallah. It is a trial, a test, a duty. And note the date, August 2012. One year to go.

Well, as Chairman Mao put it, seize the day, seize the hour. So here I am, in this restless corner of the planet, with Syria locked in a raging civil war, the Muslim Brotherhood on the rise and the Israel–Palestine dispute congealed and deadlocked.

Back home on Monday I delivered movement on Fiji policy. It was a trilateral: us, New Zealand and Fiji – three foreign ministers meeting in Sydney. The main question was whether we recognise Fiji's constitutional consultation process and their commitment to a 2014 election. My advisers pointed me in the direction of, one, restoring Australian and New Zealand High Commissioners to Suva, and two, being flexible in applying our sanctions against their ministers to travel here or to New Zealand by allowing travel by ministers on a case-by-case basis. We would favour civilian ministers, encouraging them to put civilians, not military officers, in their cabinet.

Got over the meeting in the morning (of course we did; I was in the chair). I gave them lunch at Rockpool and, over the chicken breast, insisted the communiqué include a reference to Australia and New Zealand raising media freedom and human rights. A bit of resistance but Fiji conceded.

Anyway, we put it out. Generally supported in our media. We've got engagement, we've got movement. I was sick of looking at a blank, flickering screen when it came to Fiji. So I've given myself a Fiji policy, for better or worse. See where it leads. The regime, bad as it is, is doing no more than Singapore did ten or twenty years ago – intimidating the opposition, bullying media. Still, the Pacific *is* a community of democracies, and our partners, like Samoa and Vanuatu, can expect better.

Now to get through Israel–Palestine without a stumble.

THURSDAY, AUGUST 2, 2012
Abu Dhabi, Amman

UAE Foreign Minister Sheikh Abdullah is lively and knowledgeable; seven years in the job makes him fluent, clever at a diplomat's stratagems and verbal solutions. He wears the white robes and sandals but speaks with a vaguely mid-Atlantic accent. He does high-adventure sport like bungee jumping; offering a nice bushwalk in the Royal National Park would clearly not wash. Point about the Emirates is that it is royal, it is tribal and it is tiny. Out of a population of about 9.2 million, fewer than twenty per cent are natives. I sat at a lecture by a Saudi cleric in the Abu Dhabi palace last night: me, sitting amid rows of robe-wearing ministers, with an earphone for translation. I reflected: here it is all family, all clan.

I signed a nuclear safeguards agreement – the Australia–UAE Nuclear Cooperation Agreement – and pushed our interests: getting their vote for the UN ballot (Foreign Minister Sheikh Abdullah said he would support us, publicly); selling Austal patrol boats; getting Australian property developers Matthew Joyce and Marcus Lee released from their court system (a drawn-out consular case over a nasty commercial dispute). This last we have been raising at every opportunity. At times it has been the biggest question in our bilateral relationship, our Ambassador engaged full time on it.

Just to complicate this picture of comity, they have pushed hard on one prickly request: for us to make some kind of military commitment, even a token one such as a single naval vessel, to them and the Gulf in the event of a showdown with Iran or to deter a retaliatory attack from Iran. Our approach has been that we should hold back. The notion has been aired in the National Security Committee. Within our government the consensus seemed to be: we can't slip into another Middle East war. But now they don't push on this, anyway. And the Foreign Minister suggests that the chance of Iranian retaliation against them has faded (i.e. in the event of a US or Israeli strike).

On the flight from Abu Dhabi to Amman I read cables about responses to China's truculence on the South China Sea. Washington tells us they have been told officially that the State Department has set aside the caution it showed in Phnom Penh and now concludes some anti-Chinese action is required. This is confirmed by a cable from Honolulu: the admirals are engaged. The US has been too understated on the Scarborough Shoal; this is now the consensus American view. Could be a firming up of ship visits and other activity.

A notion grows on me. 'I feel a Gareth-style plan coming on,' I tell Graeme. 'A plan for the South China Sea – about shared resource development, based on us and Indonesia and the East Timor gas deal, providing it's acceptable to the US.

I would take it to Southeast Asia.'

But on the Middle East …

We get media coverage with a visit to refugee camps in Jordan. Then we close down. Seek no more media. I want no joint media conferences in Jerusalem and Ramallah. None. And no interviews with Australian or Israeli media. None. Too many landmines in this landscape. Radio silence.

With jetlag and late Ramadan dinners, I am *beyond* tired. Patches of deep sleep – one to two hours – see me through, without Normison. Busted the wiring in my right shoulder with weights so applying heat pads and taking Voltaren.

Gore Vidal has died and I paid tribute with interviews for ABC Radio and, from an Abu Dhabi studio, for *Lateline*. I first became aware of him as the author of *Myra Breckinridge*, which was banned in Australia and which I picked up at Honolulu Airport during my first visit to America in 1970–71. Then I remember reading a profile of him in *TIME* magazine in early 1976, three years after *Burr* came out. I was fascinated by a life given over to writing, of a writer finally being recognised, as he was with *Burr*. Before long I'd read *Washington D.C.* and recognised his fascination for the world I loved, of American politics, and before long, as his historical novels came forth, he was a figure of renown in our circle of Labor operatives focused on the pageant of US history. The sheer cheek in 1996 of Bob Ellis and me drafting a letter inviting him to come to Australia, promising the company of Whitlam and Wheeldon and good food and wine, and the astonishment of receiving his reply, lettermarked La Rondinaia, Ravello (Salerno) Italy:

Dear Premier,

Plainly an offer, as we say hereabouts, that I cannot possibly refuse!

He was great fun, with all the stories on politics, literature, movies and plays. Then Helena and I spent time with him and his life partner, Howard Austen, during a holiday in Italy in early 1998. It's just sad that our last meeting at his home in Los Angeles was marred by him being blind drunk. Incontinent too. His cook served foul food. Who eats cheese soufflé these days? Yet he spoke about the historical novel he didn't get round to writing, one set at the time of the Mexican War, telling the story of an aggressively expansionist one-term Democratic President, James K. Polk, all the generals who had later become so famous on both sides of the American Civil War and a one-term Whig Congressman called Abraham Lincoln, who raised his voice in lonely opposition to America's first war of choice.

Conversations with him were hikes through the landscape of history and literature, a rare privilege.

Soon nobody will read his clever, sometimes plodding, historical novels or his agile conversational essays; or even recall his artful one-liners. For a while longer people will half-recognise his name and then it will fall off the edge of the table. He once said – and I like it – 'I'm not sentimental about anything. Life flows by, and you flow with it or you don't. *Move on and move out.*'

He said he liked my quote from Flaubert used in my book *My Reading Life*, writing about the finality of death in the antique world before people signed up to an after life:

[For the ancients that] 'black hole' was infinity in itself; their dreams loom and vanish against a background of immutable ebony. No crying out, no convulsions – nothing but the fixity of a pensive gaze. With the gods gone, and Christ not yet come, there was a unique moment, from Cicero to Marcus Aurelius, when man stood alone. Nowhere else do I find that particular grandeur.

How it ends.

We just go off into that void.

FRIDAY, AUGUST 3, 2012
Amman

The stand-out fact about Jordan: up to forty-five per cent of total government revenues are foreign grants. The US gave them $4.2 billion from 2000 to 2010. There are 6.5 million people; four million are Palestinian. Islamists gain strength – with thirty-five per cent unemployment it's not hard to understand – and the Brothers (the more accurate rendering of the Muslim Brotherhood) have fifteen to twenty-five per cent support.

On the charm stakes, their Foreign Minister, Nasser Judeh, an Arab aristocrat, is way out there. He is a Palestinian-Jordanian born in Amman in 1961. He finished his secondary schooling in Sussex, England, and graduated with a Bachelor of Science in Foreign Service from Georgetown's School of Foreign Service. Like Marty, a professional; a Foreign Minister to his fingertips, 'to the manner born'. Compact figure, aquiline nose, moustache; almost theatrical urbanity. In the Foreign Ministers' Club I suspect everybody likes him. 'Come into my smoking room,' he says. 'It's where I can smoke without giving offence.' He gestures, pulls faces, wise-cracks. 'Everyone has discovered the Muslim Brotherhood. We have them in the parliament: Been there! Done that! Got the T-shirt!' He worked in the palace as PR; married a daughter of the king's uncle; divorced her but survived as one of the king's favourites in seven governments (the ministries appointed and quickly dismissed by the king).

The news – Syria, Egypt, Jordan, Israel–Palestine – is all negative. 'It's the Chinese curse. We live in interesting times,' he says.

We do a press conference for Jordanian media. I avoid saying we support arming the Syrian rebels when invited to do so by one journalist. Instead I say the world must take notice of the pressures on Jordan created by the sectarian war over the border.

We see the king. A short, trim man. In his soft voice with its hint of English precision – hand on chin, attentive frown – he doles out his analysis. His Foreign Minister helps, urbanely: 'If I may, Your Majesty ...'

He talks about a 'Plan B' emerging from the Syrian mess: a partition. An Alawite state could run along the coast. But he isn't endorsing this plan and doesn't want this discussed now. Thinks the regime has four months to go.

SUNDAY, AUGUST 5, 2012
Amman

Yesterday one of the refugees said he was fired on by Hezbollah and al-Nusra forces. By *both* sides. Others told me of their houses bombed from the air. In the refugee camp I told the ABC camera, 'These people have been bombed out of their homes. They've fled to the border clutching their children. Australia's got to be there.' I've put around $4 million into their aid. This was at Zaatari camp in the fine dust of the tent city thrown up by UNHCR in the last weeks.

Returned to Amman through Jerash, best of the Roman cities I've seen.

The Jordanian Foreign Minister dropped in to the hotel for a tea. I asked whether we should arm the Syrian rebels. His reply: 'As the king says, "Sure – if you can give me the address and the CV of those we're arming." The arms in Libya have ended up *here*.'

We've got to look after these admirable Arab moderates, these astute survivors, these hospitable Jordanians. They are worldly bulwarks against the religious fanatics. I want to help them.

Dinner with the Ambassador and my people, where I rehearse my lines for Israel. A dangerous four days coming up. In December 2010 Kevin tripped up, calling on Israel to open itself to inspection by the International Atomic Energy Agency. Just to remind me how sensitive this diplomatic landscape is, I received a note from Gary Quinlan at the UN Mission: the whole terrain is sensitive; the Israelis will be embracing me, the Palestinians watching. My view: better to avoid media. Everything on the Middle East gets twisted; the participants on both sides back in Australia are itching to take offence.

WEDNESDAY, AUGUST 8, 2012
Jerusalem, Amman

We were invited to the home of Isi Leibler, a prominent Australian business figure who now lives in Jerusalem and, with his Melbourne-based brother, Mark, represents a Likud-oriented pro-Israel lobby. As Helena, James Larsen, Patrick Low, my media adviser, and I walked through the entrance into Leibler's apartment, an eerie pantomime was suddenly enacted: a woman emerged from the dark holding a video camera to one eye. Her smile gave the encounter a sinister cast. I've never had this experience before. I felt as if I was being accused of participating in a conspiracy, being stuck up against a wall, being forced to explain myself. We assumed that *The Australian*'s correspondent, John Lyons – the woman his partner – wanted to present my attendance as confirmation of some conspiracy between the Australian government and the Israeli right-wing – except my media adviser was ready to share the guest list with him and demonstrate that it included moderate Israelis and that I was seeing the Palestinian Foreign Minister, Prime Minister and President when I visited Ramallah. But Lyons was not going to get to interview me. Nobody was. No publicity was my preference. We didn't pursue the Fairfax representative.

I saw all the Israeli leadership during my stay in Israel: Netanyahu pointing out the window, talking about Iran on the hillline, saying if they give away the West Bank, Iran will be sitting on that hill; Barak agreeing with me completely about Israel's being branded an apartheid state – only he didn't use the term, he said 'a term used about another country on another continent' – if it did not give up the West Bank; Foreign Minister Avigdor Lieberman lecturing me in a monotone over lunch in his ministry; Labor leader Shelly Yachimovich saying she appreciated my campaign tips. She thinks she may revive the once-splendid Israeli Labor Party.

Some details ...

Ehud Barak, a small, rotund seventy-year-old who wears fashionable black casual gear, is the Israeli Defence Minister but also the link between Netanyahu's government and the Americans with his regular – even monthly – meetings with CIA Director David Petraeus. He runs US–Israel relations, not Lieberman the Foreign Minister. Barak says the point about the Arab world is that there's no ripeness for Western-style democracy. There are no Václav Havels. The Muslim Brotherhood has therefore moved in as the most organised force, not as extreme as Hamas, nor as brutal as the Iraqis or Syrians. In fact there is something more moderate about collective Egyptian society. The leadership could be less extremist than we might fear. After all, there are constraints, such as the economy and the need for US support, that would limit other instincts. They would need to balance with the military, even follow the Turkish example, although that had been built on decades of the Kemalist model.

But Iran is ticking over much faster than the world realises, and Israel is not bound by the US refusal to take action in a presidential election year. Barak says he sides with the Israeli Ministry of Foreign Affairs view that Israel needs to be doing more to show and convince the world that it is trying to reach a solution on Israel–Palestine and he says there has to be a two-state solution. He says Israel is living on borrowed time, losing public sympathy in the West as memories of the Holocaust fade.

Netanyahu is forceful, even bossy, but more intellectually supple than I had expected. Some deft touches in his conversation: for example, he said that even before the civil war in Syria, their cities were dilapidated, with few signs of shops or cafés. It was an impoverished society, degraded by dictatorship. The Arab countries have moved away from pan-Arabism – secular Arab nationalism – to Islamic regimes without missing a beat. Their first elections in various countries after the Arab Spring revolution had been free but what next? He's pessimistic. 'How could one stabilise the region given the lack of basic conceptions of individual rights as developed by Locke and Montesquieu?' he asked. 'Politics in the Arab countries were based on tribal or ideological grounds, not on the foundations of economic enfranchisement and freedom. It would take a long time to overcome the medievalism that shut out women and individual rights.'

In his view, two things stand out about Iran. One, the negotiations are not working, and two, there is no internal political pressure in the country to force a change in its policy of developing nuclear bombs. Iran is just like North Korea but North Koreans do not have a vision of global dominance. He said, 'Nuclear theocracy is more dangerous than nuclear thuggery.' Good line.

I referred to settlements and the two-state solution. I said that for decades I had fought the left wing of politics. I, and the mainstream of the ALP, had been successful. But now left movements across the world were looking for a unifying issue. Without a two-state solution, I feared that Israel would become the target. The focus would be on a burgeoning Arab population without civic rights.

I didn't use the word 'apartheid'.

Netanyahu said Israel opinion had moved. The public's position on security had hardened but had softened on a two-state solution. He did not want a unitary state that had more than a twenty per cent Arab population. Israel could not keep an increasing Arab population as subjects, but could not make them citizens. He had been arguing this since 1995.

I told him that during the last State election in New South Wales, the Greens candidate for Marrickville had been locked into boycott, divestment and sanctions in respect of Israel. We opposed this and Labor held the seat. But I was concerned about the long-term threat to perceptions of Israel. If the Palestinians don't get their state, how long before churches, unions and the whole left-liberal part of politics take up the cause of boycott, divestment and sanctions? And the longer it goes on, the rest of the spectrum? Centre parties? The Right?

Netanyahu said there were two problems to be solved. First, he did not want a bi-national state, but a Jewish democratic one. Second, he did not want a new state that would set out to eradicate Israel. Israel could not rely on anyone else to provide security if it was besieged by 'manic weaponry'.

That's when he asked someone to draw aside the curtain of his meeting room in the Knesset and pointed at the horizon. 'I don't want Iran on that hill.'

All these meetings were against a backdrop of civil war in Syria, terrorist attacks out of the Sinai against Egyptian troops and the Israeli border, and the nuclear stalemate with Iran. Israel faces the Muslim Brotherhood instead of Mubarak and could get a Syria governed by the Brothers with Salafists and armed jihadists burrowing away.

While I warned about settlements I didn't even bother registering opposition to a strike on Iran. Who am I to tell them how they should deal with a regime of apocalyptic religious leaders? And if they don't weigh the risks themselves? As it stands, their army and Mossad leadership are *against* a strike.

Managed a dinner at the Eucalyptus restaurant, just outside Jerusalem's walls, with its 'Biblical food'. Best restaurant in the world, and we had with us archaeologist Amihai Mazar, a specialist in Canaanite and Bronze Age Galilee and Judea. He said there is no archaeological evidence of the conquest of Palestine by Joshua leading his people back from their exile after Moses died during the forty years in the wilderness. But he said the Canaanites are very well known, their library of cuneiform tablets confirming that they invented the alphabet with twenty-two signs from the Egyptians. Canaan was a network of city states and these people, in turn, merged with the Phoenicians who came from the Aegean, perhaps from Mycenaean Greece, invaders from the sea. We spoke about Herodian archaeology in view of the discovery of Herod's burial place and our knowledge of Caesarea and Masada, where archaeologists have found siege camps. What are the most recent discoveries? He thinks there is a fortified site to be properly explored, which will confirm the Biblical reference to the battle between David and Goliath. Yes, absolutely – he agrees that radio carbon dating confirms a great age of archaeology is ahead of us. After all, he's made the first discovery of ancient beehives.

Fitted in a quick visit to Caesarea, the ruins of Herod's great fort and to the Israel Museum in Jerusalem for the Dead Sea scrolls.

Israel–Palestine is tribal. The solution is known to both sides but neither has the strength to swing their base behind it. So the US cannot force it. As they put it in *The West Wing*, the quest for a Nobel Prize is the quest for noble failure: Clinton beseeching old Yasser Arafat, Rabin murdered, Barak the most unpopular politician in Israel.

Fly out of Tel Aviv to Amman; then through Dubai where I will review with our Ambassador the case again of Matthew Joyce and Marcus Lee, the Australians held in the country for an insupportably long time in drawn-out court cases; then Perth to spend Friday doing fundraisers for colleagues and radio interviews.

I think I've begun to put on weight, maybe the MET-Rx protein blend I've been drinking. Last night I slept from 11 pm to 6 am, only waking once and enjoying nutty technicolour dreams. No Normison: wonderful. Foreign Minister thrashes jetlag.

Kept up the weights in hotel gyms despite a creaky right shoulder and kept up the Pilates and abs work on the floors of hotel bedrooms. Must eliminate all sugar. Must eliminate all bread: 'no flour, more power'. Not getting in any reading but carrying around Simon Sebag Montefiore's *Jerusalem* to absorb by osmosis.

I face two weeks in parliament. Then the Solomons. Then this insanely educational life – off to Cairo for the conference of Arab League foreign ministers, which I'll stretch into a bilateral with Egypt and its new ministers. I won't see the pyramids but I'll get to visit quickly the mosques and the Coptic churches, something to talk about back home with the ethnic communities.

FRIDAY, AUGUST 10, 2012
Perth

A few hours' sleep and a day campaigning: breakfast with Mark McGowan, the State Opposition Leader; then the ABC and 6PR studios for live interviews; an *Australian Financial Review* interview in a coffee shop; a visit to the mining centre at the university; a Sky studio interview; the fundraising lunch in Fremantle for local MP Melissa Parke; then a visit to *The West Australian* to talk to smart tabloid men who are fighting to win the battle for print. Afternoon tea with my predecessor Stephen Smith and a party function for him in a local bowling club.

I have more energy than sixteen gladiators.

TUESDAY, AUGUST 14, 2012
Canberra

Keating launches Hugh White's book on the US and China. He's half right – but to talk about us giving China 'strategic space'? What does that mean, 'strategic space'? Does he endorse White's view, for example, that Japan should move out of its alliance with the US? And South Korea as well? That Vietnam should accept Chinese dominance? Well, that's 'strategic space'. Beijing would relish this discussion in Australia. After all, the Chinese want to see us disoriented over our bilateral relationship. I form the view we should not react. The basics are good, we trade, we talk; 'the metrics' are healthy, as our Ambassador put it to me.

The pro-China lobby are over-egging the pudding. They want

to make us fidgety and defensive about our China policy. Make us anxious. That's not the way to respond. In this phase of the relationship, with them making us uncomfortable, a bit of benign neglect is needed, not letting the Chinese think we care too much. Until things settle

I resolve on this.

FRIDAY, AUGUST 17, 2012
Sydney

For me a grumpy week back in parliament, wrung-out, jet-lagged. A week dominated by Gillard's big, bold initiative on people-smuggling. It implements the package recommended by the panel headed by Air Chief Marshal Angus Houston. A smart piece of policy-making from Gillard's office, on the offensive and strategic. Abbott had to support it. But I was near-sleepless each night. On Wednesday night in desperation I had taken a Restoril tablet – recommended by Senator Nick Xenophon – and stumbled around like a zombie the next day, totally drained of energy. 'Xenophon, you're a peddler … a dealer,' I told him. 'I feel my brain is stuck to the top of my skull.' Could not face another 3 am sitting debating Greens amendments on a migration bill – it would have paralysed me – so I pleaded my way to a pair, a privilege from the whip's office and got home Thursday night. Some grumbles from colleagues. 'Doesn't come to Senate tactics,' they said. Yes, because on two days I had to address breakfasts on UN and humanitarian NGO campaigns, and was dead with sleep loss. But I'll be a good, cooperative little boarding-school pupil this week. Promise.

SUNDAY, AUGUST 19, 2012
Solomon Islands

A weekend in the Solomon Islands. H and I flew up Friday evening on a VIP. Busy day on Saturday: hotel gym at 6.30 am, flew to Tulagi by helicopter and visited a little hospital and made a malaria announcement, flew back to Guadalcanal and lunched with Prime Minister Gordon Darcy Lilo at a Japanese restaurant in Honiara, saw the fisheries authority in the afternoon. Then a nap and attended a reception at the High Commissioner's in the evening.

I slept a good natural sleep, waking up half-a-dozen times, then sinking back into deep, dream-filled slumber. Lots of slightly insane technicolour dreams about fighting elections and doing fundraisers and flying over islands.

Got to the hotel gym at 6.30 am and did eight reps and eight sets: squats with barbell, then walking lunges and leg curls. Good breakfast with the organic porridge we had brought, eggs, beans. No bread. Strong coffee. Then we toured the two Pacific-class patrol boats and – just fantastic, this – collected an amateur military historian, John, to tour Guadalcanal's WWII sites.

The caffeine surged. The kindly tropical sun and a cooling breeze off Iron Bottom Sound lifted my spirits. Life is good again. In the warmth I sweat out six layers of jetlag.

Here I was, walking through history: stepping down into a fox hole; inspecting rusted barb-wire; standing on the battleship-grey sand of 'Red' Beach. Later toured RAMSI, the camp of the intervention force – police and military – that was sent in as a regional intervention ten years ago to save the place.

Flying back now, on the VIP, with the Solomon Islands Prime Minister and his wife.

A learning experience, this weekend in a Pacific nation, this small island developing state. Too good to be true, this bonus to my life: I could not have told you a single thing about the Solomon Islands on Friday; I now have a working knowledge of its history and a feel for the character of the place. This is why I relish this job. This is my privilege, this force-feeding of information, this thrilling broadening of horizons, this stretching of one's capacity at sixty-four years of age.

In the VIP we fly direct to wintry Canberra, not a person to be seen on any of its streets. Box-like office blocks, deserted pavements: City of the Dead. Do Pilates lying on the floor with Sunday-night TV on, Helena in bed.

MONDAY, AUGUST 20 – THURSDAY, AUGUST 23, 2012
Canberra

Defence Minister Stephen Smith brought to cabinet a minute out of the National Security Committee. It referred to last November's announcement by Gillard and Obama about the rotation of marines in the Northern Territory. That announcement also anticipated more B52s flying into and out of Australia. This minute proposes we consider pumping this up for announcement when he and I sit down with our US counterparts – Clinton and Panetta – at the end of the year. The marines are 'in and out', as are ship visits: they are a deployment, not a base. But the aircraft deal is there for good. It involves permanency. Worse, it comes in the middle of the tensions over the South China Sea.

It represents a Big Statement. It embodies huge symbolism. Or, so I think – none of this coming from my department, but reflecting my own instincts about there now being an imbalance as we tack between the US and China.

After Smith introduced his minute I tried to capture some of this sentiment, pointing to a need for caution before we entrench this as policy. But my intervention was less than a slashing success. A pretty tepid, unconfident contribution. I mentioned Keating and Hawke and the broader position about there being not a sliver of difference between the Yanks and us. I said the minute was really about China and the prospect of a tipping point, an irrecoverable one, in our relations with the emerging superpower. I sensed I wasn't particularly convincing. I then said the Americans wax hot and cold. They don't have much to point to to prove a pivot to Asia. Therefore there's a possibility that they will spin this announcement about more B52 flights and talk it up – to make it look bigger than it is but embarrassing us with China. As the combination of two things did in late 2011: the announcement of the deployment of 2500 marines in Darwin and Obama's attack on China in our parliament. The latter angered Keating and, at the time, I took up his criticisms on my blog, writing on November 24, 2011 that:

> Like me, the former Prime Minister does not object to a
> rotating troop presence on Australia's north but is concerned
> about how it gets wrapped up in an unmistakable anti-China
> stance. Why is it remotely in Australia's interest to take that
> course?

I had tried to talk to Smith before the meeting about these reservations but we had not been able to meet. I was uncomfortable being at odds with a colleague, and such an experienced one at that.

The exchange that followed reminded me of how dishevelled cabinet discussion can get. Others spoke, but not to the point. I tried to get them to focus on how, after the marines in Darwin, we now needed to pull back a bit and how the Keating and Hawke criticisms had to be taken seriously because they had an element of public support.

Smith, a more cogent performer than I, said that no decision was being made yet. It was up to us whether to go this next step or just rest where we were with the marines – a throwaway concession to my argument. But he said – shot across my bow – he had nothing to apologise for in decisions on security that he had been part of. He said China was increasing defence spending at a rate higher than their economic growth. He was under no illusion it was serious. He made some other defensive points, like the fact that the US was shifting up to sixty per cent of its naval fleet to the Pacific. His tone suggested he was a bit stung by what could be seen as implied criticisms of his handling of this relationship. He said he stood by all his positions on national security.

At the conclusion I was eager to make eye contact; further to walk back to our offices with him.

I said my concern was the announcement – beaten up and embellished – would make us look like a continental US aircraft carrier with B52s roaring out of our airstrips, headed in all directions north.

He told me again it was an option; we don't have to proceed with it. We had an option of resting where we got to in November, with the marines announcement. He assured me that he wasn't gung-ho on these things. He said that when the option of installing American drones on Cocos Islands had leaked to the *Washington Post* in March, he had punished them by taking any discussion of the matter right off the agenda. I had hit the roof when that story had appeared and expressed my concern to Beazley. I had taken a call from Indonesian Foreign Minister Marty Natalegawa. This had implications for China and in the sea lines of communication *and* for Indonesia. As far as I was concerned, Australia should not be militarising Cocos.

Not even dreaming of it. Too disruptive to the China and Indonesia relationships. Builds us in to the controversy over drones.

Later I saw Smith perform with astonishing zeal and dash at a National Security Committee meeting as he beat off a united front of Prime Minister and Treasury to stop funding for the Growler enhancement to our fighters. This is a new capacity that enables them to knock out the electronics of any enemy. Normally a minister doesn't win against the combined forces of the central agencies (Prime Minister or Premier and Treasurer) but Smith lodged a virtuoso performance in which he took their figures apart, proved that this initiative could fit neatly within the defence budget and gave them nowhere to go. I came up to him and congratulated him and told him I'd never seen that before.

The next morning, we had a meeting on something else. He said, 'So you liked that performance.' I said, 'Well, you just don't see the central agencies taken on by a spending minister and defeated like that.'

We talked again about my anxieties over what would appear to be a big, bold announcement on American B52s roaring out of the place and I pressed, somewhat forensically, that we agree not to proceed with this. He assured me again it was just an idea, an option for us to proceed with or discard.

I reflected on the above, my first disagreement with a colleague and first serious intervention at a cabinet meeting.

The nature of the cabinet discussion was curious.

None of my colleagues seemed to understand what a strategic decision we were being asked to make here and this surprised me. I was somewhat surprised too that the Prime Minister didn't express a view. It was as if no colleagues had been following the debate initiated by Hugh White and fuelled by three former prime ministers. I was struck by the absolute assurance and ease with which Stephen attempted to lead us into what certainly looked like a big geo-strategic step, although in practice it may have been no more than affirming or embellishing what was signalled in the communiqué in 2011. But as I saw it, it would really lock us in, irreversibly, as part of the American empire. But then, I may be wrong.

By sheer coincidence Hugh White dropped into the office to give me a copy of his book *The China Choice* in which he argues that it is in America's best interests to 'remain in Asia on a new basis, allowing China a larger role but also maintaining a strong presence of its own'. And I later saw Hawke, congratulating myself that I didn't blab about this debate in cabinet, though I did hint in very broad terms that I was dedicating myself to a healthier balance in Australia–China relations.

FRIDAY, AUGUST 24, 2012
Sydney

Parliament sat Monday through Thursday. Better than last week – I attend Senate tactics at 8.30 each morning and finally get questions from the opposition, which give me a chance to perform. Days packed: NGOs about the aid program, the Solomon Islands Prime Minister, a couple of ambassadors, the pro-Israel bloc of caucus to hear about my trip. Dinner for Michelle Bachelet, Under-Secretary-General and Executive Director of UN Women.

I sent a message to the Chinese. They would have been chortling at the Hugh White–Paul Keating contribution to debate about China and the US. First, I said in an *Australian Financial Review* interview that we were sending Dennis Richardson to China to explore more consultative architecture (an annual strategic dialogue, for example) but – I carefully added – if the Chinese wanted to take more time about it, that was fine. I said, 'We are relaxed about the timing.' Richard Maude, the Prime Minister's foreign-policy adviser, told me he loved that line. So did Greg Sheridan, who took it up in a piece he wrote yesterday about my ANU speech on the South China Sea. He wrote:

> This is the right tone for Canberra with Beijing – positive, constructive but ultimately unruffled, and unintimidated.

Unruffled: that's the message with them – the perfect word and tone.

Good, so far. But returning to Sydney this morning (after a raucous party function in a Brisbane Chinese restaurant – food inedible, dripping chemicals) I let my mind play on how I can use this stance to leverage us away from another announcement about closer defence ties with the Americans. Don't fuss too much over the Chinese and feed their games; recognise that they may enjoy putting us on the defensive; but don't poke them in the eye either.

Isn't that what the whole region is doing?

SATURDAY, AUGUST 25, 2012
Sydney

Did a Sky interview and then worked in a booth at JJ Cahill High School for the Heffron by-election, Kristina Keneally's former seat, with veteran mayor Ron Hoenig as our candidate. Great fun: a steady stream of older ethnic voters who all greeted me. Electoral politics, like the old days. A young Greens woman said she wanted to see me as the Prime Minister. One guy asked, 'Will I see your name on the ballot for Kingsford Smith next year?'

A spring day in a booth, a friendly Labor mood, Julia enjoying better polls and two good weeks. Imagine running for Kingsford Smith ... the imagination races a little.

Just a little.

SUNDAY, AUGUST 26, 2012
Sydney

How to spend a precious Sunday. Gym at 10.30 am with personal trainer Arryn. Then the office for a bit of reading cables and out to Blacktown RSL to launch Filipino Friends of Labor, but poor turnout. Almost as many MPs and councillors as Filipinos. Not much life left in this party of ours.

Sometimes I think I see the ALP dying before my eyes and then I remember it was always like this, rattletrap and improvised, surviving when leadership was creative, perishing at the polls when bad. Generally our leadership has been bad. Historically, I mean.

TUESDAY, AUGUST 28, 2012
Sydney

Down to Canberra yesterday for cabinet, and Ian Watt, secretary of the Prime Minister's Department, tells me – just as the meeting convenes – 'they' want to shift Dennis Richardson from DFAT to head Defence and elevate Peter Varghese as head of DFAT. They. Who is this 'they'? Julia had been after me to talk about a 'personnel' matter. And this is it! Dennis is something of the distant Mandarin (tolerating a neophyte minister in a struggling minority government). Varghese is highly regarded, an intellectual. It's the choice I would have made. But it's made for me. By this mysterious 'they'.

Met the ACTU this morning about labour rights issues – Fiji, Myanmar, China, Vietnam. Then to airport and flight to Perth. Memorised articles from *Foreign Affairs* and watched *Mabo*.

Was interviewed at Perth ABC for tonight's *7.30 Report* on West Papua and pre-recorded a Radio National interview for tomorrow morning; met our heads of mission in Africa; met a rep of patrol-boat manufacturer Austal; did a boardroom fundraiser for WA Labor. Tomorrow a big conference for Africans on mining and Australia, Africa Down Under. Staff will show me my keynote speech in the morning. It will be mediocre. It will be devoid of rhythm and spark, humour or import.

Still, on TV I pressed the argument that while training Indonesians in counter-terrorism we also press them on humane treatment of Papuan separatists. I had my lilac tie on lilac striped shirt; navy suit. Enough to win the case on its own.

I am Foreign Minister. I trust my judgment, choose my words, soak up knowledge and recycle it. I soar above the mundane and serve my country.

The people trust me. All's good.

SUNDAY, SEPTEMBER 2, 2012
Sydney

A cable from our embassy in Washington picks up some of the conversations I've been having about us and China and the US. Beazley called on Danny Russel, senior director for Asia on the US National Security Council. Beazley writes in a cable: 'There is a hint that the Americans feel our strategic vision is being distorted by sensitivity to Chinese pressure on our political system.' Aha! At the same time he reports Russel is talking of broadening the scope of US engagement beyond security concerns – 'some idea of the direction of their thinking for AUSMIN [the annual talks of Australian and US foreign and defence ministers – our 2+2].' Now this is useful. They themselves may not want headlines about stepped-up defence ties. No roaring B52s. Serves my purpose.

On Friday I spoke to students at Sydney University, mainly ALP Club members. Some Trots demonstrated noisily over refugees, then took off before I started. Five Assangeists stood up in the back row, back to me, holding posters; stayed silent. I spoke about Australia as a creative middle power. Attendance a bit disappointing, I thought, and only one or two academics. But anything for the party, especially the kids who might be future leaders.

On Saturday I did Pilates in the studio at Bondi; first visit in months, so my Pilates instructor could correct my style. Later a gym session with Lisa Korn, one of my personal trainers at Fitness First, Bond Street; the rest of the day preparing for my interview on Sky this morning, with Sheridan, Kelly, van Onselen. I spoke to our Ambassador in Afghanistan, Defence Minister Stephen Smith, the Prime Minister. Drilled into briefing notes.

In the end I mounted a strong defence of a planned, staged transition out of the country in 2013 – not the cut-and-run withdrawal that even Greg Sheridan pushes. This is in the wake of the loss of five Australian soldiers in one day.

After the interview I hit the gym, this time with Arryn as instructor. His campaign to stigmatise all sugars was launched at breakfast on Saturday. Get sugar out of our diet and obesity is banished. I suppose I am destined to be patron. Then read in the office: Joel Brinkley's *Cambodia's Curse* and ONA reports and cables. The rest of the day free. To Egypt tomorrow night.

TUESDAY, SEPTEMBER 4, 2012
Abu Dhabi

Yesterday got myself on four drive-time radio interviews in three capitals about Afghanistan and people-smuggling, off the back of my Sunday interview on Sky. Then took off from Sydney at 10 pm, Etihad upgrading Helena and me and my staff to first. Helpful given the demands coming up. Toyed with Arabic vegetarian dishes and watched a movie about lifers in a Rome jail putting on a performance of *Julius Caesar*. Reminded me what a cold political play it is, spare in its language, no interior monologues as in *Hamlet* or *Macbeth*. I popped two Normison and, tired anyway, sunk deep; when I emerged, just lay in a half-drugged afterglow. Watched TV comedies *Miranda* and *Modern Family*.

During the three-hour stopover I talked with our UAE Ambassador, as usual, about the Joyce–Lee case; read cables: got a head and neck and foot massage; showered and got my clothes ironed – because in Cairo we get off and head straight to meet President Mohamed Morsi, then his Foreign Minister, then the Secretary-General of the Arab League.

Purpose of these four days is to get the votes of Arab League foreign ministers, meeting in Cairo, for our Security Council candidacy. Our quixotic candidacy. Doomed to fail. We entered the race too late, after Luxembourg and Finland had years travelling and sewing up commitments.

During this stopover I also rang Dennis Richardson, my former department head, now head of Defence. Talked about his upcoming move to Defence; I told him about my line on China. He agreed. Told him about my approach to the November talks with the Americans. I said I don't want blazing headlines about B52s roaring from Australian airfields to terrify and galvanise the Chinese with what would appear a new lurch in policy. Any statement about planes would only get confused by the media with the territorial dispute boiling in the South China Sea. Why don't we just rest where we were with last year's decision on marines? Steady as she goes. Consolidation. He agreed strongly. He said we don't have to put the air force dispersal into our communiqué; it was announced last November. Saying something on aircraft would be bigger with the Chinese than the 2500 marines in Darwin (because more US planes mean something for China's sea lanes of communication, their ships ploughing from Africa and the Middle East to Chinese ports). He said *our interests are different from a great power's*. Acute.

This is good. This is astute.

Our interests are different from a great power's.

'You might keep an eye on it,' I suggested.

Our Etihad A330 lifts off for Cairo, with its Muslim Brotherhood government, its frightened Copts, its bursting population sustained by its wrecked, looted economy.

THURSDAY, SEPTEMBER 6, 2012
Cairo

Got up at 6 am and did forty minutes of intervals on the cross-trainer. Then ate a hotel breakfast – carrot juice, omelette, lentils, salad, salmon – with no bread, no croissant; my new resolve on diet. My ambition: to have a *concave* abdomen defined by deep-cut obliques. Read cables and ONA reports. Some of the global trivia I love. Indonesia spends fifteen per cent of its income subsidising fuel, double its infrastructure spend. Chinese academics say their foreign ministry recognises their 'nine-dash line' claim on the South China Sea is impossible to defend internationally. Tunisian Prime Minister Hamadi Jebali says he supports our UNSC candidacy. Solomons Prime Minister Lilo is still buoyed up about being conveyed by me to Australia on our VIP aircraft, describing his visit as 'the nation's greatest honour' and he looks likely to survive in parliament. The Israelis have evacuated the Migron outpost, a settlement, in compliance with a High Court decision.

Fuelled with a double espresso, absorbing this while overlooking the Nile: this is as good as life ever gets.

Yesterday I had been in the palace that, I guess, Nasser, Sadat and Mubarak had inhabited. The man I faced – the only one democratically elected and the only civilian President – was short, bearded and suited, an engineer, perhaps an accidental President. It was terrific to get this meeting, access at this level, for Australia (solid work by our embassy, just as Washington had done great to get me that meeting with Romney). The formal notes of our exchange record it:

> Thanking President Morsi for his generous welcome, Senator
> Carr offered his congratulations to Morsi on becoming
> Egypt's first elected civilian president, which was truly a

historic achievement. Senator Carr also congratulated Morsi on his robust denunciation of the Assad regime at the recent NAM Summit in Tehran: this as the kind of leadership the world appreciated from Egypt.

President Morsi thanked Carr for his comments, noting that Egypt was aiming for a more balanced foreign policy, opening new doors without shutting others, and this wasn't an easy task. In response to Carr's question, President Morsi confirmed he would be attending Leaders' Week at the UN General Assembly in late September ...

Senator Carr said Australia was and remained a strong supporter of the new democratic Egypt. He was aware of the Egyptian government's developmental priorities, and believed Australia could help: had in mind the Australian ambassador working closely with his counterpart in Canberra to explore ways of drawing the attention of Australian businesses to opportunities in Egypt. Australia had considerable expertise in mining, dry land agriculture and in the financial sector, for example, and these were all areas of potential cooperation.

President Morsi fully agreed. Egypt had noted and appreciated Australia's early support for Egypt's transition; on a personal note, he recalled that the previous Australian ambassador (Ms Shwabsky) had been the first ambassador to call on him when he became leader of the Freedom and Justice Party. He knew of Australia's commercial and technological expertise; he also knew that, because of Australia's balanced position on the Palestinian question, it was seen as an acceptable partner ...

Commenting on the quality of Australia's higher education

sector, President Morsi said he hoped that far more Egyptians would be able to pursue postgraduate studies in Australia; he specifically meant PhDs as opposed to short courses or Masters-level degrees. That was the best way of promoting technical and knowledge transfer, he thought, and very much hoped Australia might be able to provide annually about 50 full scholarships to this end. Senator Carr said this was something that needed looking into.

Recalling his visits to Israel and the Palestinian Territories, Senator Carr said Australia was contributing some $300 million to Palestinians over the next five years, including $120 million in budget support for the Palestinian Authority. He said he had told his Israeli interlocutors that, unless Israel allowed a Palestinian state to come into existence, it would find itself playing host to a burgeoning Arab population, and one denied basic civil rights; this would lead to an erosion of international sympathy for Israel. Moreover, unless Israel halted its settlement building, it could provoke a third intifada. Some of his interlocutors had accepted this point, others less so.

In response, President Morsi said Egypt was an established, stable state and a founding member of the UN, which respected its treaties and undertakings. But, he went on, there was no ignoring that the continuing Palestinian problem and Israeli attitudes were giving rise to growing public anger in Egypt and elsewhere. Israel and its supporters had to realise that Israeli policies made it hard to sustain Egypt's position towards Israel. He hoped they had understood Carr's message: dragging things on would be dangerous. The peace treaty promised a comprehensive peace, and nothing of the sort had yet come about. Egypt's position was quite clear,

Morsi said: it respected the peace treaty, but things were likely
to get more difficult ...

In closing, Senator Carr said Australia's many Copts
appreciated Morsi's comments on religious tolerance.
President Morsi, observing wryly that 'there's always a
"but"', said he knew full well the Copts in Australia and
elsewhere had misgivings about his government. In this
context he emphasises he was doing all he could to persuade
the Copts that he meant what he said: he was a president for
all Egyptians. Morsi said all Egyptian citizens were equal;
he wanted Copts to stand for and be elected to the next
parliament in their own right rather than being appointed.
He hoped at least 40 or 50 Copts would win seats. He was
certainly prepared to make appointments but preferred to see
Copts make use of their right to stand for office and win seats.

Wishing Senator Carr well, President Morsi said emphatically
that Egypt was neither a military state nor a religious state: it
was a civil state, and he was 'digging deep' to sustain it. Egypt
was not and would never be a theocracy.

My bilaterals with the foreign ministers of Yemen, Iraq and Sudan
went according to script; however, Dr Adnan Mansour, Foreign
Minister of Lebanon, delivered a defence of the Assad regime that
left me nowhere to go. It was at the end of a long day crowded
with appointments and I was in no mood to raise objections since
there was nothing at stake except antagonising him and losing
any chance of Lebanon's vote for the Security Council. I confined
myself to asking questions. Dr Mansour represents the Shi'ite
Amal party led by Parliamentary Speaker Nabih Berri (which in
turn reflects the division of political offices in Lebanon according to religion – the President a Maronite, the Prime Minister a

Sunni, the Speaker a Shi'a).

It's known as *confessional* politics.

Unhappy country.

SUNDAY, SEPTEMBER 9, 2012
Sydney

Half dead, stumbled into the DFAT office in Sydney to look at papers for tomorrow's conference with the three Singaporean ministers in Canberra. Also worked on material for the 2+2 (the annual meeting of foreign ministers and defence ministers) with Japanese ministers later in the week. I focused my resistance to a Defence Cooperation Treaty. I am opposed to provoking China and opposed to feeding any Chinese notion that we are all ganging up to contain it. I don't care about the games they play with us – making us think we must choose between them and the US – and I'm not having a nervous breakdown because of what Keating and Hugh White say about the desirability of a tilt to China. But I don't want to make it look like containment by injecting the idea of new defence cooperation with Japan *at this time*. Although I must quickly add: first, the Japanese don't seem too excited about the prospect; second, Stephen Smith does not seem to be pressing it; third, it is still being picked over, not in a shape to be announced anyway; and fourth, the Japanese government is likely to fall soon. Still, these notions develop lives of their own. And if it got out – in the context of excitement about Japan's dispute with China over the rocks in the East China Sea and the agitation over the South China Sea – there would only be one Chinese perspective: Australia entering into a defence pact, albeit a very weak one, with one of China's neighbours; this is containment.

James tells me he's communicated my views to the Defence Minister's office and it is not a priority for them.

Cool.

MONDAY, SEPTEMBER 10, 2012
Sydney to Canberra

Forget elegant living if you're a working politician. I enter through the front door at home and climb our steps from the entrance to the living area; I pass piles of briefing papers, periodicals and books sitting on the steps that I've never been able to take back to the office because, when I leave the house each morning, my arms are already full. There are half-unpacked bags and suitcases down-stairs and in the bedroom. In the lounge room books I've bought in New York, Japan, Turkey but have never read and probably never will. The bathroom shelves have airline toiletry bags and their con-tents. One trip follows the other and when we return it's packing all over again for a week in Canberra. Serious packing, because unlike other ministers I don't have a home there and we stay in the Realm Hotel. Moments of extreme jetlag and travel weariness have me pining for the old regular life of weekends catching up with work in the quiet Bligh Street office, regular workouts, healthy home-cooked meals and my program of Jeffersonian self-education. But seize the day. The old life will return fast.

Email to Henry Kissinger

Wednesday, September 12, 2012

Dear Henry,

I hope you and Nancy are well.

I thought I would brief you on a few of my activities.

This week I enjoyed a meeting with Singapore ministers including Foreign Minister Shanmugam. He briefed me on a visit to China last week by himself and Prime Minister Lee. Shanmugam believes the Chinese position on the South China Sea is 'more nuanced' than is being portrayed, and that the media portrayal of China as the transgressor does not bring out all the facts.

He also said that he thinks the Chinese may not have fully understood the Singaporean position which says these disputes ought to be settled in accordance with international law including the UN Convention on the Law of the Sea (UNCLOS). When the Chinese see only a reference to UNCLOS they get unhappy. Singapore has pointed out to them that the Singaporean position speaks of the dispute being settled with reference to international law including UNCLOS – not under UNCLOS alone. He said that Australia should also make clear that it is not advocating the position that only UNCLOS governs the issues.

I attach an article by one of our commentators in response to a paper I gave on the theme of sharing resources in the South China Sea while setting aside the competing territorial claims. There are half a dozen precedents in Southeast Asia which demonstrate this can work, plus the precedent of Antarctica. This has got to be the final settlement: share development, set aside arguments over sovereignty. The challenge is to get the parties to agree to a code of conduct first. Some good news: China may have agreed to informal talks with ASEAN on a code of conduct to be concluded before the East Asia Summit in November.

I've been devoting a bit of time to Myanmar, having our UN Ambassador help the country win better treatment in the annual resolution that passes the UN General Assembly. President Thein Sein has taken risks for reform and deserves encouragement. Last June I lifted – and didn't just suspend – our sanctions on Myanmar, and started using the new nomenclature instead of Burma. I've urged European foreign ministers to do the same with their sanctions. If they persist in talking of 'suspension' instead of 'lifting' there will be no flow of investment from Europe into mining and infrastructure.

Last week I met President Morsi. I expressed support for his criticism of Syria in his speech to the NAM Summit in Tehran a few days earlier. With a wry smile he asked which translation I relied on. He was bemused that the Iranians reported his criticisms of the Assad regime but substituted 'Bahrain' for 'Syria', an example of Tehran's ridiculous heavy handedness.

I am told that Iran got no kudos from hosting the NAM Summit. In fact I'm advised that while the Iranians had sought to push a new Tehran–Cairo axis to advance the Islamic awakening across the Middle East, Morsi had only attended because as outgoing NAM chairman he had no choice but to personally hand the NAM baton to his Iranian successor. The Iranians had proposed 20 meetings for Morsi in Tehran;

he had two, and that with Ahmadinejad was an unhappy one. Morsi stood up to Supreme Leader Khamenei. The Iranians had also proposed cooperation with Egyptian banks to work through international sanctions and the Egyptians turned them down flat. There should be no worries about an Iranian–Egyptian rapprochement.

Another interesting nugget (I don't know if this has reached the international media) is that Iran proposed to host Palestinian reconciliation talks but this was rejected by both Fatah and Hamas. Tehran's relations with Hamas have been in decline for about a year and, according to Egyptians, Hamas is very close to closing its office in Tehran.

The reports today that Vice President Xi Jinping has gone missing seem to confirm your thesis that in 10 years' time – when China next changes leader – the rules will have to be different – more transparent – than now.

Cheers,
Bob Carr

SATURDAY, SEPTEMBER 15, 2012
Sydney

Yesterday I gave a speech to a conference on China hosted by *The Australian* and the *Wall Street Journal*. 'My job is not to get headlines,' I joked to Macquarie Bank's Nicholas Moore before the conference started. It's Gareth Evans's old advice: 'Dare to be dull.' With the Chinese chargé sitting in the audience and a dozen senior journalists from News Limited, the whole thing being filmed by ABC News 24 and Sky, I knew if I strayed off the path, it was going to be reported, in Beijing and Washington as much as here. I had Graham Freudenberg – the country's finest speechwriter and now on the payroll as a consultant from his Bribie Island home – give me a very elegant introduction and conclusion, disguising the fact I was saying nothing new. I defended Chinese investment in Australia in the wake of the government decision to allow a Chinese firm to buy Cubbie Station. And, courtesy of Freudenberg, I was able to remind people that Zhou Enlai had invited Gough Whitlam to move away from America and Whitlam had firmly declined – a pre-echo of the current debate, and reason on its own for having Freudenberg, who's written for Labor leaders for forty years, on the staff; no one else would have dredged this up.

> In Beijing in 1971, Premier Zhou did in fact – very skilfully and politely – invite Whitlam to repudiate the alliance by 'suggesting that America would prove an unreliable ally' as the Soviet Union was proving an unreliable ally for China.

> We sometimes hear echoes of this argument today from Chinese commentators.

> But note Whitlam's immediate reply – and remember this was back in 1971:

> 'I must say with respect I see no parallel in the Sino–Soviet Pact and the ANZUS Treaty. There has been no similar deterioration between Australia and the United States as between China and the Soviet Union.'

I didn't know about this exchange. Freudenberg is our tribal memory.

Then I went to the brisk 2 + 2 with Stephen Smith and our two Japanese counterparts, the meeting I'd prepared for on the weekend. They need friends, with China and South Korea at odds with them over some useless rocks in the East China Sea, and they've got a comfortable relationship with Australia. Very comfortable. I took pains, however, to see that we didn't advance talk of defence cooperation, something that, as it happened, suited the Japanese anyway. And when Stephen Smith alerted me that Defence Minister Satoshi Morimoto had made some reference in their bilateral to an exercise with Australia in the East China Sea, we both agreed that this had to go nowhere, absolutely nowhere. In the end, the Japanese didn't pursue it anyway. I don't think Japanese Foreign Minister Gemba had been in on the proposition. After our talks at the Four Seasons Hotel, we whisked them to lunch at Quay restaurant, hovering in full view of the Opera House and the Harbour Bridge on a beautiful spring day. The poor guys had to fly back to Japan overnight because six Chinese warships seemed to be manoeuvring in sight of the Senkaku Islands.

Terrible riots in the Middle East following this week's tragic killing of the US Ambassador in Libya, all provoked by some crummy little anti-Islam film produced by an American nobody and uploaded on to YouTube. I asked our embassies to step up any relevant work on interfaith dialogue. What else can you do?

SUNDAY, SEPTEMBER 16, 2012
Sydney

Had my best night's sleep in ages and woke up eager to bust into the news cycle. On the way home from the city last night we heard Hillary on the news declaring in her bold way on the riots of Muslims over the anti-Islamic movie: 'This has nothing to do with us!' It was the Hillary I love, the battling candidate from the 2008 primaries, the victor in the Texas contest fought on national security issues, speaking out forcefully as she did at the Paris conference of the Friends of Syria. What she's saying is so patently true, I was itching to join the battle.

I got my media adviser, Patrick Low, to organise a media conference in the DFAT office and I condemned yesterday's nasty demonstrations in Sydney by extremist Muslims, painstakingly defended the majority of Australian Muslims, said Australia would redouble its efforts for interfaith dialogue and – itching to do this – said the Obama administration had done more to reach out to Muslims than any previous one. *This video has nothing to do with them.*

I'll poke around in the office, go to the gym and Helena and I will have dinner tonight with the family of Peter Benic, my old bodyguard.

TUESDAY, SEPTEMBER 18, 2012
Canberra, Sydney

Both Nielsen and Newspoll yesterday saw the government recovering and Abbott slumping. An encouraging trendline although, interviewed on ABC Radio National about the Muslim riot in the Sydney CBD, I said we had a long way to go, polls go up and down etc. But the mood of the whole government has lifted, the Rudd challenge receded, Gillard's standing and status on the climb. 'Hold her back from publicity, give her a bit of voice production,' I advised one of her staff who I bumped into on the plane to Canberra yesterday. It's true. When you're ahead in the polls you don't have to be grinding out messages every hour of the day. Especially if your voice antagonises people.

Revenues have collapsed and Swan wants – needs – more cuts in government outlays for the mid-year statement. Even after the $2.9 billion cut in the aid budget in May, they are circling me again. Aid, like defence, is an obvious target. At a meeting of the Expenditure Review Committee – officials told to leave the room, only half-a-dozen ministers present – I told them that a six per cent cut would give them $300 million and be manageable, but a ten per cent cut would devastate programs. As for a twenty per cent cut which would deliver $1 billion in savings – unthinkable.

I also challenged them that we had to look at the level of assistance we lavish on asylum seekers. I said, 'No cohort of migrants in Australia's long history of immigration has ever received as much in government handouts as they do. Only Belgium gives asylum seekers more. But if we take a billion dollars out of aid, the bulk of our aid is going to be spent onshore – on them and on students who win Australia award scholarships.'

Swan, who chairs these meetings, and does so very efficiently, said we didn't have to make a decision today.

Myanmar's Speaker, Shwe Mann, was in Canberra. I had met him in Nay Pyi Taw in June. He's seen as a future President. He's deeply conscious of all the things I've done in my boutique diplomacy for the country. We've made a big investment here, of time, effort and aid.

The announcement of the new departmental secretary Peter Varghese, with Dennis Richardson shifting to Defence, began to leak in Monday's press so we brought it forward. There's been a good reaction. This is a vindication of the Prime Minister's tactics in shuffling these jobs. Yes, it made sense to fill the DFAT post instead of allowing speculation. But Stephen Conroy, chatting at Question Time, alerted me to what goes on here. The public service fills its own vacancies, and this is an example. Dennis Richardson agreed to go and head Defence and, very obviously, told Julia he'd do it if he was able to fill his old job with his own choice of successor. Now, his choice is the right one and I look forward to working with Varghese, who I met for the first time briefly today (he's on leave from Delhi and won't return to Canberra permanently till the end of the year). But Conroy's right: the bureaucracy has got used to managing these successions. Conroy said if he lost his departmental head he would be told by his bureaucrats who he was going to appoint!

WEDNESDAY, SEPTEMBER 19, 2012
Sydney

Out of the blue. Today's edition of the *Daily Telegraph* splashes with a front-page poll – only fifteen per cent of voters think Barry O'Farrell is living up to his promise 'to make NSW No. 1 again'. It also shows a six per cent swing back from the Coalition to Labor, which would give it twelve seats. A normalisation of politics, and very welcome. But the most appetising part for me is the answer to the question: who would you rate as the best Premier of New South Wales in the past twenty-five years?

> On that question, Mr Carr led with 32 per cent, followed by Mr Greiner at 16 per cent. Mr O'Farrell then came third with 8 per cent, followed by his predecessor Kristina Keneally on 5 per cent.

> Morris Iemma and John Fahey recorded 4 per cent, Barrie Unsworth 2, while Nathan Rees, who has ambitions of again becoming Labor leader, recorded just 1 per cent.

So much for that trashy *Herald* 'Carr crash' vilification launched against me just after I resigned. Without that campaign I may have been inclined to accept Mark Arbib's offer of the seat of Blaxland in the 2007 election. With the backing of the New South Wales Right, Rudd would have had to make me Foreign Minister – in 2007. All these years, in this job. And who knows?

A gym workout under Lisa's guidance, an interview by Graham Richardson for Sky, a haircut and a dash to the airport for the 2.50 pm Etihad flight to Paris.

THURSDAY, SEPTEMBER 20, 2012
Paris

To fly into Paris from Sydney and go straight into two meetings: my big fear was that I would be so tired I would not get my words out. First at three o'clock with the French Minister for Development, Pascal Canfin, then five o'clock at the Quai d'Orsay with Laurent Fabius. H, my advisers James and Patrick, and I had flown in at 7.30 am and met Ambassador Ric Wells, then struggled in peak-hour traffic to the Hotel Raphael near the Arc de Triomphe. We were able to lie down for an hour before we went off to lunch with the embassy team at a local Moroccan restaurant. Never, I thought, have I ever attempted serious work on so little sleep.

I began my meeting with the Development Minister by saying I noticed he came from Arras. This was the city of Robespierre. He just muttered something along the lines of, 'Yes ... rugby ... very popular.' My pronunciation would have been way off. But then what was I expecting? That he'd tell me the Robespierre tradition, imbued in a local school, had turned him into a Green Party ecological radical? Stick to the script. We talked around aid policy. I wrapped things up by asking him whether he had to battle to maintain funding within his government, but my point went nowhere.

Laurent Fabius, veteran Socialist Party politician, was livelier. Our meeting exceeded my dreams. Fabius is a heavyweight, a Mitterrand-recruit who had served in the first government of Mitterrand–Machiavelli in the 1980s. I'd met Fabius in Sydney in 1999, having him to lunch in my office in Parliament House when he was serving as Speaker of the Assembly. Recently we'd met in Tokyo and chatted on the phone. He's elegant and charming and given to a Gallic puffing out of the cheeks and a shrug of the shoulders. I'd heard from the scholarly Sydney businessman John Azarias in Sydney that the French had agreed that Australia, Mexico and Vietnam were countries they were going to work on. Interesting choice. And this raised the possibility we may get their vote in the Security Council ballot.

Fatigue in abeyance. I glanced at the monumental beauty of the city as we sped behind our motorcycle through Paris traffic to the Quai d'Orsay.

In my tailored pinstriped navy suit – quite up to the occasion, ironed by H in the hotel – I bounded up the steps flanked by the uniformed guards with raised sabres, and was greeted by Fabius and ushered into a gallery full of on-loan Renoirs, before sitting at a table in his eighteenth-century office with its view of the garden courtyard. He was unabashed about reading his briefing cards, so I relaxed into my notes too as we ticked off the issues: Australia's UN Security Council candidacy, G20 priorities, bilateral economic exchanges, Africa, the centenary of WWI, university cooperation, cooperation in the Pacific, China, Afghanistan, the Syrian crisis, Iran, Mali, Myanmar, Indonesia and unrest in the Islamic world.

I'd cobbled together a four-point plan to give Arabs an alternative to demonstrations in the streets and attacks on embassies when they hear their Prophet attacked. I said that Muslims could be invited to respond peacefully via the following means:

- » funding explanations of Islam in Western languages;
- » producing formal online responses to anti-Islamic material;
- » funding institutes that promote tolerant Islam through teaching publications and seminars; and
- » using available legal avenues.

I broached this with Fabius and he said he liked it and ticked it off. But the best: our Security Council bid. In response to my routine reminder that we were in this ballot, he said his government had discussed it and they see Australia as 'a serious country'. In other words, it's a country that does peacekeeping and nation-building and runs a big aid budget. A country that can work creatively with France, which luxuriates in its status as a permanent member of the Security Council. I was thrilled by this and relaxed even more into the rest of the agenda. The most disturbing part of it was Mali; he said the world could not allow Mali to become a potential Afghanistan, with the term 'Sahelistan' being used.

We left the palace, I walked across the road and did two TV interviews. Then, with two motorcycle escorts, assailed the peak-hour traffic – as on the last visit, we didn't get to spend even one night here – and charged for Charles de Gaulle. The speed and the weaving through vehicles made me nauseous. We were at the airport in time to grab some dinner in its restaurant before catching the 8.35 pm flight to Geneva.

'Do you remember picking us up at Buenos Aires Airport in 1986?' I asked Peter Woolcott, our Ambassador to the UN agencies in Geneva, the son of veteran diplomat Richard. Yes, he recalled meeting me when I was Minister for Planning and Environment on my ministerial study tour through Latin America. 'I remember you saying at the time you were being sucked into domestic politics and being drawn away from the federal arena.' He drove us to the Hotel d'Angleterre. I managed some patchy sleep.

FRIDAY, SEPTEMBER 21, 2012
Geneva

Drained with jetlag, fuelled by a double espresso, this is what I got through:

A bilateral meeting with UN High Commissioner for Refugees António Guterres at the Hotel d'Angleterre; a signing ceremony for a Partnership Agreement with the UNHCR; a bilateral with UN High Commissioner for Human Rights Navi Pillay and a speech to the Human Rights Council at the Palais des Nations; a short tour of the Palais des Nations, including the Conference on Disarmament; a lunch roundtable discussion on International Committee of the Red Cross priorities with ICRC Director-General Yves Daccord and others at the Vieux Bois restaurant; and a signing ceremony for a Partnership Agreement with the ICRC.

The setting made me think of the Frank Moorhouse novel *Grand Days*, which I would like to have finished. Public life makes long novels too hard. I am actually poorly read, despite *My Reading Life*, despite all efforts at self-education.

SUNDAY, SEPTEMBER 23, 2012
New York

Got here late yesterday after a seven-hour flight from Geneva on which I watched – for the fourth time – *All the President's Men*, the Watergate movie. Naturalistic dialogue and a clever score introduced to the movie only towards the end. The movie enlivens the opening rounds of Watergate better than any of the books. No sleep at all on the flight and I was at the outer limits of jetlag – a pre-cancerous, total, draining exhaustion – when, after a shower at the Ambassador's residence at Beekman Place, my advisers and I hit the TV studio on East 31st Street to do *Insiders* with Barrie Cassidy. I'd tightly rehearsed questions on the old China–US theme but he just got me on my four-point plan to engage the Islamic world.

Back at the Ambassador's residence, I got a deep two- to three-hour sleep. Totally dead to the world. And then was woken up by the banshee traffic noise on FDR Drive. All the louder because we'd turned off the air-conditioning because of *its* clatter. I ended up raging to Helena about moving to a hotel in the morning and went downstairs with a blanket and three pillows. I stuffed in earplugs and lay on a couch in the Ambassador's library. I sunk into an oblivious three-hour sleep on the polished leather and woke in bright daylight energetic enough to take on the task of calming contending kings and re-drawing the world's boundaries. Tomorrow we'll kick my media adviser Patrick out of the smaller, quieter bedroom and cram in there.

A splendid Sunday in New York, a cloudless sky over the East River. My *Insiders* comments got on three TV stations last night, not a bad KPI.

MONDAY, SEPTEMBER 24 –
SATURDAY, SEPTEMBER 29, 2012
New York

We walk from the Ambassador's residence in Beekman Place for a block, past apartments and Beekman Tower Hotel, and turn left up First Avenue into 44th Street, the entrance to 1 United Nations Plaza. It's a windy autumn morning in New York. There's a demonstration opposite the UN building, organised by Tibetans. A mesmeric voice fills the air through a loudspeaker:

Shame, shame, Ban Ki-moon.

It is high-pitched and penetrating. It could be man or woman. But it's powerful and rhythmic. Back comes the full-throated response of the crowd:

Shame, shame Ban Ki-moon.

And without a second's pause, the leader lets fly with:

Shame on the nations of the world.

And immediately, back comes the full-voiced response from the crowd:

Shame on the nations of the world.

But it's impossible to see them through the police cordon and we are soon in a stream of well-suited visitors – from the nations of the world, so heartily condemned – passing security and entering Oscar Niemeyer and Le Corbusier's 1952 Secretariat building, the famous slim, 39-storey, green-tinted glass and steel structure with white marble panels. The flags of member states decorate the steel fence, starting with Afghanistan and ending with Zimbabwe, and, in the streets running off the avenue to the right, the unique retail clutter of Manhattan – flower shops, fortune tellers, delicatessens, pizzerias and Indian restaurants. Inside the UN building, an industrial design interior, littered with artwork gifted from various governments with noble internationalist messages: poverty, disarmament, peace.

This is Leaders' Week at the UN, a succession of meetings conducted (on my part) through a veil of severe intercontinental jetlag, and there's no drinkable coffee anywhere. The 'bilaterals' take place in makeshift booths created by felt panels erected in the corridors. Here I sit and follow my notes, checking off subjects of 'mutual interest', with the foreign ministers of Liechtenstein, Greece, the Philippines, Mauritania, Mongolia, Panama, Togo, Afghanistan and others. Those done through an interpreter are pretty stilted. Others are possible to relax into, for example with Albert del Rosario, the urbane professional diplomat who represents the Philippines. Each checklist ends with me putting the question: will you support us for the Security Council, the ballot only a month away? For all his charm, del Rosario greeted this with a blank look (and our UN mission thought they had his commitment!). Mostly they say they are supporting us. I've got to persist and ask for support on the *first* ballot, not the second, and this is the hard part because we entered the race so long after the Luxembourgers and Finns, and many nations made a commitment to them. This is our biggest obstacle.

The bilaterals ease my relationship with other members of the Foreign Ministers' Club. I'm now very comfortable, for example, with Uri Rosenthal, Foreign Minister of Holland, who's brisk and modest and was able, in a tentative and courteous manner, to make representations for allowing his parliamentary colleague Geert Wilders, the anti-Islamic crusader, into Australia. He also asked us to provide some certainty to the Dutch-owned fishing vessel *Margiris* that is threatening to vacuum up the fish stocks of Australian waters.

The Foreign Ministers' Club is a reality, a kind of reality. We recognise and salute one another. I'm able to hail William Hague as I see him with his delegation about to cross First Avenue and elicit from the Turkish Foreign Minister Ahmet Davutoğlu 'Ah! The loud voice of the Foreign Minister of Australia!' when I see him out on the street approaching the building. Arriving at the German reception I re-introduce myself to their Foreign Minister, Guido Westerwelle, and he says, 'Of course, of course … you're famous.' The Foreign Ministers' Club … it means you can make that phone call when your nation needs a favour and have an agreeable conversation and get some consideration.

John Baird of Canada and I are great buddies, and Murray McCully of New Zealand too; I'm on first-name terms with Susan Rice, the US Ambassador who may be the next Secretary of State; and Marty Natalegawa and Koichiro Gemba are now tested colleagues. This was apparent in the 'multilaterals' with Marty, for example. I sat down at a trilateral with him and the Foreign Minister of East Timor, José Luís Guterres, then at a Friends of Myanmar meeting. Later I welcomed him as the chair of the Comprehensive Nuclear Test Ban Treaty Ministerial Meeting.

As well, on the first night after our arrival I attended a dinner in honour of President Yudhoyono. I sat next to Marty at the official table. Apart from the East Timorese Prime Minister, I was the only foreign government representative as President Yudhoyono was honoured for his achievements for nature conservation. Good for Australia.

At the dinner I bumped into my old friend imam Feisal Abdul Rauf, the (Sufi) Islamic leader in America. He invited me to visit a Fifth Avenue cigar bar and have a non-alcoholic drink with Anifah Aman, the Foreign Minister of Malaysia. Anifah – a Sabah politician, intelligent, easy to deal with – repeated what he had told me in Phnom Penh and has apparently been repeating to people in Kuala Lumpur: that he would back Australia in the Security Council vote, and do so against the advice of his officials, who have been reminding him they pre-committed to the Europeans.

I got to address the fourteen nations of CARICOM, the nations of the Caribbean. I threw away my prepared speech and, in a crowded boardroom, just reminded them of our common interest in climate change, the marine environment, and a treaty to ban the trade in small arms, and that we had financially supported a small monument commemorating the transatlantic slave trade and we'd be honoured by their support on October 18. I glowed when the Ambassador of Grenada, Dessima Williams, said that they were pleased to support us. She said Australia did indeed support their memorial to the transatlantic slave trade. They in fact expected that from a country, Australia, that had ethical policies … as shown by 'The Apology'. So The Apology resonated all the way to the Caribbean. Beautiful! Must pass this on to Kevin.

Co-chairing the nuclear meeting with Gemba, the Japanese Foreign Minister, I had one of those moments: is this me? Am I chairing this – a UN forum? Me, a kid from the sandhills of Matraville? A bit of self-indulgence just for a moment, and back to the slog.

But always the mystery: the luck of this transformation. Sometimes life can deliver surprises, good ones.

But the best fun in chairmanship was a Commonwealth meeting, this time a full conclave of foreign ministers, fifty-four nations – actually, some represented by officials – to get that Commonwealth Charter up and in place. This was Saturday, the last day in New York, and I was determined to get through the agenda briskly. Just as with Young Labor, just as with Kingsford Smith Federal Electoral Council, just as with State Cabinet – I knew that people want a strong chair who keeps pressing forward. And I did! Finished by lunch! They were congratulating me on getting the business done in half the time allotted.

And a nice touch, the lovely Louise Mushikiwabo, Foreign Minister of Rwanda, said when we came to 'other business' that there were two Commonwealth countries running in the UN ballots in October, Rwanda and Australia. She said she thought everyone at the meeting should support them. I said from the chair that I wouldn't dissent from this plea. Good-natured laughter.

At the buffet lunch I ate hastily, sitting with a table of the Caribbeans. But later, with a plate of third helpings, I joined Sri Lanka's Foreign Minister, Professor Gamini Lakshman Peiris, who was sitting alone. He invited me to visit.

Not all the meetings were so happy. I chaired a meeting with the Gulf Cooperation Council – the nations of the Gulf, excluding Iran – in a boardroom at the Waldorf. On the wall, black and white photos from the '50s of the Duke and Duchess of Windsor who lived in this hotel. We got through business pretty briskly. Then towards the end the Foreign Minister of Oman, a wily critter, asked what attitude Australia would be taking on the status of the Palestinians. Ah, the question we dreaded. I replied with the diplomatic but wholly inadequate answer that we'd have to see the resolution and consider it. But the Arabs all know that on Palestinian entry to UNESCO last year we didn't even abstain; we voted 'no'. So all this effort for nothing? I quietly resolve that back in Australia I'm going to have to persuade the Prime Minister we need an abstention on the resolution on Palestinian status.

On September 25 President Obama's address to the UN General Assembly opened with a tribute to the slaughtered US Ambassador to Libya, Chris Stevens. The President said:

> Chris went to Benghazi in the early days of the Libyan revolution, arriving on a cargo ship. As America's representative, he helped the Libyan people as they coped with violent conflict, cared for the wounded, and crafted a vision for the future in which the rights of all Libyans would be respected. After the revolution, he supported the birth of a new democracy, as Libyans held elections, and built new institutions, and began to move forward after decades of dictatorship.

And then the President wrestled with Muslim resentment of attacks on Islam, specifically the YouTube video clip mocking the religion, and how this could be reconciled with the American value – no, he insisted, the universal value – of freedom of speech:

> [W]e believe that freedom and self-determination are not unique to one culture. These are not simply American values or Western values – they are universal values.

He then said:

> I know there are some who ask why we don't just ban such a video. The answer is enshrined in our laws: our constitution protects the right to practise free speech.
>
> Here in the United States, countless publications provoke offence. Like me, the majority of Americans are Christian, and yet we do not ban blasphemy against our most sacred beliefs …
>
> We do so not because we support hateful speech, but because our Founders understood that without such protections, the capacity of each individual to express their own views, and practise their own faith, may be threatened. We do so because in a diverse society, efforts to restrict speech can become a tool to silence critics, or oppress minorities. We do so because given the power of faith in our lives, and the passion that religious differences can inflame, the strongest weapon against hateful speech is not repression, it is more speech – the voices of tolerance that rally against bigotry and blasphemy, and lift up the values of understanding and mutual respect.

The writing was masterful, a riveting sequence of short, declarative sentences marching in rhythm. Here again was what I've taken to calling the charm – the pulling power, the appeal – of American values. That is, American values at their most generous and noble, as opposed to things like universal gun ownership or religiosity. I recall Nicholas Moore telling me, in simple summation, that there would never be a question: 'Australians will always prefer American values.' That is, over Chinese values. And when I raised this speech with Kissinger he reminded me that universal values – freedom of speech, for example – don't exist in the Chinese world view. Chinese civilisation enunciates codes of behaviour, not principles for spreading democracy. Sheer wisdom, this distinction. Again, sitting in the body of the hall listening to President Obama, I was struck by how good the US leadership can be at its very best; the same impression I formed back in April meeting Kerry, McCain, Zoellick and Hillary Clinton. Their sense of responsibility for what happens in the world shines through – their liberal internationalism. Of course, in writing this I have to banish from my mind the swivel-eyed neo-cons and ultra-nationalists: George W., Donald Rumsfeld, Dick Cheney, Sarah Palin, Newt Gingrich and the ghost train of *Fox News* horrors.

SUNDAY, SEPTEMBER 30, 2012
New York

Sunday morning – a warm, breezy, clear-skied day in New York. James and I do a one-hour walk more or less along the East River and back. At two o'clock we'll catch the Korean Air flight to Mongolia, with a stopover at Seoul. I've kept going on Pilates, weight training, good diet and no alcohol; plus the capacity of a 65-year-old – my birthday was September 28 – to survive on dramatically less sleep than a younger Bob Carr.

On balance I think being Foreign Minister will only take two years off my life. No big sacrifice, everything considered.

TUESDAY, OCTOBER 2, 2012
Ulaanbaatar

The ominous letter from the Palestinian delegation had arrived at our UN Embassy on Thursday. It had asked simply: will Australia vote in favour of giving them enhanced non-state status? We were never going to be able to avoid facing this. It was always going to come up. So much for our whole Security Council campaign, so much for the push into Africa, so much for enlisting the whole Caribbean. What if we collared the Palestinians and said, 'Listen, we're giving you $300 million over five years … my colleagues in Canberra wouldn't allow this to continue if Palestine cost us this vote'? But no, a Canadian source told me they tried that last time and it doesn't work. Supporting their bid for increased status – the political gain – is all that counts and if we vote 'no', as we did last year in their bid for UNESCO membership, we will lose all Arab votes, over twenty. And lose our bid. My job is to get the Prime Minister to shift from 'no', which is where she's at – thanks to the Melbourne-based Israel lobby – and which leaves us in the company of a handful of nations: US, Canada, Marshall Islands, Guam.

Meanwhile, I'm in Mongolia.

SATURDAY, OCTOBER 6, 2012
Sydney

These days I don't even open the review sections of the newspapers. A night at a concert or an opera or a play in Sydney would be torture. I haven't been to a movie in the seven months I've been in this job; to spend a Sunday afternoon or evening like that would be anathema. I prefer to soak up global trivia from CNN or to idly channel flick during the jetlagged hours.

I read the department's collation of international stories from the Australian press and very occasionally get time to read their suggested articles from the international press, or descend on the *Herald Tribune* from my iPad, or pick at the articles reproduced on the American website Real Clear Politics. I devour *Foreign Affairs*, the journal of American internationalist orthodoxy and, over breakfast in hotels, read the *New York Review of Books*. I catch up with copies of *The Economist* and sometimes, to my surprise, actually get good value from *TIME* magazine – an article on the African-led, American-financed Somali peacekeeping or Joe Klein's columns on the presidential campaign.

As for books, I half-read them. Question Time is good for this given that I get so little attention from the opposition, or periods of Senate duty when a Minister has got to be in the chamber. This way I got into a book on the Australian coastwatchers in World War II, my interest piqued by my visit to the Solomon Islands. Nick Warner, the head of ASIS, gave me a few books on spies and one of them is a history of technology used by the CIA. It reminded me that getting spies to operate inside the Soviet Union was just about impossible. As late as the '60s when you did have an agent, he was totally dependent on the old-fashioned techniques of 'dead drops' and coded numbers being picked up on his Panasonic radio.

I've half-read Joel Brinkley's *Cambodia's Curse* and got value out of it. I've dipped into Richard Woolcott's *The Hot Seat*, a memoir of our senior diplomat. But the old days of spending a whole Saturday or Sunday devouring great slabs seem a hundred years away – those special times I enjoyed, even as New South Wales Premier, with the sun coming in through the lounge-room window, me sitting upright on the Biedermeier sofa, with a book propped on the cushion on my knee in a quiet house with Helena off having coffee with one of her favoured mates. Those days are gone, replaced by the jetlag and the Canberra detention, and there are the demands of the gym and distractions of the iPad. I can rarely bring myself to watch serious videos, although H and I did enjoy a DVD of *The Tempest*, directed by Julie Taymor who produced *Titus*, with Helen Mirren cast as 'Prospera'. A woman taking the place of Prospero and it worked.

There will be time.

Part of the Australian business lobby is agitating about China and the US. Kerry Stokes said he's ashamed that American troops are on Australian soil under US command. James Packer said we've got to express our 'gratitude' to the Chinese. The Chinese embassy would relish this, especially as it comes against the backdrop of Hugh White and Paul Keating's comments. From Mongolia, doing a *Lateline* interview, I actually talked up John Howard's recent speech that used the same language I've used about China: a security relationship with the US doesn't stop us from having a strong relationship with China. I'm increasingly intent on sending out a message that we're absolutely 'unruffled' – I've used this line a few times – about the relationship with China. The Chinese diplomats may even be playing games with us, trying to keep us wrong-footed, trying to make us apologetic about our US treaty relationship. I'm more and more taken with the line that I think I picked up from a report by a DFAT official in a summary of his conversation with the Chinese – that we don't object to their military modernisation, they can't object to us nurturing our treaty relationship with the US. And there's a new line I'm going to use, namely that the US–China relationship is in good working order – both sides keep telling us that – so therefore, as a result, we shouldn't be goaded into thinking we've got to choose between the two.

I read that a scholar called Edward Luttwak recently referred to the Chinese being 'autistic' in their attitude to foreigners. Maybe. On the other hand, it might be true that they're less coordinated and more divided in their policy-making than we assume.

Of course, the US can be 'autistic' in its approach to foreigners. The miscalculations of the Bush administration prove the point.

SUNDAY, OCTOBER 7, 2012
Sydney

Got up this morning at what we thought was 6.30 am so I could get to the Sky studios for *Australian Agenda* to be interviewed by van Onselen, Kelly and Sheridan. Plenty of time, I thought, as I lay on the floor in the sun trying to soak up some Vitamin D and counteract the horrific impact of all this plane travel. I had the radio on and it turned out it was daylight saving. It was 8 am and I had to be there. Now! Threw the suit on and charged out, Helena pressing peanut butter on spelt bread into my hands. I walked into the studio as the program was starting, makeup being dusted on me ...

We sailed right into it. Covered everything. An excellent format, lots of give and take: China, India, domestic politics (Tony Abbott and women, Alan Jones) the US presidential elections, the Security Council seat and why it wasn't a guaranteed win for us. I really enjoyed it and they thought it was good too. Came to the office and absorbed briefing notes on Syria for a *Four Corners* interview this afternoon but ducked down to the gym for an hour for a workout with Arryn – chest and back, really hard. Yesterday I did Pilates in the morning at Bondi Junction, a legs workout with Lisa in the afternoon. Last night we ate kangaroo cooked in coriander, turmeric and cumin while watching *Breaking Bad*. I tweeted about this and found that British Foreign Secretary William Hague picked it up and tweeted, 'What Aussie foreign ministers eat.' Why not, William? It's lean protein.

Paul Monk's article on China in *The Australian* on October 1 takes up Luttwak's view that China is an autistic nation and has been bad at strategy, locked up as it has been in its own Middle Kingdom mystique and totally unused to dealing with other powers as equals. Luttwak had said, 'Constructive dialogue with China is important ... the problem is that China is tone deaf in strategic matters.' Paul Monk, I think, is one of Australia's best intellectuals – no, the best; this is another case of him leaping over the various divides and factional camps, the culture wars.

He says: 'China has never broken the centralist, authoritarian, repressive mould of politics dating back to the Shang dynasty ... it has never developed an open, pluralist politics of the kind that dates back to classical Greece in the West.'

MONDAY, OCTOBER 8, 2012
Canberra

I dance, I sing, I fly through the air. I am the master entertainer. Yesterday, after the *Australian Agenda* broadcast on Sky, Greg

Sheridan rang me when I was back in the office to extract a few more details about Dennis Richardson's recent trip to China about more regular consultations with the Chinese leadership. After ringing Dennis, I phoned Greg back and gave him a few details and thought no more of it.

I got a run on Sunday night saying the attacks on Abbott for misogyny had made their point. But nothing prepared me for the sweeping front page of *The Australian* today that declared:

Carr Plan would put Beijing on similar standing to Washington
ALP seeks tighter China ties

Or Greg Sheridan's assessment that 'Bob Carr is in the process of delivering a masterclass to Australian politics.' And tonight I ran on *Four Corners*, interviewed by Kerry O'Brien on Syria after a documentary. I said this was a crisis for the 'dictator for life' model that Arab nationalism had imposed on the Middle East.

Had Monday off for a bushwalk in the Royal National Park, sun and surf and striding over the rocks to beat the jetlag.

TUESDAY, OCTOBER 9, 2012
Canberra

My antenna at caucus picked up that the Prime Minister was upset with me. In her report she mentioned her time at the UN seeking support for the Security Council ballot but didn't mention that I'd been there. Suspicious. So she wasn't just shrugging off yesterday's blazing *Australian* front page – or today's editorial that praised Carr's China policy as 'adroit and measured'. So much for dancing, singing, flying through the air. Damn! The nuisance of serving in someone else's government, not your own! As the caucus meeting broke up, I dragged myself out and sat next to her on the lounge that faces the room. It may have been what Alan Clark refers to in his diaries, facing an angry Thatcher, as a 'pre-caning moment'. Still, I explained that I had no idea Sheridan was going to put that huge spin on my modest comments. 'And Dennis went there as *my* envoy,' she said, aggrieved, and I guess rightly so. Yes, I said, and I had no idea that Sheridan was going to make that his lead and portray it as a Carr initiative – and I didn't. I apologised for Sheridan's over-enthusiastic endorsement. She asked whether I thought he was going to be Abbott's foreign-policy adviser if he wins; she quoted Sheridan saying he'd been asked to do it but hadn't made up his mind. I said I had no idea.

All this intersects with another delicate matter almost laboratory-designed to sow tension between us: Palestinian status. They have now said in their letter to our UN mission they want the sort of status the Vatican enjoys in the General Assembly. Last year we voted 'no' when their bid for membership in UNESCO came up, putting us in a minority of fourteen with the US, Canada and the Marshall Islands. Another fifty-two nations abstained but an overwhelming 173 voted 'yes'. The Arabs are on to us. We're not going to fudge this. They will probably lobby and caucus against us as they apparently did against Canada two years ago; that is, if we can't at least say we will abstain.

I want us to say we'll abstain. To at least say, we *won't oppose* your resolution.

This is a battle I've got to win with the Prime Minister because of the influence on her from the Melbourne-based pro-Israel lobby.

I seek a meeting.

WEDNESDAY, OCTOBER 10, 2012
Canberra

I went to the Prime Minister's office after Question Time. Her chief of staff, Ben Hubbard, bustled out and said, 'No, she said she spoke to you after caucus.' I said, 'It's not about that. It's about something very important. I need to see her.' I sat down with her, Hubbard and Richard Maude. I made the case on the Palestinians. She grew uneasy as I explained it was coming to a head; we could lose all twenty-one votes of the Arab League and more from the Organisation of Islamic Cooperation. I told her I'd spoken to Yuval Rotem, the Israeli Ambassador, yesterday and urged him to cut us some slack, to accept we would abstain and not kick up a fuss. He said he'd speak to Netanyahu. I explained to the Prime Minister our intelligence confirmed that earlier this year the Israelis were *expecting* us to abstain. We wouldn't surprise them in going this route. So abstaining would be no big deal. We'd be part of a small minority if we didn't – that is, if we voted 'no' – and we would blow our support from all those Arab states, and that would cost us the Security Council election. Her eyes shifted worriedly. At least she allowed me to explore the idea of the Israelis agreeing to let this slip through.

THURSDAY, OCTOBER 11, 2012
Canberra

The issue dominates my life. Yuval hasn't got back to me to give me the decision I want, namely advice that he's spoken to

Netanyahu and Netanyahu thinks in the greater good he can live with Australia moving from the opposition to the abstain column. For God's sake, I repeat to him, you get us on the Security Council for two years where we can do you some favours. Parlimentary Secretary Richard Marles, who's part of the pro-Israel Victorian Labor Right, agrees with me and likes the strategy of getting Yuval's consent (pathetic though I think this is). Mark Dreyfus, an intelligent supporter of Israel and Jewish to boot, takes some more arguing. I have a minor explosion of anger and frustration and point out that it's an appalling position if Australia allows a group of businessmen in Melbourne to veto policy on the Middle East.

And then a visitor arrives in my office with the air of a conspiring cardinal on coasters, sniffing out a useful heresy: our beloved former Prime Minister Kevin Rudd, purse-lipped, choirboy hair, speaking in that sinister monotone. A *chilling* monotone. He was once friendly with Australia's pro-Israel lobby but fell out with them badly as he shifted our vote on eight – I've made it nine – UN resolutions that touch on Palestinian status. He's interested – morbidly so – in what the Prime Minister will do with this issue and how it might affect our Security Council vote. We share our anger at the extraordinary position where 'The Lobby' has this influence.

By the end of the day, I see less chance of Yuval – the cunning Yuval, the omnipresent Yuval – delivering on what I asked for. And I doubt the Prime Minister – now heading to the airport for Bali and India – would summon up the will to ring Netanyahu. Helena and I go off to a dinner at the Singapore High Commission for visiting Prime Minister Lee Hsien Loong; Simon Crean, Martin Ferguson and Penny Wong are also in attendance. The conversation is all China. This dinner in Canberra on Thursday night mandates we drive for three hours to get back to Sydney. Sitting in a car all this time, shifting in my seat, mad with desire for bed, listening to a CD of *The History of the Decline and Fall of the Roman Empire*, is a better option than another night in the Realm Hotel – even though I've had them install organic steel-cut oats in their kitchen and I like the Mexican beans in their buffet.

SATURDAY, OCTOBER 13, 2012
New York

On the flight to New York I watched parts of two Oliver Stone movies, *Born on the Fourth of July* (surprisingly good) and *JFK*, in which gullible Stone idolises the fruitcake New Orleans attorney Jim Garrison.

Stopped at Los Angeles for a shower in the first-class lounge, I brought up this message from the Prime Minister on my mobile phone:

> Dear Bob and Richard [Marles] – I have read the letter [the letter from the Palestinian delegation] and noted what is and isn't in the cables. I have also done a quiet check-out re the Israelis. I don't think we're at a tipping point re UNSC campaign. Our lack of clarity re the Palestinian resolution has been an ongoing problem for us and will continue to be. So no flexibility there. We should just hasten slowly and not respond to the letter prior to the vote. I will call Bob tomorrow morning. I'm on Bali time. Julia.

Then slept from LA to New York and fell out of the plane to have one of our mission's staffers ask me, 'How was your flight?' What am I supposed to answer? The highlight of my life? A delight?

A joy? Pure frolic from wheels up to touchdown? Singing and dancing for a joyful fourteen hours? Jetlag makes me grumpy. But on Sunday I had the energy to take Helena, Graeme and Patrick to The Cloisters for Romanesque and medieval art. Beautiful autumn weather.

We talk with Gary Quinlan over an Italian dinner on the Upper East Side, inevitably about our Security Council chances, about the Palestinian resolutions. Up close, I allow myself to think that we could win this one. I expect, however, at any moment to hear news of the Arabs caucusing and blocking us: general pessimism fills me.

SUNDAY, OCTOBER 14 – TUESDAY, OCTOBER 16, 2012
New York

So a last desperate week in New York. Surly pessimism dominates my thinking, mixed up with the fever of jetlag. This time we are escaping the traffic noise at the Ambassador's Beekman Place apartment and staying at the quaint and gracious Carlyle Hotel on Madison and East 76th Street. With its petite foyer, high-ceilinged dining room with its banquettes, and Lilliputian lifts, it's out of another era. John F. Kennedy is linked with the place, his 'Jack Rabbit' sex – over in seconds, in the woman-astride position to protect his back – must have been practised in its suites. On Monday nights Woody Allen plays in their jazz bar.

My big job of the day is to host the last-ditch reception in the marquee in the grounds of the UN. This is the traditional gathering before a ballot.

I had been memorising the names of ambassadors so I can deploy special attention as required. I write down names I must remember: the Albanian Ambassador who visited Australia in March is Ferit; the Austrian, who says they sometimes get confused with Australia in UN ballots, is Martin; the Belarus Ambassador, who gives every hint of voting for us, is Andrei; the Indonesian is Desra – Desra Percaya – and very likeable. I'm getting to know them. The large-framed athletic ambassador from Barbados, Joseph E. Goddard, calls me Bob; I call the Cuban Pedro. I remember that the formidable, penetrating Chinese statesman is Li Baodong; Stuart Beck from Palau, with his American accent, is a great ally on climate change. Sofia Borges from East Timor, Australian-born, couldn't be a stronger supporter and we count her a friend as we do Robert Aisi, the Ambassador from Papua New Guinea.

For the reception I'd been given an utterly mediocre speech, but its staleness of language did not matter when I got up on the stage. No matter how resonantly I soared, how vigorously I modulated, half the crowd kept talking their heads off. Cavalier rudeness. Puts me and my pretensions in their place. I junk a few paragraphs, end their irritation – and mine. One of my least successful orations.

Still, some good, lively conversations before I left. Africa looks uniformly good, the Pacific Islands are holding. My phone calls to European foreign ministers have elicited some very specific commitments – like, 'We will switch our support to you on the second ballot if you come second on the first.' Vatican intelligence says we are well ahead. But they don't know about us letting down the Arab League on Palestinian status.

Our embassy staff was heartened by the turnout. But leaving the reception, I have no sense of momentum or inevitability. Finland is said to be glowing with confidence.

Glowing.

Traitorously, I speculate on how better off we'd be if I'd been able to pull out of Rudd's whole quest the week I'd taken over. Deep within, I know this is going to be a disaster.

WEDNESDAY, OCTOBER 17, 2012
New York

Had dinner with Col Allan, former editor of the *Daily Telegraph* in Sydney and an extraordinary success as editor of the *New York Post* for what? Now eleven years. Keating and I had spoken at his farewell in Sydney. He confesses plainly to loving Rupert. Why wouldn't he? A boy from Dubbo installed in New York, one of its opinion leaders, courted by Republican nominees. Good luck to him. When he started rubbishing Obama, his wife, Sharon, sailed into him, which brought smiles to a pair of eavesdropping Democrats at an adjoining table.

Met Harold Caballeros, Minister of Foreign Affairs for Guatemala, and made a bid for a vote; then a courtesy call on Jan Eliasson, UN Deputy Secretary-General, a former Swedish Social Democrat Foreign Minister – and looks and sounds it: seventy-two years old, lean, alert. Out of the country of my soul, Sweden: its lean, competitive private sector, red barns and immaculate fields with no billboards or litter; its glittering global citizenship and ostentatious good governance. Poster child of European social democracy, now fading fast. He's off to Mali tomorrow. I put in a bid for a medical pact to guarantee ambulances and doctors into Syria. He flatters me by saying that he read my release. He reminds me that it is, of course, international law anyway.

Those refugees in Jordan flash into my mind. Kids in the dust, parents squatting in tents, packaged food and portaloos. Perhaps no hope of return to their homes, living now as Middle Eastern refugees, in camps for life.

All my feeling about this ballot is bad, plain bad. The people at the reception talking loudly over their drinks as I made my drab speech; the notion that diplomats lie for their country – of course they tell you they'll vote for you; the queasy sense that we've let down the Palestinians and the Arabs by our craven position on Palestinian status; the reminder that Canada lost two years ago and maybe the General Assembly does not like clean-cut, English-speaking middle powers like us.

Over breakfast in the belle époque dining room of The Carlyle, I talk to Richard Marles, who's worked strenuously on the bid, to his staffer and Caroline Millar, head of DFAT's United Nations Security Council Task Force. 'Don't worry folks,' I tell them. 'I'll handle it. As Premier I had to explain train crashes and poison in the water supplies. A defeat in a UN forum is nothing compared to a bushfire emergency or a crisis in child care. Leave it to Bob.'

I've got the Australian media accepting that, because of our late entry – six or seven years after Finland and Luxembourg – and because we're not part of any major bloc, our chances are not good. One bit of good news, though: it seems we can probably get by without Palestinian status coming up. If true, this would be a relief. To have the Israel–Palestine agenda dragged into this would be distasteful, all round. So far there's been no evidence of the Arabs mobilising because we've failed to reply to the Palestinian letter.

THURSDAY, OCTOBER 18 –
SUNDAY, OCTOBER 21, 2012
New York, Tennessee

Dinner with the Kissingers at La Grenouille and Henry reminds me he is ninety at his next birthday. I ask him what Hillary will do after she leaves the State Department – work for an NGO, a non-profit, perhaps? He looks right at me and breaks into a smile. No, perhaps not.

He said it appears to him that Obama has got three foreign-policy objectives should he be re-elected. First, a Palestinian state. Second, climate change. Third, non-proliferation (which explains his consistency on Iran). But the Palestinian state? Kissinger says he has no evidence on this, just a hunch.

It's Thursday, the day of the vote. At 9 am, after my raw muesli, poached eggs and chicken sausage – an army marches on its stomach and my theory is you kill fatigue with protein and fibre – we fill the car and van and head downtown.

What will be, will be.

Walking into the UN I chat with the Australian news teams, again talking down our chances because I couldn't believe we were going to get this. Too good to be true, if we did. Thirty nations told us 'no' up front, mainly because of our late entry. The Europeans will surely lock in behind Finland and Luxembourg. Our Palestinian position must surely be poisoning the Arab world against us although, interestingly, our mission still has no confirmation of this.

I took my seat in the auditorium next to Gary Quinlan, with Graeme Wedderburn and Richard Marles sitting behind me. Gary instructed us not to let expressions show up on our faces. Cameras would be focused on us throughout. The chairman went through the motions: he said there were 193 nations present and read out the nominations for the different constituencies. The ballots were brought around and I carefully wrote *one* name only, what's known as a 'short vote' as opposed to putting one of the others on it as well, and the ballot box came round and I deposited the ballot paper. We settled in for a long wait. In fact, I left the auditorium to sit down for a meeting with the Argentine Ambassador, who told us he'd voted for us. We spoke about cooperation and I reminisced a bit about some of the Australian–Argentine comparisons that had been made over the years and that had once interested me. He reminded us we had been neutral on the Falklands/Malvinas and asked that this continue during the British plebiscite.

Then, standing outside the hall, we heard a rumour that we'd won by one vote. I didn't know how to take that. When we returned to our seats, we got the rumour that our vote was 140 out of 193, an unambiguous, very happy first-ballot win. Ha! The wind *was* blowing in the right direction. A positive gale!

'You're so lucky,' Graeme whispered, leaning across. I knew what he meant: the 1991 and 1995 State election outcomes when he was on my staff. But Gary warned we had to be expressionless and have it hit us like a surprise. The chairman read out the result. There was no punching of the air or leaping around. I just beamed and shook Gary's hand, congratulating the man who did it, the professional diplomat. While the other ballots continued to be called, a procession of well-wishers came to our table to congratulate us. Quite moving, this. Suffering little Mali; some Caribbeans, including Dessima Williams from Grenada who had counted The Apology as a reason to vote for us; our good friend Susan Rice, the US Ambassador (old friends the best friends) … And when that was complete, I was free with my colleagues to stroll out and face the media and declare a big, juicy, decisive win for Australia; congratulate Australian diplomats who brought it about; declare it a win for Australian embassy and consular staff, aid workers, military personnel and police officers who'd served overseas, creating a positive image of this country. So it goes.

Naturally, I did non-stop media interviews, most from the little TV studio on 31st Street. All good, all positive. Then on Friday morning, we flew to Washington, collected the Beazleys at the airport, and on to Knoxville, Tennessee, where we were staying with Senator Lamar Alexander and his wife, Honey, who we got to know when he had taken a sabbatical, after two terms as Governor of Tennessee, in Sydney in 1987. He lives amid glorious Tennessee forests in dropped autumn colours in a landscape with rail-fences, authentic log cabins and antique barns. We get a little walk in. We see bear tracks. Over breakfast, we chuckle at the Australian papers. Peter van Onselen says that the Security Council win means that if the party's sick of Julia, they won't turn to Rudd; they'll turn to me.

Diplomat Carr a blocking agent to Rudd comeback
(*Sunday Telegraph*)

… Perhaps the most significant political implication of Carr's success this week is what it does to his standing within the Labor caucus. So far as leadership candidates go, he now moves into the category of number one blocking agent to a Rudd comeback. If Gillard again falters in the polls, this time such that her leadership becomes terminal, watch her supporters scramble for an alternative to prevent a Rudd return, such is their hatred of the man.

Carr's good week helps elevate him into being that person…

It sounds far-fetched but it's happened before: when the late John Gorton became PM in 1968 while still serving in the Senate.

Ego-balm, soak it up while it's good.

Charles Waterstreet in the *Sun-Herald* writes a hilarious piece about how I should be given responsibility for the Australian swimming team.

At Knoxville Airport, starting the journey home, I notice everybody is obese. Everybody else, that is.

WEDNESDAY, OCTOBER 24, 2012
Sydney, Canberra

I bought two primers on Tennessee history at Knoxville Airport but, of course, I will never read them. These days I read nothing. Feeling very chuffed, very fulfilled, only a nagging worry that the publicity may create tension between the lady and me.

We just had this text-message exchange:

JG: Bob, I have seen a list of pending diplomatic appointments that has names next to a number of positions on which I am supposed to be consulted. Please take no further action on these and instruct the Dept to take no further action until we can sort this out. Ben will speak to Graeme re this tomorrow morning. Julia

BC: Sure. No problem. I am not attached to any. They were submitted by Dennis before his departure. Ben might want to talk to him about any that concern. Bob

Later I added:

BC: And Dennis certainly did not tell me that any were to be submitted to you. I repeat: not one of them was a Carr initiative! All were Dennis recommendations.

JG: Understood – thanks Bob.

SATURDAY, OCTOBER 27, 2012
Sydney

Last week the Foreign Minister of Myanmar visited Australia. He told me, almost in passing, that he sees Australians as Asians.

It was a confirmation of the way this country has transformed itself. It confirms our capacity to meet all the goals outlined in yesterday's Australia in the Asian Century White Paper. If our partners already see us as being part of their region and their future then we are more than halfway there.

In fact, last week we not only had this visit from Myanmar, we were also visited by the President of the Philippines, Benigno Aquino III, and their Foreign Minister. In addition, I hosted the Secretary-General of ASEAN.

The habit of consulting Asia, of linking with Asia, is upon us. This habit will be enhanced by our decision to send a full-time ambassador to Jakarta for relations with the ASEAN Secretariat and the ten members of the Association.

Australia recognises ASEAN's centrality in the architecture of Asia. We are committed to their master plan on connectivity – for example, by involving ourselves in initiatives in the Greater Mekong subregion. I have recognised the ASEAN lead in assessing the changes that President Thein Sein has pursued in Myanmar.

The ASEAN nations were right to see the reforms as irreversible, to lead the rest of the world on engagement with Thein Sein, to advise and encourage and nurture his government. I said this to the Friends of Myanmar at the UN.

The biggest challenge the ASEAN nations have is to avoid the middle-income trap. While their growth has been impressive, they have to see that it's not choked off by institutional rigidities and corruption so that they're held back from rich-country status.

SUNDAY, OCTOBER 28, 2012
Sydney

Sometimes, being a member of the Foreign Ministers' Club – all those bilaterals with talking points – turns out to be useful. On Friday, a pirated boat arrived at Cocos Islands with fifteen Sri Lankans. We want to return them. It's a priority – the Prime Minister is driving this with telephone hook-ups with ministers. But when our High Commissioner went to see Foreign Minister Peiris in Colombo, she served him a list of requirements before we could send them back, seeking a *written* guarantee that various laws and conventions would be applied. He very understandably took umbrage. Yes, they want to take them back but don't like, understandably, being put on the defensive like this. I had had a cordial chat with him after the Commonwealth meeting in London, over the buffet lunch when I found him sitting alone. I was able to pick up the phone to him later on Friday night. I was happy he took my call and was not offended by our High Commissioner's brisk efficiency in these things. I told him that all we needed, to satisfy Australian legal requirements, was a record of him reaffirming that Sri Lanka adheres to conventions, will give them due process and does not apply capital punishment. No problem. He agrees to take them back. After our conversation, I dictated a note that goes in the files. That's all that's needed to satisfy our system. But here's the thing: I doubt if the conversation would have been as useful if we hadn't gotten to know each other and got on well. It's the value of the Foreign Ministers' Club. You meet your colleagues in a circle of cordiality and it's not hard to beat a path to them to solve a problem. At the very least they will pick up the phone. They will be disposed to help if it doesn't cut across any competing national interest.

'Kevin Rudd is running you down,' a business contact said. 'He's rubbishing your performance as Foreign Minister. I have it on impeccable authority.' Well, it doesn't surprise me. It'd be hard for him to do otherwise. How could he talk up the role of someone who succeeded him as Foreign Minister? It's probably against human nature; certainly against his. That makes it hard for me to track him down and finally talk to him about the Security Council vote, giving him credit for initiating the bid. So I drop the idea. Ringing him after this intelligence would be against human nature, against mine.

FRIDAY, NOVEMBER 2, 2012
Sydney

From a departmental paper on China, some cold blasts of realism. Here's what it concludes: China's rulers see us as being less important than Canada. Only slightly more important than New Zealand. Their reliance on our resources only feeds resentment of us. While they will not ever enjoy us being close to the US, it is the one thing that would make them respect us. (This realism stands at odds with the obsequiousness of part of the business world, the 'compradors' who suggest we build our foreign policy on expressions of gratitude to the Chinese). The paper repeats our 'hedging strategy' of being prepared for a nasty chauvinist China as much as a mature, cooperative, multilateral one.

I doubt the observation that we are so unimportant to them.

Gareth Evans recommended a book and I found it in The Strand in New York, the world's best bookshop: Samantha Power's *A Problem from Hell: America and the Age of Genocide*. Beginning with the mass murder of Armenians by the Turkish government in 1915, it's an account of the development of the concept of the crime of genocide and moves across the landscapes of the Holocaust, Rwanda, Bosnia, Cambodia.

May become the only book I read cover to cover in this job.

The big old-fashioned fundraiser in Fairfield was a pro-Labor ethnic festival – I sat next to the Melkite bishop; there was a leader from El Minieh in Lebanon, which I visited in 1997; and whole tables of other Lebanese; the Fuzhou community was there – Hokkien-speakers like Helena – and leaders of the Indian community who had been back there on Gillard's recent visit. I told them Chris Bowen, whose re-election fund should make $40,000 out of the evening, was a future Treasurer and Prime Minister. Got out by 9.30 pm and headed home. Helena had finished packing for Malaysia–Bali. We are leaving tomorrow.

Most of the time I am impressed by the efficiency and public-spiritedness of my minister-colleagues. But on a teleconference cabinet meeting about people-smuggling, on a Friday afternoon at the end of a sitting week, everyone tired, their voices – flattened by the sound-system – came across as querulous and grating. They've been working with one another since 2007 – which, in federal politics, means living with one another – and before that in opposition. There must come a time when they all find one another disagreeable and monotonous. But to see them – us – replaced with the blowhards and mediocrities of the other side?

SATURDAY, NOVEMBER 3, 2012
Sydney to Malaysia

Flying from Sydney to Malaysia. Up here at 30,000 feet, a chance to reflect. Bit like looking down at crawling humanity from the ferris wheel in Orson Welles's *The Third Man*. Dennis Richardson had recently told my friend Michael Easson in respect of me, 'And I thought Rudd was a media tart!' Yeah, Dennis, but the medium is the message, in this job as much as any. So I'm reported in the *Australian Financial Review* on Friday saying we are aligning our foreign policy with ASEAN, we take the organisation seriously, we recognise its centrality, they were right over Myanmar and we followed them. Merely *saying* it in the *Australian Financial Review* means that becomes Australia's stance. That's Australian policy. The medium *is* the message.

Last week I commented on the US super storm that hit ten east coast states in the last days of the presidential campaign. I told TV that there were no reports of casualties among the 26,000 Australians over there and that we would offer America assistance on recovery. Led TV news bulletins, ran on radio all day. The notion of the politician as *the commentator*, even as the entertainer – well, it's part of the job because it gives you more authority when you have to win an argument with colleagues or put some other proposition in the media. The easy stuff is money in the bank. My media adviser, Patrick, understands this instinctively, like providing a comment on another fraught consular case with an Australian lawyer, Sarah Armstrong, being detained by my old friends in Mongolia. Anyway, it works – as confirmed by the people who stop me at airports and in the street and tell me I'm doing a good job for Australia. This *'for Australia'* is the thing. The publicity translates into authority is what I'm trying to say. Stephen Smith was better prepared for being Foreign Minister than I, more meticulous, more knowledgeable, but there may be truth in Michelle Grattan's assessment he is an introvert. Just speaking up and being interesting may be sixty per cent of being a political leader.

Joel Fitzgibbon, the caucus whip and the chief numbers man for Rudd, saw me about one of those consular issues. Jock Palfreeman, the son of one of his constituents, on holidays in Bulgaria, saw a gypsy being beaten up by a crowd. He was charged with whipping out a knife, entering the fight and killing one of the attackers. We discussed the affair: we think his family has probably got to pay a $30,000 fine before the Bulgarians will even consider a transfer and we shouldn't argue for improvement in his conditions because they'll probably hold that against the poor bastard. As he leaves, Fitzgibbon talks about The Leadership. He says the improved poll position means there's less toxicity but the electorate will defeat Julia nonetheless. I want to tell him that he should stop the mischief-making and get Rudd to stop generating the low-rent stuff he goes in for – street walks and articles for the *Sunday Telegraph*. Trying to couch it positively, I say, 'You're playing a waiting game.' He says he agrees. He says there's no end-of-the-year deadline for Gillard but March next year looms. Uh oh. I may have given him the impression I'm not opposing his venture. I didn't want to make this commitment. But then …

MONDAY, NOVEMBER 5, 2012
Sabah

Malaysian Foreign Minister Anifah Aman is smooth, well spoken, deeply friendly. At our first meeting, back in Phnom Penh in the margins of the East Asia Summit's foreign ministers' meeting, he had firmly said he would vote for us for the Security Council, even over the frowns and thrusted notes of his advisers sitting with him. He stuck to it, too. We got their vote.

He is apparently part of the wealthy political elite, his brother the Sabah Chief Minister. The Barisan Nasional holds twenty-two out of twenty-five federal seats in the state. Thus East Malaysia is the 'fixed deposit' in favour of the coalition. But Anifah was off last night to three village meetings that would keep him out till 3 am, talking broken bridges and new roofs. He fears a protest vote that goes too far from voters flirting with 'time for a change sentiment'.

'You mean an over-correction?' I ask.

'Yes.'

The federal elections are due by April. Still, the coalition has the media and the cash.

In our talks yesterday we were locked in agreement on people-smuggling, South China Sea, peace in the South Philippines, Myanmar, their own candidacy for the UNSC for 2014–15. And today in the *Borneo Post* and *New Straits Times* there are big positive stories: 'Malaysia Praised for Countering Human Smuggling'; 'Praise for Peace Maker Role'; 'Carr Commends Malaysia for Combating Human Smuggling'.

Exactly what I want: a pragmatic alignment of Australia and ASEAN. As Myanmar Foreign Minister U Wunna Maung Lwin said to me, 'We see you as Asians.' And Anifah said, 'You are a bridge between Southeast Asia and Europe.'

Today, Anifah's flying to Melbourne for the Cup, we to Sandakan for the Australian memorial, then to Kuala Lumpur.

WEDNESDAY, NOVEMBER 7, 2012
Sabah to Bali

Heard that Obama had won Ohio and Florida while we were on the tarmac at Kuala Lumpur, en route to Bali. The lucky bastard becomes a two-term President. Democrats keep the Senate too, the Republicans the House. Fills me with foreboding about the possibility of a deal to reduce the deficit. Debt is the biggest threat to American security.

I deeply doubt this political system can resolve it. If America sinks into a decrepitude of inflation and no growth, what happens to our security?

Well, a ring of prosperous, resilient societies in Southeast Asia with a stake in Australia. Their supermarkets full of our products. Our kids in one another's universities. Their defence forces training in our north. Their companies becoming multinationals by investing in Australia. This is the goal: a strong, sympathetic region to the north. Which is why Gillard and I are here, in Bali, at SBY's fifth Democracy Forum.

THURSDAY, NOVEMBER 8, 2012
Bali

An idea takes hold: that Australia be seen by the Europeans and Americans as expert on Southeast Asia. Not Asia as a whole. That's presumptuous. How could we compete with the US knowledge of China? But expert on Southeast Asia. That this – us being part of their narrative, us knowing them intimately – be seen as a competitive advantage for Australia. That we should aspire to such authority. Part of my alignment with ASEAN. Why not?

Miles Kupa, our High Commissioner in Kuala Lumpur, tells me the British mission is selling its great old grand colonial property and retreating to a floor in a high-rise. Our understanding of Malaysian politics – the High Commissioner's cables are top rate – can't be beaten. Anifah says he sees us as a bridge between Asia and Europe. Here in Indonesia, the Norwegian Ambassador just told me he looks to our Ambassador for clues. Our people talk the language.

Tonight at Yudhoyono's dinner at The Westin, Helena and I sit at a table of foreign ministers: the European looks familiar but he wasn't on the list. Who is he? The Rolodex in my head spins. I've met him … he's from a *small* country. Kosovo? A Balt? He tells me he's just come from Myanmar, even got to Pagan. Then the Balinese dancers romp in, he's distracted and I get to glance at his name card. Switzerland! I remember we voted against him and for South Korea on the hosting of some green event. But that's alright. They didn't vote for us for the Security Council.

Also at the table, Afghan Foreign Minister Zalmai Rassoul who smiles but doesn't make contact; Mongolian Foreign Minister Luvsanvandan Bold who beams, perhaps shamed that he couldn't deliver his country for the Security Council vote; and Marty, who looks exhausted at managing all these guests and satisfying the

President, and his charming Thai-born wife, Sranya.

But I take my seat next to the lounging Zimbabwean Foreign Minister Simbarashe Mumbengegwi, who tells me he knows Sydney. 'How?' I ask. Turns out he lived in Glebe as a student. Then he asks, 'When are you going to lift sanctions on my country?' I reply, 'When you approve a constitution.'

President Yudhoyono has organised Indonesian dancers and songs so beyond this we get no conversation. Marty stares bug-eyed with fatigue. The Afghan minister looks worn, makes no contribution, gazing off in the distance, thinking – I guess – of the Taliban slaughter ahead; the Mongolian minister just thinks – I guess – of how unbelievable it is to be here, having been trained in Marxism–Leninism in East Germany under communism and having been elected to government in a democratic Mongolia only last June. The dinner ends at nine. As we get up, someone I don't recall introduces me to ... to Ahmadinejad? It's got to be Ahmadinejad! The beard, the deep-set eyes, the gaze. Are there cameras? How do I handle this? 'Do you recognise him?' asks the interlocutor. I'm now certain it is the Iranian President. I say, 'Er ... um ... he's ... wearing a tie,' which Ahmadinejad never does, thus explaining my confusion. I hope. Then the Ambassador from Morocco – for he is the interlocutor – tells me it's *his* Foreign Minister, who I had met in Rabat back in June. But he *looks* like Ahmadinejad. Very bad form, by the way, this challenging you to remember someone. A smooth diplomat would start, 'I'm sure you remember our Foreign Minister ...'

As we get up, I tell the Zimbabwean if he helps bring democracy to his country, I will get him an honorary degree from an Australian university. No, a number of them. Honorary degrees will be showered. He expresses satisfaction.

FRIDAY, NOVEMBER 9, 2012
Bali

When Hillary Clinton says 'Marty's decisions can be somewhat complex', or Julia Gillard says 'Marty reminds me of Johnny Depp', or Stephen Smith says 'I understand Marty is alright with this one', they can only be discussing one person: Raden Mohammad Marty Muliana Natalegawa, the 49-year-old professional diplomat who's been Indonesia's Foreign Minister since 2009, appointed by President Yudhoyono. Even the English-language Indonesian press refers to him as 'Marty'.

My briefing describes him this way:

> Natalegawa, 50, is a polished and adroit Foreign
> Minister. An experienced problem-solver and savvy media
> performer, he has established good relations with the often
> prickly Indonesian parliament. Well-versed in regional
> idiosyncrasies, Natalegawa is an effective operator when he's
> on familiar ground, such as dealing with Myanmar or helping
> fellow ASEANs manage conflicts. Even so, he can overreach
> at times, compounding perceptions held by some ASEANs
> that Indonesia's regional leadership efforts are self-serving.

I first met him on March 15 in Canberra, just a few days after I was sworn in to federal parliament, for the annual 2+2 meeting between Australia and Indonesia. I was afraid I was under-briefed for my first meeting. Marty made it easy.

He's a small, compact figure with black hair, brushed straight back. His hallmark glasses and his tightly fitted bespoke double-breasters hint at a cosmopolitan fashion statement. When we looked at a portrait of Indonesia's founding fathers in the Dutch-era foreign ministry building, he said with a smile, 'I like that one with the round glasses.' I asked him where he got his glasses and he confirmed it was New York, where he served as diplomat.

He was born in Bandung, West Java, where his father had been a former director of a state-owned bank. He told me his parents had been regents (heads of local government, elected by the people). He went to boarding school at Ellesmere College in England. He told me that students were once taken on an excursion to London and set loose. Some boys went to the museum. He went off to enrol in Amnesty International. Later he studied international relations at LSE where he met his wife, Sranya Bamrungphong, the daughter of a Thai diplomat. At Cambridge he did his Masters of Philosophy on conflict intervention. This is a large part of the international agenda – Syria, Libya, Rwanda, Bosnia; the whole question of when to intervene and how, endorsed by the General Assembly in 2005. How noble the sentiment and carefully sifted the arguments: but how bloody difficult to apply as confirmed by the escalation of massacres in Syria.

Marty rounded this off with a PhD in nuclear arms control at the Australian National University, living in Canberra with his wife. The former Indonesian Ambassador to Australia said he recalls Marty volunteering to write speeches for him. One evening he gave him an assignment and the next morning the immaculately typed, word-perfect draft landed on the Ambassador's desk. At the ANU, he once left by bus to Adelaide to watch the Grand Prix, when it was washed out by rain, wrapped up in ten minutes. He had to return, seeing more of the Australian countryside than can be forced on any international visitor. He is still interested in automobiles. No, he said, he does not play golf. He laughed about that with his wife. Despite his glittering academic credentials, I have never heard him talk about anything other than foreign affairs. 'So you're interested in history?' he asked me last night. But then stopped short of pursuing the subject. No hint he shares this love of history.

The degrees mean he has the perfect academic preparation for being Foreign Minister of the world's fourth largest country (and a reminder of how modest my own).

His diplomacy had been immediately apparent in Canberra, when the two of us had walked straight into our 'tête-à-tête'; that is, a meeting without advisers. Marty slices up an agenda: some items are bilateral, some regional, some multilateral and global. Some get pulled out to the next meeting, when we'll be sitting with defence ministers and a brace of colleagues; some issues can be resolved between the two of us. He raises human rights in the two Papuan provinces before I am able to. He disarmingly accepts responsibility for police work and the need for more sensitivity. Each side is allowed to register the politically important expressions of concern on sensitive questions. Later, he can tell Indonesians he raised the question of minors in detention. And I can tell Australian media, if asked, that I raised the question of jailed Australians in Bali.

It is a 'Bob–Marty' conversation. His softly spoken English is perfect and accented. His conversation is littered with some diplomatic jargon, which I find myself drifting into these days. He comfortably uses words like 'optics', 'modalities', 'synergising' and 'changing dynamics'. I once said 'forward leaning' in a radio interview, as in 'William Hague's forward leaning on Syria.' But haven't brought myself to use one of Marty's favourites, 'modalities'. He said in our Jakarta discussion that our developing bilateral relationship had several 'propellants'. Not sure whether I could recruit that either; still, 'modalities' would be sweet.

Marty may have his own anxieties. At the official dinner he hosted last night, I told him the sheer pleasure of the job was that it was a learning experience. It was the best job in politics because of the interesting content loaded down your gullet each day. He agreed but, looking off in the distance, said something about not liking the internal politics. I imagine that in any presidential system – I'm thinking of that of the US, France, Russia

– a Foreign Minister has to compete with advisers and influential ambassadors to maintain his influence with the palace. After our first meeting in Canberra I received a call from him a day or two after the *Washington Post* had featured a front-page story alleging an Australian plan to allow the Americans to militarise Cocos Islands. He wanted to know – needed to know – whether it was true (a reasonable enquiry, given that we were not able to consult Indonesia before the 2011 decision on marine deployment in the Northern Territory). And, when I told him it was only speculation and there was no Australian decision on this even under consideration, he enquired whether, when I make a public statement making this clear, I might mention that the Indonesian Foreign Minister had enquired about this. We all have domestic dynamics. They count as much in Indonesia as anywhere.

Marty probably lacks influence beyond the foreign-affairs portfolio, the wording of communiqués, fretting about reference and the Bali process or the centrality of ASEAN.

He succeeds in giving any international visitor the impression they're the most important person in the room. He never pushes too far, and hence dissuades you from pushing him too far. He is the most unflappable protector of his President. No one gives a more sure-footed speech of welcome or vote of thanks – for example, to the Prime Minister of Cambodia for hosting an East Asia Summit – and he seems to embody the Indonesian disinclination to take sides, just possibly a Javanese trait. No ASEAN Foreign Minister will be better placed to take off to Manila, then hit Hanoi, Phnom Penh and Singapore, to try to negotiate an ASEAN communiqué on the South China Sea as he did after our bilateral in Jakarta on July 16.

That's what he's off to do at 1 am, so I allow him to wrap up this official dinner as soon as guests have sipped their coffee.

I told him I thought it must be a marvellous time to represent Indonesia: 'You're a robust young democracy,' I said. But we can only guess about his country's chance of pulling it off, or about his prospects of serving under another president. Still, Marty's style means you are willing him to do it, and his country.

SATURDAY, NOVEMBER 10, 2012
Singapore to Sydney

Flying from Singapore to Sydney. Our stance on the Middle East is shameful, in lockstep with the Likud, designed to feed the worst instincts of Israel and encourage it to self-destruct, placing us with the Marshall Islands and Canada and rejecting the entire Arab world and the Palestinians. First the Prime Minister stopped a message to the Palestinians before the UN vote that we would 'not oppose' enhanced Palestinian status. She was right tactically because not responding did not destroy our chances; and our mission to the UN was wrong to think it would. I readily concede all that. But it would have been the better course to have told them it was our intention to abstain, the better policy, the honourable one, the position in Australia's interests. Then she swiftly overruled my approval for our UN mission voting in favour of an Egyptian motion on non-proliferation in the Middle East. We had to tell the Egyptians the reversal had been made 'at the highest level'. In other words, the Prime Minister had overruled her Foreign Minister. I'm advised by our UN mission that Egypt and the Arab League are forming the view that having been elected to the Security Council, Australia has now walked away: 'after you got elected this is all we get.' This made me wince.

Netanyahu is spreading more settlements and this week I wanted to issue a statement using the word 'condemn', as the UK did. The UK under a Conservative foreign secretary. But all statements on the Middle East have to be threaded through the Prime Minister's office. Back came the reply: one, we don't use the word 'condemn'; two, it must go past her staffer Bruce Wolpe and Cabinet Secretary Mark Dreyfus; and three, whatever we do, advise the Israeli Ambassador first. But this morning I ring James from the airport lounge in Singapore to move things along and I get the advice that *any* statement on settlements – even that 'we express concern' – is vetoed by the Prime Minister. He was told this by Richard Maude, her foreign-policy adviser, the diplomat on her staff.

Extraordinary. We can do nothing.

Gareth Evans sent me a copy of an email he had sent Bob Hawke – by coincidence it arrived on my iPad this morning – urging Hawke to plead with Julia to get us to at least abstain on the UN motion to lift the Palestinian status. It will come up at the General Assembly on November 29. Evans wrote:

> I am passing through New York and have just seen the draft text of the resolution circulated today – seeking Palestinian observer-state status in the UN General Assembly – which seems certain to go to a vote in the General Assembly later this month. The text seems to be unexceptionable in its detail, e.g., being clear that full membership of the UN remains to be determined and final status issues remain to be negotiated, and containing no remotely offensive language. It will clearly be carried by an overwhelming majority, with most of our friends either voting yes or abstaining – with the exception, of course, of Israel itself, the US and maybe 15 to 20 others at most of the 193 members.
>
> …
>
> Any argument by the PM that we cried wolf before without adverse consequences would be quite misplaced in the

present context: the almost universal expectation around the UN, as I have picked it up, is that the only question for us is yes or abstain – and real shockwaves will go out if we vote no.

I have tried in the past to talk to Julia about this issue without any noticeable effect. I honestly believe that you are [that is, Hawke] the only person on the planet that can possibly persuade her (a) that the resolution will not damage Israel's interests or undermine its negotiating position on all the relevant final status issues, and (b) that it will be terribly damaging to our international position, and anything we might be able to achieve on the Security Council, if we do not at least abstain on this vote.

High hopes, pal. I emailed him that the Prime Minister had just now vetoed even a mild criticism of the latest settlement expansion. We can't say we *condemn* it; we can't even say it *concerns* us.

We are not running an Australian foreign policy. It's not even pro-Israeli, in the deepest Rabin-style understanding of the country's survival; that is, an acknowledgment that without a Palestinian state, Israel will morph into an apartheid state with a burgeoning captive Palestinian population denied civil rights.

Helena says I should go and see Julia and have a showdown.

Subcontracting our foreign policy to party donors is what this involves. Or appears to involve. It sours all prospects.

Resignation is clearly an option, when you disagree as Foreign Minister with something forced by your Prime Minister. But it involves hurting the party and denying me the choice to run guerrilla activity against the shabby policy.

Stayed overnight in Singapore to avoid an overnight flight out of Bali on discount airlines but it also let me have a relaxed talk with Foreign Minister Shanmugam over a protein shake – I brought a sachet of the powder – in a coffee shop, without coat and ties, without staff. He's a smart lawyer, good brain and this was our third meeting. Eighty per cent of our talk was about China, its internal dynamics – the tremendous challenges that China's leaders face. We also discussed their so-called 'nine-dash' line claim on the South China Sea and how it is unclear what exactly China's claims are. He cautions on the need to avoid coming out negative on China at this month's EAS.

Today's *Financial Times* – which I read on the plane – refers to 'the outlines of a Chinese-style Monroe Doctrine' taking shape. That is, the Chinese objecting to any outside powers being present in Asia as the Americans under President Monroe in the nineteenth century objected to any European powers in Latin America.

On CNN this morning, David Petraeus, Director of the CIA, resigns because of an extra-marital affair. So an affair is elevated to a hanging offence. Their best military commander, the author of the text on counter-insurgency, the leader of the surge in Afghanistan, a dedicated public servant. Next step – chemical castration mandated for cabinet appointees? The New Puritanism claims everyone in its sights. Or maybe it was a plot by the fat people of America against a greyhound-fit public servant who could run rings around them.

THURSDAY, NOVEMBER 15, 2012
Sydney

Any time with Hillary is pure champagne, pure quality.

I'm just back from Perth where Stephen Smith and I had Australia–United States Ministerial Consultations (AUSMIN); the Americans represented by Hillary and by Defense Secretary

Leon Panetta. She stepped off her big plane, eyes hidden behind large-framed oval sunglasses, her hair pulled back, an outsize light blue jacket and black slacks. She knew all our names, she didn't complain about the fatigue, she said she was delighted to be here. For God's sake, we've made her travel for thirty-five hours to reach Perth to give Stephen Smith another triumph for his hometown – and even with touchdowns in Hawaii and Guam she projected freshness and charm.

When we sat down with the Prime Minister and canvassed a few subjects (interesting that Gillard raised the Palestinian vote in the General Assembly – maybe I've got her thinking this through) Hillary was bright-eyed and engaged. It struck me: she's someone of my generation – the same debates at university, Vietnam teach-ins, the flirtation with Whitlamism, or, in her case, McGovern-ism, the rebuilding of left parties by reaching for the centre, the hunger – our hunger – to know about the whole wide world. Of course with the briefings she gets, and the four years in the job, she *would* know her stuff. Anyone would. But there's not a doubt in my mind that she'd be a breezily confident President. Speaking with authority and interesting to her electorate.

Over dinner at the Matilda Bay Restaurant – about a dozen Americans and a dozen Australians – I said to her, 'I loved it when you said about that anti-Islam video "this has NOTHING to do with America!"' I told her that I'd been driving around Sydney when I heard that on the radio and I quickly convened a press conference and repeated it. And I added, 'Sometimes vigorously stating the obvious has a real healthy effect. It just resonates even if you think you're telling people something they already know.' She agreed and she said they tracked that comment in the Arab world and they found that even in mosques there were people saying, 'Well, this had nothing to do with the Americans.'

The next day our talks were easy as we canvassed the whole agenda: the protection and promotion of Asia–Pacific security, support for regional dialogue, the advancement of global security, the promotion of global development and the enhancement of Australia–US bilateral defence cooperation.

Paul Keating gave a speech – the Keith Murdoch Oration – at the State Library in Victoria yesterday. He was decent enough to give us advance warning. Today it's plastered everywhere. It has some very strong material in it, like the reminder that before Keating became Prime Minister the Australian Prime Minister only attended two international gatherings, the British Commonwealth Heads of Government meeting and the South Pacific Forum, and in no multilateral fora would he or she ever sit with the leaders of the US, Japan, China or Indonesia. He referred to Australia being over-deferential to the US, repeating criticisms he made at the time of President Obama's visit in 2011 – with which I agreed. He said:

> Whichever way we cut it, Australia must lay a bigger bet on
> its relationship with Indonesia. And this has to be cultural
> and commercial as well as political. The Australian people
> are unlikely to beat a path to Java or to Sumatra without
> public policy in this country divining the way.

It gave me an opportunity to respond on *AM* and, by the end of the day, a dozen other places. I stated that Australia's objectives had not been surrendered to the US. I said: 'We are in a treaty relationship with the United States because we've got a major task and that is the security of this continent, a small population, a large continent, an uncertain region, an uncertain world. And since the early twentieth century the response of Australia has been to seek a relationship with the United States.' Besides, it was easy to work with the Obama team because they are multilateralists and have a decent agenda (the argument about the *charm* of American values).

On *AM* I also defended Australia's relationship with Indonesia:

> In Jakarta we have the largest embassy, we've got the largest
> concentration of Australian diplomats. Indonesia is the
> biggest recipient of Australian aid. We are building schools
> in Indonesia. We have a high level of cooperation with
> counterterrorism that has assisted Indonesia jail over 400
> terrorists and Indonesians and Australians are safer as a
> result. And we've got a process of consultation with Indonesia
> that means I exchange text messages with my Indonesian
> counterpart.
>
> And we've had more – we have a ministerial exchange
> with Indonesia, an Indonesian minister coming here or an
> Australian minister going to Indonesia, on average every
> three weeks since 2007.
>
> The relationship with Indonesia I think is very satisfactory
> to both sides and the Prime Minister's relationship with
> President Yudhoyono is another confirmation of that.

It was several months ago that Stephen Smith brought to cabinet the paper on an agreement to boost US military aircraft flights into and out of Australia. That got me hot and bothered about the prospect that this AUSMIN would have projected to the world – China and Indonesia – searing and savage headlines about massive new defence deals between the US and us. I intervened in that cabinet debate, I spoke to Smith, I later discussed the matter with Dennis Richardson, who agreed with me that this AUSMIN should not contain another big strategic initiative. 'This will be a successful AUSMIN if we have the media complaining there was no big announcement,' I recall Dennis saying to me. He and

I were locked in agreement and it was no bad thing that he was headed off to take over as boss of the Defence Department to keep an eye on what had become our joint strategy: no repeat of last year's boldness that saw headlines about 2500 marines in Darwin and more ship visits.

And I did something else. I went straight to the Americans, putting it to them that the last thing we need is another shock to the system about military cooperation. I had in mind the effect on the region; I also had in mind the effect on domestic political opinion in Australia. I was pleased that Ambassador Bleich agreed with me so readily; in other words, even on the American side, there's no appetite for ratcheting up the strategic cooperation.

Then just before the start of the second day of AUSMIN, over breakfast I blanched when I looked at the newspaper summaries and there were big headlines based on Stephen Smith's comments about more US ship visits to HMAS *Stirling* at Garden Island. Dennis and James shared my concern. This was not tracking as we had intended. 'How does that get read in the Chinese Embassy?' I asked them. In fact, the communiqué that had been negotiated between the two sides was cool-headed on this. It referred to the prospect of more American naval use of HMAS *Stirling* simply as a matter for further study. This was the wording already agreed upon:

> We also discussed potential opportunities for additional naval cooperation at a range of locations, including HMAS *Stirling*. All of these possible areas of cooperation would require substantial further study and additional decisions by both capitals.

At breakfast, Dennis gave me some advice. 'You're speaking first at the press conference [that is, ahead of Hillary Clinton, Leon Panetta, Stephen Smith]; *you* can frame the way this announcement gets made.' And I did, by telling the media this was a steady-as-she-goes, business-as-usual AUSMIN with no big strategic surprise. It was all about consolidation. The decision on HMAS *Stirling* was subject to a long-term study and any rise in its use by visiting US ships 'would be years *or decades*' (I insisted on adding the *decades*. Smith preferred *years*). This certainly framed it. Framed it good and hard. On the way to the VIP aircraft to fly back to Sydney I rang both Greg Sheridan and Peter Hartcher to drive home the message: there was no new strategic initiative in this announcement because the Americans had no appetite for it. And Greg didn't like that.

FRIDAY, NOVEMBER 16, 2012
Sydney

My AUSMIN strategy worked. A big feature article by Cameron Stewart in *The Australian* today records that the AUSMIN meeting contained 'not a single big announcement' and 'underscored the fact the Gillard government wants speed limits placed on the move towards a greater US military presence in Australia'. Stewart went on to write:

> Almost a year after the Obama visit, Smith said in Perth this week that preliminary discussions for greater access for US planes to Australian airfields in the north was 'just starting', with no clear timeframe for concrete results.

> The notion of more visits by US warships or nuclear submarines – or even the semi-basing of such vessels at

Perth's HMAS *Stirling* – was an even more distant prospect. This idea, Smith said, was a 'third cab off the rank', which was 'years away'.

And further on he wrote:

> Taken together, these things make it difficult to conclude anything other than that Australia is choosing to build up the presence of US forces here without fanfare, without headlines and, in the words of Smith, 'step by step'.

What I wanted. Mission accomplished, although it must be said Smith sensibly was not working for any more forceful positions.

SUNDAY, NOVEMBER 18, 2012
Sydney

After a Chinese fundraiser on Friday night, a quiet weekend. Almost a return to a normal life. I read some pages of Samantha Power's book on the history of the crime of genocide, and at night we watch a bit of the BBC's *Cymbeline*, I think one of the only thirty-nine Shakespeare plays I've never seen or read, other than *Henry VIII*. But only a bit – in this job I haven't read a single book cover to cover, seen an opera or been to the movies. I devour parts of books, read cables as if life itself depended on them, see movies on planes.

Today a press conference – just like a Premier's life, this Sunday media – launching an advertising campaign warning Australians to buy travel insurance. Then Helena and I had lunch with my former staffer Walt Secord. He had advice on me speaking on the Armenian genocide. He said the verbal formula Armenians repeat is the one used by Obama: 'You know my personal views …' Then he goes on to say Obama's administration does not take a stand between Turkey and the Armenians. This is useful. As Foreign Minister, I have to tell the Armenian community that Australia takes no side in their historical dispute with Turkey. But that doesn't mean I can't remind them of my years of attending Armenian commemorations and giving them a memorial to their genocide on the roof garden of State parliament. Walt advised that whatever our differences with the Jewish community about Palestinian statehood, I must always continue to see their delegations. What got Whitlam into trouble was keeping them waiting for hours and even then not seeing them.

On pure intuition Walt knew I was writing a diary. Interesting, this. They work for you for years. They hear you thinking. I went to the gym and, without a trainer, did a tough legs workout. My favourites are walking lunges, sumo squats and one-legged Romanian deadlifts.

Later back in the office – good time to work, Sunday afternoons – I spoke to Gareth Evans. He had been at an Australia–China Council meeting in Beijing when the news from AUSMIN came out. He said the line in the communiqué about no containment on China was appreciated. I then gave him the full story of my work to see that a new raft of strategic initiatives with America had not emerged. Like Keating – to whom I spoke about this on Friday – he appreciated the importance. We joked that we were getting criticised in *The Australian* for going slow on our strategic integration with America. On Palestinian status, he said he'd spoken to Anthony Albanese who is 'hot to trot', now fully briefed and ready to engage with the Prime Minister. I then polished off a telephone interview with *AM* to be broadcast tomorrow morning where, with some nervousness in my voice, I carefully wove my way between the imperative of condemning the missile assaults on Israel by Hamas and other associated terrorist entities and calls for Israel to be cautious and proportionate and minimise civilian casualties.

Home for an early night and then off to a week in the Senate.

TUESDAY, NOVEMBER 20, 2012
Canberra

The second-last sitting week of the year. Only the Senate sits, so this echoing palace-mausoleum of a building – Helena thinks it's an oversize circus tent – is largely empty. Only half the caucus colleagues strolling the corridors. I have the gym to myself. I've banned coffee from my diet to see if I can escape episodes of atrial fibrillation. So far this has given me lethargy and headaches. To live is to lose ground.

To feed my gloomy irritation I sustain another defeat at the hands of the Likudniks. This is over how we vote in the UN in a dispute between Israel and Lebanon. When I met the Lebanese Foreign Minister in Cairo in September I told him we would be more sympathetic than we'd been in the past on the annual General Assembly motion that deals with the 2006 destruction by the Israeli air force of the oil-storage tanks in the Jiyeh Power Plant in Lebanon. This caused an oil slick along the Lebanese and Syrian coasts. This motion calls on Israel to provide compensation to Lebanon and Syria. We had voted against the resolution on the grounds that we do not consider the General Assembly the appropriate forum. But this implies we are unsympathetic and in my view Lebanon is a country with which we have friendly relations.

Moreover, we have over 181,000 people of Lebanese ancestry living in Australia. I wanted to abstain.

For some reason this motion got threaded through the Prime Minister's office – even though it doesn't deal with Palestinian status or the Israel–Palestine dispute – and today I got a message that we were not to shift our vote to an abstention but were to continue to vote *against* this resolution. This would place us with only seven nations. I've sent Julia a text message – she's in Cambodia at the East Asia Summit – saying:

> Julia – motion on Lebanon oil spill raises no Palestinian or Israel security issues. In that context I gave commitment to Lebanon. Need only abstain. If oppose we will be with half a dozen only. Terrible signal to the Arab world and with other votes to Arab background voters. Can you take a minute to reconsider this?

She replied:

> In an EAS session. Re resolution – Australia has always voted against it. No reason has been given to me to change. We do need to discuss Middle East issues – had a good chat with Obama. Will ensure we do when I get back. Julia

The rest of our exchange:

> Julia – not so simple. I as Foreign Minister gave my word. I was entitled to because it had nothing to do with Palestinian status or security of Israel. We have friendly ties with Lebanon and they have a big population here. Moreover we are about to take our SC seat and had won support from a lot of the Arab world. This is an ideal issue for a symbolic shift and doesn't touch on Israel's security one little bit which is why

I felt free to make a commitment. Cop it – and blame it on your Foreign Minister. Cheers, Bob

Bob – still in EAS – my jurisdiction on UN resolutions isn't confined to ones on Palestine and Israel. Any shift of significance needs to be checked with me. And our only refuge on ones closely followed is to have policy justifications. On this we have none.

Julia – But (1) our relationship with Lebanon and (2) our opening to the Arab world and (3) new UN status is policy justification. Separately, policy justification definitely exists in spades for condemning these new settlements. Not to do so is departure from policy. Bob

Bob – I agree re working on settlements.

This comes against the backdrop of first, being overruled on 'con-demning' 1500 apartments being thrown up in East Jerusalem, a brazen expansion of settlements; second, being overruled on sup-porting an Egyptian policy on a nuclear-free Middle East; and third, the approach to a vote on Palestinian status.

This last one has been the subject of discussions I've had all day with colleagues. Tony Burke believes we ought to be voting 'yes' for this. He agrees with me that there is a big gap between the New South Wales Labor Right and the Victorian Right, wedded as it is to the pro-Israel line. Chris Bowen, in danger in his seat of McMahon, endorses this. So does Jason Clare. Then, out of the blue, Ed Husic, Member for Chifley, rings me to say he has spoken to the Israeli Ambassador and told him they need to go easy in Gaza, that they won't advance their cause by bombing houses and killing children – a brave statement for an MP with a Muslim background (Bosnian). I briefed him on the above, as I did

Richard Marles, my parliamentary secretary who is from Victoria and part of the Victorian Right. Sam Dastyari, the New South Wales General Secretary, agrees with me, especially in view of the horrific polling figures in Sydney's multicultural melting pot of the south-west.

We'd have nothing to say to these voters if we were part of half-a-dozen nations supporting Israel, as opposed to another 158 – this was the vote on the Lebanon oil-slick resolution last time. Melissa Parke, MP for Fremantle, a member of the Left, is going to move a motion in caucus that we 'not oppose' the Palestinian status resolution.

I rang Gareth Evans and he said a 'no' vote by us would be the worst Australian foreign-policy decision in a generation. He told me to fight all the way.

WEDNESDAY, NOVEMBER 21, 2012
Canberra

Striding down the corridor of the press gallery at Parliament House, I gave a cheerful greeting to Laura Tingle, chief correspondent of the *Australian Financial Review*. She replied, 'Ah! Someone in the place who is enjoying himself! You just don't give a fuck what happens!'

THURSDAY, NOVEMBER 22, 2012
Canberra to Sydney

Spent much of yesterday – here in Canberra, Senate only sitting – ringing colleagues, Steve Smith and Wayne Swan included, to build support for a 'yes' vote on Palestinian status. At eleven o'clock last night, in the Realm Hotel with Helena in bed, I sat at the desk and rang the UN Mission, getting Ambassador Gary Quinlan out of bed at 6.30 am New York time. This is about the other question: how we vote on the resolution covering the dispute between Lebanon and Israel on the 2006 oil slick. When is the vote, I asked, and did he have an instruction from the Prime Minister? The vote will be on today, he said – and he had received an email from her office. So *I* cannot give you an instruction – that is, to vote 'yes' or abstain? No, it has been determined. On the instruction of our Prime Minister we will vote, I guess, with a handful of nations on the Israeli side.

Despite the hour, I rang Gareth who railed at the insanity.

Now today in the office I get the report from the UN mission: 152 nations voted yes, a few abstained, seven voted no. In this last category: the US, Canada, the Marshall Islands, Nauru, Micronesia, Israel and – disgracefully, shamefully – us. *The shame.*

I use this in calls to colleagues. On Chris Bowen's suggestion I rang New South Wales backbencher Daryl Melham. He's a veteran left-winger, an old factional partner of my friends Rodney Cavalier and Peter Crawford and he's got Lebanese ancestry. He is in the cart instantly. He will speak in the caucus debate on Palestinian status.

I accept an invitation to a Chinese-community dinner in Sydney tonight. This gets me out of a late-night session of the Senate and an extra night in Canberra. A night at home.

FRIDAY, NOVEMBER 23, 2012
Sydney

A day in the Sydney office full of mostly routine meetings and a smallish charity lunch. This lunch was a prize raffle and an events company won. And here I am – listening to people talking about their holidays and their favourite restaurants until, ten minutes before I am due to leave, the organisers finally get round to suggesting people ask me questions. The exhaustion of this kind of stuff. But the guy from a finance company sitting next to me tells me that he thinks I'm doing a great job representing Australia and this makes it all worthwhile. Kindness of strangers.

A frustrating afternoon. The meetings run late and overlap but I had a visitor from the Arab world – Wadah Khanfar, former Director General of Al Jazeera, who heads a foundation in Qatar and knows the whole Arab region. I could have talked to him all day. We got to discuss President Morsi, who brokered the truce in Gaza this week. I hint to him and the Arab-background Australians who brought him to me that I'm a little shame-faced about Australia's voting record at the UN, knowing that it's going to get a whole lot worse if Gillard gets her way on the big vote coming up next week, November 29. I go off to do the Wran lecture at Parliament House, not a boring paper but a PowerPoint and improvisation. Jill Wran is there but a poor turnout. I mean, to hear a former Premier and Foreign Minister talk on one of our legendary leaders, under 200 party people turn out. A reflection on my star appeal. Or the whole show may be dying.

SATURDAY, NOVEMBER 24, 2012
Sydney

I do nearly two hours of Pilates this morning, have lunch at home and come in for a hard legs workout at Fitness First with my trainer Lisa. Squats, lunges, leg raises, calves – the works. At 3.30 pm, back in my silent, empty Bligh Street office, I take a phone call from the Prime Minister. 'I'm just settling back with a peppermint tea,' she tells me, the 'I' enunciated as a perfectly shaped 'Oi' in her trademark broad Aussie vowels. I tell her to keep cool as she plans her defence in parliament about the latest blow-up of the AWU scandal, again in the media in the last twenty-four hours. I barely understand it and can't bring myself to read more than the first five paragraphs of any of the stories. I tell her if I can help her staff, canvass any defence lines, I'm happy to.

Then I say that we should address two matters: first, a process for dealing with our difference on Palestine and, second, the substantial issue itself. She tells me that she's discussed the matter with Obama, who's going to work strenuously to defer the vote because it would force America to withdraw funding to the Palestinian Authority and to the UN. She tells me the Jewish community remains very important and they won't settle for anything other than a 'no' vote, that they figure prominently in fundraising and they're big in Victoria. I reply that the vote's going to be carried anyway and we'll find ourselves in the degrading position of being ranked with six other nations in a pathetic minority. She says that she hears that some Europeans want to vote 'no'. I say I hear the Europeans are gravitating to a consensus position – namely, that they'll all abstain.

We come to process. I suggested we have a meeting in her office on Monday with a selection of ministers. We agree on Albanese, Burke, Smith, Swan and, at her insistence, Conroy and Dreyfus.

I suggest Sam Dastyari but she says no one from the party organisation. I suggest we have a paper prepared and we agree that the paper can establish a basic factual position on, first, what the Europeans may actually do, and, second, what increased status might mean – she thinks it could give them some rights in civil aviation and this would worry Israel.

Appalling. She is wedded to voting 'no'. I can't bring myself to ring my mentor Evans and share this.

Home tonight. Walt Secord rings and suggests that instead of me getting done over by the Prime Minister, why don't I come out now and say we'll vote against Palestinian status? 'Because I've got to live with myself,' I reply. Curious; who suggested he phone me?

SUNDAY, NOVEMBER 25, 2012
Sydney

An appearance on *Australian Agenda*, a gym session with my other trainer, Arryn and a meditation class – this may save my life – at Double Bay. No media are wise to the big difference on the Palestinian status vote between Gillard and me. It's a mystery: how and why some things *don't* leak.

TUESDAY, NOVEMBER 27, 2012
Canberra

Manic activity yesterday as the contest over our vote on Palestinian UN status bubbled up and consumed everything. Sitting next to me in the Senate, Steve Conroy – a member of the Victorian ALP Right and, on Israel, an ultra – blasted me that my position is monstrous, a betrayal, a deceit and warns that the Right faction will bind all its members to vote against the Palestinian bid; that is, forcing every member of the faction to vote for Australia voting 'no'. 'I think you might find the New South Wales Right takes a different view,' I responded meekly. Later I rang Dastyari and Fitzgibbon to prepare them to resist this outrage, a binding position imposed on the National Right.

After Question Time four members of the falafel faction (the pro-Israel grouping in the caucus) were milling around excitedly and Senator Glenn Sterle asked whether they could see me. I promptly agreed to a meeting in my office. With four of them sitting around I expostulated that their lobby was wanting to claim victory on everything. Block the slightest hint of a criticism of Israel. 'You stopped me making criticism of Israel's settlement policy two weeks ago and you stopped me putting a vote behind the Lebanese on a matter that had nothing to do with Israel security or Palestinian status. No wonder tensions are boiling over ... You're insisting that every policy shift gets passed by the Israel lobby in Melbourne!' They argued they hadn't participated in these attempts to block me. I responded that the Prime Minister's office had and I presumed it had happened with their involvement. They insisted they had not, I think sincerely. I made it very clear that I supported an abstention in the UN. They were entitled to know it. But my complaint about the two other matters meant they left my office somewhat on the defensive.

By the evening the agitation was more and more intense. Joel Fitzgibbon and Ed Husic, both in the Rudd camp, were circling, exploiting this as an opportunity to open up leadership. I received a call from the former Prime Minister himself, again speaking in that sinister undertone that bodes no charity. Darkly he commented on the state of affairs, rehearsing the history of his relations with the Israel lobby, once so happy, now so gloomy. How much of this is about money, I asked him. He said that about one-fifth of the money he had raised in the 2007 election campaign had come from the Jewish community. On the numbers in the caucus, he said, the National Left had about forty votes. As for the Right, it was important to remember the outer ministry, junior ministers and parliamentary secretaries, did not get bound by a cabinet decision. So some of the Right were free to swing behind the motion. For the motion to win we would need twelve to defect from the Right. He was aware that figures in the New South Wales Right – Chris Bowen, Tony Burke, John Murphy – wanted to have something positive to report to the bursting Arab and Islamic populations in their electorates.

Meanwhile Gareth Evans and I stayed in contact, he bemoaning that getting overruled on this would warrant me resigning. He's coming up to brief caucus this evening, something I suggested, but not likely to help much – only a handful ever turn up to this kind of briefing. But my other plan was, of course, the motion in caucus. It was always clear that I couldn't shift the Prime Minister without some pressure, couldn't win in cabinet alone. She could ignore – and would – a cabinet majority. A motion in caucus was that pressure. On Tony Burke's advice I persuaded Melissa Parke, *not to move it* – Tony Burke warned me that she is seen as something of a surrogate Green – but to cede that right to Andrew Leigh, who is non-aligned. Harder for the Right to shrug off a motion coming from him. In turn, he told me he was eager.

This news got around.

That evening, coming out of a Senate division, I bumped into Leigh. He told me he was now 'under pressure' to drop his motion in caucus tomorrow. Uh oh, this meant pressure from the Prime Minister's office ... this meant pressure from Dreyfus ... this would mean, if it succeeded, all my leverage would evaporate. If it was just me and cabinet she was dealing with, the Prime Minister would get her own way. But if it was a motion, gathering support by the hour, in tomorrow's 9.30 am caucus meeting then she would have to consider a compromise.

'You can pull it off. This is a matter of principle. They can't pressure you,' I told Leigh. 'Meanwhile think of how we get to amend your motion and turn it into a bid not to support a vote of support at the UN but *to abstain.*'

To *abstain*.

Because a motion supporting abstention would be easier to get carried.

He agreed that in the caucus the next day he would amend his own motion to seek an Australian abstention. He wouldn't be pressured into backing down.

He's what the inimitable Keating would call 'a principled little bugger'.

As agreed, the Prime Minister and I assembled for our discussion with other ministers at 4 pm in her office. In attendance were, at my suggestion and with her agreement, Stephen Smith as a former Foreign Minister who had steered us through UN votes on Middle East questions; Anthony Albanese, as a senior minister representing the Left; Tony Burke, who represented that element of the New South Wales Right that supported my proposition for an opening to the Palestinians. On the other side of the argument were Stephen Conroy, the firebrand of the Victorian Right with an umbilical attachment to the cause of Israel; and Mark Dreyfus, the Cabinet Secretary, who is close to the Jewish community in Melbourne but who, up till now, I had thought might reflect a more liberal perspective on these issues than – for example – his colleague Michael Danby (who was not at the meeting, it being for ministers only).

The Prime Minister outlined the issues in her characteristically neat, brisk manner. Then the discussion opened and covered all the familiar territory – what the UN motion would mean and would not mean, what the available positions for us would mean in terms of winning votes/losing votes in Australia. After being very civilised, the discussion degenerated into a dispute between Burke and Conroy versus Dreyfus about whether the Arab community in Sydney deserved the same consideration and treatment as the Jewish community in Melbourne. At the end of one-and-a-half hours the Prime Minister said she was unmoved. She still adhered to a position that we should vote 'no' because the motion wouldn't achieve anything, it would complicate a two-state solution, the Americans would retaliate against the Palestinian Authority, etc. Deeply depressing to me. Conroy insisted, as we walked across the corridor into the cabinet meeting, that I should say nothing when this was discussed in cabinet because there would certainly be a leak that would have the Foreign Minister at odds with the Prime Minister. This was not unreasonable, I thought, on the assumption that she and I would be the only speakers. So I agreed. My spirits were low.

We got through other business and came to the political discussion. The Prime Minister made reference to this vote on Palestinian status and said that UN votes were things that she determined and, as agreed, asked me to give an account of the pros and cons of the options before us. Opening a file of briefings from the department, this I proceeded to do in a sing-song disinterested voice that belied my passion and resolve. Then when I finished, the Prime Minister asked for comments.

Sometimes in life, unexpected things can happen. Sometimes the cause of truth moves forward, without prompting.

My colleagues started to speak.

Craig Emerson first. He acknowledged that it was the Prime Minister's prerogative to determine these things – this I found astonishing but so it goes, everyone was to say it – and I expected him to chime in with support for Julia's position. Nothing doing. He quoted Gareth Evans, who he had seen in the corridors, saying that if we voted 'no' it would be the worst Australian foreign-policy decision in a generation. Then Albanese gave a no-holds-barred robust presentation of the case for voting 'yes' or abstaining. The Prime Minister repeated her mantra: 'I have made a judgment call.' Then Chris Bowen came in, putting in a low-key but very cogent way the case for us taking into account the interest in this of Arabic-background Australians. Martin Ferguson then made as strong a presentation as any of the others, saying a lot of people have moved on this subject and quoted Bob Hawke as an example.

I saw Steve Conroy getting restless, signalling to Bill Shorten that he should speak, as if he was in a Kingsville branch meeting itching to do in the local lefties. Peter Garrett chimed in. I had not the remotest notion of his position. He said – quite correctly – that there is big symbolic significance in the resolution. He said abstention is fine but he'd be happier if we voted 'yes'. Shorten and Conroy made their comments on the theme of sticking with the simple pro-Israel messages and the General Assembly vote not making any difference but – this is the significant point – *they were the only ones*! One after the other, Tony Burke, Mark Butler and Simon Crean (a surprise because he's been assumed to be part of that Victorian right-wing pro-Israel lobby) all spoke against the Prime Minister's position. Crean!

Moments like this – moments of clarity and outspokenness – make it possible to love the party.

I then said that I had not intended to speak because I didn't want to allow people to leak the fact that I, as Foreign Minister, was at odds with the Prime Minister. I pointed out, however, that the contribution of my colleagues made it impossible for me to sit there silent. I made three points. One, Australia has interests in the Arab world. Two, an abstention by Australia offers some hope for moderate Palestinians on the West Bank. Three, if we voted 'no' it would take pressure off Israel to do the right thing and stop settlements and enter serious negotiations. I referred to the settler violence directed against Palestinians.

So nine ministers spoke against the Prime Minister's position and Smith had spoken at the earlier meeting. That was ten. On the other side, only two had spoken for her. But the Prime Minister repeated that it was her right to decide and she would adhere to her previous position. Her brisk efficiency descended into a style that was icy and robotic. I found this moderately astounding and made a plea that she think about it overnight and settle on an abstention. If we abstain our Ambassador could outline any 'eloquently worded qualifications and explanations' in his speech and that would make it easier for her. But no, she continued to adhere to her mantra and the meeting concluded, as unsatisfactory as any I've been at, although remarkably well conducted. Also passionless and lacking in vitriol.

All these repetitions of 'it's the Prime Minister's call' and 'it's the Prime Minister's prerogative' are a reminder that what we have is not *cabinet* government but *prime ministerial* government.

Around ten o'clock I gravitated into Martin Ferguson's office and we discussed the extraordinary cabinet meeting. 'What about Emerson?' I asked him. Emerson took on the Prime Minister; I was assuming he would be loyal to Julia. 'You're forgetting,' said Martin, 'Bob Hawke is his first love.' We agreed that I should go down and see Wayne Swan. I did. He had already changed from his suit to jeans, sitting at his desk having a beer with Stephen Smith. Both of them were in their mild ways astonished by the cabinet meeting we went through, by a Prime Minister adhering to a position that had the support of only two other cabinet ministers. But they reacted with distress when I told them I would have to join the debate in caucus tomorrow, defying cabinet discipline. 'You can't do it.'

In the corridors, I bumped into Tanya Plibersek, very upset. 'Now I know what you were leaving messages about on the weekend,' she said. She told me she had been to see the Prime Minister to beg her to change her position. Nothing doing; this mystery runs deep.

At around 10.30 pm, I left with Graeme Wedderburn for the Realm Hotel, Graeme going off to ring Joel Fitzgibbon and Andrew Leigh to ensure there was no caving in to prime ministerial pressure to withdraw the motion and no pressure by the Victorian Right to bind the National Right to their pro-Netanyahu stance. From the phone in my room I tried to reach Penny Wong, who was doing *Q&A* in Sydney, but without success. On Graeme's suggestion, Joel Fitzgibbon phoned through at midnight and confirmed he was standing firm – he, of course, with a different agenda, that is, the reinstatement of Kevin Rudd.

I attempted ten minutes of transcendental meditation and fell into a patchy sleep. Woke before dawn and meditated for half an hour.

When I turned on the iPad I saw that there was a suggested motion being touted by Dreyfus. This was the device the Prime Minister wanted as a right-wing fudge on the whole issue. That's what she'd said in the meeting in her office with the half-dozen ministers: 'This is what the Right does. It blunts left-wing thrusts in conference by coming up with a fudge motion.' Which is true enough but, in this case – sorry, my dear Julia: I'm going to sabotage this tactic. So I tapped out an email to Dreyfus saying: 'Alarm! Alarm! – the draft says nothing about settlements!' I offered to provide him with a form of words on settlements. This was mischief-making on my part. Having been through the manic process of drafting resolutions on so many occasions, I understand how a naïve suggestion from the sidelines ends up complicating things hopelessly and ties you in knots.

In the Realm's café I wolfed down my organic steel-cut oats with fruit and yoghurt plus poached eggs and Mexican beans. My stomach bulging with this fibre and protein – energised by an espresso – I went to parliament and made more phone calls: to New South Wales right-wing Senator Matt Thistlethwaite, telling him to feel no obligation whatsoever to vote for the Dreyfus motion, and to Jason Clare, telling him that as a parliamentary secretary he was not remotely bound by cabinet solidarity and to stand up for the interests of the New South Wales Right. Then, at 9.15 am, I reluctantly went down to keep a request by the Prime Minister to meet her by 9.20. My anger bubbled over when I encountered Bruce Wolpe, actually an old friend, in the foyer to her office. The Prime Minister arrived and asked what we were arguing about. 'Oh, settlements,' I said. She and I entered her office.

She tried an explanation of her position. Kevin had made commitments to the Jewish community. Then as Foreign Minister, Kevin had kept going to Israel, driving Netanyahu mad promoting a batty peace plan and promising to commit Australian troops to patrolling borders. I quickly agreed this was nuts; however, I cut to the chase: she should – must – retreat to an abstention. This is not about Kevin's leadership, it's about protecting her, I said. And then I let it drop. I said the motion in caucus would no longer be for Australia to support a 'yes' vote at the UN ... but for Australia to support an *abstention*. I saw fear dance in her eyes. She had not been expecting abstention business. Who was going to move it? 'I'm not sure,' I fibbed. 'I've just heard it ... but I think that makes it ... harder for you.' If I told her the mover of the motion was Andrew Leigh, it would sound as if I organised it.

She was quite distressed. She saw that her fightback was now undermined. The chances were now strong of a motion getting through, even with all the cabinet locked in. I then said, 'Julia, on the bottom line, I can't put my hand up against the Palestinians.' That is, I cannot vote against Andrew Leigh's motion. I cannot vote for the Dreyfus fudge motion.

This sunk in. Slowly she enunciated, 'Right ...'

'I can't vote against the Palestinians. I won't speak in the debate. But I can't vote against the Palestinians.' I had no idea where this would lead but it was the truth. I believed she would not have wanted to sack me or felt strong enough to do it. There was no question of me resigning. I relished this brinksmanship – the existential spirit – as I did when I defied the union blockade that locked my MPs out of Parliament House over my workers compensation reforms. 'Throw the dice high' is sometimes the best in politics. She asked for time to consider. I apologised for making her life complicated – I meant it – and left and walked through the corridors to the caucus meeting.

People were gathered in conversations. The meeting was delayed by the Prime Minister's absence. I managed to say encouraging things to Andrew Leigh. I deliberately sat next to John Murphy of the New South Wales Labor Right and found an opportunity to engage him on the issue. 'I've got thousands of Arab voters,' he said and then launched into a criticism of our cravenness towards Israel and said that if Julia lost on this ballot it would be an opening for Kevin. He said he would hold his seat under Kevin. I avoided engaging on this. This was not my agenda, at least for now. It was a long wait till Julia arrived. When she did, she sat on the couch and Conroy engaged in conversation with her with the friendliest atmospherics. Too friendly – were they talking about this? It then came time for her report. She defended the government's record because it was the fifth anniversary of the government. She did it well but it was pretty boring and then she came to this question. She spent a lot of time spelling out what a 'yes' vote on Palestinian observer status would not do. In other words, the downside of what I was asking her to do. This locution is okay if it suggests the speaker is then going to remodulate and say nonetheless, all things considered, in the final analysis ... they will take the opposite view. This did not seem likely in her case. Damn it, I thought. This is an appalling loss.

And then ... she said, after considering all the facts she favoured ... abstaining.

We would, in the final analysis, not oppose Palestinian status.

At this moment the bells rang for a House of Representatives division and the meeting adjourned. I and others quickly agreed no motions would be put – not Andrew Leigh's, not Mark Dreyfus's. Left-wingers were congratulating me. For a moment at least, the universe was moving in accordance with the laws of justice.

The Prime Minister returned to the meeting after the division in the lower house and had a word with me outside, saying that she wanted help in seeing that the story wasn't pitched in terms of her being done over. I promised to do all I could and went off with Richard Marles to meet with a bunch of foreign correspondents visiting Canberra, and then to launch the Pacific Growth and Employment Project, and then attend the Australian International Cultural Council meeting with Minister Crean.

Then I did media.

The reporters were on to the fact that the Prime Minister had failed to get her way. They knew about the cabinet meeting where the bulk of ministers had opposed her line. They knew that she had changed her position minutes before the caucus meeting this morning. So I praised her for listening to her members, for crafting a policy based on their desires, for rigorously consulting, and so on. I said she had shown real leadership.

I rang the local ambassador of the Palestinians to tell him the decision. He was thrilled. 'I can show my face in the Arab world,' I joked. I rang Jeff Bleich to break the news that we won't be sticking to them. But he had been primed with a good line, I guess from the Prime Minister's office. 'I hear you and the Prime

Minister stopped a "yes" vote getting up,' he said. Er, yes, I concurred. I told him it confirmed a shift in thinking in my party – tired of Netanyahu and the bellicose right wing and sick of the spread of settlements. He agreed Israel had lost the public relations battle. He said we couldn't be accused of changing our vote to earn Security Council votes – we didn't promise anything. That's right, we got elected without a commitment and simply delivered. I got a message from James that Yuval was unhappy with the decision and my role in it. It had been my doing, he said. Correct.

The column of ten nations, die-hards, glued on Israel supporters – Micronesia and the Marshall Islands – had just been reduced by one. A message to the settlers and the fanatics in Israel, a message to the noble Israeli liberals and moderates, a message to a suffering West Bank population, battered and trapped, a message to the UN membership about Australia, the country they just elected to the Security Council.

WEDNESDAY, NOVEMBER 28, 2012
Canberra

In the Realm Hotel, I got up in the early hours and read the online report of Phil Coorey on the front page of the *Sydney Morning Herald* under the heading 'Backbench revolt forces PM to drop Israel support'.

One of the mysteries with the media: they can get it wildly wrong but sometimes both the reportage and commentary can be uncannily accurate.

Coorey's piece says it all.

Julia Gillard has been forced to withdraw Australia's support for Israel in an upcoming United Nations vote after being opposed by the vast majority of her cabinet and warned she would be rolled by the caucus.

As a result, Australia will abstain from a vote in the United Nations General Assembly on a resolution to give Palestine observer status in the UN, rather than join the United States and Israel in voting against the resolution as Ms Gillard had wanted.

In a direct rebuff of her leadership, Ms Gillard was opposed by all but two of her cabinet ministers – Bill Shorten and Stephen Conroy, both of the Victorian Right – during a heated meeting on Monday night.

She was then warned by factional bosses she faced a defeat by her own backbench when the caucus met on Tuesday morning.

The Minister for Foreign Affairs, Bob Carr, who met Ms Gillard before cabinet, drove the push to oppose the Prime Minister.

The former Labor Foreign Minister Gareth Evans briefed Labor MPs on Monday, warning they would be on the wrong side of history if they stood with the US and Israel against the rest of the world.

Ms Gillard had wanted to vote no while the Left faction, which is pro-Palestinian, wanted to vote for the resolution.

The Right faction, which would usually support Ms Gillard, backed an abstention, in part due to the views of its members that the government was too pro-Israel, and also because many MPs in western Sydney, who are already fearful of losing their seats, are coming under pressure from constituents with a Middle East background.

Senior sources have told Fairfax Media that in cabinet on Monday night, at least 10 ministers, regardless of factional allegiance and regardless of whether they were supporters of Kevin Rudd or Ms Gillard, implored the Prime Minister to change her view.

Inside, Peter Hartcher had written a comment piece that included this, also accurate:

The uprising was led by Bob Carr. 'He was on the ring-a-round', canvassing support for his position, said a factional convener. 'I've never seen a cabinet minister stand up to a prime minister like that.'

He noted correctly that it was an important marker in Australian political sentiment about the impassioned dispute between Israel and the Palestinians.

Inside *The Australian* it was commentary along the Likud lines with an op-ed by Mark Leibler reproducing the same old lines that people are not listening to anymore. On the front page, *The Australian* quoted one Labor MP saying:

By the time she got to the caucus, her foot soldiers were telling her that she possibly did not have the numbers. So rather than risk the embarrassment of being defeated on the floor of the caucus, she capitulated. But it was a very, very tense 12 hours, I can tell you. She came perilously close to losing the leadership this morning.

That must have been a Rudd source.

I had my staff scotch stories from the media that I had threatened to resign over the issue. Mood in the corridors fairly tense.

In the afternoon I sat in Question Time with Conroy glowering silent next to me and other members of the Victorian Right avoiding eye contact or even looking my way. I easily handled questions from the opposition about the affair:

> **Senator ABETZ** (Leader of the Opposition in the Senate):
> My question is to the Minister for Foreign Affairs, Senator
> Carr. I refer the minister to his remarks on Sky *Agenda*
> yesterday: 'There is a feeling in the Labor Party that you go
> for abstention. You even go for a "yes" vote.' Minister, what
> are the arguments in favour of a 'yes' vote on Palestine being
> granted UN observer status as opposed to abstention? At any
> stage during discussions on this issue of our vote on Palestine
> being granted UN observer status, was the effect on Labor's
> vote in western Sydney raised?

> **Senator BOB CARR:** … The decision by the government
> to abstain on this question accords with our strong support
> for legitimate Palestinian aspirations towards statehood but
> reflects our view that the only way to a two-state solution in
> the Middle East, with a strong Palestinian state side by side
> with an Israel with absolute security, is through an outcome
> negotiated by the two sides, the two sides thus having a
> commitment to the success of the outcome. You cannot get
> that through a resolution of the General Assembly, but to
> have voted 'no' would have sent a message that Australia does
> not believe in something we do believe in – namely, statehood
> for Palestinians.

... the vast bulk of Australians want a two-state solution. That is the common-sense, mainstream position adhered to by the Australian people: that there should be a Palestinian state side by side with a secure Israel. That is the view that the majority of Australians hold.

Senator ABETZ: Mr President, I ask a supplementary question. Does the minister maintain that the US understands that opinion in the Labor Party is trending towards a 'yes' vote on this vital issue and that the government's shift on this long-held bipartisan plank of Australian foreign policy will have no impact on Australia's relationship with the United States?

Senator BOB CARR: Isn't it delightful to have a question as predictable as that? The answer is simply yes. When I phoned Mr Bleich, the US ambassador, yesterday, he was entirely relaxed about the Australian decision ...

I had dinner with three ABC reporters, and then in my office I reviewed the events of the day with a very relieved, very chuffed Gareth Evans. But he simply could not believe a Prime Minister would get away with cabinet conceding she had the right to do something a big majority opposed – and he had been there right through the Hawke and Keating years. Gareth was there when Hanan Ashrawi rang up from Ramallah. She told me she would have preferred an affirmative vote. 'Listen, Hanan, this was a very good outcome for the Palestinian cause given the challenge we faced,' I told her, and handed the phone to Gareth so he could lead her through it.

THURSDAY, NOVEMBER 29, 2012
Canberra

The media continues to focus on the Palestinian vote.

Tony Walker in the *Australian Financial Review* wrote that: 'If Labor has any pretensions to being regarded as a social democratic party, newly admitted as a member of the Security Council, there was no credible way Australia could have voted "no" on the Palestine resolution. How Gillard and her few supporters could have believed otherwise is a mystery.'

He said, 'This is a signal moment in Australian foreign policy, breaking a nexus on the Palestine question where Australia was in lockstep with the US and Israel ...'

Troy Bramston wrote in *The Australian*, 'The day Carr won the Mid-East conflict':

> Carr will not be critical of Gillard's leadership. He believes she made the right call in the end.
>
> Moreover, along with eight other ministers, he saved Gillard's neck. As one familiar with the discussions said yesterday: 'If the caucus resolution on abstention didn't go under her feet, she would have gone under the ice.'

I get one weak question from the opposition at Question Time, which I bat away easily. In the chamber my colleagues from the Victorian Right avoid looking at me. They only simmer.

FRIDAY, NOVEMBER 30, 2012
Canberra

Today Laura Tingle had a funny – and true – opening to her column, invoking the corridor encounter on November 21 when she said that I looked like I didn't give a fuck:

> Bob Carr is gliding along the press gallery corridor, a look of serene contentment on his face. We are talking a couple of weeks ago here, long before cabinet was discussing Palestine and Israel.
>
> The Foreign Minister was off to talk about something or other on one of our 24-hour news channels and it was hard not to be struck by what a freak he appeared.
>
> Freak in a good sense, of course.
>
> For Carr is perhaps the only person in the federal caucus, nay, federal politics, who looks like he is having a really good time.
>
> A successful career as NSW premier, ended before the murk of the NSW Labor machine rose up to consume all who followed him; a job he has always wanted; the satisfaction of seeing a campaign for a UN Security Council seat successfully ended; clean hands in the Rudd coup; and absolutely no personal responsibility if the next election goes badly for Labor.
>
> Carr has nothing to lose. And seeing the enjoyment and satisfaction he gets from his job makes you realise how miserable the rest of our federal politicians seem.

I went to the whip's office with a packet of chocolates yesterday afternoon to thank them for their support, especially in getting pairs, and Helena and I flew out of Canberra at 6 pm.

Back in Sydney and – this came about by sheer coincidence – I am booked for a dinner of about fifty Palestinian professionals hosted by their ambassador. I can look them in the eye. 'My party's battered and wobbly and on the defensive,' I say. 'But sometimes it gets things right and becomes a forum for movement and change in Australian politics.'

Key lessons of the week are now emerging. First, a prime minister in a parliamentary system effectively enjoys the powers of an elected president. All those references to 'This is my call' and 'It's your prerogative, Prime Minister.' And that raises the question of why the leader did not prevail in this case. Simple. Because a cabinet minister felt so strongly about it he was able to set off – no, work with – a backbench revolt that took the fight out of the cabinet room, where the Prime Minister was prevailing, into the caucus room, where anything could happen. Well, that introduces the second factor: an underlying shift in party sentiment towards the Arab perspective and the Palestinian cause.

This, in turn, had been brought about by the behaviour of the Israelis themselves – all the right-wing nationalist belligerency, the religious extremism and the spread of settlements – and the behaviour of the Melbourne-based Israel lobby in Australia attempting to stand over us, to block any criticism and to win every last little argument. Part of the shift as well was explained by the rise in Arab or Islamic numbers in western Sydney electorates. Yes, and this was a split between Melbourne and Sydney perspectives. Melbourne with two-thirds of the Australian Jewish population and a politically active Jewish leadership, and Sydney with electorates bursting with Arabs, Christians and Muslims. It reflected a split in the National Right too, Victoria versus New South Wales. To be candid as well, it wouldn't have happened without a Foreign Minister committed to making it happen. 'I can't put my hand up against the Palestinians, Julia ...'

It was the penultimate touch to have the motion moved by Andrew Leigh, not Melissa Parke, and – the final touch – to switch his motion to support for Australia abstaining. Both my work.

It was exhausting. My weight had slipped back and my cheekbones showed and my eye sockets were those of a tired old man. But as I pushed things to the limit for a good cause I had the energy of a gladiator.

Power wears out only those who don't have it, as the sainted Giulio Andreotti was wont to opine.

SATURDAY, DECEMBER 1, 2012
Sydney

The Melbourne-based Israel lobby never learns. They get Josh Frydenberg, a Liberal backbencher, to write an op-ed in *The Australian* lamenting that because of my work, Australia has abandoned its old friend Israel. But Frydenberg is a fierce Likud supporter and backer of settlements; his op-ed follows those by Mark Leibler and Colin Rubenstein, each from the same wellspring, the Melbourne lobby. Patience with Israel's hardliners has run out and is dragging Israel's standing down too. The *Australian Financial Review* today runs an article by Andrew Clark that opens quoting me praising Israel for being a democracy – true, as ever – and repeating Australian friendship, but then quotes my warning:

Good friends speak the truth to one another and, as a friend of Israel, we have a duty to highlight our concern about the settlement activity which is illegal under international law.

Tony Walker, also in the *Australian Financial Review*, says that what I've promoted is in line with the 1947 General Assembly resolution creating Israel and a Palestinian state.

In the *Sydney Morning Herald*, Paul McGeough quotes me appealing to Israel to stop building settlements in the West Bank. Then – wouldn't you know it, right on cue – morning radio reports that Israel has just committed to another huge settlement in East Jerusalem to punish the Palestinians. Incorrigible. I get out a statement registering our concern and the Prime Minister, after the events of the last week, doesn't resist. But ... if we had voted 'no' to Palestinian status, we would now, thanks to Netanyahu, be caked with excrement.

Helena drove me to Bondi where I did two hours of Pilates, then to Double Bay for my third meditation lesson; to the office to read cables; to the gym; and then we go to a dinner-dance Christmas party in Kogarah hosted by the Egyptian Women's Association of Australia, which I attend as guest of the Egyptian Ambassador.

Events are turning me Arabist.

SUNDAY, DECEMBER 2, 2012
Sydney

Joel Fitzgibbon rings to review the events of the week. Why was she so wedded to Israel, I ask. Because she's wedded to the Victorian Right, he replied. Well, I said, New South Wales has interests too. Apparently Conroy was threatening to expel the New South Wales people from the National Right. Fine, Joel said, we'll sit between them and the Left and run the party. Separately, Sam Dastyari told me he's seeing her on Wednesday and will repeat what he told her at Friday's Kirribilli House Christmas Party: she should be concerned at New South Wales right-wingers thinking they will lose their seats. If that's where it sits next year ...

Jeff Bleich rang me yesterday to say the Assad forces have moved chemical weapons to airfields and will use them to bomb suburbs of Damascus. Pictures in today's paper of a street of wrecked flats in Damascus: a regime at war with its own people.

At the Egyptian Christmas party last night – all Armenians, Italians and Greeks – three people volunteered that they supported what we did on Palestine. Two told me we had to stop the refugee boats.

THURSDAY, DECEMBER 6, 2012
Papua New Guinea

Here I am, back in Papua New Guinea for the first time since 1973 or 1974 when I came as a Labor Council official to supervise a trade union training course. A waste of time – we had nothing to teach unions in PNG and I think they're less relevant now than they were forty years ago. But I should have got back here sooner. I envy Richard Marles, my parliamentary secretary, for his intimate knowledge of this place and the rest of the Pacific. My introduction to the Melanesian world has come with this job, my trip to the Solomons the single most interesting visit I've done.

At Mount Hagen I announced extra funding for maternal and

child health at their local hospital and visited a wonderful Catholic girls school, Notre Dame Secondary. It had been founded by a Sister Mary from Ohio, now at the point of retirement. 'Ohio – more Presidents than any other state and it now determines who wins elections,' I told her. What a glory the Catholic education system is, planting this happy, well-equipped school in the highlands and delivering education to these girls. Sister Mary told me that mothers work hard to pay for their girls' education because they – the mothers – have been abandoned with their girl children. Husbands move on to another wife and another marriage. They take their sons, not their daughters. The mothers want to save their daughters from this fate and do so through getting them schooling.

I inspect the school and hospital and then the Mount Hagen markets – an experience on its own. Then the drive up the bumpy road to our lodge, Rondon Ridge. There was from everyone an uncomplicated, naïve affection for Australia. This is one part of the world where Australia is simply liked. Unless I'm kidding myself, warmly liked.

On Wednesday in Wapenamanda I saw Rimbink Pato, the PNG Foreign Minister, sworn in as a member of provincial legislature. We inspected the military and gave speeches from the official grandstand. Then one man stepped forward from the audience and roared out in Enga, the local language: 'All you educated people have spoken. I'm an ordinary man and I want to say something. I want to thank Australia. I want to thank Australia for being here to see our local member sworn in. I want to thank Australia for its friendship and support ...'

Where else could you drive around and wave non-stop to pedestrians and get back a friendly wave, without an up-you gesture or a clenched fist at least once in a while? It goes back to the days when Australian district officers provided passable governance and appeared to be building things. Maybe it reflects wartime bonding. On the other hand, the country's going backwards on all the UN Millennium Development Goals, especially with maternal mortality, the stunting of children and school attendance.

In Port Moresby today I sat with Ministers Bowen, Clare and Emerson, plus Parliamentary Secretary Marles, opposite six or seven PNG ministers. We moved through an agenda that covered their Sovereign Wealth Fund, an economic cooperation pact, the defence partnership between us, health and immigration.

Foreign Minister Rimbink Pato is from the highlands. Big bodied, big head, big smile. But he speaks very softly, almost a whisper. He was a successful local lawyer who represented Peter O'Neill, who's now the Prime Minister. He was made Foreign Minister after O'Neill won his parliamentary majority in August. He's been away from his southern highlands home travelling the world, even to Russia. He liked the fact that I used every opportunity to praise Papua New Guinea for the great achievement of their elections: this topographically diverse, linguistically diverse country let its people choose its leaders. Moreover, he likes the theme I've worked up that they should play a bigger role in the region. I will discuss with the New Zealanders whether they might be included in our discussions on Fiji, turning the trilateral into a quadrilateral.

If O'Neill pulls it off and winds back corruption and entrenches the Sovereign Wealth Fund then he'll prove himself a stand-out Prime Minister. We're pushing one thing above all: getting them to set up an independent procurement authority to buy the medicines for their hospitals. We will supply them with the medicines, the authority will allocate them to hospitals. This wipes out corruption in the supply chain. And more people get access to medicine. I underlined this several times in our meeting. It could be the biggest, most important reform we steer them to.

SUNDAY, DECEMBER 9, 2012
Sydney

Billionaire Andrew Forrest was there to meet us at 8.30 am when we arrived at his apartment in Macquarie Street for breakfast. He had wanted me to go to a conference in Myanmar organised by Walk Free, an organisation he founded to oppose slavery, and to a business conference in China. His apartment looks right out on the Opera House and Government House in the Botanic Gardens. Great location and nice enough but nothing to mark it as the residence of an iron-ore magnate. I started talking on China – 'The elephant in the room,' he said.

He had sometimes complained about our policies, part of the business push for a pro-Chinese re-alignment of Australian foreign policy. I said someone in my department thought the Chinese regarded us as little more important than New Zealand and their dependence on our raw materials only made them like us less. I myself wasn't sure, I said, but regarded it as an interesting perspective. He distanced himself from the James Packer view that our policy towards China should be based on gratitude and the Hugh White view that we might one day align ourselves with them militarily. But he seemed to think that our relationship with them somehow fell short. He said, 'I tell them I know the Foreign Minister and he has a good heart. They say that's fine but what does the heart matter ... I think they want humility from us.'

I don't understand how our foreign policy could be based on humility. I would prefer self-respect and a forthright presentation of interests. Still, his interpretation of the Bo Xilai affair was something I haven't heard. He claims that Xi Jinping had Bo Xilai axed to send a message to corrupt party officials that this is what would happen as soon as he took power as Party Secretary and President. Andrew said the speech at the party conference from

Xi was forthright and sincere on corruption and the rule of law.

'The rule of law – that means getting rid of party detention centres,' I said. He hadn't heard about them so I explained that outside the judicial apparatus, the Chinese Communist Party runs camps and jails into which dissidents can be flung for an indefinite period and be denied access to the courts. 'That's where a dissident could end up simply for insisting on taking a protest note to Beijing,' I said.

I also told him that we had presented the Chinese with a letter suggesting formal consultations between our prime minister and their president once a year in the margins of the G20 or APEC or East Asian Summit. So the ball's in their court if they want to elevate the relationship, I explained to him.

He talked about human slavery. He told me about a nine-year-old girl in an orphanage in Nepal, rocking backwards and forwards on her bed, refusing to eat and trying to die. She'd been shipped off to the Middle East to be a sex slave when she was six. The Forrests located one orphanage in Nepal – a friendly place on the surface – from which they later found out children were sold into sex slavery. He's trying to stop it at many different points: by pressuring companies not to source material from firms that use slavery; by pressuring airlines to take responsibility for flying slave labour into countries that permit it. He explained how workers from the Indian subcontinent end up in the UAE, tricked by the contractors into going into debt for their airfares and working without payment, as modern slaves. I told him how we'd taken pity on them working in the sun when we saw them during my visit as Premier in 2005 and Helena and I had got all our party to empty our hotel fridges of fruit juice and water and distribute it to them.

I promised him I'd do everything to help him in his crusade here.

Today's *Sunday Telegraph* has an article by Samantha Maiden, who we took to Papua New Guinea with us, and a big colour picture of me and Rimbink being carried aloft on a sedan chair, surrounded by flowers and flags:

> The adventures of our quirky Foreign Minister in Papua New Guinea.

> One giant, show-stopping, international geek adventure.

'Geek': will never escape that.

> In this latest political incarnation as a Foreign Minister, Bob Carr gives every indication of being the happiest man in cabinet.

> His simple message of praise for PNG's recent democratic elections is hammered at every opportunity.

> His PNG visit is a blur of photo opportunities, at the Bomana War Cemetery he talks to Dickson Hango, one of the last surviving Fuzzy Wuzzy Angels. He's blogging, taking photos out the window of the charter plane with his iPad, raving about the quality of the PNG coffee on his Twitter account after sharing a cup with the former PM Paias Wingti and the Foreign Minister Rimbink Pato.

> ... All the quirk, the high-pants, the stump speech magic, the political experience of being NSW premier and the deep love of history, books and foreign affairs is being rolled into one giant, show-stopping, international geek adventure.

TUESDAY, DECEMBER 11, 2012
Sydney

Yesterday I rang the Egyptian Ambassador to let him know I had held back on criticisms of President Morsi over his attack on the Egyptian judiciary. 'I've been saying the President deserves the benefit of the doubt,' I said to him. 'He's inherited a judicial apparatus from the previous dictatorship and, in any case, is submitting the new constitution to the public in a referendum. I appreciate the time he gave me on my visit and look forward to visiting again soon.'

And I have another consideration here. I want to put myself in a position where I can continue to make representations to the Egyptians on behalf of the Christian minority, the Copts – the population estimated as high as fifteen million. They have such a splendid community here in Australia and I want to do something for them. Maintaining a dialogue with the new Muslim Brotherhood government is part of it. Our vote on Palestinian status helps as well.

I read in *The Economist* that Rahm Emanuel, Mayor of Chicago and Obama's former chief of staff, called the recent settlements announced by Israel as a betrayal of America's friendship. A woman with an American accent stopped me in the street the other day and said as a Jew she appreciates my position on the Palestinians. She knows the Netanyahu government's policies are a disaster for Israel. She's very proud of the strand in American–Jewish thinking that stuck with Obama and rejected the extremist demand for American Jews to fling him out because of Israel policy.

In the Sydney office all day. Grim polling in *The Australian* with Labor's primary vote slumping to thirty-two per cent against the Coalition's forty-six per cent. Dastyari is seeing the Prime

Minister to convey the concerns of the New South Wales party at stubbornly lousy polling in Sydney's west.

THURSDAY, DECEMBER 13, 2012
Sydney to Dili

In the smaller of the VIPs – no private compartment, no shower, no flat beds, pure hardship – we fly above the Nicobar Islands (Who owns them? Who lives there?) in the Bay of Bengal on our way to Sri Lanka. I committed to this visit when I was negotiating on the phone with Foreign Minister Peiris, asking him to take back a boatload of 'irregular maritime arrivals'. He obliged and I'm on my way.

We need to clinch this relationship – of course, still managing carefully the human-rights sensitivities of the post-civil war period – in a way so they will keep disrupting people-smuggling, interrupting boats, taking migrants back. I will have to praise them for their cooperation and make comments about human rights – I'm leafing through Gordon Weiss's *The Cage* on the bloody last days of the Tamil Tigers – without threatening the cooperation. The arrival of boats is the underlying reason we are polling badly in western Sydney, so this relationship with the Sri Lankans is important, maybe vital. The boats are coming from there.

On the plane we fill the time with trivia. I take Shakespeare, Patrick Low takes the history of *The Endeavour*, James takes the French monarchy and Simon Benson from the *Daily Telegraph* takes News Limited editors.

Trivia quiz?

Name Shakespeare's son. What is his relationship with

Hamlet? How many men did Cook leave behind in New Zealand? Name the wife of Clovis. Which News Limited editor once struck a colleague in the face?

Stopped in Timor-Leste en route and met the leadership and the Fretilin opposition. I talked with Australian troops and police, inspected hospitals and schools and visited the Resistance Museum, which tells the story of this baby state, known in diplomatic speak as a 'fragile, post-conflict LDC [least developed country]' with its Portuguese ancestry … and the haunting danger that, like most such countries, it may lapse back into the conflict within seven years. The same possibility hovers over the Solomons, where our peacekeepers are also evacuating.

I promoted membership of the Commonwealth to them. 'Less demanding than ASEAN with all those meetings,' I said to the President. 'And it's a community of democracies and you're a proud democracy! And Mozambique and Rwanda are in it. You don't have to have been a British colony!'

The fatigue produced by bursts of atrial fibrillation has not slowed down my exercise but elbow pain and a sore shoulder on my right side has. Not enough time for the physio. I am into my third week of transcendental meditation (twenty-two minutes, twice a day) but haven't noticed a difference. Will persist. Must be ways of 'de-exciting' those brain waves.

We compressed our appointments in Dili today so we could arrive in Colombo in time for a briefing from the High Commissioner over a curry at Chutney's in the Cinnamon Grand Hotel. Said to be succulent.

TUESDAY, DECEMBER 18, 2012
Colombo

President Mahinda Rajapaksa won the election in 2005 and inflicted a final bloody defeat on the Tamil Tigers and consolidated the power of his Sinhala Buddhist party, the United People's Freedom Alliance, with a fifty-eight per cent vote in 2010. No one challenges his authority; the opposition – the right-wing Sinhalese – are enfeebled.

He sits like a monarch, in white tunic and red scarf, prosperous, fleshy, toes withdrawing from sandals.

On his left, a row of seats occupied by his people headed by Foreign Minister Peiris; on his right, a row of seats headed by me.

It's like a royal audience. His bejewelled fingers caress a silver toy.

He barely looks me in the eye. He seems to drift off to other thoughts. There are pauses, when he gazes off in another direction, mulling, turning over possibilities.

I fill in. 'Where is your next visit?' I ask. 'Myanmar,' he replies. So I praise Thein Sein as a hero of reform. He agrees.

'Have you talked about the Chief Justice?' he asks his Foreign Minister with a sly smile. This is the current controversy: a move by the governing party to impeach Chief Justice Shirani Bandaranayake for corruption. It has set off ripples of criticism in the Commonwealth over breach of separation of powers. But I now hear the justification from the President and the Foreign Minister: the Chief Justice had a big secret bank account that she failed to declare.

Anyway, I make a point of elaborating my position on human rights. We will go to their CHOGM, not boycott it as the Canadians intend, and will take a more understanding, supportive position on their process towards reconciliation. On the other hand, we will need to see benchmarks reached, including the government's own as set out in the reconciliation report.

In my talks with Peiris, I stress the same approach. Give us signs of progress – like a dialogue in the New Year with the Tamil National Alliance – and I've got something to put to the Canadians and the Brits in your defence. This Foreign Minister is a professor who did his thesis on a comparison of Dutch elements in the common law of South Africa and Sri Lanka. He would have to find my approach reassuring, and a relief.

The notes prepared by the High Commissioner say it well:

Senator Carr raised human-rights issues with the Minister of External Affairs, Defence Secretary and President. He delivered a clear message that Sri Lanka could expect to remain under international scrutiny in the lead-up to the March session of the HRC and CHOGM. There would be discussions in international forums about Sri Lanka in the lead-up to both these events. Australia was prepared to help make these discussions more constructive but, in order to do so, we needed to see clear and tangible progress by Sri Lanka against the recommendations of the LLRC and the Human Rights Action Plan. It was particularly important that Sri Lanka produced concrete results on 'totemically important issues'. These included reconciliation and accountability. Concrete progress on reconciliation and other LLRC recommendations was a critical part of the way forward.

A pragmatic interests-based policy, not contemptuous of human-rights imperatives: this is what I've crafted here.

WEDNESDAY, DECEMBER 19, 2012
Sydney

Flew back into Sydney last night and this morning finally caught up with Paul Whittaker, editor of the *Daily Telegraph* for breakfast at the Hilton. He and his Canberra correspondent, Simon Benson, say there are six votes hanging between Gillard and Rudd. They know more than I. Both seem aware of Sam Dastyari's line – that the Prime Minister has got to lift the vote in western Sydney or what will happen will happen: 'Given the chance, people will jump rather than face the firing squad,' in Dastyari's words. They hint at some ambiguity in Shorten's position as well. I don't know about this.

There's the tidal pull, as well, that comes with people moving behind a likely victor. Which has them assuming a Rudd challenge, then a Rudd win – depending, of course, on the New Year's polls. But it's not just the New South Wales Right; they seemed to believe some movement on Shorten's part.

That's the problem: the whole caucus gabbles to the media non-stop. I'm as bad. Talking on the leadership I fall into saying, 'Well if they change leaders again there's only one minister who can get out and explain it to the public.'

'You – because you're not compromised.'

'That's right.'

Whittaker says Murdoch asks if Bob Carr can ever be Prime Minister. They are keenly interested in the government's thinking on media control and knew an end-of-session package had been considered. I didn't tell them the Finkelstein stuff, full-bodied media reform, has been dropped and Conroy has settled on a tort of privacy.

After the breakfast I sped home and switched to bushwalking gear for a walk in the Royal National Park. The break has begun.

SATURDAY, DECEMBER 22, 2012
Sydney

Canadian Foreign Minister John Baird rang. I'd alerted him from Colombo that, at the media conference with Foreign Minister Peiris, I'd said no, Australia would not be boycotting CHOGM like Canada. Indeed we thought *engagement* on human-rights issues was the thing. I was candid about us having an interest in the Sri Lankan government stopping boats. He, of course, has a loud domestic Tamil constituency. Different interests here and I won't allow ours to be subverted. He is cordial about this. But the Canadian approach, as we see it (I, Varghese) – their 'values-based foreign policy' – is more appropriate for an NGO.

I ring the Palestinian Foreign Minister in Ramallah to argue that after their victory in the General Assembly on status they should not attempt to join any UN organisations or the International Criminal Court. They should consolidate, not go forward. They should not provoke Israel. And I repeat the Australian position that there is no substitute for direct negotiations with the Israelis.

TUESDAY, DECEMBER 25, 2012
(CHRISTMAS DAY)
Sydney

From a review by Neal Ascherson of Jason Stearns's book on the Congo, *Dancing in the Glory of Monsters*, in the *New York Review of Books*: 'The great dying was the result not of bullets or slashing *pangas* but of displacement.' A new notion: displacing people as a means of genocide. Another mass atrocity crime.

Some of my Christmas reading.

We spend this Christmas break entirely at home, watching DVDs. There was an old play with Judi Dench and a movie about Louis XIV called *The King is Dancing*; and poking through books – Cicero's *On the Nature of the Gods*, Leonie Frieda's biography *Catherine de Medici* and W. J. Hudson's biography of Lord Casey, who as Minister for External Affairs strongly opposed Menzies' policy on Suez.

In other words, I live the previous life – my old life – except for the cables that I get delivered in batches.

WEDNESDAY, DECEMBER 26, 2012
Sydney

Lousy weather over Christmas so I'm happy to be home-bound with Helena. The phone barely rings. I listen to Ian McKellen read *The Odyssey* on tape and there are the cables …

Following Finland's defeat for the Security Council there's a discussion on whether 'the Nordic brand' in the UN is 'past its use-by date'. Russia's relations with Turkey have never been better, with close personal ties between Putin and Erdogan. Six months to the presidential election in Iran with Supreme Leader Khamenei wanting a carefully chosen candidate list. Reports that 350 Sri Lankan asylum seekers are headed to the Philippines. The interim Prime Minister of Fiji gets handed a draft constitution from his commission and, typically under the influence of his interim Attorney-General, threatens to arrest a public servant if anyone else gets a copy.

We are to have discussions in Beijing on how we handle our responsibilities on the Security Council after January 1.

No politics in the papers.

FRIDAY, DECEMBER 28, 2012
Sydney

Helena flies out of the house to see Annita Keating and Annita's mother, who lives at Coogee, Joanna Capon, other friends; and returns with food. I just stay indoors reading. Re-reading, ransacking old books such as Teddy White's *The Making of the President 1968*. He describes the decrepitude of the state and city Democratic Party machines, '... the assumption of professional control was hollow' and everything was broken springs and rust.

Even in Chifley's time the ALP was improvised, cobbled-together, rattletrap and ramshackle. What this busted machinery needs is clever, crafty, energetic leadership to bridge the contradictions and animate its arteries; eloquent speeches and punchy one-liners – to lift its spirits and direct scorn at its opponents. Leadership like that of Hawke, Wran, Keating. Others.

I think of ringing Rudd just to chat foreign policy. But that simple act would be loaded. I'll move when the New South Wales Right moves. Too much conspiring is pointless, frivolous. Picking up a biography of Louis XIV, I see this description by Richelieu of Gaston d'Orleans:

> He entered into the conspiracies because of lack of will, and he always crept shamefully out of them because of lack of courage.

No fussing about caucus numbers for the sake of it.

Tony Walker of the *Australian Financial Review* dropped in yesterday to interview me for an article on foreign policy in the new year. Over a coffee he treated a Rudd return as comical. The media are not sold on it, not campaigning for it. Hardly like the British press campaigning for Churchill's return in 1939.

SATURDAY, DECEMBER 29, 2012
Sydney

Spoke by phone to Sam Dastyari, just to catch up. He said, 'She's so much the better Prime Minister than he is. But he can win the next election – he can run arguments against the Labor Party, against politics.' He said Julia sought advice from Laurie Brereton on what would happen if she expressed lack of confidence in the party whip, Joel Fitzgibbon, who works the numbers for Rudd. Laurie warned her Joel would resign and submit his name to the caucus ballot and win re-election as whip. Simple as that. She's silly to be focused on him.

SUNDAY, DECEMBER 30, 2012
Sydney

More pleasure in re-reading. I take down John Cheever's stories and pick *The Lowboy*:

Oh, why is it that life is for some an exquisite privilege and others must pay for their seats at the play with a ransom of cholers, infections, and nightmares?

Ah, the gift of settling on those three nouns: cholers, infections and nightmares.

Former staffer Prasan Ulluwishewa tells me my visit to Sri Lanka went down well in the community here. Not publicly lecturing them on rights, not elevating the Tamil Tiger agenda, recognising them as a serious place, a worthwhile country for an Australian Foreign Minister to visit.

WEDNESDAY, JANUARY 2, 2013
Sydney

Return to the office; the year begins. Tony Walker's piece appears in the *Australian Financial Review*: a one-page feature about me carving out my own place in history, a useful summary of the things I've been doing, plus a news story about us consulting China on our new Security Council responsibilities.

The *Sydney Morning Herald* runs this little piece on Bob Carr's Sydney. They had interviewed me by phone, then cleverly reshaped it as a first-person account – and got everything right.

I grew up in a 1920s cottage near Maroubra Junction. We moved to a fibro cottage when my father got a war service loan and was able to build a house on the sandhills at Matraville.

It was a fabulous area for kids to play in. There was a great garbage tip with waste dumped there every morning. There were two sewage-polluted beaches, Malabar and Maroubra. There were power works, abandoned military stores and a sewage vent. A snake man performed at weekends, pulling snakes out of a sack. It's a peninsula, sandhills everywhere. It was a terrific place to grow up.

In my lifetime – and I still live in Maroubra – there has been about 100 years of progress. The sandhills are being grown over. The beaches are so clean they don't get stormwater anymore. The area has been sewered.

I love the coastal walk – South Coogee, Clovelly, through the cemetery, all the way to Bondi. The cliff face, in Robert Hughes's words, looks as if it's broken off like a biscuit. The red roofs of the eastern suburbs. The opportunity for running on beaches and plunging into the surf. That sense of the surf in your nostrils and in your mouth, and you can feel the sun on your skin.

There are days when, from North Bondi to Maroubra, the surf is breaking perfectly. I love going for a swim at 7 at night. The sun's still out, the place isn't crowded, there's space in the waves, and then you go home and have dinner.

The sheer ordinariness of this. A sweet corner of the planet to live in.

Last night I scored easy TV news coverage on Hillary's illness, a death in Bali, the US budget.

Easy – I'm not even trying.

SUNDAY, JANUARY 6, 2013
Sydney

I polish off a book about the North Korean gulag, *Escape from Camp 14* by Blaine Harden, and tell James I want the department to vacuum up everything on the country's cataclysmic human-rights violations so we're as informed as possible. Get it put on the agenda for our talks with the British later this month. Spoke to Beazley about it too; I asked him to have one of his senior people do the rounds of every NGO based in the US working on North Korea. A horrific story: 200,000 people being starved and worked to death, the camps vaster than Auschwitz, visible on Google Earth.

Apart from a Pilates class, finishing that book and watching a DVD of Spielberg's *Lincoln*, I have totally wasted this weekend.

THURSDAY, JANUARY 10, 2013
Sydney

Working in my Sydney office I met a delegation from the Council of Churches, recently returned from Israel–Palestine, to press the Palestinian case with me. They showed photos of a Hebron street divided with a waist-high concrete wall; photos of deserted Palestinian shops, bankrupted by the wall; a photo of a Palestinian farmer separated from his date farm but still beaming a beatific smile. The Salvation Army Major, Kelvin Alley, spoke about 'the grace' of these Palestinians. He went on to talk in my language about the Middle East – the drift away from a two-state solution, the drift towards an Israel practising apartheid over a big Palestinian population. I told them to put their case to every Australian politician they could reach.

These were conservative evangelicals.

Later I spoke to Peter Varghese, head of my department, about our agenda. He concurred that when I meet William Hague next week I might indeed agree on a communiqué that calls for American leadership to make peace in the Middle East. But, he warned, our national interest really requires an America focused on Asia. My view, of course – but the US can do both. We then discussed how we could work with Singapore and perhaps Indonesia to press the new American Secretary of State, John Kerry, to make East Asia his first overseas visit. Even to include Southeast Asia in that symbolic first trip.

Had an Italian lunch down the road with Nick Warner and talked spy stuff. The wind blasted down Phillip Street and nearly picked us up. January winds and high temperatures are a disaster for the forests in New South Wales facing their greatest fire danger ever. The biennial or triennial bushfire crisis used to be a big part of my life as Premier.

FRIDAY, JANUARY 11, 2013
Sydney

In Sydney, bushfire threat somewhat abated, I have lunch at Rockpool with Ratu Inoke Kubuabola, Foreign Minister of Fiji. We look at the transcript of his Prime Minister's remarks yesterday junking the draft constitution that would have returned the country to democracy. In fact, this is not quite the case. The Prime

Minister has the view that the recommended parliament is too big, that there should not be an unelected consultative assembly sitting alongside the parliament and the President should be elected by the parliament instead of such a body. He's right on all this. Sadly, he won't accept our new High Commissioner, probably because he's aggrieved we didn't vote for him as chair of the International Sugar Forum. He seems still committed to the timetable for elections in 2014.

I cross the bridge for my get-together with the Prime Minister at Kirribilli House, the cottage that passes for the residence of a head of government. Still, with the breeze coming off the ocean through the flyscreen doors – harbour on two sides – it's a nice enough way to live through an Australian summer and, for God's sake, the job has got to have some perks. Before I could get on to my checklist of foreign-policy concerns, she raised hers: stating that our offices weren't working together, that hers had not heard about yesterday's press release stepping up Iran sanctions, that we've got to let her people know what we are doing. I was surprised. I told her I didn't think the increase in sanctions was a story and hadn't made any fuss about it myself, wouldn't have suspected her office would want it – not big enough. Still, she thought it would have been useful in the Jewish community at least. That's fine and I told her I'd get Graeme to coordinate to see that our people work more closely.

We then got on to the agenda. I briefed her on Sri Lanka and quoted from an intelligence report that said, after my visit, the Sri Lankan police in Negombo were now worried about accepting bribes to assist people-smuggling ventures, whereas previously they did it with impunity. Moreover, after my visit, Australia's policy of returning irregular arrivals has been widely publicised and fewer people are prepared to risk people-smuggling ventures because they know they'll be deported from Australia.

I told her how our position differed from the Canadians and

she said she didn't like Stephen Harper anyway, finding them – the Canadians – bossy and arrogant. We discussed the Middle East and agreed on the need for contact with the Jewish community and appropriate criticisms of Hamas. I handed over a transcript where I'd done precisely that in a media conference earlier in the week. I told her about my meeting with the Council of Churches and their pro-Palestinian agenda. We agreed on more activity in the Arab community given what we'd done. I briefed her on my interest in a campaign to protect Christians in the Middle East. I told her that Hague and I were interested in calling next week for US leadership towards a return to negotiations on the Middle East. I told her about my interest in a campaign on the North Korean gulag and also pressing the new US Secretary of State to make his first overseas trip to the Asian region and Southeast Asia in particular, if we could pull this off. We discussed her travel for the year. She underlined the goal of having the Chinese tick off on our bid for a strategic dialogue. 'It would be a clear foreign-policy success.' It would indeed.

We discussed her problems with Joel Fitzgibbon, the party whip and putative leader of the Right, who's so doggedly in the Rudd column and such an irritant to her. I insisted she'd be better off ignoring him, sad as it was that she didn't have a single leader of the Right she could do deals with.

Her complexion is perfect, she's focused strategically (asked me to build a campaign on Abbott and his interest in the Anglo-sphere – as proof that he's old-fashioned, doesn't understand today's world, has no affinity with Asians or Arabs or Africans). Her eyes are fresh; she never shows fatigue. We drank herbal tea, her little dog played with a green tennis ball and I left in the good spirits that normally arise after an amicable encounter with authority.

WEDNESDAY, JANUARY 16, 2013
Sydney

Last Sunday, as I moved through my agenda with the new Japanese Foreign Minister Fumio Kishida, ticking off the issues through a translator, briefing notes in front of me, I speculated how my old dad would have responded, being told when he was steering landing craft through the islands of Papua New Guinea that his son, nearly seventy years later, would be talking to a Japanese leader about Papua New Guinea's future. History teases us and jokes with us; the universe is loaded with paradox; and the rate of change sometimes exceeds our imaginations.

There was nothing in the agenda pushing us to a military alliance. We have continued to keep a defence cooperation agreement out of the communiqués. And they haven't chosen to salvage Prime Minister Shinzo Abe's old notion of a quadrilateral pact (the two of us plus America plus India). That seems – happily – to have been forgotten. In the press conference I went out of my way to reject any notion of containing China. Yes, I told the media, we can have improved relations with China and Japan. 'International relations does not have to be a zero-sum game,' I said.

On Fiji, Peter Varghese advises that we more or less have to accept that the interim government has dictatorial instincts and work out what concession from them we can live with. 'Well,' I said. 'That's got to be a free and fair election. There's not much we can do to fine-tune their constitution. If they want to put in a benign reference to the role of the military then we can't stop them.'

'What we want,' Peter said, 'is an election in Fiji, the results of which are going to be universally accepted.'

Mali pushes through on to the front pages with the French sending troops and planes to hold the advance of the Islamist columns until the West African nations can throw their forces into it. Now that we're on the Security Council we are at the heart of this. Is this what membership of the Security Council is all about? Running the sanctions on al-Qaeda? Shaping an intervention in Mali? Gary Quinlan, our Ambassador to the UN, put it best in an interview when he said that chaos and crisis is precisely what you deal with on the Security Council. These are its business. He quoted former Secretary-General Dag Hammarskjöld who in 1954 said: 'The United Nations was not created in order to bring us to heaven, but in order to save us from hell.'

I've revived the gym. First legs workout in five weeks and quads, hamstrings and calves ache so much I can hardly walk. Feels terrific.

THURSDAY, JANUARY 17, 2013
Sydney

Sometimes – only sometimes – my department springs to life in ways that reveal its hidden personality. Back in November 2012, Paul Keating gave a speech suggesting Australia join ASEAN. I was then asked to comment on it. On November 15 I said, 'Yeah, the day may come, but they're very proud, the ten ASEAN nations are very proud of what they call ASEAN centrality. And you don't force your way into a community before time … I suspect now is not the time.'

Later, on another television program, I said, '… the chances are we would be rebuffed and ASEAN would say "That doesn't fit our vision".' But up comes a ministerial submission asking me to clarify that 'Australia has no plans to seek or even consider membership even in the long term and that doing so is not necessary to pursuing closer engagement with the region.' The submission says membership of ASEAN would 'subordinate aspects of Australian foreign policy to ASEAN. It would require Australia to refrain from any real criticism of ASEAN governments (e.g. on human-rights issues) and from putting forward alternatives to ASEAN positions. It would require Australia to accept other ASEAN countries, notably the ASEAN Chair, representing Australia in discussions with external parties such as the United States, China and international organisations.'

It then goes on to warn that membership of ASEAN would involve with it Australia having to set up an 'ASEAN National Secretariat' to implement ASEAN decisions at the national level and that in general it would cramp Australian independence. It also warns that ASEAN countries would be strongly opposed to Australia joining. It says the Singaporean High Commissioner was twice asked informally if recent public commentary is as a result of policy consideration with the Australian government.

I wrote on the bottom of the submission, 'My comments were in response to remarks of a former Prime Minister – who I chose to treat with courtesy – and didn't reflect any desire to shift Australia's position. No need to pursue or clarify.'

SATURDAY, JANUARY 19, 2013
Perth to India

I sat in business class on Singapore Airlines, flying to India, glancing at newspapers full of reports about yesterday's talks between us and the UK. This was the fifth Australia–UK Ministerial

Consultations (AUKMIN), foreign and defence ministers of Australia and the UK, an annual consultation held this time – at Stephen Smith's insistence – in his home town. A pleasure to deal with UK Foreign Secretary William Hague. I've known him since about 2000 when he was Leader of the Conservative Party and followed his stint as Opposition Leader against Blair. Today he was determined to mount a call for the US to resume the Middle East peace process. It was his idea but I fastened on to it, drafting language for the communiqué strong enough to make it a story for the Australian press. I fashioned a strong criticism of Israeli settlements, including a reference to them *all* being illegal. I carefully drafted a sentence stating the UK and Australia voted the same way on Palestinian status; I added a call for Palestinians not to do anything provocative (code for going to the International Criminal Court) and inserted an insistence that rocket attacks from Gaza not be resumed.

I wanted this to be the story of the day. To be so, it needed pumping up with this strong language.

A Conservative Party Foreign Secretary of the UK in lockstep with us on the Middle East peace process. It confirms my position on the UN vote last year.

This is a challenge for Abbott: the UK Tories agree with me on Palestinian status and settlements.

'No need to run it by the Prime Minister,' I told James over breakfast. 'We're not a nanny state.' But later Stephen Smith queried the sentence about the UK and Australia having voted the same way at the UN. He suggested it might set off those inter-party tensions that boiled over a month ago. I relented – this was over morning tea – but it turned out the UK party liked my words and wanted them kept in. Smith then said it should be run past the Prime Minister. When it was presented to Richard Maude, her foreign-policy adviser, he said there was no difficulty. Later I learnt that Dennis Richardson, in his role as head of the Defence

Department, had also taken it on himself to call Maude about the Middle East wording. Yes, we are a nanny state. But it was ticked off twice.

Clearly last year's battle cleared the air. I no longer have a Prime Minister's office running interference.

On Thursday, sitting on the big VIP flying from Sydney to Perth, Hague and I had conducted our 'bilateral' – Sri Lanka, Fiji, Indonesia. I had been worried he would try to pick up our support for the UK on the Falklands. I'd been briefed by the department that we shouldn't move from our neutrality (I hadn't known we were neutral; I had assumed we were backing the Brits). Hague opened the subject as we flew over the Great Australian Bight. I distracted the issue. 'Yes, the Falklands,' I opined. 'You can judge people by their enemies. Think of Margaret Thatcher. She took on the IRA, the communist leaders of the miners' union and the Argentinean generals,' I joked. 'Great enemies.' The subject passed.

One of Hague's best notions is that of nurturing in the foreign policies of developing states (India, Brazil, Indonesia) some concerns for human rights and a responsibility to protect. This is a concept that Hague had aired with Kevin Rudd. I said you can see this already at work in Indonesia – their president goes to Myanmar to advise the army to return to barracks; and in Malaysia – they broker peace with Islamist rebels in the southern Philippines. But (this was Hague's view) would you get India or Brazil to contemplate humanitarian intervention anywhere? Syria? Mali? Do they ever think about the lessons of Rwanda that, of course, haunt the West?

According to UK intelligence chiefs the outcome in Syria will be: a Lebanon-style long-running civil war; a weak Sunni Muslim Brotherhood-style government; a fractious informal coalition. Hague says the only immediate hope may be a defection of Alawite generals and an assassination. At any rate, according to one of their boffins, we are witnessing 'an attritional battle that will end in a messy way … it won't be Lawrence of Arabia entering Damascus.' The opposition are light infantrymen up against a 'Warsaw Pact-like army' (with a Warsaw Pact-like attitude that chemical weapons are normal weapons).

I scribbled a note to Mike Rann, former Premier of South Australia, who I made High Commissioner to the UK in December: 'More interesting than COAG.'

In Perth I did ABC radio in the morning and a studio interview with Howard Sattler of 6PR in the afternoon. The magic medium: you project personality with your voice, you tease out complexities, you underline for emphasis. I rang Yuval, the Israeli Ambassador – who would be unhappy at my words on settlements – to let him know I'd carefully written into our communiqué demands for the Palestinians too. I rang the Sri Lankan High Commissioner, Thisara Samarasinghe, to let him know that – due to my efforts, I implied – Sri Lanka was not mentioned in our communiqué even though his president had just sacked their Chief Justice. This brought forth a suitable expression of appreciation. It would win him points back home. His reputation as master diplomat swelled.

Now off to Delhi, Davos, Berlin and London, where I've kept an evening for theatre and I had told Hague on the plane to Perth I was looking forward to seeing Pinter's *Old Times*, which I had seen with Ralph Richardson and John Gielgud in London in 1975. (My memory failed me; it was *No Man's Land* I saw with those two greats.) Hague had said when he and Ffion, his wife, have dinner in the Wolseley, 'London's best restaurant', they always see Antonia Fraser (Pinter's widow). 'She *lives* there,' he had said. 'But Ffion's there three days a week for breakfast – she sees everyone in London business.' (His wife runs a successful consultancy that measures the effectiveness of company boards.)

I wonder how long he wants to do his job? How many times

can you do these 'bilaterals'? He had to leave early because the Algerian hostage crisis had trapped several Brits.

During the four-hour stopover in Singapore, I had a curry lunch with Shanmugam, Singapore's Foreign Minister. I was driven to a big union-owned country club in his electorate where, in open-necked shirt, he spends Saturdays working his constituents. This is part of the professional playbook for the People's Action Party (PAP), a grassroots approach to politics that's possible in Singapore's concentrated confines. The PAP MPs are out there with big 'open surgery' events during the weekends designed to capture different groups – the old, the young, the young families. They do a block visit every week or every other week, covering every household over four years and are expected to report back to party headquarters on crowd size, crowd enthusiasm. And also, in another reflection of party discipline, about twenty-five per cent of the party MPs will be asked to step down every general election to replenish the gene pool. Of course, this playbook has been supported by seven to eight per cent economic growth. Now, with the maturing of the economy, growth has slowed to three per cent. Globalisation has an effect here as everywhere.

Shanmugam said that China's investments in Southeast Asia are significant and Southeast Asia is linked very closely to China, economically.

He also said that his view was that Sri Lanka should be engaged by the world community. Which supports my strategy of engagement with them. They should be encouraged to undertake reforms, and help their Tamils in Sri Lanka. That cannot be done by isolating Sri Lanka.

I communicate all this to Philip Green, our High Commissioner in Singapore, in the car to the airport.

Groaning at the airline's plastic business-class food, we fly to Delhi.

TUESDAY, JANUARY 22, 2013
Delhi

Flying Lufthansa 763, the daytime flight from Delhi to Munich, en route to Davos.

Last night a dinner at the High Commission with four Congress Party ministers and a few heads of think-tanks. The ministers talked – as if we Australians were absent – of Rahul Gandhi's speech to the weekend conference of the Congress Party, a party losing its base with the rural poor to parties based on caste and regarded with distaste and cynicism by younger, better educated, urban Indians. Rahul is the scion of the Nehru-Gandhi dynasty. His speech called for more openness and less centralisation. The ministers referred to him as 'Mister Gandhi' and spoke with a reverence suitable for royalty. I was struck by how deeply dynastic the Indian system is.

Then they moved on to China. There was reference to it being in *competition* with India although there is also partnership in the relationship, and cooperation. 'But we *are* competitors,' intervened one voice. But another entered a reservation: 'Let us not lock ourselves into a narrative of pre-determined hostility.' Just like the debate at home.

'China's future is bound up with whatever happens to the US,' said one. 'But don't count on the US being in decline,' responded another. 'America has recovered before – after 1975, in the '80s,' he said. There was a consensus that China's difficulties are formidable – no, terrible: the monumental errors that have left huge over-capacity in the economy, the environmental catastrophe, less arable land than India, food insecurity, a 'decrepit' banking system with someone, sometime, having to absorb the losses.

Then it got more interesting. One referred to 'the loose coalition' that has formed as a result of more assertive Chinese behaviour: India, the US, Australia, some of the ASEANs. And one mentioned that China has no allies around the world, in contrast with the US with its signed-up friends in Europe and Asia.

This 'loose coalition' is interesting. Or, as another put it, the idea of 'a countervailing coalition'. Another conceded, 'Incipient containment is there.'

All this, without any reference to me, sitting as host.

And then, one by one, in quick succession, the ministers got up to leave – to appear on TV, to go to party meetings.

Yet earlier that day, in solid discussions followed by lunch with Foreign Minister Salman Khurshid, I couldn't get a comment – not a single benign one – about China. The new leadership? The economic slow-down? Nothing. No response from across the table. And yet we talked Fiji, Sri Lanka, Afghanistan, Iran, Middle East peace process. Still, one of our staff said that eight years ago you couldn't get an Indian to talk strategic stuff with Australia. They'd clam up. Our interests are 'converging' (a term I used) and we are invited to be strategic partners. Khurshid even proffered that India would now sign up to 2+2s with us. But Khurshid did not respond when I raised the prospect of a trilateral with them, the US and us, and I only did so tentatively. The official High Commissioner's note records:

> Senator Carr raised the possibility of US, India and Australia
> trilateral discussions at senior officials' level, noting this
> would provide an opportunity to discuss a broad agenda
> including cyber, Indian Ocean, maritime security and
> Afghanistan. Khurshid did not respond on this point.

Here, I guess, is the key: they don't want to send a message to Beijing that they are moving abruptly into something that may be seen as containment. Hey, I can understand that! Isn't that what we do when we side-step the Philippines' suggestion of a strategic partnership in the middle of their fraught relationship with the Chinese? Or cool the recently discovered ardour of the Japanese for a defence agreement? In this fashion we daintily tread: not wanting to provoke the prickly, half-distracted behemoth, yet nervously hedging our bets in case it becomes nationalist, strikes out, and each needs all the friends he can get.

When I got to see 80-year-old, two-time, triple heart-bypassed Prime Minister Manmohan Singh – sweet it was to be in dialogue with a world-historical figure (think Morsi, Clinton, Blair, Netanyahu, Barak) – I again ticked off a checklist of interests. Our negotiations towards a Civil Nuclear Cooperation Treaty will begin in March, we would like more political support for the free trade agreement, we are ready for joint naval exercises, we both want a strengthened East Asia Summit, we offer a Water Technology Partnership …

I refer to my notes but Singh has none. He leans forward, his petite face intent and focused. It's as if he has memorised the script. World-historical figure, truly. He lifted millions out of poverty when he liberalised the Indian economy. He favours reconciliation with Pakistan. He refuses to play to the mob. And – to focus on his view of Australia – in 2009 India erupted over the violence against its students in Melbourne but he stayed calm. He wants a free trade agreement with us. He likes our relationship. I texted the Prime Minister that he is 'still glowing' about her visit last October.

WEDNESDAY, JANUARY 23 – SATURDAY, JANUARY 26, 2013
Davos, Switzerland

Easy to think the whole world should be like Switzerland. The world's cities should be Swiss cities: solid brick and stone buildings; smoothly gliding, almost noiseless trams; columns advertising art shows and opera; well-dressed bourgeoisie in heavy coats; newsstands with the dailies in all European languages. And hotels like the Baur au Lac with the heavy Germanic doors to its rooms, a sunlit breakfast room with the smells of roast coffee and limitless varieties of bread, and an old-fashioned newsstand–cigar shop in the foyer. With Peter Woolcott, our Ambassador to Geneva – it's a post that covers human rights, refugees, climate change, WHO and ILO – we travelled from Zurich (this urban ideal) to Davos by train, luggage being sped by van.

To be here as Australian Foreign Minister instead of just State Premier is sweeter by far.

Louise Arbour succeeded Gareth Evans as head of the International Crisis Group. In a private meeting she uses the term 'humanitarian paralysis' to refer to the deadlock over Syria. My plan for medical aid is blocked by this paralysis. Her advice is that the West should not vilify the Russians. We should '*de*-antagonise' the Russians. She warns that Iraq is most at risk from the fallout from Syria. Iraq – where bombings are back to the levels of the war. She referred to the Democratic Republic of the Congo as 'the biggest UN Mission ever, but not much to show for it though'. Millions are unaccounted for since 1994 by wholesale displacement, accompanied by sexual violence.

I go to dinner with the heads of some of the world's biggest aid organisations including that of the US Global Fund, and am seated next to Bill Gates and Saudi Prince Turki al-Faisal. He asks me, 'When did you last visit the Kingdom?' I reply, 'Oh, a few months ago and the highlight was spending time with your Foreign Minister who has served in that post since 1975.' And his Royal Highness replies, 'He's my brother ... and he –' he points across the table to a younger Saudi prince, 'is his son.' Gates talks about how the Global Fund can help wipe out two of the oldest plagues known to humankind, malaria and tuberculosis, and one of the newest, HIV/AIDS. Gates tells me he's committed to the final six-year plan to wipe out polio. Gates is one of the finest global citizens. Modest, even shy; a Christ-like glow.

In the corridors and at one-on-one meetings and panel sessions I mix with my old mates from the Foreign Ministers' Club, including Nasser Judeh of Jordan and Ahmet Davutoğlu of Turkey. I meet Myanmar Minister U Soe Thane, who asks me to do more work to persuade the Europeans to lift and not simply suspend their sanctions against his country. I get a chance to do this almost immediately when I have a one-on-one meeting with Mark Rutte, the new Prime Minister of the Netherlands, who chats as if we are members of the same cabinet. He's sympathetic to lifting EU sanctions on Myanmar.

'The most important events of 2012 were the things that didn't happen,' says Professor Joseph Nye, the eminent American historian, at an evening session devoted to history. 'Iran was *not* bombed. And Japan and China *didn't* go to war. These were the two dogs that didn't bark.' It's like Eisenhower, he said, choosing not to use nuclear weapons in 1964. This is a gathering of about fifty people. I contribute with a declaration that nothing that happened in 2012 was as important as the mounting evidence of global anthropogenic climate change. Richard Haass, the President of the Council of Foreign Relations in New York, is there and we talk, with him inviting me to visit; the editor of *Scientific American*, Mariette DiChristina, is there; and I discuss tweeting with Gideon Rachman of the *Financial Times*.

The Arab World is a mosaic. Syria could disintegrate completely. We have to accept an Islamic-flavoured government in Egypt. The US has got to drop talk of remodelling the Middle East on Turkey. In Afghanistan the CIA created a wave of fanaticism and we are living with it till this day. I don't know who delivered these pearls. Someone in this ski-city. Someone at one of the panel sessions. But I have them in front of me in my notebook. That's my point about Davos. It's a concentrated education. Glancing at the notepad I also see that Joseph Nye made this observation about Obama on Libya and I think it's good. Praising the President's policy, he said Libya could have been a story summed up as 'US invades third Muslim nation in a row'. Instead, Obama waited for the Europeans. He then led from behind, and leading from behind – as Eisenhower's presidency demonstrated – can be a good strategy.

I tweeted that Kenneth Roth of Human Rights Watch told me that five million died in post-1994 conflicts in the Democratic Republic of the Congo. I was inundated with tweets from people who told me this is a defamation directed at Rwanda and his methodology was flawed. I sometimes regret getting into this tweeting business. But now that I've discovered how to paste photos on the tweets after snapping them on the iPad, it is entirely addictive. Twenty-six thousand people are now receiving these telegraph messages and mad Liberals waste time and energy sending me hate messages.

And from Roth I collect material I'll need to launch a campaign on North Korean human rights. He calls it the most oppressive place on earth. All these meetings take place between the conference centre and the hotels. The sky is a perfect blue, the snow is piled high but I can get between the venues without an overcoat because the journeys are so short.

Lunch in one of the hotels has me seated as a guest of the *Washington Post* at a table that has the President of Israel, the Prime

Minister of the Palestinian Authority, former Israeli Prime Minister Ehud Barak, and the Foreign Minister of Jordan. Our host, Lally Weymouth of *Washington Post* fame, roams the tables with a microphone. She has David Gergen, a US political commentator, speak. I guess the audience is 500. Gergen talks about how the Foreign Minister of Australia is quoted by Clinton (I think he means Bob Zoellick) declaring that America is one budget deal away from banishing talk of American decline. Her eyes light up and she invites me to be the next speaker. So I get up and develop this argument, which, as always, Americans find hugely flattering.

SATURDAY, FEBRUARY 2, 2013
London

Picking an Aboriginal woman athlete, Nova Peris, to go into the Senate from the Northern Territory dissolved into negative publicity for the Prime Minister. *Nothing* ever goes right.

The Prime Minister set September 14 as the election date; then Craig Thomson gets arrested. Then yesterday Nicola Roxon and Chris Evans resign their ministries. As the *Daily Telegraph* puts it spitefully, 'Government in chaos as cabinet crumbles'.

Helena and I gave ourselves Tuesday to Saturday in London and while the days were packed, we saw Pinter's *Old Times* and I hung on the swooping inflections of the actors enunciating the playwright's crafted lines. Talked about the play to Sir Tom Stoppard, who we had to dinner at Stoke Lodge (the High Commissioner's residence, where we stayed). He referred to Pinter's technique of having a character who had not yet entered the action stand onstage, behind the two other characters, just still, and looking out the window. 'I remember finding that technique surprising at the time,' he said. That is, in 1974. 'But it doesn't surprise today.'

'That's like your shock techniques in *Travesties*,' I said. 'Astonishing when we saw John Gaden do them at the Nimrod in Sydney in 1976 but routine when we saw Antony Sher at the National Theatre twenty years later.'

Stoppard said he is seventy-five, smokes and gets no exercise and is 'walking out' with a 58-year-old woman. He looked at Helena. 'Your wife has the most intelligent face,' he said. I looked across at Helena who was in conversation with Ros Kelly, the former Sports Minister who lives in London, and caught her sweet profile. We had once joked about a reference to 'small-nosed ferreting animals' in a nature documentary. I explained she is half Chinese (cute flat nose) and Indian (coffee skin and flashing brown eyes). But he had picked the intelligence.

I had insisted on seizing the weekend for a trip to Stratford so we caught a matinee of *The Winter's Tale* – an entrancing, intelligent production – in the new theatre and a disappointing *A Life of Galileo* in the Swan Theatre that evening: the sort of jerky, broadbrush, frantic acting that you get in Sydney. Fled at the interval, as we do regularly in Sydney.

After Mike and I spent the morning with spies in the country, our wives caught up with us and we dropped in to see Bletchley Park then drove back to London. Out of London at 9.30 am on Saturday, arriving Sydney at 6.55 pm on Sunday.

WEDNESDAY, FEBRUARY 6, 2013
Canberra

A cabinet discussion on tactics devolves into complaint about State governments unfairly attacking us for their cuts and claiming credit for our infrastructure. Really? They would do that? A sad discussion. The states wouldn't matter if we were seen as a strong government with authority under a leader who could shape narrative and argument. The Newspoll on Monday was disastrous, putting us back at thirty-two per cent. Rudd circles.

Last night I went to a meeting of the Right caucus. It was held around a table in the office of Joel Fitzgibbon, party whip and convenor of the New South Wales Right. Half-a-dozen backbenchers and ministers picked at potato chips and drank beer, coke or water. Party Secretary, Sam Dastyari, dissected the dismal news. I looked around the table. Half of them were going to be gone. Fitzgibbon said Gonski and the National Disability Insurance Scheme don't shift votes and 'attacks on middle-class welfare' only alienate miners in his electorate. The Obeid scandal being examined by ICAC is on the front pages every day. I hate to use this cliché but an existential crisis erodes the very notion of a Labor Party.

I struggle with jetlag and work on the cables. One in from Washington says that Joe Nye of the Harvard Kennedy School – who became something of a buddy in that Davos session – is in contention to replace Kurt Campbell at State. Beazley spoke to him and reports:

> Nye said China policy for the US was 'a manageable problem'. The US actually had a stronger hand than most gave it credit for. As he had written in a *New York Times* op-ed (25 January) the US did not need to organise a regional coalition against China. If China misbehaved, the US could

rely on a natural balance of power mechanism and China would end up 'encircling itself'. This was a feasible outcome. The main dangers to US China policy were: (a) a diversion of US attention or pull-back due to budgetary problems; (b) the US pushing too hard; or (c) a policy mistake over the Senkakus, which left Japan feeling abandoned, with consequent knock-on effects for other US allies. He thought the probability of (a) or (b) was low; (c) was also not too likely.

Nye said China's leaders could not bear to lose face, and would keep pushing on these border issues. They needed a face-saving way out. He did not think this would lead to conflict, but there was always the danger of an accident or miscalculation, similar to what occurred in 2010 with the collision between a Chinese fishing boat and a Japanese customs vessel. Nye was part of the group of 'Wise Men' who visited Japan and China last October. In Beijing they had met Vice Premier Li Keqiang, who was acutely aware of the likely costs to China of ongoing tensions with Japan, including trade costs. Li had said China needed another thirty years of peace to develop its economy, but at the same time it could not compromise its sovereignty.

I like this Nye, trust his cool-headedness.

FRIDAY, FEBRUARY 8, 2013
Sydney

A famous Australian business-figure visits to talk about activities in Asia. He says I need to pick some arguments with the US to show the Chinese we are not in a camp hostile to them. 'Er, don't think that's the way to go about it,' I venture. 'I know what you mean ... but there are other ways.'

WEDNESDAY, FEBRUARY 13, 2013
Port Vila to Sydney

Now returning from a quick Papua trip, in the smaller VIP aircraft, flying from Vanuatu to Sydney where Helena will get off; I'll fly on to Canberra.

The romance of the Pacific Islands. The spray of islands under the plane, the kids at the local tech in Kiribati breaking into song as they sat in rows while we inspected their workshop, the fragile social advances funded by our aid: these vulnerable peoples in cultures degraded by colonisers. And their cautious, shy, appraising leaders. But through AusAID we are seeing the youngsters all learn English and get an Australian-level trade qualification so that if their atoll goes under they can come here or to New Zealand as sought-after skilled migrants, not as desperate environmental refugees.

In Apia after a reception I grabbed two historians and sat them down to dinner and got them talking about the history of the Pacific. They talked about the DNA, linguistic and botanic evidence that the Polynesians originated in Asia before coming to this 'continent of islands'. These people settled in Samoa 3500 years ago. This was, of course, the second wave of settlement, the first wave being the Melanesians who walked on a land bridge from Southeast Asia to Australia 50,000 years back. The second wave, the Polynesians, were those who got here with marine technology. It enabled them to sail against the wind. Because they found Papua New Guinea and the Solomons already occupied and were pushed away by those occupiers, they kept moving east. The Tongan ocean-going canoes may have been superior, the technological basis for Tongan colonialism. Tongans settled the eastern part of Fiji and part of Samoa. For 600 years, this colonising lasted, based on their repute as superior warriors. I savoured the stories of early Europeans who were adopted by villagers, donating their own DNA to the mixed races. I heard this in Kiribati as well: the story of the German coconut empire, Samoa, a German colony officially from 1900 to 1914 before the New Zealanders grabbed it.

Had a long breakfast discussion with Samoan Prime Minister Tuilaepa Aiono Sailele Malielegaoi that focused on Fiji's 2014 elections.

THURSDAY, FEBRUARY 14, 2013
Canberra

A night in the Realm Hotel and then a full day of Senate Estimates beginning at 9 am and dragged out till 10.49 pm. A process where any senator can turn up and ask anything of me and my bureaucrats.

No revelations, no scandals. The most Liberal Senator Helen

Kroger could come up with was the old stuff about Helena travelling with me. I bit back the temptation to say, 'Get used to it, sister! She travels with me, full stop!' But I calmly pointed out that when this news had broken last year Tony Abbott didn't criticise it and Alexander Downer and Amanda Vanstone supported it. It's the entitlement, it's accepted practice, so Helena has come on every trip but two. 'There's an election in September,' I said. 'It's up to Senator Kroger to announce this practice ends with the next coalition government.' Then questions meandered over the UN Security Council seat, last year's terrorist attack in Bulgaria, diplomatic relations with North Korea and Myanmar.

But the process is about accountability. I sat back and listened to my bureaucrats, learning a few things.

I'd only had half a chicken for lunch in my office and I was getting ravenous as the afternoon dragged on with questions about travel advisories and the political situation in Venezuela, mainly directed at my public servants. I started dreaming of a great steaming pasta with tomato and eggplant. There was a one-hour break for dinner and the nearest Italian restaurant was far off in Civic. I retreated to the parliamentary dining room where there were a few other downcast senators, trapped at the Estimates Committees for other portfolios. On offer was a leg of soft, blubbery pork and some prawns cooked in a kind of chilli paste laden with sugar and salt, but I was ravenous and even downed spoonfuls of – this is not to be believed – fried rice. The immobility and tedium of the day unleased an animal force of greedy restlessness. I went to the dessert corner and found some miniature ice-cream cones: strawberry, chocolate and vanilla. Then a little ginger pudding: worse than raw sugar. I felt like retreating to the toilet and tickling my throat with a feather.

FRIDAY, FEBRUARY 15, 2013
Sydney

I flew back to Sydney this morning for lunch with John Alexander, the former editor of the *Sydney Morning Herald* who works for Packer. He thinks the Gillard government is a joke, he despises the Prime Minister as someone who failed the smell test at a low-level legal firm and had lingered with the Communist Party for years. He says she had neither the competence nor experience to run a pie shop, let alone the biggest company in the country: the Federal Government. The latest disaster is that the mining tax will produce barely any revenue. He thinks the class-warfare rhetoric is despicable; he thinks Gillard and Rudd have done enormous damage to the country destroying the Hawke–Keating philosophy of growing the pie, instead stealing it from others.

This must be the conventional wisdom of the boardrooms. Again, Labor's missed opportunity. This generation – Rudd, Gillard – were not canny enough to neutralise the business sector. Wran did it, Hawke did it; and Keating divided and bedazzled and distracted. We have not been *canny*.

I cancel my afternoon appointments and go home to try to get some sleep so I can perform at the Sydney Institute tonight. Not offering them a lecture. Offering them question-and-answer: puts me on my mettle and keeps them focused.

Bob Carr

FRIDAY, FEBRUARY 22, 2013
Bangkok

'How is Australia seen from here?' I asked them last night at the embassy in Bangkok. 'Super-close to the Americans?'

The guests were academics and government advisers, all of them – the Ambassador, James Wise, had told me – more comfortable with us and the Japanese than they are with the US or UK.

'Australia flip-flops about Asia,' said one.

'We still remember "deputy sheriff",' said another, to general laughter.

Extremely close is the impression. That is, us and the Yanks.

Does it hurt, is the thing. I wasn't alert enough to press that question.

Still, if I ever make a diplomatic blunder it can hardly be as lasting as Howard's nod in response to Fred Brenchley's question for that 1999 *Bulletin* interview. So we are America's deputy sheriff in the region, Brenchley had asked and Howard did not quickly rule it out. The story exploded, and as this encounter in Bangkok showed, the opinion leaders still remember it.

Forget the paid demonstrators in the red and yellow T-shirts, and the exiled Thaksin in Dubai running the country with his twelve telephones, and the corruption. Thailand is a serious country. That is the takeaway from our Ambassador.

I met four big companies with investment in Australia: one was in coal mines, another in power stations, a third in off-shore gas, another in sugar. More serious than our investment there. One of the academics last night told me she is charting how Thailand is building multinationals, including some through investment in Australia. Last year's growth was over six per cent. Over the last thirty years this growth was the highest in Asia. The Pheu Thai Party – that is, Thaksin's – will win eighty per cent of the vote at the next election in 2015. In other words, the country does not lack political stability. 'The Red Shirts are driving more equal wealth distribution, and it's needed,' said one of the guests.

Why isn't this more widely known?

Yes, Thailand is a serious country. Of course, it is – but I don't think that's been the impression.

One of the guests said they are lucky being close to China but not sharing a border. They don't trust the Americans to be consistent about deeper engagement with Asia; after all, the US let them down in the 1997 Asian financial crises. On the US, one academic said, his students were all sceptical. Meanwhile, China keeps pumping in trade and investment. The Thais are deeply, traditionally, instinctively of the view they don't have to choose. Said one, 'Thailand survives during uncertainty. That's what we do.' They could never produce a White Paper on defence or foreign policy; a unified national position remains elusive. And why can't the US be more subtle, asks one. Why have bold statements about pivot? Rebalancing? An Obama Doctrine? Just do what you must do and do it quietly.

That goes to the heart of it. The short answer is … because they're American.

Home on a daytime flight, Thai Airways International. A plastic-cheese omelette in a crêpe. Then minced meat (it may be chicken) swimming in MSG. All I can do is set a record for water consumption while I read papers and cables and watch all their documentaries. The best is one on Prince Charles and Dumfries House, the 1750s aristocratic mansion stuffed with treasure in Scotland, which he risked everything to restore and which Helena and I have visited. On TV Charles is the best public-figure communicator I've seen, probably because he's talking about things he's committed to: restoring a house of his favourite century and delivering social justice to the locals who get jobs running it. Helena snoozes. The flight is 'longer than sorrow', as someone said in a Márquez novel.

SATURDAY, FEBRUARY 23, 2013
Sydney

Unintended brilliance by me, to be in Laos and Thailand this week. Nobody in the media could trap me on leadership. When one Australian journalist asked me about it at my Bangkok press conference I just said I don't talk domestic politics when overseas. And got away with it.

Everything's gone wrong for Julia. The government's back on thirty per cent. The slow death of the old party.

Two things are clear. The public seems just not to like her despite all her hard work and resilience (a phenomenon I've witnessed in State politics with opposition leaders or ministers, when 'the mob' just settles on visceral distaste for a public performer). And as Prime Minister she has not produced enough policy wins. Any government needs some. In my first term I made heaps of mistakes (tolls, Government House, a failed hospital closure, a bed tax to pay for the Olympics) but balanced them with policy wins (solid budgets, curriculum reforms, environmental gains, a sound privatisation of the TAB). If you struggle on some fronts you have to chalk up victories elsewhere. Lately she can point to none.

Reports in the press suggest Rudd's challenge will be after June. Must nag Fitzgibbon on the need for *a plan*. Plans are not Kevin's strong suit.

MONDAY, FEBRUARY 25, 2013
Sydney

Last night a huge Chinese dinner to celebrate the New Year, held in the Shangri-La Hotel in Sydney. On closer examination it turned out to be a gloriously successful Labor fundraiser – how strange to use the words 'Labor' and 'success' in the same sentence these days – orchestrated by Sam Dastyari, to raise $100,000 for Chris Bowen's campaign in McMahon and $100,000 for the ALP Head Office. The other guest was a round-faced Kevin Rudd, infused with the inevitability of his return to the prime ministership, smiling jovially and delivering a speech in Mandarin that covered all bases including – important for me – that with me as 'the great helmsman', Australia–China relationships were secure for the future. His demeanour was very friendly. It confirms he's picked up from Fitzgibbon and Dastyari my own shift across the caucus divide.

'I must have a talk to you about Prisoner X,' he said as he departed for a debate with Joe Hockey. I told him there was a suggestion from the bureaucracy that his office, when he had been in government, had been kept informed about this affair in Israel. A look of dark concern crossed his face. 'Don't worry,' I said. 'It's not serious.' He remarked that it looked like bureaucrats trying to cover their backsides and he was off.

I gave a speech but the interpreter, translating paragraph by paragraph, lost her way and couldn't remember what I said. Meanwhile, I began to fear each dish of Chinese food was swimming in MSG – confirming that as Sydney's Chinese population has grown larger the Chinese food has grown worse – and I was beginning to get a headache. Helena and I took off early and I had grass-fed beef with salad at The Cut, a steakhouse in The Rocks.

I haven't asked for a guarantee through Dastyari; my assumption is Rudd keeps me.

Email from Kim Beazley

February 28, 2013

Dear Bob,

Peter [Varghese] raised with me a question you raised with him about why we had been unsuccessful in having Secretary Kerry conduct his first tour in Asia. I understand he has shared with you my note to him. In that failure we are among many, including some in the White House. I am attaching an article that appeared this week in *Politico* which created a stir in a number of camps including Hillary's. She did not appreciate the notion she had been engaged in 'odometer diplomacy'.

This week for me has been a week of these questions. In a robust call on a variety of matters, Wendy Sherman raised a complaint that in a private forum I had expressed the hope that Senator Kerry would maintain the Asian focus but had doubts. I told her the report was true and, like most of the Asian ambassadors, I was worried. She sought to reassure me, reference the conversations the Secretary had had with you.

From a different angle, I did a farewell dinner at the Residence for Kurt Campbell. In attendance, apart from Kurt and Lael Brainard, there was a bevy of officials who were friends of Kurt. They included Tony Blinken, the new Deputy NSA; Steve Richetti, Shailagh Murray and Evan Maureen Ryan, who are counsel and advisers to Biden; Jake Sullivan, late Director of Policy Planning in State and now senior foreign policy adviser to Biden; and Samantha Power who, rumour has it, will emerge with an Undersecretary job in State. Their emphasis was on the proposition that while the White House and Hillary had been critical in initiating the pivot and the move of the US into the EAS, it was Kurt Campbell's nuts and bolts diplomacy which drove it. I would agree with that, which makes his successor critical.

Kerry is a formidable intellect and a very energetic man. He was the Senate's most experienced foreign policy spokesperson. He has been a senior figure for years, frequently undertaking the role of bearer of messages from the President. These have mainly been delivered in the Middle East and Pakistan. He has been largely inaccessible to us. I and we have not found it hard to get to Senators and Representatives with visiting Australians or on our own (Republicans easier than Democrats). Kerry has been impossible. In the three years I have been here, without question about the most useful visit we had was yours. (He would not see Kevin on one of his visits). He likes you. In his pecking order, however, unlike the situation with Clinton, Australia does not rank highly.

Kerry wants big achievements. Erroneously, Asia is not perceived here as the locus of big achievements, just intricate, often-frustrating spadework. He probably sees Europe and the Middle East providing him with these opportunities. He cannot avoid North Asia with the North Korean issue, Sino–Japanese and Japanese–Korean disagreements. He will give them focus but, one suspects, not from a wider Asian perspective. With the pivot, it is South and Southeast Asia that counts.

We need a formula to press on him to change his mind. One aspect is the basic statistics in our White Paper on the rapidly growing economic weight of Asia. Given his fascination, another is the possibility that he can leverage his Middle Eastern initiatives in the much more important Muslim communities in Indonesia, India, Pakistan, Malaysia and Bangladesh. In a decade's time, Asia moves from being 70 per cent of the market for Middle East oil to 90 per cent. The fact that the US plays a role in the Middle East on preserving stability and access to oil might also be a selling point in Asia and a string to his bow from an angle that he understands.

When the appointments at State are nearer complete, I will send a cable on what we think it means for us. In the meantime, it is worth looking at the attached article. It has got our dilemma pretty well.

Kim Beazley

SATURDAY, MARCH 9, 2013
Sydney

Yesterday up at 5.30 am to fly down to Hobart. One of our Tasmanian senators, Lisa Singh, organised a visit to Ogilvie High School – 1930s buildings in generous green parkland, suitable for a fine public school, the land of grounds all public schools deserve – and I speak to about 150 girls on International Women's Day. I told them about the prejudice against women in Afghanistan and the Melanesian world. I told them about news I had last week from Amnesty International that seventy women leaders had been killed in the last year in Afghanistan. I told them how AusAID was training midwives in Cambodia to bring down the rate of maternal death from 220 per 100,000 births to something like eight per 100,000 births as it is in Australia.

I said that whenever Australian-funded doctors and nurses operated on blind people to remove cataracts in Cambodian villages there was an extra unintended outcome: within days, the number of girls at schools shot up. 'Why is this?' I asked the assembly. One girl saw the point straight away. She said it was because the girls had been kept home to look after blind grandparents or parents. I told them about our program to train women in Papua New Guinea to work as village magistrates. The number had gone up from ten in 2004 to 700 today. In this most male-dominated warrior culture we are leveraging change that helps women.

I was joined at the high school by Jane Austin, the Labor candidate against Andrew Wilkie, who sensibly stuck by my side when I faced TV interviews on the lawn to talk about the Security Council vote on North Korea.

Later I saw a business delegation concerned about the effect of new biosecurity laws on Tasmanian salmon farming; and we managed a quick trip to David Walsh's Museum of Old and New Art. I then went on to Parliament House to answer questions from representatives of NGOs assembled by Senator Singh – Amnesty International, Friends of Tibet, the Women's International League for Peace and Freedom, a youth wing of World Vision, United Nations Youth. A sheer pleasure, a sheer treat; these people were the best of Australia. I looked out the window at a swathe of parkland in the sunlight and asked, 'How do we justify our privileges as Australians? By helping the less well-off. It's the right thing to do and it's in our interest.'

I then went to the ABC studios for an interview with Louise Saunders, one of those easy, sincere, relaxed interviews when you're too tired to give a damn about selling messages or straining for effects. Again, the magic of this medium, radio – space, immediacy, personality. Then ABC TV caught me to talk about North Korea's nuclear tests. A studio interview to run on the national news that night – another bonus.

Then off to the University of Tasmania. I stare down my exhaustion and give a lecture on International Women's Day themes in a nice auditorium with good acoustics before an audience of sensible idealists. I leant over to Lisa and said, 'It's good that it's us talking here – about these issues – and not the bloody Greens.' I told my stories about Cambodia and Vanuatu and Papua New Guinea again, with only passing references to the sad, boring speech someone in AusAID had served up without a narrative or a rhythm or a fresh phrase.

On the way to the airport I spoke by phone to Foreign Minister Peiris of Sri Lanka, who was seeking assurances in respect of the Commonwealth's treatment of his country's human-rights record. I laid the assurances on with a trowel. This is pragmatism on our part. We need them as a friend. And moreover, the best way to get progress towards reconciliation in Sri Lanka is to engage, not force the Rajapaksas into the welcoming arms of China or leave them isolated.

Flew out of Hobart on a 7.35 pm flight and arrived home in French Street, where Helena had some slow-cooked lamb and delicious vegetables ready.

I texted Julia about what I'd done and she replied:

Hi Bob – just landed in Sydney – going to [Peter] Harvey memorial. Glad you did the stuff in Hobart. We can take Denison off Wilkie and the 'Left' constituency is important to that. Jane Austin is a good candidate, we wouldn't have lost that seat in 2010 with her.

SUNDAY, MARCH 10, 2013
Sydney

A wipeout for Labor in the Western Australian elections. Naturally, a first-term government managing a mining boom was going to get back – with a personable leader as a bonus – but by all accounts, federal Labor's unpopularity helped produce an 8.7 per cent swing. And to worsen things for the Prime Minister there will be a Newspoll on Tuesday, and it's a parliamentary sitting week.

Just do my job, I tell myself; just take every opportunity that comes with being Foreign Minister for another six months.

But at home this morning I had a chance to push on with a re-reading of *The Brothers Karamazov* in the newest translation by Richard Pevear and Larissa Volokhonsky. I'm up to the scene when the quarrelling Karamazovs call on the Elder Zosima in the monastery on the outskirts of their town. (In September 2011 Helena and I visited Staraya Russa to see the Dostoevsky house and the monastery in the forest that inspired this account.) I even got a chance to watch another scene of David Tennant in *Hamlet* directed by Gregory Doran, which I have on BBC iPlayer on my iPad – by far the best *Hamlet* I've seen. And then to the city to do a press conference on our support for Schapelle Corby's parole application, not that I think she's going to get anything after the public reaction in Indonesia last year when President Yudhoyono cut her sentence by five years. The Indonesian public does not like narcotics traffickers, even the garden-variety version.

TUESDAY, MARCH 12, 2013
Canberra

This is insane. There was an 8.30 am cabinet meeting this morning. It was going to be devoted to coal seam gas. I opted not to get on an earlier flight to Canberra to make it. I had nothing to contribute to the subject. When I arrived I found that Stephen Conroy's media changes were the story of the day. They had been dumped on the cabinet meeting – without warning – and adopted. We are committed to a wholesale war with the newspapers. In that pre-election phase when we should be friends with all.

I said to a colleague, 'My view as Premier was to do three things with the media. One, persuade them. That is, let the editors and commentators know why you are doing things and sell your case as strongly as possible. Two, keep a flow of stories, arguments and ideas. Three, exploit divisions in the media so that, for example, when Alan Jones was assailing you, you had decent relations with the *Daily Telegraph*. Or, when all the papers are against you, the TV news bulletins carried your stories every night. Or, when the radio commentators were ganging up on you, the radio newsrooms were accepting your phone calls and broadcasting your seven-second comments on the news of the day.'

That's it. The Carr Doctrine: persuade and charm, and throughout it all, simply entertain. Instead we're choosing to antagonise all the media six months from the election. There could be a brilliance behind this but I'm not going to ask.

I shouldn't have expressed my dissatisfaction. The atmosphere is hothouse. Colleagues talk.

WEDNESDAY, MARCH 13, 2013
Canberra

Steve Rosen, a former official of the American Israel Public Affairs Committee (AIPAC), now director of the Washington Project at the Middle East Forum, was around Parliament House. I bumped into pro-Israel lobbyist Colin Rubenstein and got him to bring Rosen to my office. Rosen says there's been a convergence in the Middle East, there's a new government in Israel, there's now a consensus for an 'interim Palestinian state with temporary boundaries'.

Some hope, in other words.

Earlier in the day I spoke to UN Under-Secretary-General Terje Rød-Larsen. He told me that the American Jewish leadership – both AIPAC and the Conference of Presidents of Major American Jewish Organisations – is united in criticism of Netanyahu. He said, 'They understand the catastrophe that awaits Israel if there's no two-state solution.'

Yes, a catastrophe – which was the point of my argument on Palestinian status.

THURSDAY, MARCH 14, 2013
Canberra

The end of the parliamentary week and leadership speculation swirls. Walking down to Question Time I notice three TV crews standing in the corridor aiming their cameras at the entrance to the Prime Minister's office. What's going on? A few more steps and I encounter Paul Kelly, editor-at-large for *The Australian*, and he asks me whether I've heard anything about a delegation to meet the Prime Minister. Throughout the week people spoke openly. Even Kim Carr, sitting down to Senate Question Time, suggests I'm ill-advised to be going to America on Saturday, to expect to be called back. Dastyari tells me he's heard nothing. I ring Joel Fitzgibbon to advise him it would be crazy for Rudd to take over before the budget. Later, bumping into Chris Bowen in the corridors, we discuss this and he tells me it's too hard to unpack a budget and there's no alternative but to take over now. 'Besides,' he says, 'Thérèse is in two minds. She tells Kevin it's not time, it'll be too late to take over and that he's got to give up so much.'

On the plane out of Canberra I see John McTernan sitting next to Jason Clare. Earlier in the week I'd told Jason that the disastrous media changes had me moving from one camp to the other. What is going on in McTernan's mind?

Helena is fuelled up against a Rudd return. Really angry. Even to the point where I've got to warn her against the danger of sounding hot and obsessive. Her objection may go back to an occasion when she and Rudd met in my other office in my last months as Premier. He was not leader of the party at the time but would vigorously maintain his contacts – and I was one of them – and press his case, nagging the party to consider him as leader. He had casually remarked to her something like, 'Gee, what's Bob done to upset so many people ... they're all getting stuck into him.' She says she sprang at him and said, 'You wait till you've been in power for ten years and they gang up on you.' She recalled that the way she sprang reminded her of her cat in Taiping when she or her brothers goaded it. She's definitely in the Gillard camp, unmoved by my argument that it's all a pragmatic judgment and it's about which leader minimises harm for the party. My view: we're in survival mode – as a party, an institution – and he offers the better chance.

FRIDAY, MARCH 15, 2013
Sydney

Had breakfast with Kurt Campbell at the Park Hyatt: for me, organic oats with yoghurt and berries, then an omelette; for him, a defiant patriotic statement of flapjacks with maple syrup. He's touring Asia sending messages for the Obama administration as he slides off into private life. Which means making some money before joining Hillary's campaign and becoming her Secretary of State in 2017. As, apparently, he will. He says North Korea is now terribly dangerous. He says the leader suffers vehement mood swings. The political leadership – 3000 leading families – is being purged. The real leader, the kid's distant relative, Jang Song-thaek, expects to be executed any time soon. Meanwhile, South Korea is now more feisty. Kurt says it is very, very serious. 'North Korea is the real deal.'

He gave me some advice about meeting John Kerry in Washington next week. Kerry should get on with me because of our common interest in climate change and ocean environments; his reputation as an intellectual. He said Kerry won't want it to be implied that he falls short of the Hillary standard when it comes to engagement with Asia. Plainly, he has a deeper interest in the Middle East. But it might be good for me to talk about Asian involvement in that process, using Indonesia and Malaysia as case studies. He advised that I look at a *Politico* article called 'John Kerry: the Un-Hillary Clinton', which he believed reflected badly on the people around Kerry for wanting to send a message that the new boy was better than his predecessor. But he suggests that in the meeting with Kerry I say we support and encourage his leadership on the Middle East and *then* lead him into our real abiding interest, namely whether America's involvement in Asia will continue.

I got him to advise me on two questions. I asked him, first, whether it was feasible for us to talk up resource-sharing agreements between the Chinese, on one hand, and, on the other, the Filipinos and the Vietnamese. He strongly recommended I proceed, referring to some discussions between Sinopec and the Philippines. He said, 'Talk up a Track Two dialogue and start seeding institutions to pursue it. Let it be known that you're doing this, keep repeating that the goal is progress towards a code of conduct. And highlight other programs on resource management, marine management etc.' I then asked him whether my 'unruffled' policy on China was the best one. He agreed it was and he said that Australia was moving on 'mil-to-mil cooperation' with the Chinese even faster than the US.

He told me that he's had scores of meetings with former Thai Prime Minister Thaksin. 'Where?' I asked him. He said, 'Everywhere. Sydney, New York, London, Moscow.' Great idea. I'll get Graeme to line up the same thing in Dubai.

It was a year since my first meeting with Campbell – over breakfast at the same hotel – where he talked non-stop and barely let me get a word in. This was a better experience. In fact, his advice was strikingly useful. I can see why Beazley depends on him so much (but he says Beazley must now cultivate other sources).

After breakfast I headed to Fitness First then went around the corner to have coffee with Sam Dastyari. Dastyari says there's a ten per cent chance of the leadership issue erupting next week but it's still hard to bring on a show of hands against Gillard in the party room. The mechanics aren't settled. Of the seventeen New South Wales members of the caucus – that's Left and Right – only four would be in the Gillard camp now and two of those – Tony Burke and Chris Hayes – are open to persuasion.

I told him I had terrific meetings lined up for Washington next week, including with Vice President Biden, and didn't want to have to come home.

SUNDAY, MARCH 17, 2013
Sydney to Washington; Dallas stopover

Joel Fitzgibbon, Rudd's campaign director, rang to warn me the chance of action on Monday has increased. What action? A delegation to Gillard. And they would want me to fly out of Washington Monday night, after my meeting with Kerry. Long groan. I'm now in transit in Dallas, already crippled with jet fatigue and a world-class headache. Helena keeps up her anti-Rudd propaganda and insists Fitzgibbon is just talking things up.

I remember that in 2007, after Rudd assumed the leadership, Mark Arbib had pressed me to take pre-selection for the seat of Blaxland, to go into parliament at the 2007 election and become Foreign Minister. Helena wanted me to do it. I held back. After all, in the early months of Rudd's leadership it was by no means certain that he would beat Howard. But Arbib had passed on to me that Rudd wasn't altogether enamoured of the idea of me entering parliament. Well, I thought, that's enough for me. I want to be Foreign Minister, nothing else. And if there's a lack of enthusiasm from the Prime Minister then there's a danger I could be trapped in federal politics without securing the only job I would want there. Helena put that down as a mark against Rudd.

Patrick checks the Sundays and Rudd's in them everywhere, with the implication he's about to take over. I need to insinuate the notion that, after he takes over, I should be allowed to stay in the US to complete my juicy agenda – speaking in the Security Council, dinner with the Kissingers and Bloomberg, seeing a raft of senators; above all, my meeting with Vice President Biden.

Gillard has not had a political success all year. The media package, and how it was adopted, has destroyed any confidence I could have in her office and instincts.

MONDAY, MARCH 18, 2013
Washington, New York

'So foul and fair a day I have not seen.'

A few hours of patchy sleep, even after swallowing a Normison, under the blast of the cyclonic air-conditioning of the Willard Hotel. It's the last time we stay in this tourist-class joint; I had insisted on it because Lincoln had checked in here in 1861, so memorably captured in Vidal's *Lincoln*. But under the gilt it's just a bit shabby, the gym cramped, breakfasts are undignified scrambles – although they do pass the test of offering oats and berries.

To meet the new Secretary of State, John Kerry, at the State Department at 11 am. The same routine as with Hillary last April. We stand nervously in the holding room on the eighth floor with its museum-quality furniture and paintings of former Secretaries of State on the panelled walls. There's a talk with Danny Russel, in charge of Asian policy at the National Security Council, who is happy to be the new Assistant Secretary for East Asia (that is, Kurt Campbell's successor). Every time a door opens we come to attention in preparation for the newly minted Secretary. Lots of false alarms.

Then Kerry arrives with a bustle. I met him in April in his role as Chair of the Senate Foreign Relations Committee. I had also met him at Davos in 2001 with his wife Teresa, formerly Teresa Heinz the heiress. He is tall, and as lean as I, wearing a tailored dark grey suit with a white shirt and pink Hermès tie. He has a helmet of grey hair and baby-fresh skin. The surgical scars under his eyes I noticed in April have faded in a triumph of American cosmetic surgery. Here is another advertisement for the supercharged and charming American internationalist, although as Kurt Campbell had insisted on telling me, he can make the occasional mistake, like telling the *Boston Globe* that the President had decided on him a week before Susan Rice withdrew from consideration, thus embarrassing the President and diminishing Rice, the US Ambassador to the United Nations. Reassuring, though, that American policy titans can make mistakes.

We sit down at the long table in the meeting room and he recites the catechism about America having 'no stronger ally or friend than Australia'. He adds that he had personal experience of this in Vietnam and said he meant his comment seriously. I say I recall President Obama's speech at the UN Security Council last September, which eloquently defended freedom of speech in the backwash of Arab agitation over the YouTube video mocking Islam. The strength of the speech ('worthy of Lincoln,' I said) and the fact that only an American president could have made it highlighted the shared values at the core of the US–Australia alliance. 'It's values as well as interests that commit us to this alliance,' I tell him.

He bounces straight into North Korea, asking, 'What do we do?' I tell him we stand ready to apply autonomous sanctions on top of those of the Security Council. We will lobby Asian powers to have them enforce sanctions: the search of any vessels headed to or from North Korea. I say that while there would probably be benefits from allowing a reopening of the North Korean Embassy in Canberra in the future, now is clearly not the right time. Secretary Kerry agrees. He says he spoke earlier today to his Chinese counterpart, the new State Councillor Yang Jiechi. Every indication is that the Chinese are very upset with the regime in Pyongyang. The US judgment is that Kim Jong-un is irrational and unpredictable.

Taking Kurt Campbell's advice I raise the Middle East – to applaud Kerry's initiative in heading there, this evening as it happens – instead of starting with Asia and appearing to lecture him on making it his priority, a criticism he is apparently sensitive to.

He laments yesterday's remark by the Israeli Minister for

Housing, which committed the government to throwing up still more settlements. 'Yes,' I say, 'that's why we voted not to oppose increased Palestinian status.' He says that the vote was fine by him and if the vote were held today the Israelis wouldn't get a vote from anyone except themselves.

We get on to Asia and I pass across an analysis of Indonesian politics and of the likely contenders for the presidency – Aburizal Bakrie, Prabowo Subianto, Megawati Sukarnoputri, Joko Widodo – and suggest our missions in Jakarta reach towards them, their potential ministers and their advisers. Secretary Kerry says Indonesia is a country whose great importance is vastly neglected by most, but not by Australia. 'It is a big piece of the future puzzle.' He agrees with my argument that Indonesia is a successful, democratic, moderate Muslim nation. He asks about signs of religious intolerance in Indonesia and I tell him they exist but these need to be carefully assessed. Some attacks, on churches, for example, have appeared to be gang-based crime, not religiously motivated.

On the South China Sea I hand over another piece of paper, an analysis of resource-sharing proposals that would enable China on the one hand and Vietnam and the Philippines on the other to vault over their disputed sovereignties and get straight on to exploiting the resources and sharing the benefits.

I've noted Secretary Kerry's interest in the world's oceans and offer Australia's active assistance with any initiatives the US plans to undertake. I say that if the US was to hold a major conference, we would be willing to fund attendance by the representatives of small island states who otherwise would not be able to afford to get there.

The agenda is brisk; we have no more than half an hour and his style is to move through it quickly. As we are nearing the end, Kim Beazley at my side scribbles a note to remind me to raise the Trans-Pacific Partnership.

Then the next part of the ritual. A secretary enters the meeting to hand him a yellow slip of paper. Time to wrap things up by saying, 'The media are waiting for us.' Each party then takes ten minutes to go off and prepare for the media conference. The Secretary of State returns. The double doors are opened and we walk through to our lecterns facing the media. They have been told there will be one question from US reporters and one from the Australian. I get a double-barrelled question that has me declare my loyalty to Julia Gillard and I get a chance to praise the Secretary of State for being as committed to the rebalance to Asia as his predecessor.

He tells the media he has always been interested in Asia. He talks about helping force regime change in the Philippines in 1986 at the end of the Marcos dictatorship. He recalls working with John McCain for ten years on reconciliation with Vietnam. I think this exchange is helpful to Kerry in warding off criticism he's not committed to the rebalance in Asia.

The leadership stuff out of Canberra rattles on all day. Peter Hartcher had put on the front page of the *Sydney Morning Herald* and *The Age* that I (and two other ministers) had swung against Gillard. We put out a rebuttal declaring he had never checked the story with me. I go off to the downtown ABC studios and do an interview where I bat it away. I say that if Hartcher had checked I would have denied it and the story could not have run.

I see John Kerry again at a reception at the *National Geographic* to promote protection of the Ross Sea in East Antarctica, a New Zealand–US initiative. I get to speak from the lectern, announce Australia's support. Kerry gives an elegant speech, mentions his record on marine protection. Once again I find myself admiring Washington's ruling caste – their internationalism, their knowledge, their reach beyond America's interests to a full global agenda. The charm, at their best, of American values.

I wish John Kerry well as he takes off to the Middle East. Then we drive to the station for the train to New York with provisions the embassy got us from Whole Foods: turkey, salads, crab cakes. On the journey I receive a text from the Prime Minister's adviser John McTernan that Hartcher's verballed me, virtually claiming on radio I have lied in my rebuttal and have been complaining about Gillard's leadership to colleagues. I have, of course – especially since the stupid media policy was adopted last week. I don't respond. Only time is going to sort this thing out. Interesting ... when you don't return calls of the leader's staff. Power is ebbing, is shifting from her.

WEDNESDAY, MARCH 20, 2013
New York

In New York at the UN for a speech at a conference to wrap up work on an Arms Trade Treaty. Our Ambassador for Disarmament, the diligent Peter Woolcott, is in the chair. My remarks open the debate. This work is a pushover. I take a speech from the department that had been revised by my staff, I cast an eye over it and then, when called on, read it out with the modulation and pacing I learnt from my voice teacher, Gina, back in the late '70s and early '80s and practised battling away in the Legislative Assembly. Then I wait a respectable time and slip away. Other UN duties: meetings with Valerie Amos, UN Under-Secretary-General for Humanitarian Affairs; with Ray Chambers, Special Envoy for Malaria; and with US Permanent Representative Susan Rice.

Yesterday I was interviewed live on *Lateline* – early in the morning, New York time – from the little 31ˢᵗ Street studio in Manhattan. I had to declare again that I supported Julia Gillard. As we drove from the studio I got a pained call from Sam Dastyari. 'Mate,

mate ...' This, of course, the mating cry of the New South Wales Right. He went on: 'What are you doing ... I'm getting phone calls ... you should have just batted it away ... you've given a strong endorsement ...' He had just taken calls from Bowen and Albanese complaining that I had undermined their pro-Rudd campaign. But after being warmed up by the interview I was in full voice. I lashed out: 'What on earth do they suggest I say when asked whether I support her? I got out of bed two hours ago. I don't know what *they're* planning! How *would* I know? They should know that if I failed to endorse her – to express my *full* support – that brings on the leadership challenge ...and I'm not doing that.'

It turned out that Dastyari hadn't even seen the program.

The Rudd forces are freebooting when it comes to sticking my name in the press. But they're not smart enough to understand that putting me in the papers as a Rudd supporter puts me in a position where I'm going to be asked whether it's true. Have I shifted my support from Gillard? And I can only say that I have not. All week Fitzgibbon had been urging Graeme that I get a seat on a plane and return. Ridiculous – that's me bringing on the challenge. Me dashing back to Australia actually provokes it (why else would I be returning?).

In the Rudd camp now, I simply see him as the least bad alternative. The better choice in mitigating the loss we face. But he hasn't spoken to me, I haven't spoken to him; his troops have not communicated that they have a strategy and want me to be part of it – an invitation I would refuse anyway. As we drove from the studio to the Ambassador's residence at Beekman Place I wrapped up my phone conversation with Dastyari by saying, 'If the Rudd forces see me playing a role in this they should give me the courtesy of phoning me. If these geniuses have got great ideas for a form of words, they should pay me the courtesy of ringing me. Not sticking my name on the front page of the paper as a Rudd supporter and then expecting it to fall into place!'

Anyway, I recover my equilibrium in the Ambassador's residence: breakfast in the dining room, on the corner of this 1930 building. The Manhattan sunlight pours in. There's the modulated traffic noise: distant honking cars and police sirens. A moment of grace, out of a John Cheever story. All that's needed is cigarette smoke. And like lowering myself into a warm bath, I sink into the mass of global trivia in the crisp pages of today's *New York Times*. If this – New York light through the canyons of Midtown buildings and the liberal internationalism of the newspaper – is not perfection, I don't know what is. All this – plus my cables. And organic steel-cut oats with blueberries and goat milk yoghurt, unflavoured, and espresso coffee. This is a voluptuous moment.

Yesterday I sat in the Security Council – the only Foreign Minister present – for a debate on Afghanistan. I am greeted by the Permanent Representative of Rwanda who promises when I visit (can't see this happening) to take me to the gorillas. Gary Quinlan, our Ambassador, takes me across the room to Ban Ki-moon and the Russian Permanent Representative who this month chairs the Council. I greet US Ambassador Susan Rice. She is being considered as Obama's National Security Adviser.

Our mission helped in drafting the resolution. A UN resolution, in this case, is fifteen pages of paragraphs 'recalling' this, 'reaffirming' that, 'welcoming' something and 'encouraging' something else again. After speeches by Ban Ki-moon and the Afghan Permanent Representative, the resolution is adopted by all fifteen votes. I get to raise my hand in my first Security Council vote.

Then the speeches are given, me first: my speech drafted by the department and worked on by James and Patrick on the train on Monday night. I glance at it once before delivery. Once. No one listens. Then read it for the record. I note the progress the country has made. I note the challenges including the 2014 election, improving governance and Afghan forces assuming responsibility for security. I acknowledge the work of the High Peace Council in moving to reconciliation with those insurgents who are ready to renounce violence. High hopes.

Similar speeches follow from all other fifteen.

While Azerbaijan speaks I banish my irritation with the squabbles of the ALP leadership. I allow myself to enjoy the moment, representing my country, sitting in the forum. And I flick through my papers. An ONA report says that Afghan insurgents are making gains, taking back areas vacated by the International Security Assistance Force as it draws down. The Taliban has little incentive to negotiate. They must be laughing at us.

In the evening Helena and I go off to dinner at Erminia Restaurant on 83rd Street with the Kissingers and Bloomberg. It's a cosy Italian place, too few tables – barely twenty – to be a serious business concern. Is it run as a tax loss?

We speak about Syria. Henry says America should pick one side – army, militia, coalition – and arm it. Both he and Nancy suggest the Obama White House may be slow to activate 'the situation room' in crises like that over Benghazi. As a result, there may be less than optimal leadership on foreign policy.

Bloomberg, this small, neat, handsome man who Kissinger seems to be coaching in foreign policy, is counting his last days as Mayor. He seems to think his replacements are mediocre. I tell him again – as I did when I met him at dinner at the Kissingers' home last year – how much I admired his leadership on smoking and obesity and climate. I tell him the thing that struck me most when we stopped over at Dallas Airport on the way to New York was the large number of pathologically fat Americans, walking between fast-food outlets dispensing different mixtures of sugar and fat.

Back at the hotel I take great pleasure in tweeting a picture of us as we stood outside the restaurant. Just to push Carr-haters and Kissinger-haters over the cliff into madness.

Meanwhile madness had broken out in Canberra. Simon Crean had held a mid-morning press conference to speak on 'Labor values' and call for an end to leadership tension. Two hours later he called another to demand a leadership spill, endorse Rudd and propose himself as deputy leader, noting that the job had actually been promised by Rudd to someone else. The strategy here was not immediately obvious. His second press conference was held immediately before Question Time, appallingly cruel to Gillard, as I noted to Helena.

She called a caucus meeting that afternoon for a leadership vote. But ten minutes before it convened Rudd announced he would not stand. Crean was sacked and Richard Marles, who had that afternoon declared himself a Rudd supporter, resigned as Parliamentary Secretary. Gillard and Swan were re-elected unopposed.

'Confusion now hath made his masterpiece,' as someone says in *Macbeth*.

MONDAY, MARCH 25, 2013
Washington

Packed our bags again and got the train back to Washington. We arrived at the White House gates, were met by protocol and shown in. I breathed in the atmosphere of James Monroe's times, the rich, elegant colours of the early nineteenth century, the paintings of maritime scenes, a breakfront mahogany cabinet. Then, we were ushered into the Vice President's office, a cosy set-up with a fire crackling away and his staff seated in armchairs, his in one row, mine in the other, facing one another. Biden's welcome was flamboyant. He looked at James Larsen and declared he could have been President with hair like that. He carried on with boisterous irony about how America was 'abandoning the Pacific', the rebalance wasn't going ahead, America was pulling out of Asia. Blah, blah, blah. Then, having had his fun, he said soberly the US presence was the one reason there had been stability in Asia. 'It sounded chauvinistic,' he said. 'But the reason was the US, period.'

He recalled spending a lot of time with the then Vice President Xi Jinping, telling him that the US was a Pacific power and that it was time the US refocused its resources accordingly. Interestingly, he said that Xi had spent a lot of their discussions asking about how the US exercised civilian control of the military. He thought Xi was 'going to school' on civilian control of the military. Biden had told him there was a risk of an accident, which could threaten everything in the US–China relationship. When President Obama had asked him about Xi, he had told him that Xi had the look of a man about to take a job that he knew would not end well. Biden said that he thought the reform process in China would be uneven and patchy, two steps forward, one step back.

He asked me what I thought about this. I said I was struck by one thing above all: the difficulty they would face in getting institutional reform. The government was unable to enforce pollution control because the state-owned corporations would not stop pumping out filth. If they couldn't control their own state-owned enterprises, they would find it hard to implement the World Bank report that recommended they be privatised. I knew how hard it was, I told him, to attempt privatisation of the state-owned electricity system in New South Wales up against institutional barriers – union power, employee resistance. Imagine how hard it's going to be in China.

Biden said twice he thought Australia had a very deep knowledge of China. In the end I contradicted him. I said, 'No country knows China better than the United States. You've been trading with it since the Empress of China sailed out of the East River in 1784 to go off and buy porcelain, tea and silk in exchange for furs and Spanish bullion.' I said the American universities had an unparalleled knowledge of China and its culture and its civilisation. I told him that Australia was very happy with US policy in Asia and pleased to see the President move to revive efforts towards Middle East peace.

He said he hoped we had listened closely to Obama's speeches in Israel. He had just spent an hour with the President reviewing the trip. They had aimed to be realistic and had not told the parties the way to peace. The President had told the Israeli people that 'they had to want' the outcome. The US objective was to get direct talks started between the parties. And then he said that he understood Australia's vote on the Palestinian-observer-state resolution – fascinating that he'd picked this up in his briefings – and our view that it gave us some leverage. He said that in his last meeting with President Abbas, he had asked everyone else to leave the room. He then asked Abbas if Netanyahu gave him everything he needed, could he do the deal? Abbas had shifted uncomfortably in his seat. Looked sideways. Then he stuttered out, 'I think so.'

He said the Arabs had to step in with measures to give Abbas space. Australia's credibility with the Palestinians and Arabs could be useful. I said I'd be happy to exercise that.

Finally I put in a plug for the Arms Trade Treaty to place accountability for the first time on the trade in small arms around the world and the Vice President said, 'We would find a greater willingness in the final days to "lean into success".' Great phrase that, 'lean into success'. He said he did not want the US to be the impediment in getting agreement on an ATT. He said he admired what Australia had done domestically on gun control and wished the US could do the same.

Then he got a message handed to him. Ah, that call from the

President, to end a routine meeting. But he was smart enough to say, 'But this is not the normal "the President wants to see you ... wrap the meeting up".' He told me that his state, Delaware, was the only state in the union that didn't have a national park and today the President was signing one – a small one – into existence. He said, 'All politics is local. Gotta be there for this.' I thought of telling him that I'd declared 350 national parks as Premier but my legendary and hallmark modesty prevented me.

Biden was embracing, ebullient, knowledgeable. I could understand why he's seen as a politician's politician. 'Yes, he'll run for President,' Beazley told me as we crunched outside in the snow. 'He just enjoys politics and campaigning so much. He'll run even against Hillary. Even if he knows he's going to lose.'

Love it, the circus of primaries and caucuses and debates and conventions.

I did a quick press conference and we sped to Union Station for the Acela Express 2166 train back to New York again. Beazley stood on the station waiting to wave me off. He said, 'This has got a bit of the John Curtin style to it – politicians farewelling one another at a railway station.' In overcoats, too.

THURSDAY, MARCH 28, 2013
Sydney

Beazley is very upbeat about my visit. He said the Americans took it very seriously, as confirmed by Vice President Biden's willingness to meet me. In a cable, he said 'he simply does not meet foreign ministers in DC unless they're associated with trouble spots in which the US is enmeshed, or China.' It does reflect the fact that 'we are slowly rising up the totem pole of the US's viable allies.' He added:

> We are valued because of loyalty and delivery on our part but also location. Gradually, the Asian orientation is sinking into policymakers here, even as the Middle East – Iran, Afghanistan – dominates their daily lives. Things are absorbed slowly in this giant bureaucracy and polity. It's interesting to see arguments we were making years ago gradually being regurgitated back to us by interlocutors as they raise matters like the TPP, APEC, engagement with China, and the correct way to approach Southeast Asian regional organisation. A map incorporating Australia's strategic geography is back in their heads.

Reminds me again of Paul O'Sullivan's notion of Australia as 'a different kind of ally' to America, the all-weather, totally reliable one, and it being in our interests to be in this space. Then I think of George W. and Iraq, the neo-cons and Fox News and also of Dennis Richardson's 'our interests are different from a great power's'.

MONDAY, APRIL 1, 2013 (EASTER MONDAY)
Sydney to Bali

Arrived back in Sydney on Qantas on Thursday morning. Went to the physio at Randwick for treatment on my shoulder and to receive prickling electrical currents from a machine that may help with jetlag. Will try anything. But the fatigue was still excruciating over the three days of the Easter weekend. Did nothing –

except a Pilates class, body weight exercises and lying in the sun in the backyard. Declined TV requests on North Korea – I am too exhausted, having woken at 2 am each day. Still, great healthy cooking by Helena. Ocean trout with turmeric and cabbage. Slow-cooked chicken with aniseed. French herbs and broccolini, sweet potato, tomatoes and Brussels sprouts. Yesterday I slept two hours in the afternoon, lay in the sun and met one of my trainers for a workout in the park at Maroubra Beach: boxing, kettlebells, body weight leaping around. Slept okay with a Normison.

Devastating polls confirm that for the ALP it's an existential crisis. Party support slumped to thirty or twenty five per cent: the party of Australian social democracy receiving backing from only a quarter of the electorate. And no revival in state support in New South Wales or Queensland. A leader with no electoral resonance, disliked by the community. Unbelievable to me that six months out of an election instead of settling controversies, consolidating support, befriending everyone (what I did, as Bracks, Beattie, Rann, Gallop did – and from the Neville Wran textbook anyway) we launched a war against the media and played with a tax on super. This is not politics.

I have had no conversation with Rudd – not this year, except for that corridor encounter in Davos; not through the leadership crisis – until Thursday when he rang from Beijing to say the South Koreans had asked him to pass a message to the Chinese: tell 'em to curb the DPRK or all bets – all promises of restraint – are off. If attacked by the north again, the south will respond. We agreed to talk when he returns but didn't touch on the messy failure of his bid for the leadership.

It was a fine week to be away. Apart from ringing Richard Marles, who stepped down as Parliamentary Secretary (that is, as my assistant) because he had backed Rudd, and his replacement Matt Thistlethwaite, I have spoken to no parliamentary colleagues. Not Gillard, not Swan, none.

I will work on my own agenda.

At the airport, Graeme reminded me it's twenty-five years to the day I was elected unopposed as leader to the New South Wales Labor Party. That was in 1988, after the smashing of the Unsworth government at Nick Greiner's hands. A quarter of a century ago and I'm still at it. No Federation-era politician who entered a colonial legislature in the early 1880s was holding federal office in 1913. But time is running out fast. As I filled the date on the departure card before boarding the Virgin Airlines flight to Bali, I thought there goes another month; September 14 bears down on us – if we can last.

After Bali, then to Jakarta, and to China with the Prime Minister. Now reading Pankaj Mishra's *From the Ruins of Empire: The Intellectuals Who Remade Asia*; a brilliant account of intellectuals like Liang Qichao, Jamal al-Din al-Afghani and Tagore, who led the first assault on Western imperialism in Asia. Tilts one's view of the West. In fact, makes it possible to hate the West, the 'ravening wolves' who tore at China, sold opium to its populace, destroyed an Arab–Persian civilisation in Delhi in the 1850s and reduced China and India, towering civilisations and advanced economies, into 'shadow countries'.

TUESDAY, APRIL 2, 2013
Bali

With Arctic air-conditioning of the Westin Hotel in Bali blasting away I get only patchy sleep – jetlag from the US east coast (fourteen hours' difference with Sydney/twelve hours' difference with Bali) jetlag from Sydney (three-hour difference with Bali). My circadian rhythms are bewildered. Still I take a Normison. And who needs eight hours anyway when you've other tools: meditation, exercise, dietary rigour, no alcohol, a morning espresso? Irrepressible curiosity? Yesterday I did twenty-five minutes of intervals on the bike at home before leaving for the airport; and a legs workout in the gym at the Westin Hotel when I arrived, those wonderful one-legged Romanian deadlifts, my favourite. Another workout at 6.30 am.

Then breakfast with Dr Dipu Moni and José Luís Guterres, foreign ministers of Bangladesh and Timor-Leste. The Foreign Ministers' Club again. Relaxed. No real business. Pleasant talking outdoors by the sea, stoking my system with a fruit-and-vegetable juice, muesli, fruit, yoghurt, eggs.

Right now I'm co-chairing with Marty Natalegawa the Conference on People Smuggling, Trafficking in Persons and Related Transnational Crime. Thirty-nine nations represented by ministers or officials. A big auditorium in front of me.

It's April and I'm in the business of extracting everything from this job before it's wrenched from me.

Meanwhile from the cables – the global trivia I'm addicted to – I note that the CIA is going to relinquish its drone program to the military and concentrate on giving the President better intelligence on North Korea (where it seems to admit to 'flying blind'). From Syria there is now an assumption chemical weapons have been used and sarin gas is being tested. As for Iran, the time for an effective Israeli air strike has run out.

From one report on Iran, an American source has it:

Every bit of optimism is confounded by the fact they are on the path to a nuclear weapon.

The CIA.

I've enjoyed the exchanges I have had with Petraeus and his

successor as director, John Brennan. But one must not be seduced by spies and their agenda. Best I keep thinking of the book I read on the agency's record of failure called *Legacy of Ashes*. The CIA, it argued, has no successes to point to. It has all been failure. And to remember one exchange with Kissinger, as I recall it anyway:

> Were you ever served up intelligence that was a real revelation?
>
> No.

While I chair the conference in the Westin Hotel ballroom, I flick through press clippings from home. Disastrous, all disastrous. Crean, now out of the cabinet, bitterly attacking changes in super policy that are being canvassed for Swan's budget, due on May 14. God, it's months from an election and the feuds and policy blunders continue. Labor polling in Victoria now awful. Why, oh why, would Gillard want to stay on? Just hand over, slip aside, allow Rudd to do what he can. Think of the party.

WEDNESDAY, APRIL 3, 2013
Jakarta

President Yudhoyono sits in the front. The Australians sit in a row on his right, me and Defence Minister Stephen Smith at the head of the queue; the Indonesians in a row on his left, facing us, Marty and Defence Minister Purnomo Yusgiantoro at the top end. The President invites his Foreign Minister to report on our talks, a bit like a principal calling on a head boy.

Then the President says he's just returned from Europe where governments were adopting a 'look east and go east' doctrine. He had also met with leaders of South Korea and Japan who had adopted a 'look south' policy to capitalise on trade and investment opportunities in the region. He raises the Papuan Provinces. He says he gives the matter a lot of thought. He would like to see that they achieve 'special autonomy plus'. This is our goal too and we express our support.

Good bilateral.

During the day I meet with Aburizal Bakrie, Chairman of the Golkar Party. Bakrie is a short, nuggetty, reddishly tanned man with a big jaw, the Golkar Party candidate for President but apparently not performing that strongly in the polls. Nonetheless, he called on me when he visited Canberra and it's important to keep in touch. We talk in his office in Bakrie Tower, full of modern Indonesian artwork. According to our Ambassador, Greg Moriarty, he would have been satisfied that an Australian Foreign Minister had called on him.

Later I meet with Joko Widodo, the Governor of Jakarta. There is speculation about him becoming President and a suggestion of Obama-style charisma in the man.

FRIDAY, APRIL 5, 2013
Jakarta to Hainan Province

Woke up at 3.30 am in Jakarta, left the hotel at 7 am and it feels like I've been a day on a plane getting here to Hong Kong for a six-hour stopover on the way to Hainan. So I'm wrung-out with fatigue. Have read about fifty cables, some more of Pankaj

Mishra's *From the Ruins of Empire* and listened to Derek Jacobi on my Walkman reading *The Iliad*. The rattling of North Korea's nuclear-armed dictatorship is the news. I really should charge north to the DMZ and inspect the border of the Koreas; it's all the media cares for.

My flight is about to take off. I will join the Prime Minister and a big Australian delegation at the Bo'ao Forum in Hainan. Then Shanghai, Beijing.

Indonesia was a rich experience – the President, the deepening relationship, especially with Marty, seeing the potential successors to Yudhoyono and hearing the lively commentators and think-tankers discuss the 2014 presidential elections at the Ambassador's last night. The joy of being Ministre des Affaires étrangères even in a disintegrating regime about to spill us all into obscurity.

SATURDAY, APRIL 6, 2013
Hainan Province, Bo'ao Forum

Once we'd finally made it to Hainan, it was a further two-and-a-half-hour drive to the conference-centre hotel. This was unbelievable, beyond endurance. We arrived at 11 pm. That means close to twenty-four hours without sleep.

This trip is about the China relationship.

Australia occupies a floor in the hotel, a slightly dank four-star tourist hotel, bristling – we can assume – with hidden listening devices even on the balconies. This morning a briefing with the Prime Minister, the Trade Minister, Craig Emerson, the advisers. And then the Australian delegation meets the International Monetary Fund's Christine Lagarde, this week on the cover of *TIME*.

Lagarde talks. She says the financial crisis in Cyprus shows 'small countries can raise major issues'. Italy struggles with a weak set of leaders. Slovenia could be in trouble next but, unlike Cyprus, is small and self-contained. Meanwhile there can be no reforms – I guess in banking or the IMF itself – until after 'Angela's election'; that is, the German election in September. The good news is the US economy. She sees more of a recovery than six months ago. She says, 'Climate change is regaining ground [after Copenhagen].' Thank God. By the way, my line to Zoellick – that America is one budget deal away from greatness – is now conventional wisdom. She uses it. It is quoted everywhere, generally without attribution.

When I get her to sign my copy of *TIME* – her on the cover – she says that at a Washington dinner party Colin Powell remarked she should have worn make-up for the picture. She *had* been wearing it, of course – nobody would be photographed for a cover or campaign poster without thick, professionally applied layers. Gillard tells her own story. She said this reminded her of a campaign encounter on a wet, windy day when an old constituent looked at her, then at her poster and said, 'That was taken on a good day.'

Later we have meetings with Australian business, the New Zealand Prime Minister, the President of Mexico. The food in the hotel is inedible, laced with the curdling poison of MSG. Fibre and protein are impossible to locate; the musty fitness room – a single cross-trainer – is the least salubrious in any hotel I've ever stayed in.

SUNDAY, APRIL 7, 2013
Hainan Province, Bo'ao Forum

We get up at 5 am so I can do a live interview with *Insiders* at 7 am. I decline flatly to answer three questions on domestic politics – my new policy, to distance myself from the political disaster my colleagues seem intent on inflicting on themselves – and I talk the China relationship, North Korea, Indonesia.

Back at the hotel over breakfast I bump into Peter Costello. 'All Labor can say is 'Don't elect Tony Abbott', but it doesn't work; the electorate has moved beyond that.' I joke that with six months to go our strategy is obviously to repel as many voters as possible – hostile media laws, a new tax on super. 'It's the normal practice to consolidate support before an election. I did it myself. But we're obviously trying something else.'

All Abbott says – needs to say – is, 'Your super is safe with us.' Must be worth an extra five per cent. At least.

At 4 pm we drive to the State Guesthouse for the formal meeting with President Xi Jinping. The Prime Minister moves through the checklist – our commitment to a 'constructive, comprehensive and cooperative' relationship, the new bilateral architecture we seek, the FTA, investment, our interest in human rights, North Korea – pausing after every chunk for the interpreter to translate for the Chinese. Concluding, she uses the words 'our strategic partnership', which is the shorthand description of what they want from us, and what we will agree to in order to get them to give us guaranteed annual leaders' meetings.

We sit across the table, the two teams facing each other. The nine Chinese include my old interlocutor Yang Jiechi, just promoted from Foreign Minister to State Councillor. In May, on my visit as newly minted Foreign Minister, he had lectured me on 'the exclusion of Chinese companies' (code for not letting Huawei supply equipment to the NBN) and on 'strengthening Cold War alliances' (code for rotating US marines through the Northern Territory). Also among the nine Chinese is the new Foreign Minister Wang Yi, who I will sit down with in Beijing.

There is a formal structure and a one-hour time limit. With the slabs of translation, there is absolutely no give and take. No short, sharp exchanges. All is scripted. No spontaneity. The way these things go.

After Gillard speaks Xi responds. He says they are our biggest trading partner, source of tourists, source of tourist revenue. There have been good relations for forty years; we need to 'take our relationship to a new level ... scale a new height ... a new relationship that carries through the traditions that we have ... similar to our relationship with the US and the European Union.'

He says we have to approach human rights 'in a constructive fashion ... based on mutual respect ...' He points to our agreement to have annual meetings but seems to caution that in their system he occupies a position different from the Australian Prime Minister, as President of the Republic and General Secretary of the Communist Party; and that their State Councillor is higher than Foreign Minister (this is not our contention – the Australian Foreign Minister is a senior member of cabinet). Then, back on the world situation, he says they are 'highly concerned' about the situation on the Korean peninsula. He hopes 'all relevant partners will work for peace and stability ... China will continue to work on the parties to have them avoid making extremist remarks ... remain committed to the six party talks process ...'

That's it.

Our Prime Minister thanks him.

We troop from the State Guesthouse, back to the noisome hotel.

We fly out of here on the big VIP jet – the 737 – with the departmental heads, press gallery and ministerial staff who travel with the Prime Minister. To Shanghai overnight.

WEDNESDAY, APRIL 10, 2013
Beijing

Here in Beijing we formally and officially get what we want from the Chinese – a commitment to an annual leaders' meeting; and give them what they want – the term 'strategic partnership' to describe Australia–China relations. My meeting with new Foreign Minister Wang Yi was stress-free. He's new to the job and learning the routine, as I learnt it in my first meetings a year ago. Consult your talking points, move down the list editing as you go, give your interlocutor time to say what he's obliged to say. In this case he started by touching on China's core interests, Tibet and Taiwan. I restated our policy. This is satisfactory to them. My priority is to press the destabilising effect of North Korean bellicosity.

We continue our bilateral over lunch. I diverted to dynastic history – fall of the Ming (1644) the three great Qing emperors (Kangxi, Yongzheng, Qianlong with a combined rule 1661 to 1796). He knows it intimately and we canvass history.

After a pleasant diversion I say, 'We'd better get back to our agenda or our advisers will get restless.' But his response on North Korea was very much party-line. Of course, why would they share any of their intimate dealings with North Korea with me? Or our Prime Minister? These exchanges – these bilaterals between foreign ministers – are full of generalities and happy agreement and cautious fine shadings.

For example, Wang on the strategic partnership we were now committed to:

As strategic partners China and Australia firstly should view each other as constructive partners, not as a threat or as an adversary. Secondly, should respect each other's core interests and key concerns, properly handle differences through dialogue and not engage in military activities directed against the other side. Thirdly, we should jointly champion peace ...

And then I respond thus (I quote from our formal record):

> Senator Carr said he fully supported Minister Wang's views on implementing the Australia–China strategic partnership. In particular Australia hoped to further develop our highly valued cooperation on international issues, including the United Nations Security Council (UNSC) G20, Asia–Pacific Economic Cooperation (APEC) and East Asia Summit (EAS).

At the meeting with President Xi in Bo'ao, headed by the Prime Minister, it had been the same. But here in Beijing at our meeting with new Premier Li, I thought there was just a hint of a reformism path. So, for example, when our Prime Minister made the obligatory, almost ritualistic reference to human rights, he said China had made progress on human rights and – this is the thing – would make more. In the context I thought this encouraging. He might have been dismissive, told us to back off.

Media attitudes to this visit were going to be important.

Our Ambassador Frances Adamson and Richard Maude carefully briefed the media. The journalists liked the briefing from the professionals. 'It wasn't spin,' one said. At the media conference the first question to the Prime Minister was something like, 'How do you explain your triumph?' They asked me one question and I declined. I simply said, 'The Prime Minister said it all.' She deserves to bask. She enjoys so few wins.

Why were the Chinese so open and obliging?

Had they reached the view that the 2500 US marines being deployed in northern Australia was not as big a deal as we and the Americans made it look when announced during Obama's visit back in 2011? Did they note our studious neutrality in the disputes in the East China and South China Sea? Our open door on investment? Our declining to meet the Prime Minister of the Tibetan government-in-exile? Was it part of a charm offensive in Asia?

Then I had my meeting with newly promoted State Councillor Yang Jiechi in the leadership compound at Zhongnanhai. As if to confirm the different atmospheres it was a dramatically different encounter from the one last May when he was Foreign Minister. He started by expressing appreciation of my knowledge of Chinese history and culture, my work on the relationship back when I was State Premier and for my 'cautious' policies on Tibet and Taiwan. 'Cautious'. I like this 'cautious'. It is a fair assessment, an accurate rendition. There were *no* disagreements, he said. I made a point of ramming home Australia's openness on Chinese investment. No proposals rejected since 2007. Big ones approved, like Cubbie Station.

Then there was an absolutely scripted meeting with the Prime Minister, me and Minister for Financial Services Bill Shorten and Chinese and Australian CEOs. This was a very pro-forma set-up. After it, Shorten and I were accommodated in a holding room while the Prime Minister met the leadership of Huawei. Shorten said our meeting had been 'fantastic'. This was a bit rich – it had been formal presentations by both sides, over in under an hour. He emphasised he saw it as 'great experience' or 'great preparation'. That is, for him. For him, as a future Prime Minister.

I didn't respond.

The jejune comment suggested he does not sense how deep the defeat, how hard the haul back, for the first leader in opposition. In any case, we talk as if there is a consensus he will be our next leader.

FRIDAY, APRIL 12, 2013
Singapore

It boils down to this: the Australian dream is good US–China relations. It's the same for Singapore. Our nightmare is some kind of breakdown in this bilateral relationship – China and the US. If this was to happen, a nightmare for us, Singapore, I guess the whole region. The China–US bilateral is the most important one in the world. To us, and the world.

This was the consensus over breakfast at our High Commissioner's in Singapore. I stopped here in Singapore to experience a bit of their hard-headed realism. Tommy Koh, their Ambassador-at-large, made this point. He said that Singapore and Australia should help China to understand the US, to steer them away from misreading the US. As an example, when the Philippines decided on arbitration of their dispute with China over the South China Sea, it was their own initiative. It was done without consulting America. Yet the Chinese see it as part of the wide-ranging American plot to isolate them, to contain them. We had a long discussion about the South China Sea, backwards and forwards. No easy answers. The Chinese case is that they've enjoyed rights in the South China Sea for centuries and that these historic rights prevail over any rights defined by international law. And as Koh pointed out, in the real world the law does not always prevail. Lee Kuan Yew is quoted in the book *Lee Kuan Yew: the Grand Master's Insights on China, the United States, and the World*, edited by Graham Allison, Robert D. Blackwill and Ali Wyne – as saying:

> Peace and security in the Asia–Pacific will turn on whether
> China emerges as a xenophobic, chauvinistic force, bitter
> and hostile to the West because it tried to slow down or abort
> its development, or educated and involved in the ways of

the world, more cosmopolitan, more internationalized and outward-looking.

I had lunch at an old-fashioned Indian curry house with Foreign Minister Shanmugam. We canvassed everything. He was very interested in the cordiality of our reception in China. I talked it up. One objective is to make Singapore understand it doesn't hurt itself in Chinese eyes by getting closer to us, the notable American alliance partner in the region.

We discussed the Malaysian elections. We talked about the attempts by the Canadians to organise a boycott of CHOGM in Sri Lanka. And as in our previous conversation, we discussed the challenges that faced the Chinese.

SATURDAY, APRIL 13, 2013
Singapore to Sydney

Flying Singapore Airlines back to Sydney. 'Why do we always get put at the back of business class?' I asked the attendant, half joking. 'Why do you always deny our request for a window seat?' He locates a volunteer to shift. With sunlight I can read my precious cables. That's my chief pleasure.

From Brussels about next week's trip to Europe, one cable advises:

While our brand recognition is growing in Brussels, we operate in a crowded space, with an audience absorbed by its internal and regional difficulties. Europe does not yet fully comprehend the significance of Asia's rise for its interests.

Our deep integration to the region is our comparative advantage to Brussels.

From Tel Aviv an account of John Kerry's visit to Israel and the Palestinian Territories. But all Israel's officials are downbeat. One in the Prime Minister's office told our post:

> Whenever Israel offered the Palestinians something, it was never enough for them. For example, the Palestinians were currently asking for the release of pre-Oslo Palestinian prisoners, but this was extremely difficult for Israel politically.

The report notes, however, that Israel has currently been quiet on the settlement front. Yet Naftali Bennett's inclusion in the cabinet and Barak's retirement mean the government is *more* right-wing.

It's a mystery to me why Kerry is elevating the Middle East peace process – his third visit; even talking shuttle diplomacy. It's his safety zone, I guess, a familiar landscape. The line from *The West Wing* rings true for me, when Bartlet's staff discussed the pursuit of a comprehensive Middle East peace. One of them warned that the road to a Nobel Prize is the road to noble failure.

Another cable is really gloomy. Lashkar-e-Taiba, the Pakistani terrorist group, is training Rohingya, a Myanmar Islamic minority group, hoping to win them for their anti-Western version of Salafi Islam. No evidence they are making progress but it could destabilise a community, feeding into irregular migration and people-smuggling.

The latest P5+1 (the five permanent members of the Security Council plus Germany) talks with Iran were a flop and Khamenei sees the West as weak and is focused on his country's June presidential election.

MONDAY, APRIL 15, 2013
Sydney

I participate in a National Security Committee meeting of cabinet by video conference from Sydney. We approve a Defence White Paper that contains none of the H. G. Wells science fiction about blockading Chinese ports and shooting off missiles and churning up the seas with state-of-the-art submarines that was in the 2009 document at the insistence of Rudd. Instead it states: 'The Government does not approach China as an adversary.' It uses language I've been using for the better part of a year, like the reference to China translating its economic growth into military power and that this is an unsurprising development. It always happens when nations rise economically. And that the relationship between US and China will determine our strategic environment over coming decades. It reflects the idea, reinforced in Singapore, that our nightmare – Singapore's as well – is a breakdown in the US–China relationship.

Meanwhile Immigration Minister Brendan O'Connor reports that Iran does not accept the return of failed asylum seekers. He reports that members of the Iranian cohort in our detention centres are racist and arrogant and behaving as you'd expect people with military training. Most irregular maritime arrivals are coming from Iran. They might rise to thousands a month. They are not fleeing persecution. They are seeking economic improvement. Understandable that they should do this. But we have a regular immigration program that must be favoured over people-smuggling businesses. Talk about nightmares. How many would we get if there were a real war in the region: a total breakdown in Pakistan or Afghanistan, a US strike on Iran?

FRIDAY, APRIL 19, 2013
Sydney

The *China Daily* suggests that over time it might be possible 'to make Australia the one Western country that is the most friendly to China'. The nationalistic *Global Times* wrote that Australia should 'make clear it would not be a party to any US military build-up ... or partake uncritically in any US-led wars'.

I was in Melbourne for two days. I addressed a lunch of South Asians – that is, Indians, Sri Lankans, Pakistanis – in Rob Mitchell's electorate of McEwen (which we will lose on a swing of 9.1 per cent, that is to say, to be lost) attended a fundraising cabinet dinner at a table hosted by a Chinese–Australian entrepreneur who is opening a chain of stores selling vitamins and food supplements, and the Australian architects he's hired to design them for him. This is, after all, the Asian Century: Chinese–Australians investing here, hiring Australian firms to serve them. This was confirmed the next day when I attended a lunch for Anna Burke in the seat of Chisholm (which we will lose on a swing of 5.8 per cent, that is to say, to be lost). As at the meeting with the South Asians, I warned that Abbott's talk of an Anglosphere would send a message that we weren't taking the Asian Century seriously.

The others ate pork and beef; my advance work had won me fish steamed in ginger. Through the incremental power of such small decisions may we cheat the Angel of Death and secure ourselves one extra year or two to play and work and squabble and fret.

On Wednesday morning, had the awkward, challenging meeting: a breakfast in the boardroom of Arnold Bloch Leibler for thirty or more members of Melbourne's Jewish community.

Mark Leibler runs the lobby and had booked in a meeting the afternoon *before* the breakfast. To prime me? To rehearse me? I didn't know that this would be necessary. But I turned up, with James Larsen, my principal adviser and, as it happens, a former Ambassador to Israel. So we sat down in the Collins Street office of Arnold Bloch Leibler. Mark began by acknowledging my long history of support for Israel but, that out of the way, surprised me with a 'how dare you' tone; as in, 'How dare you put out a statement saying that Australia had chosen not to block enhanced Palestinian status at the UN because of Israeli settlements?' I was nonplussed. It was Israel's aggressive settlement policy that made it – in my view – absolutely untenable to side with them and a handful of other nations and vote down the Palestinian bid. In fact, I couldn't see the point he was making, couldn't understand his objection to me saying we wanted to use our vote to send a message about settlement policy. He astonished me further by taking up the case of Ben Zygier – more of the 'how dare you' tone – the dual Australian–Israeli citizen who had worked as a spy for Mossad and had then been jailed by them. 'This is incredible,' I told Leibler. 'I downplayed the affair as much as possible. Did everything to understate it. The only alternative to my approach would have been a bare-knuckled fight with the Israeli government over how they treated an Australian citizen.'

I was at the point of saying there didn't appear to be much point to our breakfast tomorrow if it was going to be like this. However, he defused things by saying these matters would not be, in fact, raised at the breakfast. He wanted to have the disagreement over now. In a sense, I appreciated the candour of this, and I'm happy he felt he could talk to me with this candour. On the other hand, why can't he and his lobby understand that their aggressive take-no-prisoners approach does their cause immense harm – the way they apparently blocked the slightest criticism of settlement policy through their influence on Gillard's office and the way they blocked me voting with Lebanon against Israel in the dispute over the oil spill, again through their influence on Gillard's office.

This breakfast was going to be tense, my first meeting with the community after the eruption over our vote on Palestinian status. Even the Israeli Ambassador, Yuval Rotem, had warned James that the Melbourne Jewish community were really hard-line. But I began by saying in effect, 'Look, we disagree about settlements ... and about our vote on Palestinian status ... but there's a lot we can talk about.' And when the third or fourth question got off West Bank and Israel–Palestine issues and on to Syria, I knew this was a serious exchange. Mark Leibler's introduction had been a model of impartiality – Carr's been a long-term friend of the Jewish community, he campaigned on Soviet Jewry, we are disappointed by the vote on Palestinian status but we welcome him today etc. All fine. And their tone was sophisticated and civilised. 'They're very smart, this group,' I told Leibler when I took my seat at the end of a question-and-answer session. I told him he had handled this very intelligently. It could have been a sour exchange. But there was, I think, a fair bit of intelligence in the room. As we left his building on Collins Street I said to James, 'My fondness for the Jews resumes all over again.'

Took yesterday off for a bushwalk in the Royal National Park. Windy, with rain threatening, and too cold to go in the water. At Big Marley I just lay in the sun. The wind off the ocean filled my lungs on the walk back to Bundeena. Antidote to the hours of recycled air in the fuselage of 747s and baneful hotel air-conditioning from half-century-old, rat-infested ducts with congealed dust.

From today's *Australian Financial Review*, an indictment of the government I serve in, an account of the growth in public-service employment in Australia since the GFC: since 2008 public servants have increased by 406,000. It makes me toy with the opportunity I missed. Carr as a fiscally conservative – no, just conservative – Labor Prime Minister who might have maintained a dialogue with the Australian people about living within our means, not spending more than what we've got, brave enough to wear the criticism of being a Liberal in Labor clothing. No carbon tax, just an extension of my New South Wales greenhouse gas emissions trading scheme that applied to the power industry but with the opportunity of adding aluminium, steel, transport over time, when it suited us. A more cautious stimulus package. No tax review – I *hate* open-ended reviews – and therefore no sudden unveiling of a mining tax. Instead of Gonski, a package on teacher education. No war with media, no cosiness with unions. Also on the list of things, a tightening of the indefensibly lax guidelines that mean any asylum seeker who arrives here gets to stay, thanks to the courts and the tribunal.

With a bit more deftness in the period after my victory in 2003 I might have managed the planet-alignment needed to leap from Premier into the federal caucus. Except that Mark Latham and Rudd were sitting there and their seething ambitions made the federal caucus a den of treachery and jealous resentment. Walk into that cave and the panthers would have pounced and clawed your throat open.

SATURDAY, APRIL 20, 2013
Etihad: Sydney to London

A brisk dinner last night with Timor-Leste Foreign Minister José Luís Guterres in the Intercontinental. We talked migrant workers; plans for a study of economic connectivity between them, us and Indonesia; their bid for ASEAN membership. This bid is opposed by Singapore. Unlike Rudd, I've never lectured the Singaporeans on the need to let the Timorese in and the Singaporeans appreciate it. After all, it's ASEAN's decision; we're not a member.

Incidentally, my comments in yesterday's *Straits Times* ought to elevate our Singapore relationship:

> Singapore has set out quite self-consciously to make itself an intellectual centre. It aspires to be a brainy nation.
>
> This is the country that set out to give itself centres of expertise in strategic thinking.

The journalist wrote:

> Singapore holds many layers of attraction for Mr Carr. 'The reason I stop over in Singapore as I criss-cross the region is to bring myself up to date and see what the think-tanks are saying, and what my colleague, Foreign Minister Shanmugam, is saying.'
>
> The two men met on Mr Carr's first overseas visit as Foreign Minister in March last year and obviously struck up such a rapport that the veteran Australian politician said: 'I made the point of stopping over, even for four hours, in early December.'

Shanmugam texted me his thanks and I replied he would always buy me with a good curry.

Guterres last night got through our meeting and dinner without raising the nasty simmering dispute between us concerning the validity of the 2006 Treaty on the Timor Sea. They must be ring-fencing it as an exchange between our respective Prime Ministers.

Downstairs outside the hotel Helena was in the car with our luggage. We got to Kingsford Smith and got into our business-class

Etihad seats and I popped two Normison. Woke to watch BBC documentaries on the iPad.

Then the sweetest nostalgic movie about an historical episode. It had a cast of characters I know as well as my own family: *Hyde Park on Hudson*, the Roosevelts and the 1939 visit of George VI and Queen Elizabeth. Oh, Franklin and Eleanor: my dear old friends, soldiers of freedom, on some level my own mother and father, glorious in their flaws and heroic in their instincts for liberty and the anti-Hitler cause. The supporting cast was on screen as well. The President's secretary, Missy LeHand; his mother, Sara Delano Roosevelt; the late-night scene of a president charming and reassuring a stuttering, insecure king – with the war coming, the kingdom never more at risk since the Armada. Comes the heart-wrenching moment when the President in his wheelchair, Eleanor and Sara at his sides, waves goodbye to the young king and queen, standing on the platform at the rear of their train. They're going off to face the catastrophe of World War II. 'Good luck to you!' beams the President. 'All the luck in the world!' What a poignant moment, on the brink of war. Also scenes of family disputes, overheard by servants. Was he simultaneously running real love affairs with secretaries and an old flame? He was a normal, hard-wired human, and – Gore Vidal told me the President's son had told him – sexually active despite the polio.

The greatest President after Lincoln. In 1973 I remembered being so saturated with FDR stories as a result of reading two books on him simultaneously that I dreamt he came to our flat in French Street and Helena and I straightened the blanket over his legs as he sat in his wheelchair.

SUNDAY, APRIL 21, 2013
Luxembourg

Bertrand Russell wrote about the difficulty of absorbing the inhumanity of our species. Mitterrand said '*indifférence*' was the most important quality in a political leader.

Horror upon horror. This was a small meeting in the Château de Senningen in Luxembourg, ten foreign ministers plus representatives of UN agencies and we were devoting ourselves to the humanitarian consequences of the civil war in Syria. The worst statistic: at the present rate of displacement there will be nine million people out of a population of twenty-two million by the end of the year who will have had their homes destroyed. And here is another statistic so dire I had to ask the head of the EU's humanitarian agency to confirm it for me: at the present rate of refugee flow, Lebanon will host a refugee population equivalent to thirty per cent of its own population, Jordan twenty-eight per cent; both governments will totter as a result, the Jordanians especially vulnerable. We're looking at a proxy war between Shi'a and Sunni with implications for the whole region. Or, seeing it yet another way, we're looking at a government with a Warsaw-Pact style army setting about demolishing the housing stock of its people by aerial and artillery bombardment. Certainly that's how an observer from Mars would be justified in seeing this conflict.

Here's a grotesque tragedy for the Palestinians, the lost people of the Middle East. Syria is the third-largest host country for them after Iraq and Pakistan. It has a population of 520,000 Palestinians. Someone said that there were reports of Palestinians being forced off buses and out of food queues. Two Palestinians were found hanged in a refugee camp in Syria after a sharia trial.

Meanwhile trucks with medical equipment and supplies are

looted by representatives of the Assad government when they head to rebel-held territory.

I was the first Foreign Minister to speak and argued strongly for a special plan to protect medical supplies, medical personnel and the status of hospitals. I was heartened that the Australian plan for a medical pact – that I had been pushing for months – was widely known and acknowledged. I said we faced a deadlock over attempts to get a ceasefire and attempts to get a political transition plan. Surely the UN can salvage something out of this – 'a bare-bones deal to get medical personnel and supplies into the country'. The Swedish Foreign Minister Carl Bildt came in strongly and said the UN should go to see Assad and argue for something like this.

On Monday we drove to Brussels. A NATO meeting on Afghanistan and meetings by me with EU officials.

TUESDAY, APRIL 23 – WEDNESDAY, APRIL 24, 2013
Brussels

Because my thoughts keep turning to Asian policy, I quizzed Duncan Lewis about Indonesia. He's our former head of the Department of Defence, now Ambassador to Belgium, the EU and NATO, based in Brussels. As a lieutenant he'd studied in a Yogyakarta military academy with Yudhoyono and Prabowo. He spent a year studying Indonesian. He's been back there many times. He claims there is a Javanese world view that is as distinct as China's concept of the Middle Kingdom. To some extent an Indonesian president assumes the mantle of Javanese king. If there's a paranoia at work in their politics it's about the centrifugal forces, the satellite states at the extremes of their empire: Aceh, Sulawesi, Papua. Their strategic concerns are the role of China and the existence of radical Islam, especially in eastern and central Java. Four hundred years of Dutch occupation exposed them to the West. The appeal of the Non-Aligned Movement is now fading, as reflected in the fact that they are not as sensitive to the US presence in Asia as Malaysia, for example. In short, they are inclined to tolerate the US in the region. They want to secure foreign direct investment as the key to maintaining six per cent per annum economic growth. One of their big assets is their young population.

And they don't look south, don't dilate on us.

Brussels is much ritual and some substance. This afternoon the meeting on Afghanistan comprised over fifty representatives sitting around a glass table, barely able to see the furthest ends. Platoons of advisers sit behind. We all get to give three-minute speeches that all say the same thing. We hear from John Kerry, NATO head Anders Rasmussen, Afghan Foreign Minister Rassoul and ISAF Commander Joseph Dunford. Then I get to say:

Australia remains committed to the transition process as agreed by our Leaders in 2010, and reaffirmed last year at Chicago …

We look forward to continuing to work closely with partner nations and the Afghan government in guiding the Council's work on this important element of the UNSC agenda.

…The next 12 months will be crucial as the Afghan government prepares for the presidential elections, works to manage the economic impact of transition, and continues to implement reforms agreed with donors at Tokyo.

We look forward to working with the government as it
leads the way to credible and inclusive elections, which
are accepted by the Afghan people, and as it continues its
progress to fight corruption, strengthen human rights, and
build the capacity of state institutions ...

Transitions are hard. There is much work to be done. The
insurgency remains tenacious, and big efforts will be needed
to train a sustainable ANSF and strengthen capacity and
governance ...

We remain resolute.

The lights have been switched on in Afghanistan. They will
not be switched off. The country will not go back to what it
was in 2001.

The Afghan people themselves, who have suffered so greatly,
have the desire and the capacity for a strong sovereign
democratic state.

That's all. No interchange and no questions. It's done. All ritual.
As for substance ...

I sit down in a room and get to meet for the first time Foreign Minister Sergey Lavrov of the Russian Federation. I tell him
I want to elevate the relationship, and my proposal to do so in
cabinet (this notwithstanding all the advice that Russia has very
little interest in us and there is effectively no common ground).

He raises a complaint about the difficulty they've had getting
visa access for people to work on their embassy in Australia. I
groan at getting another complaint about Australian visas and in
all naïvety promise to look into it (after he leaves I get advice and
understand completely).

Then I raise Syria and say that Australia wanted to separate humanitarian issues from the political struggle and ensure that, as per international law, medical supplies reached the sick, and medical professionals and hospitals were protected. I cited an example from Aleppo, where one side shot dead a doctor and nurses treating the wounded from the conflict. All nations should be able to agree to enforce the protection of medical workers.

Lavrov's reply is instructive. He said this issue had been discussed for a number of months. Consistent with the principle of protecting medical workers, Russia supported OCHA in its dealings with the Syrian government. The problem was that the attitude of the opponents could not be guaranteed. The opposition was highly fragmented. Parts of the Free Syrian Army were not under a unified command; for example, the terrorist groups Al-Nusra and the Islamic Caliphate of Iraq. He said there was no way to get these groups to respect the protection of medical professionals. I replied saying there was a burden on the Europeans and the US to enforce these principles where they had influence. There were now thirty-six doctors in Aleppo, whereas previously there were thousands. Lavrov said the reason for the problem was that the removal of Assad had been made a priority. Instead of a humanitarian priority, many in the international community were focused on a geostrategic objective. This would cost lives. The international community needed to unite in its efforts to stop the conflict and arrange talks that included the government, which Russia supported. He said if all the countries that had met in Geneva last June followed their conclusions and pressured their clients on the ground to do likewise, then there would have been a change on the ground by now.

He added that Russia did not accept any no-fly zones or humanitarian corridors because these amounted to interventions. International law required international humanitarian support to be administered with the consent of the authorities on the ground.

This pre-condition was not filled. He said the international community should fight the root causes, not the symptoms. This was a war of ethnic and sectarian cleansing. Two Christian priests had just been killed. The opposition had mutilated the corpses of dead government soldiers. I remember Kissinger's advice that there's no point to be gained demonising the Russian position. And there's a strong internal logic in it. And they are right about some of the forces lined up against Assad.

We catch the TGV to Paris on April 23.

Next day at the Quay d'Orsai, once again the troop of guards at either side of the steps, the red carpet, the urbane Foreign Minister waiting to greet me. This time, as we've spoken before, I have a relaxed meeting with Laurent Fabius where we tick off the issues: Syria, Iran and then China, ahead of Fabius and Hollande's visit there.

Then to the station and the TGV to Amiens. Time to look at the cathedral before a bad dinner – a really bad dinner – at a seafood restaurant and an early night before a 3.30 am start to the day.

THURSDAY, APRIL 25, 2013 (ANZAC DAY)
Amiens, Villers-Bretonneux

I've got a fine speech from Freudenberg. The sterling Labor wordsmith, the master of rhythm, linkage, pace and romantic historic reference. His words are perfect for this occasion, delivered by me – if I say so myself – in a slow, deliberate tone, no, say it, a masterly tone, the baritone burnished to bass by sleep deprivation, before the white stone of the War Memorial at Villers-Bretonneaux at 5.30 am, chilly enough for an overcoat and with the dawn just creeping into the sky. An estimated 4000 Australians and our French comrades, including the Minister for Veterans Affairs Kader Arif, are here.

I send Graham's words airborne to the audience in the crisp morning air:

> Through [the Anzacs'] eyes and words, we may see the
> deeper meaning of the Australian idea that our national
> identity was forged in the battlefields of Gallipoli and France.
>
> Not only by their prowess and bravery, but by the immensity
> of the human tragedy called the First World War.
>
> The seminal catastrophe of our civilisation.
>
> How could they not be changed in the crucible?
>
> How could their young nation not be changed with them and
> by them?
>
> Australia would never again be able to isolate itself from the
> rest of the world.
>
> The most heartfelt of the inscriptions on our war memorials
> is 'Lest we forget'.
>
> The English poem 'Recessional', from which it is taken, is
> more than a call to the duty of remembrance.
>
> It is also a warning against the arrogance of power.
>
> Today, we bear in our hearts and minds both meanings,
> in this consecrated ground amidst the peace and beauty of

France, when we say: 'Lest we forget.'

Then a stand-up breakfast with the local mayor. Ravenously hungry – I had only wolfed down berries at the hotel in Amiens as we struggled out with our bags at 4.30 am – I slapped some butter on a baguette and speared some delicious ham, washed it down with criminally bad coffee. Then we did functions non-stop, concluding with a long service standing up in baking springtime heat at the village of Bullecourt and then a repeat a few feet away before a statue of an Australian digger. The same reading of the ode, speeches, national anthems, the full works duplicated within spitting distance of the earlier service for the same audience with the same participants. Not entirely sure what our embassy had in mind. Sleep deprived on top of jetlag, on top of standing-in-the-heat exhaustion, we drive to the station in Lille and catch the train to London.

SUNDAY, APRIL 28, 2013
London

Staying with Mike Rann at Stoke Lodge. Friday was devoted to the meeting of nine Commonwealth foreign ministers in Marlborough House, the headquarters of the Commonwealth. A breezy spring day outside and before the Commonwealth meeting starts I get to know the new Foreign Minister for Vanuatu, Edward Natapei. He's very strong in his criticism of Bainimarama's Fiji regime.

The Commonwealth agenda is basically agreed but Canadian John Baird delivers an attack on the government of Sri Lanka and suggests we should not be having our CHOGM meeting there in

November. This is his oft-stated position and we have agreed to disagree, which I now do. I say the country's been through three decades of civil war and has been traumatised by that experience. And there was support for a decisive ending of the war, which was no doubt accompanied by atrocities as was every stage of this 35-year-long conflict. It was a terrorist insurgency against the government. It was targeted at women and children and religious monuments and invented suicide bombing. It's not just the Tamil narrative, I point out. I say Australia will continue to raise human-rights issues but we will do it by engagement with them, not by isolating them.

I remain good friends with John Baird but we can't go along with the Canadian line, and no one else around the table agrees with him. Indeed, outside, one of the Caribbean High Commissioners says to me, 'It's an honour to be at a meeting with a man like you.' And Dipu Moni, the Foreign Minister of Bangladesh, who is chairing the meeting, and Secretary-General of the Commonwealth Kamalesh Sharma insist on me being present at the table of a media conference so I can handle some of the expected questions on the subject. Which I do.

Helena and I drive down to Chevening to have dinner with William and Ffion Hague and John Baird. It's an early seventeenth-century mansion, gifted to the UK, now granted to ministers by the Prime Minister. The Hagues share access to it with the Cleggs. So after Baird, Hague and I conduct our trilateral we have dinner at a table where British aristocracy had talked about the outcome of the Seven Years War in 1763 – which helped create Baird's Canada, as it happens. Their portraits look down on us from the wood-panelled walls.

The foyer is decorated with the pistols, rifles and armour of an entire regiment, surrendered in the 1720s. 'Looks like the proceeds of one of my gun-buyback schemes,' I declare. After breakfast we drive with Baird to Chartwell, where Randolph Churchill,

Winston Churchill's great-grandson, shows us around. Then leaving Baird, who is heading to Heathrow and back to Canada, we make the statutory trip to Stratford to see an unglamorous production of *Hamlet*, which works pretty well.

This morning, walking the streets of Stratford, I have a conversation with the Prime Minister on the phone. I tell her time has run out on her notion, which we have discussed, of appointing a former cabinet colleague as Ambassador to Turkey. In other circumstances, it might have been okay but this is too close to the election; the opposition would say they'd recall the person; it would give them a head of steam. It simply can't be done. It's the first time, apart from the climactic fight over Palestinian status, that I've had to press on her such firm advice. I think she'll take it. I still wish I'd had the chance to do it about media reforms.

Sunday afternoon we see *This House* – a play about the minority Labour government preceding Thatcher's Conservatives – and have a curry with the Ranns, Ros Kelly and David Morgan.

MONDAY, APRIL 29, 2013
London

When I was a kid growing up in Maroubra we had a great-aunt – a spinster, sister of my mother's mother – who lived with us and worked as a cleaner at the Prince of Wales Hospital. She had a little room in the filled-in verandah and had plastered it with photos – quite nutty by the standards of our age – of the royal family: the Queen and the Duke and the little Prince and his sister. This was the early '50s. It must have been this aunt who gave me a coronation book in 1953, which had pop-up models of royal carriages.

I grew up knowing that Prince Charles, the heir to the throne, was a contemporary of mine. I was to meet him in Sydney twice. On his visit on Australia Day 1994, a man dashed at him from the crowd. The then-Premier John Fahey tackled the potential assassin, who turned out to be unarmed and just mentally disturbed. John's quick response made the front pages the next day, adding to his lustre for winning the Olympic bid and saving Sydney from December bushfires. The day after this I sat gloomily in my office staring at the headlines. Bruce Hawker, my chief of staff, walked in and said apropos of Fahey's glorious publicity, 'Take it from me as a gambler. No run of luck lasts forever.'

Mike Rann and I drove to Highgrove, the Prince's home since 1980, through a gracious Gloucestershire town of honey-coloured stone, out of Janes Austen. The entrance – with a sign reading 'GM free' – took us through a working farmyard. The road circles to the façade of a three-storey house with big bay windows and cream-coloured pilasters. Prince Charles, ruddy-faced in a double-breasted suit with pocket handkerchief – blue striped shirt and tightly pulled striped tie – is waiting on the steps to greet us. Like Obama, Petraeus and Kerry (and his father, the Duke) he belongs to the elite of the flat-stomached: men who've looked at the prospect of swelling belly fat and settled on strategies to stay slim. The intimate room we sit down in is an apotheosis of interior design: flowers, plants, cameos, paintings, framed photos. We enter a conversation that covers climate change and our encounters with the deniers, my creation of 350 new national parks in New South Wales, some quirky matter about the succession law in Australia that I had not followed, John Kerry's interest in ocean environments ('He's a good man') and the Joyce case in the UAE (Joyce is an old boy of Charles's school in Australia, Geelong Grammar, and the Prince has been recruited to make representations to the UAE about it). I said we favoured CHOGM going ahead in Colombo, engagement being the better way of dealing with the Rajapaksas. The three of us talk, sitting on low sofas facing one another across a low coffee table with old books and an old illustrated *London News* with a cover story about royal activities from the 1940s. For a second, Camilla's blonde hair appears at the window, peering in, then vanishes. She is returning from a morning walk in galoshes. As he sees us out, after about forty-five minutes – he's off to Holland for a coronation – we talk Wagner ('Oh, *you're* a fan!') and he suggests I come to a fundraising concert for the Philharmonia Orchestra in Buckingham Palace in November. 'But we might ask you to bring a corporate representative to make a donation,' he suggests, slightly stooped, in his self-deprecating and gently ironic style. I congratulate him on his support for the Royal Opera and the Royal Shakespeare Company, those icons. On the way out, Mike tells me, his private secretary says that I should keep in touch.

I think back to those days in Robey Street, Maroubra, and Auntie's pasted-up photos of the little Prince as a toddler holding the hand of his sister, probably in the garden at Windsor or a railway station, waiting for Mother to return from a tour. Sixty years later – sixty – both of us were meeting to talk about our battered planet. A sort of closing of a circle. History teases us.

Mike said in a meeting with the Queen, she had referred to the abdication in Holland, an old queen making way, and said, 'It's not something we do here.'

More's the pity. Think on it, Ma'am, think on it.

Charles would be a good monarch. My republicanism wobbles. Who would we elect in his place? A general? A tennis star?

TUESDAY, APRIL 30, 2013
Etihad: London to Sydney

From David Shambaugh's *China Goes Global*:

> ...China is *present* and *active* in various parts of the globe and
> in various functional spheres – but is not (yet) *influencing* or
> shaping actors or events in various parts of the world.

(My emphases.)

He argues China punches 'well *below* its weight'.

On this leg I watch *The Wind That Shakes the Barley*, a drama set in the time of the Black and Tans, the Anglo-Irish Treaty of 1921 and the civil war between pro-treaty and anti-treaty forces. After an endless flight – longer than sorrow – we get home in the early evening. I fling open the balcony doors; fresh air blows in, flavoured with Maroubra surf.

SUNDAY, MAY 5, 2013
Sydney

Home for two days, then flew up to Port Moresby on Friday to do a fundraising dinner for the Burnet Institute to raise money for maternal and child health. A PNG woman is eighty times more likely to die during childbirth than an Australian woman, and for largely avoidable reasons including haemorrhage, sepsis and obstructed labour. In PNG, one in five children won't reach their fifth birthday. But there is hope. In 1990, the mortality rate for children under five in developing countries was ninety-seven deaths per 1000 births. Today it's down to sixty-three deaths per 1000 births. That's a thirty-five per cent reduction in thirty years.

The trip was an opportunity to talk to Foreign Minister Rimbink Pato, Planning Minister Charles Abel and the Prime Minister Peter O'Neill, each of them giving priority to getting more infrastructure through Australian aid. Big road projects, a new hospital, a court complex. This is fine, I tell them, but there is 'an opportunity cost'. Neither of us wants it hung round our neck that we've reduced funding for AIDS or maternal health or textbooks in schools. I hope I clarified this choice for them. Prime Minister Gillard will be going there next week.

A cable from one of our posts quoting the views of a prominent American presenting a picture of Kerry's recent visit to Asia: 'A deal less successful than Kerry evaluated himself.' There had been no 'breakthrough' in shifting Chinese attitudes on North Korea. China's pressure on North Korea was still in the range of 'normal quiet inducements and subtle pressures rather than any forcefulness'. Kerry had been reluctant to press home policy points and confined himself to asking questions. In China there seems to be a view that 'the pivot is over', shown by Kerry being critical of Japan and fairly soft on requirements on North Korea. The source said the Secretary of State's style was 'senatorial', preferring to question rather than issue direct statements. The source expected him to quickly come up to speed in gaining confidence. On the new Chinese leadership the source has formed the view that the coming man in foreign policy is Wang Huning, who has not yet got a portfolio. Gossip has him as the man with Xi's ear and the new State Councillor Yang – my friend – has an awkward relationship with Xi, who saw Yang as forced on him by his predecessor. This could now put three layers on foreign-policy advice.

The source said that Japan was now very hard-line on China and believed that if they took the hardest line, China would eventually back off. Finance Minister Taro Aso was particularly virulent. He even argues at length about World War II history, in which he believes Japan was the victim, not the aggressor. He told our source he was tired of Chinese complaints about the Senkakus.

Flying back from PNG I watched Helen Mirren in Shakespeare's *Cymbeline* on the BBC iPlayer app, the first time I've seen the play in full after seeing a bit of it six months ago. In London I bought a DVD of the Globe's production of *Henry VIII*. When we see that it means I can say I've seen all thirty-nine. Nobody else on the planet can.

WEDNESDAY, MAY 8, 2013
Sydney

Giulio Andreotti died on Monday, seven-time Prime Minister of Italy, known as Beelzebub and Il Diavolo, who I got to know through the eerie 2008 movie *Il Divo*. The Papal Nuncio in Australia said he remembered vividly a conversation with Andreotti at a dinner in Havana and it was mesmerising. Kissinger told me he found him frail, small, unprepossessing; hardly what you expect in the titan of Italian cabinetmaking and factional politics, the 'spider figure' at the heart of the Italian state.

Andreotti once said, 'If you think ill of others you commit a sin. But you often get it right.' I savoured the fact that he collected all his theatre programs and in his disgrace over alleged Mafia links lamented, more than anything, being removed as the head of the Ciceronian Society. The movie showed him as a daily communicant, rising at 4.30 am and making his way through the dark Rome streets surrounded by twenty bodyguards to say

confession. In church his mentor De Gasperi had sat silent, pray-
ing. But Andreotti talked to clerics. 'Priests vote,' he said. 'God
doesn't.' He was a great survivor, living with cataclysmic migraine
attacks, cultured but with mobster links and who might ultimately
warrant Napoleon's description of Talleyrand, *'une merde dans un
bas de soie'*. Which means 'a shit in a silk stocking'. His abandon-
ment of colleague Aldo Moro to the Red Brigade killers certainly
met François Mitterrand's requirement for political leadership:
indifférence.

Mitterrand. He also once intrigued me, charmed me from
a distance. When I led the opposition in New South Wales I
savoured stories of his arid, lonely years in opposition. After an
overnight trip on a train he might arrive at a town in regional
France, with a change of shirt in his briefcase, to greet a handful of
Socialist Party locals, just as I flew around to meet country branch
members across New South Wales. Once a year he would travel
to have dinner with a railway worker with whom he had served in
the Resistance. He might visit a gallery to view a single painting.
He could list all the kings of France, knew all its literature and
spoke a classic French, or so a Socialist Party insider once told me,
talking in their headquarters in the Rue de Solférino. No matter
what region of France he visited, this admirer said, Mitterrand
knew the precise thing to order on the menu. Mitterrand told Elie
Wiesel that *The Brothers Karamazov* was the greatest novel ever
written. When I met the Archbishop of Paris he told me Mitterrand's knowledge of the Bible was deeper even than his. The prize
he won was the richest elective politics offers: fourteen years in the
Élysée, 1981 to 1995. Not even 1600 Pennsylvania Avenue beats
that.

Thus his portrait hung in my office when I was Opposition
Leader. Then one day I read about his long-term friendship with
René Bousquet, a shadowy Parisian banker who had been Vichy
police chief in Paris. Bousquet was thus the organising force of the

notorious round-up of Jews in mid-1942 that filled the Velodrome and Drancy with men, women and children marched from their homes by French police, not Germans. He was responsible for the picture of the kindergarten toddlers walking, guarded by French police, to Le Bourget railway station. Mitterrand had kept him as a friend. Money may have figured.

The Mitterrand portrait was consigned to my wastepaper basket. Shit in a silk stocking, I thought, looking at an erstwhile friend.

THURSDAY, MAY 9, 2013
Adelaide

The UK has confirmed it will attend CHOGM in Colombo in November. One of the reasons is the trilateral discussion with me and the Canadian Foreign Minister in Chevening, where I'd argued as forcefully as I could against accepting uncritically the Tamil narrative and in favour of the notion that we'll do more for human rights in Sri Lanka by engaging, as opposed to isolating, Sri Lanka. This comes on top of another success (precious few in this business), which was the European Union deciding to lift its sanctions on Myanmar. I had raised this with every EU Foreign Minister I had met and with Cathy Ashton, the EU High Representative for Foreign Affairs and Security Policy. And I did it at the request of our friends in the Myanmar government who thought investment in mining and manufacturing would not flow their way while the sanctions were simply in a state of suspension.

I wish I could point to a comparable breakthrough in my plan to get a medical pact for the desperate people of Syria. This side of the business is so hard. Talk about slow boring through hard boards.

Wayne Swan told me the fiscal situation is ruinous. The high dollar has wiped out company profits. On the plane back from Brisbane on Tuesday I sat next to a CEO who told me some think if European troubles worsen it could go higher. 'How much higher?' I asked. 'Oh, $1.50,' he said. Federal government revenues have collapsed. We're being swamped with asylum seekers and each of them costs $100,000 a year, another hit on the budget. Swan's urging me to drive my department to come up with diplomatic interventions to stop this flow – 6000 last month dumped here by people smugglers from Afghanistan and Iran which, unlike Sri Lanka (as a result of my diplomacy) will not accept returnees. So the government struggles with problems beyond its capacity to solve: a stratospheric Australian dollar that could go even higher because Australian bonds are among the few in the world to be AAA-rated and the inability of Australia to turn back asylum seekers. The government is being dragged under by forces beyond its control, and has few political skills and no public goodwill.

Nonetheless, I dashed down to Adelaide today to perform for Steve Georganas, Member for Hindmarsh, at a pleasant community gathering on foreign aid. I love the aid lobby. They'll be bitterly let down in next week's budget but the truth is you can't run aid on borrowings. Georganas will lose his seat on a 6.1 per cent swing, which is to say, he will lose it. Another poor bastard about to be swept into oblivion.

Later today on a street corner in Sydney I bumped into Martin Ferguson. He said his backing for Rudd – he left the cabinet when the Rudd leadership challenge petered out – was all about saving the furniture so that the next generation on the Labor frontbench might get back into office sooner than otherwise. 'I wanted to see the Bowens and the Clares saved,' he said. He suggested he would not be recontesting his seat but making way for someone younger.

He also said there could still be a change in leadership. This, I know, is *not* Dastyari's view.

Helena has prepared grilled salmon and piles of vegetables; we watched the 1968 cult classic *The Swimmer*, based on a John Cheever story. At 9.30 pm I put on a meditation tape and fell sleep sitting up.

SUNDAY, MAY 12, 2013
Sydney

In the car returning from Swan Island to Melbourne Airport, a discussion with senior people about Afghanistan. They agree that, after twelve years, the whole war has been a waste. The Taliban is laughing. Said one of them, who has been there twice a year over the last ten, 'We spent a billion dollars in Uruzgan province. It has a population of just over 300,000. We could have achieved the same result if I'd been sent up there with $10 million to distribute bribes.' They agree that after September 11 we could have had a special forces intervention to take out al-Qaeda. Instead it became a huge, expensive exercise in counterinsurgency and nation-building.

Shakespeare, from *Troilus and Cressida*, on the Trojan War: the whole thing was 'a cuckold and a whore'. Huge armies mobilised, the largest coalition in history for ... nothing.

It does not bear thinking about.

TUESDAY, MAY 14, 2013 (BUDGET DAY)
Canberra

I sat yesterday in what must be the last caucus before the election.

The Prime Minister gives one of her neat, compact reports – mainly about deals with the states on disability – that would suggest things going swimmingly for a government headed to an orderly re-election. But there's no dash or authority, none in Wayne Swan's preview of the budget either. Lower House MPs must be looking around the room thinking this place will be cleaned out, half of 'the colleagues' gone from the next parliament, they themselves. I haven't even gotten to learn their names.

Richard Marles, sitting by my side, says he thinks he will hang on. John Murphy, in the row in front of me, talks about his Tamil community in Reid but he's gone on a swing of 2.7 per cent, which is to say he's gone – Tamil support or not. John Faulkner says the meeting is like a mausoleum but not to quote him because he plans to use it in his book.

In caucus I get a couple of questions on the aid budget but while we've delayed by another year reaching the target of 0.5 per cent of GNI, Swan has capped the spending of aid money on onshore asylum seekers – something sought by aid advocates, and increased aid spending by 9.6 per cent. There's big support for aid in the caucus and he would have risked a Ruddite revolt otherwise.

Dastyari told me another challenge is not on, although Kurt Campbell, the just-retired US Assistant Secretary of State, talking on the phone, told me he sat with Rudd for three hours in Beijing and he said he would strike before September. Dastyari confirms there are double-digit swings in western Sydney.

Meanwhile, some advice about China from Singapore think-tankers, this from a cable out of our High Commission.

Assertive actions by China in the sea get praised inside China but concessionary ones do not. Nationalism rings strong. China's Central Committee had never succeeded in coordinating all the agencies (navy, coast guard, fishing vessels) active in the area. A lot we see reflects 'bureaucratic politics' and the ill functioning of the Chinese system as well as 'an underlying, untutored, nationalist sentiment'. They were not the result of centrally coordinated policy-making. For example, the Hainan declaration on maritime administration last year had to be submitted for provincial government approval. The provincial representative of the Ministry of Foreign Affairs was supposed to be present but missed the meeting and his deputy attended and let the declaration through. The controversial passports showing the famous nine-dash line – the line on the map asserting Chinese sovereignty over the sea – were no longer being issued in China and the person responsible for the decision to issue the passports in the first place had apparently been sacked.

The source says China is aware that if it roughs up Vietnam or the Philippines it will worsen relations across the whole region. It would drive the ten ASEAN members closer to the US.

I am writing this during Senate Question Time. Today a boat with asylum seekers has docked on Croker Islands, a reminder that boat arrivals are soaring, and a reminder of the cost of them to the budget as well.

WEDNESDAY, MAY 15, 2013
Canberra

I attend Senate tactics at 8.30 am, the Senate caucus at 9 am, Question Time at 2 pm where the opposition leads with the government's failure to control boats or the deficit. As with Monday's caucus, the atmosphere is weirdly subdued. Walking down the corridor I comment on this to Gary Gray, who will lose Brand on a swing of 3.3 per cent. 'It's gallows humour,' he says, but that's not quite right. It's fatalism.

Yesterday, Budget Day, ended with the regular ALP budget-night fundraiser in the Great Hall. Bill Shorten introduced the Prime Minister, who spoke briefly in her monotone before handing to an exhausted Wayne Swan. The tone was flat, suburban, worn out. It's sad; no authority or flair. Nothing memorable, nothing with spark. We used to be the interesting party. It was so depressing, I ate half the cheesecake dessert.

Today I use my time to brief myself on Asia: a farewell call from retiring Korean Ambassador Taeyong Cho; a visit from Jeff Bleich, the US Ambassador; George Yeo, the former Singaporean Foreign Minister; Wahidullah Shahrani, the Afghan Mines Minister. I devour cables on Myanmar and Bangladesh and plan visits to both countries, plus the Philippines and Brunei, maybe China.

Dinner tonight with the Arab heads of mission. The life I wanted, the life I lose in four months.

SUNDAY, MAY 19, 2013
Abu Dhabi

The headline in *The National*, the local English-language paper: 'Iraq on the brink as sectarian violence grows'.

The story reports 130 dead in three days in the Shi'a–Sunni violence.

Last night I took to dinner in our hotel the 24-year-old son of murdered Pakistani Prime Minister Benazir Bhutto. He – Bilawal – is chairman of the Pakistan People's Party, a softly spoken graduate from Oxford in politics and history, accompanied by his Ambassador. He had campaigned in their recent elections from here, Abu Dhabi, aware he'd be murdered by the Taliban if he did rallies at home. Then today we woke up to news of one of Imran Khan's MPs killed, shot dead overnight. How can Pakistan survive as a democracy when secular politicians are shot or bombed? Routinely. Meanwhile, Syria bleeds and may spill Shi'a–Sunni warfare into its two fragile neighbours, Lebanon and Jordan.

Today the UAE Foreign Minister, Sheikh Abdullah, talked Egypt and said that not just a military coup but outright civil war is an option in the country. Of course, the UAE disdains the Muslim Brotherhood. He is pessimistic about Libya too. He said the June elections in Iran are irrelevant because the President is a mouthpiece for Supreme Leader Khamenei. 'He is like "the spokesperson" for your government,' he said. He said as the Iranians see it, 'There is an Orthodox bomb, a Protestant bomb, a Hindu bomb, a Buddhist bomb and a Sunni bomb. They believe there needs to be a Shi'a bomb.' But he added he would rather see half the UAE destroyed than have Iran get nuclear weapons.

Again I press the Joyce–Lee consular case. Gone on too long. Bad procedures. The Victorian Supreme Court decision. Suffering of families. He says it's in their judicial system. Will look at it again. The UAE is a bastion of tolerant Islam and elevates women. Abdullah even expatiated to me on the plight of Christians in Egypt, a favourite theme of mine. As Platonic categories are concerned, it's an aristocracy, I guess. The UAE does not 'do' democratic politics. In the Arab world today that's still better than anything else on offer.

Abdullah invites me to his desert retreat in November. But I may not be minister then, I tell him. 'But I hear you'd have a chance of winning if you changed leaders,' he said. 'Yes. But our mate Kevin made himself somewhat disliked by colleagues,' I reply. He knows Kevin. He laughs.

Off to Qatar.

MONDAY, MAY 20, 2013
Doha

News from North East Asia: the DPRK has not tested its ballistic missile, thus ending 'its escalation cycle' at least for now. Chinese pressure? Promise of engagement? Budgetary difficulties?

Last week I read a cable reporting the Indonesian Foreign Minister, Marty Natalegawa, was castigating the UK Ambassador in Jakarta because a West Papuan group had opened an office in Oxford. It had nothing to do with the British government, of course. These provocateurs, who encourage Papuans to put their lives on the line while they are safe working in universities in the West, will likely think of hanging up a shingle somewhere in Australia. Coincidentally, DLP Senator John Madigan asked me a question in parliament on Thursday filled with shock-horror allegations about Indonesian management of the two Papuan provinces. I rebutted these urban myths. Like, for example, a story that Australia had provided C-130s that were transporting youngsters from Papua to elsewhere in Indonesia to be inculcated in Islam. And again I put on the record that Australia and the whole world recognised Indonesian sovereignty over West Papua.

But I want to anticipate a provocateur opening an office here and, if one does, see that it doesn't become a barrier in the Australian–Indonesian relationship. I rang Marty, who was in Washington, and told him we should not be captured by provocateurs and we've got to start thinking about them opening an office on Australian soil because – and this was the essence of the message – there was no way the Australian government could stop it. I also recommended he look at my answer in the Senate and said our embassy would get it to him. 'One option for you, if this does happen,' I told him, 'might be to say that the Australian Foreign Minister has already spelled out it has nothing to do with Papuan secessionism.' He absorbed this and said he'd still prefer us not to allow an office to open. I hope I have averted something.

THURSDAY, MAY 23, 2013
Beirut

Our Ambassador had planned a trip to Tripoli and north to El Minieh. But there is fighting between Alawites and Sunnis in Tripoli so we abandoned the coastal option and drove up the Bekaa Valley instead, a Shi'a heartland run by Hezbollah. I looked at the non-descript housing and the refugee settlements. I thought about how wondrous this valley would have been in Roman times, at peace with travellers moving north and south from the great city of Baalbek, with its towering temple complex, through a land full of crops, a granary of the Roman Empire. History doesn't record progress; Hadrian or Marcus Aurelius would have found our world hideous. Apart from motor vehicles and planes and anaesthetics, little sign of 2000 years of human progress, little elevated beyond their own second-century strivings and achievements.

On the Zahle highway we visit an encampment of eighty Syrian families living in wooden frame huts with cloth or canvas walls, squatting inside on rugs or mattresses. The kids play in the dirt and miss school; the men wait at the crossroads to be picked up for day labour for 10,000 Lebanese pounds or six Australian dollars a day.

I thought of the deformity of an Arab model of dictatorship for life, crumbling after decades. There's also the smouldering war – inexplicable to us – of Sunni and Shi'a, these confessional hatreds challenging the post-Ottoman nation states. There's the intrusion of family, clan, sect.

Unleashed, these forces are pushing people over the borders. The women I met in Baalbek who entered Lebanon this morning, fleeing the fighting in Qusayr between the FSA and al-Nusra and, on the other side, the Assad forces and Hezbollah. One woman in a hijab wailed at me, 'They call themselves Party of God. But God will take his revenge on them.' She said world war was preferable to what she had gone through.

I was reduced to ticking off the arguments against intervention – it's not legal, Assad's too strong, al-Nusra is getting stronger.

The Lebanese are hosting a population of Syrian refugees soon to become equivalent to one-third of their own. In Australian terms that would mean us hosting seven-and-a-half million. It could grow a lot worse. As Edgar in *King Lear* puts it, 'The worst is not/So long as we can say, "This is the worst."' Someone told me if the fighting around Damascus turns savage, another half-million could present at the Lebanese border, about fifty kilometres away from the Syrian capital. But a member of the Lebanese parliament told me, 'Make that one million.'

I announced $9 million more in Australian aid to help with refugees, bringing our humanitarian support for the Syrian crisis to a total of more than $78 million. In Beirut I met the President; the retiring Prime Minister; the Prime Minister-designate in his private home; the Foreign Minister and Ziad Mikati, a nephew of the Prime Minister, currently on his staff. Mikati, a Sunni, showed me the reconstructed buildings in the heart of the city. He said he was running a program to give imams a broader education in psychology, criminology and English language. And, in terms of thinking of the future of the place, I enjoyed a meeting with Kazem Kheir, a young Sunni MP. We ate an omelette in the Place de l'Etoile café which Prime Minister Rafik Hariri had left minutes before a truck bomb killed him and twenty-one others.

Robert Fisk, the legendary correspondent for *The Independent*, drops in for coffee at our hotel, the Phoenicia, which overlooks the site of this 2005 assassination. He's been in and out of Syria with his wife. He's sceptical about Western claims that chemical weapons are being used. He tells me the FSA always retreats but the bearded al-Nusra soldiers, recruited from Saudi, Yemen and Libya, stay put and fight hard. He speaks about atrocities on both sides – the killing of prisoners, the eating of an enemy's heart, the barbequing of butchered opponents' heads. He speaks with respect for Assad's army and says its officers in the field are not Alawites but Sunnis. He speaks with contempt of the Israeli army – they were defeated by Hezbollah, after all – but acknowledges their air force is supreme. One of the Australian correspondents we spent time with thinks Fisk is the prisoner of outdated leftism, who believes that oil is the key to Western behaviour in the Middle East and is reluctant to admit that the disaster in the Islamic world has nothing to do with America.

At the airport flying out, I meet the Maronite patriarch and extend greetings from the fine Maronites in Australia I got to know well from my seventeen years leading the State ALP. The community and I go back a long way.

On the plane I read Nicholas Blanford's *Warriors of God*. It's about Hezbollah and introduces me to the history of the Shi'a.

SUNDAY, MAY 26, 2013
Sydney

Flew in last night. I can now claim to have visited ten Arab countries (Oman, the UAE, Saudi Arabia, Qatar, Jordan, Egypt, Libya, Morocco, Algeria, Lebanon). Before the job I had only been to Lebanon, as Premier. I had had dinner with the Arab Ambassador in Canberra before I took off and they were all delighted; of course, it helps that we voted the right way on Palestinian status and that we correctly describe all Israeli settlements as illegal, as they are under the Geneva Convention. This goodwill towards Australia will be flushed away, of course, come September as, under Abbott, Australia reverts to voting the way Likud wants, all self-respect gone and moderate Israelis (who support my position) snubbed and their positions rejected.

MONDAY, MAY 27, 2013
Sydney

Working in the office in Sydney, I read a cable summarising Obama's May 23 speech reviewing US counter-terrorism policy since 9/11. The President outlined a US strategy on the use of drones, the prevention of violent extremism and the closure of Guantanamo Bay. He said beyond Afghanistan it was important not to define the situation as a 'boundless global war on terror', but rather as a series of persistent, targeted efforts to dismantle specific networks'. He said foreign aid was not a charity but fundamental to US national security policy. He called on Congress to close Guantanamo and said he would appoint a senior envoy whose sole responsibility would be achieving the transfer of detainees to third countries, with judicial review available for every detainee.

Another reason it's hard to be at odds with America this time, under this President.

Cabinet tonight – I attend by way of teleconference – was about options for tightening up refugee status determination. About time. If I'd been Prime Minister it would have happened years ago. We have been giving every asylum seeker, including plain economic refugees, the benefit of the doubt. Ninety-five per cent of arrivals get to stay. Of applicants who get rejected by migration officials, eighty-nine per cent get their rejection overturned. The tribunals and the High Court have created a situation where a sovereign nation cannot control its borders; the elected government cannot say no to people who are clearly not refugees. We've acquired a reputation in the region as a soft-touch, a honey pot. So they keep coming. Easier to get in and out of Australia than Canada, even with its vaunted Charter of Rights, or any other nation.

But fancy fixing this up now: the tightening up should have happened under Rudd. This confirms the lack of judgment that has brought us to this politically catastrophic position.

It should have happened under Rudd.

WEDNESDAY, MAY 29, 2013
Sydney

Four Corners broadcast some kind of a report on Monday night that alleged cyber espionage from China against the new ASIO headquarters building being constructed in Canberra. I didn't see it. I had some sort of memory of being briefed on this issue but – under Gestapo torture – could not have recalled whether the espionage was successful or not, or how conclusive the evidence of it was. The ABC and Sky interviewed me at the airport on the way to Canberra for a busy day of appointments (Parliament was not sitting). They were talking about other issues but threw in a question on this and I answered insouciantly with something like, 'I don't comment on matters of intelligence or security.' And when Kieran Gilbert of Sky pressed me, asking what does a strategic partnership with China amount to when they can launch cyber attacks at us, I replied with something like, 'Our relationship with China is very robust ... it can withstand many things.' Something like that.

Then in Canberra I had back-to-back appointments all day. In the afternoon at a little gathering on oceans policy, the Chinese Ambassador, Chen Yuming, seemed to be moving nervously when I greeted him. As I departed he took the time to say he appreciated my response on 'sensitive issues'. I hadn't had time to be briefed about *Four Corners* but picked up on the run that the Prime Minister had said in parliament some of the *Four Corners* allegations were plain untrue.

There's nothing to be gained by elevating this and generating a searing front-page headline, in any case. I later heard that my comments were broadcast from one end of China to the other, even with footage of me from the Bo'ao Forum with voiceover. 'You were all over Chinese TV,' a friend of mine reported.

Improvisation rules.

MONDAY, JUNE 3, 2013
Sydney

David Bradbury's lunch at Penrith Cricket Club on Friday should have been bursting with local businesspeople crossing over from their normal conservative alignments to acclaim their local Labor MP as a man above partisan politics, a legendary, good local member. I'd done scores of these types of campaign lunches or dinners in my elections in 1999 and 2003 but ... nothing doing. It was a crowd of union officials and the retired Labor MPs Peter Anderson, Faye Lo Po' and Ross Free. There was the sweet smell of a political corpse enshrouding the gathering. With only a 1.1 per cent margin he must know it is not worth campaigning.

That was lunch. Then in the evening, in the first-floor of a function centre, I addressed a big, bursting, mainly ethnic gathering for Julie Owens, Member for Parramatta, who's got a margin of 4.4 per cent. I spoke about our foreign-policy achievements and about the threat that under Abbott these would be reversed.

On Sunday I did *Australian Agenda* on Sky and told them that if it would end the suffering of the Syrian people any earlier, we should allow President Assad to live in a gilded palace with

peacocks strutting on the lawn. I then went to a Coptic mass at
Arncliffe to tell the community from the pulpit we stood by them,
given all their anxieties about the Muslim Brotherhood in Egypt.
A lot of applause. I told them my first phone call as a minister-designate to an Ambassador had been to Ralph King in Cairo, asking
him to check up on the Coptic community's welfare by visiting its
churches and monasteries in Cairo and Alexandria.

A well-placed Singapore source tells our High Commissioner
that, as they see it, the US–China relationship is the key one for
the region and that it was 'characterised by complex, competitive
interdependency'. The Singaporean decried Hugh White's 'overly
mechanistic analysis of how China and the US should settle their
futures' and said, 'If he had learnt anything in his long career, it
was that "all foreign policy is a series of improvisations".' He said
everyone in the region had to find a new balance and Singapore,
like Australia, needed good relations with Beijing and Washington, but that was difficult because of US–China competition. He
said that China had benefited from the US role, especially when it
came to Japan and South Korea.

Our position as well.

'All foreign policy is a series of improvisations.'

TUESDAY, JUNE 4, 2013
Sydney

Last night, I was hooked up by telephone to the cabinet meeting
in Canberra and heard them discuss last-minute reforms to electoral law. Again, an air of unreality here. The proposal is changing
the law so that people can get on the electoral roll and vote on

the same day. I said, 'We are in a mad pre-election period when everything we do will be magnified on the front page of the Murdoch press ... how's this going to be interpreted? And why wasn't it done two years back?'

No answer.

Why wasn't it done earlier?

It's like the moves to tighten up the regulations that cover IMAs (Irregular Maritime Arrivals) – the people brought here by people smugglers, mainly these days economic refugees, not people escaping persecution. After cabinet, genuinely curious, I rang Brendan O'Connor, the Immigration Minister, and put the question to him: 'Why are we doing this now? Why wasn't it done two years ago? Why wasn't it done under Rudd?' He agreed with me completely. The sensible reforms he's brought to cabinet will benefit an Abbott government. That leaves us to say after the election we introduced them. This is a half-credible position. But ... why wasn't it done before now?

Each paper is running a front-page story about a different opinion poll. It is pointless to reach for adjectives – 'catastrophic' or 'disastrous'. Lay bets on when the first journalist will write about an 'existential' defeat.

This afternoon I've got to fly into this wretched mess – Canberra – for dinner with Gareth Evans (loquacity, perfect sentences, sound insights) and two days of Senate Estimates Committee.

Bob Carr

WEDNESDAY, JUNE 5, 2013
Canberra

A sad, dysfunctional building, this federal parliament. Does all ambitious contemporary architecture end up with unhappiness institutionalised? My office, to start with. Its most important function is to receive visitors such as a Swedish Foreign Minister or a UN Under-Secretary-General. Yet there is no waiting room. They and their delegations stand in a telephone-box reception area, looking at a receptionist and sprawling into the corridor. There is no conference room to use for the meeting, just my smallish public-service office with, admittedly, a view of the eucalypt forests and the mountains, with a flag on a stand for photos. Then in the public spaces the architect or his client got the scale completely wrong. Why such a vast hall separating the two chambers? When I'm striding across it for a division, there's often nobody there. A handful at most. A bad attempt at a Mughal mausoleum. More wasted space in the Senate chamber itself. The architect gave it a ceiling as high as a Romanesque cathedral. Beneath it is acted out the banal discourse of the party hacks. There is a mismatch between the grand ecclesiastical scale of the chamber and the aldermanic tone of the exchanges. The building is crammed with artworks; it's a fair bet that no one has looked at them, apart from the portraits of the Prime Ministers. There's no magical electrical aura about either chamber; sterility prevails.

I want the cosy, conversational Westminster feel, the red-leather and wood-panelling of the chamber in the old Parliament House. In my mind, it had an atmosphere redolent of pipe smoke, waistcoats and afternoon newspapers.

Malcolm Turnbull told me that visiting the Korean parliament, he entered an amiable tearoom; there is no comparable socialising space in this building. No, not completely true. There are little lounges on either side of the Senate chamber that are cosy and enjoy natural light and have newspapers. But I've never seen anyone use them! There is no communal space, no area for mixing apart from a crummy little café with its spillover of chairs and tables in an echoey corridor. There the food is as unappetising as it is in the parliamentary dining room. Whether you're hosting an international visitor or grabbing a meal with colleagues, you know the food will be dismal. No one would dare improve it – MPs' perks, can't go there. At the official lunch for the Chinese Minister for State Security they served fish with an excremental deposit of cream – not yoghurt – on its burnt skin.

The acoustics in the cabinet room are so lousy you can miss out on whole sentences and, listening by video or telephone link, you might pick up one-quarter of the conversation if lucky.

I would have given anything to have been a member in the cramped, gossipy Art Deco building opened by the Duke of York in 1927, the old Parliament House down the road.

THURSDAY, JUNE 6, 2013
Canberra

The gruesome polls flavour everything and news gets even worse. People-smuggler boats have been the biggest mark against us but now one asylum seeker turns out to be a convicted al-Qaeda terrorist! And he's being held in low-security detention! We're not only losing control of borders – 3000 arrivals a month indict the idealism of the refugee lobby and the soft-headedness of the High Court – but now, worse, the people smugglers are bringing in

379

convicted terrorists. The courts and tribunals make it impossible for an executive government to turf them out. Again, why wasn't it fixed up five years ago under Rudd?

And the Prime Minister apparently still wants me to give a former cabinet colleague a posting as Ambassador to Turkey.

She raised it months ago; I told her in late April the person was as qualified as any of the political appointments of the Howard era but it was politically wrong. When I checked with Swan a week ago he said, 'She's still keen on it.'

In this febrile pre-election climate if she was to force this through – force it on me – she would ignite a firestorm. Jobs for mates on the eve of an election.

Locked up at Senate Estimates for two days. Only challenge is to avoid getting waspish and generating a poor TV story. Avoid hunger is my tactic. Helena has sent me to Canberra with cooked kangaroo and vegetables plus avocados, organic almonds and eighty per cent cocoa Lindt chocolate; and I have a mid-morning protein shake with an espresso brought into the committee room. I send staff out to get roast chicken from Woolworths and curry from the Punjabi Hut in Manuka.

The Estimates Committee starts at 9 am and drags on until 11 pm. The questions to public servants (and occasionally to me) drone on and I read Michael Fullilove's *Rendezvous with Destiny* about FDR's use of personal envoys during the war. And I read cables. Interesting that Chinese Foreign Minister Wang Yi was very conciliatory in talks with Vietnam, the new soft Chinese line that they signalled when the Prime Minister and I were in Beijing. Interesting that Vietnam is not progressing the use of Cam Ranh Bay by the US. Like us, like others such as India and Singapore, they have no wish to provoke China even while wanting the US in the region and needing to hedge against China turning bossy. Sitting next to me at Estimates, Peter Varghese says yes, the Chinese are using softer language but on the reefs and shoals and mountain borders across Asia, they are maintaining a forceful presence, giving nothing away.

FRIDAY, JUNE 7, 2013
Sydney

In the Qantas Club lounge at Canberra Airport last night I watched Rudd in a *7.30 Report* interview, strutting his stuff for a return to the leadership. Jason Clare was there, a staffer or two, and a member of caucus – a tall, statuesque blonde – I couldn't name. Rudd nailed Abbott for lying about sending the boats back and it was a contrast with the strained, scratchy monotone of Julia, the voice that the public has just stopped listening to. I took Jason and Graeme into a corner of the lounge and phoned Dastyari. 'Listen, it's no contest,' I said. 'He cuts through.' Sam read latest polling that showed us losing every western Sydney seat; Jason's two-party preferred estimate is down to forty-four per cent – that's the Labor bastion of Blaxland, Keating's old seat!

The statuesque woman, leaving to get her plane, told me, '*That's* our only hope. You will have to speak.' She meant speak up about the need to switch to Rudd. I said, 'Crean did and nobody followed.' She said, 'You've got gravitas.' I asked, 'What margin are you on?' She said, 'One per cent. I'm gone.' I asked Jason who she was. He said he didn't know. What? I don't know half the caucus – even more. But I've got an excuse: I'm an elitist arriviste. He's been here since 2007 and is spoken of as a potential leader.

Who is she?

Flew home. H had prepared slow-cooked lamb with layers of vegetables – cherry tomatoes, sweet potatoes, fennel, celery.

TUESDAY, JUNE 11, 2013
Sydney

Wayne Swan called me on Saturday, loyal deputy shoring up support for his boss. But in this dire climate, I had nothing to lose by gently nudging forward some truths. I said I wouldn't want Julia to be having an internal conversation for the rest of her life about whether things might have been different. 'Here's what I would do,' I said. 'There are only 100 days left as Prime Minister. The polls are unanimous. Just let Rudd take over. If he achieves a half-decent result – a conventional loss – then she can bask in having done the right thing. God, she only foregoes 100 days. Leaves a bit of a hero. If he fails, well, that's a vindication too. But why hang on *just to keep him out?*' His response was pretty mild. He just said, 'But it would be handing the party over to a madman.' 'Forget that,' I said. 'The party should be left in some condition to fight back at the election after this. It can't be rendered as weak as the New South Wales party.' We left it at that. He didn't resist my arguments. Presume he'll pass them on.

My friend Marty Natalegawa flew to Sydney to have a breakfast meeting at the airport with the Foreign Minister of Vanuatu to talk about Indonesian Papua. He had some hours before boarding a return flight to Jakarta so we invited him home for morning tea with his Ambassador and senior adviser. I had the normal reservations: our house is small, in a nondescript suburb, no servants, no paintings, books everywhere. He presumably lives in a bit more elegance. Everyone does. On the other hand, all the beachfront coffee shops would be raucous with holiday crowds and Helena had bought two cakes from Infinity Sourdough Bakery, Victoria Street, Darlinghurst – a flourless chocolate cake and an almond butter cake. These proved a hit.

In our lounge room on the Biedermeier sofa, Marty said the

Vanuatu policy on Papua is to see it as a matter of human rights, not a matter of sovereignty. This is good all around. Human rights, not sovereignty. He spoke about his own plan for a treaty across the Indo-Pacific to build confidence, to minimise the chance of accidental disputes and to manage change. He spoke on this at the CSIS in Washington and I felt a momentary irritation that I had not been briefed by our Washington post. They can find someone to sit in at the Bradley Manning trial to pick up espionage erotica (which I told them to terminate forthwith when I heard about it at Senate Estimates) but not report on a speech by the Indonesian Foreign Minister in the heart of Washington's think-tank land.

I raised the issue that concerns us most: 6000 Iranians arrived in Indonesia under their Visa on Arrival (VOA) scheme and 2000 of them came on to Australia as IMAs – that is, clients of people smugglers. I said this has got out of hand and it has to end. Marty promised to review the way VOAs operate in Indonesia.

He liked the cakes and Helena had one for him to take home to Sranya. I texted the Prime Minister on Marty's commitment. She replied she would like things to move fast.

It was a long weekend. I got a bit of exercise. I ploughed through Michael Fullilove's book and Robert Kaplan's *Monsoon*. I did Channel 10's *Meet the Press* where I refused to comment on the polls or leadership, and did a long interview with Ellen Fanning on SBS. Last night we watched a DVD of Ibsen's *Little Eyolf* with Anthony Hopkins and Diana Rigg, full of wintry angst. We went to bed listening to Phillip Adams interview Tim Bowden about the Australian POW experience under the Japanese. My mind filled with the stories of the Eighth Division – an army of 20,000 marched to Changi on the darkest day in our history, the fall of Singapore – and how the survivors were haunted by the memories when they returned to suburban homes or farms.

All dead now, and their stories fading, sinking into the sediment of all the other war histories from the start of time.

Sometimes I've thought of death as wholesome, beautiful in its finality, creating space for the new generations; but lying in bed I thought of the stories, lost with the veterans, and how irrevocably sad to have all this experience ground to dust.

In turn, this had me think of all the dead I've known. As did the character Gabriel at the end of James Joyce's story *The Dead*:

> His soul had approached that region where dwell the vast hosts of the dead. He was conscious of, but could not apprehend, their wayward and flickering existence. His own identity was fading out into a grey impalpable world: the solid world itself, which these dead had one time reared and lived in, was dissolving and dwindling.

By my side my little friend slept untroubled.

WEDNESDAY, JUNE 12, 2013
Sydney

No movement from the Shorten camp. So leadership remains deadlocked. Yesterday Gillard gave a speech in Sydney to a women's group, raising abortion rights as an issue of the campaign, trying to copy Obama, I guess. Badly advised. In the 12-month countdown to an election, you don't raise nasty, divisive issues – this is the Wran model and I and other Labor premiers learnt from it: in the lead-up to an election *you are friends with everybody*. I ring Dastyari who agrees with me and adds that abortion is like guns and (until recently) immigration – it's a consensus issue that the parties don't use against one another. I told him it sounded awful on TV last night, like a desperate last-minute bid for votes. Moreover, playing so obviously for feminist votes makes men think she's hostile to them. Or, at least, that's my view. Dastyari assures me that the polling for Victorian seats is so horrific that it will force Shorten and the faction to move on her.

I talk to no one else about it and stick to my job: lunch with PNG Foreign Minister Rimbink Pato yesterday, a meeting with the Laos Vice Minister for Foreign Affairs, Sounthone Xayachack, today where I will press her about their recent shocking decision to send home nine young North Koreans. I'm going to hand her a copy of *Escape from Camp 14* and go a bit further than I would in any other diplomatic setting. As time runs out I want to maximise the good.

US Ambassador Jeffrey Bleich briefed me by phone that the Americans believe Russia has agreed there should be a transitional authority established in Syria with full executive power. That it should take over all executive authority from the existing government in Damascus. That Assad would not be part of the process. He claims this had been agreed to by the Deputy Soviet Foreign Minister. I simply do not believe it. It does not ring true. It is too big a concession by Russia and I cannot believe that Assad is ready to depart. Jeffrey assures me. We'll see.

MONDAY, JUNE 17, 2013
Canberra

For a week the leadership deadlock has continued. I congratulate myself on avoiding conversations with cabinet and caucus colleagues and staying out of the media. This morning Sam Dastyari told me that a resolution on Friday – MPs staying an extra night in Canberra – is a possibility. The Prime Minister's misjudged speech on abortion keeps getting attention. According to the polls today it produced a seven per cent drop in male support. She now has a sixty-one per cent disapproval rating and Labor is at twenty-nine per cent, down from thirty-eight per cent at the 2010 election. Our proportion of seats in the House of Representatives would be the lowest ever. We are being led into a barren defile where we are going to be exterminated. Media dwells on Bill Shorten, a delight for a hothouse ego.

Over the last week I saw six foreign ministers in Sydney: those of Indonesia, PNG, Laos (the Vice Foreign Minister) New Zealand, Morocco and Fiji. I addressed an Islamic function in Bankstown on Thursday night and pounded out a speech defending multiculturalism, denouncing racial discrimination and boasting of our support for enhanced Palestinian status. This tub-thumping effort left Bronwyn Bishop, representing the opposition, with nothing to say except to read out a mealy-mouthed letter from Abbott, which had the audience talking over her. It was sweet to see the Liberal candidates for these Labor-held seats – full of hope at the start of the evening – leave with their tails between their legs. A bit of old-fashioned Labor professionalism won the audience. A sweet tactical win but it counts for nothing if we stick with Julia, sadly.

That US intelligence that Russia would sign up to a Geneva II conference on Syria – I was sceptical when US Ambassador Bleich put it to me. Now my doubt is confirmed. I'm told today, 'The Russians have not delivered.' Why would they? My instincts were superior to State Department intelligence. This gives me something of a glow.

WEDNESDAY, JUNE 19, 2013
Canberra

On Monday night at cabinet Gillard announced curtly she would not be affected by the media and would stay in the leadership. There was no comment on this. Through the meeting ministers were talking in a relaxed fashion and laughing skittishly as if entirely removed from the wintry political climate, living in an alternate universe. Her selfishness struck me. If disastrous polling had been given to me – say in my third year as Premier – I would have handed over the leadership. To save the party from a catastrophic defeat (which is what she's looking at) but also to save myself from the opprobrium that would be dumped on me the Sunday after the election.

What's going on in her head? Surely, she can't believe she can turn this around. The public polls are conclusive and are reinforced by what she hears from the party about its polling. Is she incapable of seeing how her reputation will suffer? Or, on the other hand, incapable of imagining her hero status if she makes a statement in the house announcing her resignation, putting the old party first? The motivation can only be a deeply ingrained detestation of Rudd. At once understandable … and unworthy.

Yesterday in this surreal atmosphere people met cheerfully enough for a national Right meeting, for the caucus, for the daily Senate tactics meeting. The only groaning and eye-rolling took place when one was out of the crowd with another Rudd supporter. Dastyari tells me Shorten is resolved it must happen and he knows that I am prepared to talk to him about things, but – this is important – that I will not be part of any delegation to call on the Prime Minister. I am the elder statesman, the equestrian statue, after all.

Meantime, in another part of the Emerald Forest …

We entertain the Sri Lankan Foreign Minister, Professor Peiris. His delegation includes President Rajapaksa's son, Namal. Yesterday I gave another briefing to Julie Bishop – might as well assist the transfer of power in the national interest – telling her about my meeting with Marty and what Vanuatu is saying about Papua and our contact with the Sri Lankans. On the last, she is in agreement with our scepticism about the narrative being put forward by Tamil activists.

The Sri Lankans appreciate that if we had taken the same hostile tone as the Canadians then the UK could well have wobbled about CHOGM going ahead in Colombo in November. 'Australia coming out so early made a big difference,' their Foreign Minister said. I think not enough weight has been given to the trauma of thirty-five years of bloodthirsty, terrorist assault on Sri Lanka and its people. We continue to press them on reconciliation and human rights. There is evidence of progress. Less happy evidence as well. Still, better to engage.

Our High Commissioner in Colombo, Robyn Mudie, is a terrier – which is terrific – when it comes to keeping the pressure on. So after my formal meeting with the Sri Lankan Foreign Minister, as we break for the lunch, she pushes me strongly on keeping the pressure on human rights. I tell her to scribble me a note so we can move down the checklist over lunch in one of the parliament's antiseptic dining rooms. She approves the strategy and gives me this:

Minister, as discussed

For CHOGM

» free speech at People's Forum and free and open accreditation for all who want to take part;
» freedom of media – no barriers to accreditation, no

attempt to restrict reporting;

» clear commitment to free and fair Northern Province Council.

All of these are very important leading up to CHOGM and beyond.

» e.g. Media freedom is a real concern
   - recent attacks on Tamil paper in the north
   - self-censorship.
» Accountability – concrete steps to help give answers to the many families with missing/disappeared.
» Also long-term accountability broadly will be critical for reconciliation and without it the future stability and prosperity of SL is not guaranteed.

Good Ambassador. Useful notes, and I deploy them.

At a meeting of the National Security Committee last night, we looked at a voluminous set of recommendations dealing with the people-smuggling disaster. Here the Prime Minister was at her best, briskly ordering the decisions that we had to make. It's all about persuading the Indonesians to take back returnees we send to them by air, a hard task. Again, I'm driven to wonder why it wasn't tackled a year or two years back.

THURSDAY, JUNE 20, 2013
Canberra

Still no movement. At the Press Gallery Ball last night Simon Benson, the *Daily Telegraph* correspondent who's close to Shorten, told me Bill is consulting the unions to square off with them before he switches to Rudd. This should not be taking place; they should have no role in this. Anyway, this would mean the melodrama continues into next week. And I'll be in Indonesia if it happens after Wednesday.

In a dubious move, the Prime Minister has all our Indonesia plans about stopping boats on the front page of today's newspapers:

> Julia Gillard is planning a trip to Indonesia in two weeks to discuss with President Susilo Bambang Yudhoyono ways to stem the rising flow of asylum seekers coming by boat before the September election.

This makes it very hard – probably impossible – for the Indonesians to agree with anything we put up, given their internal political pressures. It raises the bar very high and therefore involves a high risk of public failure. The only reason her office may have elevated this story is to create a distraction from the Rudd challenge.

At DFAT headquarters today I addressed NGOs on human rights, an annual consultation organised by the department. I was asked a question by a refugee advocate who was repeating a claim broadcast on the ABC that 300 of the 1000 Sri Lankans that we had sent back have been stuck in prison. This is simply an untruth and I told her. I said we returned 1000 people; only four had complained about mistreatment. The High Commissioner had investigated and found that in three cases there was no basis to the claims; the other case was still being investigated. I am struck again by the vast web of urban myth being spun here. As I said at the meeting, not even Tamil advocates have made this claim.

Meanwhile, what's left of the Tamil Tigers is drawing on the funds raised by the Tamil diaspora and feeding this kind of propaganda. I'm increasingly impatient with it. Whatever the flaws of the Rajapaksas they did bring an end to nearly three decades of terrorist insurgency – an insurgency full of atrocities that the world chose to ignore.

Later, I read further evidence that my instincts on Russia and Syria were right. A report says:

> Moscow's support for the Syrian regime was rooted in the belief that Western intervention in Syria would threaten Russian national security, would enable and embolden Islamic extremists, and could serve as a precedent for future Western intervention in Russia itself. This conviction, combined with Moscow's greater confidence about the Syrian regime's ability to survive, meant Russia still saw more benefit in supporting Assad than in cooperating with the West.

Today I meet the Afghan Finance Minister, Dr Omar Zakhilwal. And then – I was able to escape Canberra, with only two-and-a-half sitting days next week for me, and what will probably be my last visit to Indonesia as Foreign Minister.

SATURDAY, JUNE 22, 2013
Sydney

Last week, several reports about the threat from extremist Islam.

On Thursday the Afghan Finance Minister, Dr Omar Zakhil-wal, told me that there was a surge in suicide bombings in Afghanistan with several Taliban fanatics convening on a target and then blowing themselves and the target sky high. Why the surge? Well, the Taliban madrassas – religious schools – in Pakistan had closed for the summer holidays and their young students had streamed off to Afghanistan to do their bit for the cause and to take themselves to heaven. One father heard that his boy had gone off to Afghanistan so tracked him down and took him back.

On Friday I had talks in Sydney with the Mauritanian Foreign Minister Hamadi Ould Baba Ould Hamadi, and pressed him about Mali: al-Qaeda pushed out, reconciliation with the Tuareg minority now taking place, elections in the offing. The minister spoke about the origins of al-Qaeda in the Islamic Maghreb. It grew out of a Salafist group in Algeria during the 'years of embers' then moved into Mali, its leaders having met bin Laden fighting the Russians in Afghanistan. It adopted the name of al-Qaeda in the Islamic Maghreb in 2007, committing its allegiance to Osama bin Laden. Mauritania calculates that in one year al-Qaeda made $150 million from crime. That amount is bigger than the defence budgets of four countries in the region.

This weekend I resumed Kaplan's book *Monsoon* and read about the rise of Wahhabi Islam in Bangladesh, taking over from the syncretic Hindu-influenced Islam that had prevailed there for centuries. Kaplan notes, 'From jeans and T-shirts a decade ago, women in the capital of Dhaka, in the port city of Chittagong, and throughout the countryside are increasingly covered in burkas and *shalwar kameezes*.'

SUNDAY, JUNE 23, 2013
Sydney

Now the weekend and I haven't had a single conversation about the leadership challenge, still expected to come when a delegation of ministers, including Shorten, sees the Prime Minister on Thursday with Rudd being installed on Friday. I've stayed out of the media on this. This morning, giving some grabs to the ABC Radio newsroom on the consular case involving six young Australians accused of throwing a hotel doorman off their balcony, and the legal system of Peru, the reporter switched topics. 'Caucus is meeting this week, Mr Carr. What do you think the chances are of a leadership challenge?' I simply hung up.

TUESDAY, JUNE 25, 2013
Canberra

The annual Lowy Poll says that eighty-two per cent of Australians support Australia's US alliance. In today's *Sydney Morning Herald* Peter Hartcher says, 'This is as close as you get to consensus on any matter.'

He also writes that Australians are increasingly 'wary' of China. China has dropped from the eighth most warmly regarded country in Australia to thirteenth in one year, and in the international poll, positive views about China fell as well.

Professor Qiao Mu of Beijing Foreign Studies University said a story quoting a BBC poll on China's international standing had put China in an 'embarrassing' position:

It seems China is getting rich fast but its influence ranking
is dropping dramatically. China is drawing more attention
globally, for its increasing foreign aid and participation in
international affairs, but now it turns out that the values and
the political system China holds are not accepted by the world.

Yet China's values haven't changed. They are just the same as they
were a year ago. The new element must be Beijing's assertiveness
in territorial disputes with its neighbours.

For their part, Australians will always prefer American values.
And our interests have predisposed us towards an alliance with
America, something that was evident as far back as our response to
the victory of Japan over Russia in 1905. To put it more broadly, we
have always sought an alliance with the dominant English-speaking maritime power. We didn't leave the British Empire; they left
us. And even after Iraq, George W. Bush, Afghanistan and other
embarrassments, eighty-two per cent of us still want a US alliance.

On the weekend I came across a different approach to this in
Edward Luttwak's book *The Rise of China vs. the Logic of Strategy*. He devoted a whole chapter to Australia. He said that 'for
all its ever-increasing ethnic diversity, it fully retains the Anglo-
Saxon trait of bellicosity'. Gasp! That, he says, explains Australia's
involvement in so many wars.

And then he astonished me with this conclusion:

It is not surprising, therefore, that Australia has been the
first country to clearly express resistance to China's rising
power, and to initiate the coalition building against it that is
mandated by the logic of strategy.

He then makes reference to the 2009 Defence White Paper and
enhanced links with Japan, Indonesia and Vietnam. I said to
Stephen Smith as we went into cabinet yesterday, 'Do you know

about this book by Luttwak? He says that we've *initiated* resistance to China's assertiveness since 2009. He's got a whole chapter on it. He says we got there first, we put it together.'

Stephen wasn't aware of it.

I passed Michael Pezzullo, head of the Australian Customs and Border Protection Service, and invited him into the office. I knew he was a defence expert and adviser going a long way back into the Labor years. More crucially, he had been the Deputy Secretary of Defence, responsible for the 2009 Defence White Paper. I asked him about the Luttwak reference and he gave me a useful guided tour of the China relationship. He said the key concepts when it came to responding to China's growth or assertiveness were these: hedging versus over-hedging versus containment. He said, 'Take the 2009 Defence White Paper. That was a case of over-hedging.' By this he meant the controversial chapter talking up Chinese strategic assertiveness and the prospects of major power conflict, and the commitment on 'force structure'; that is, to buy twelve submarines and new aircraft. That was over-hedging but the 2013 Defence White Paper, which pulled back a bit (but not in respect of its commitment to those defence acquisitions), would be an example of plain hedging.

He went on. He said that 2009 was a response to two deeply felt Australian anxieties. One was the prospect that Indonesia could one day turn malevolent, specifically by Islamist forces joining with its army. The issue would be what we would do if the US failed to provide us with 'lethal assistance' in the case of a conflict with a different, aggressive Indonesia. The second anxiety: a threat from China, which he defined in an interesting way. He expressed it in these terms: a dispute in Asia between the US and China that results in Chinese attacks on joint US–Australian facilities in the Northern Territory and Western Australia, those of Pine Gap and Exmouth. A little Star Wars? A touch of H. G. Wells? Still, that's what strategists are paid to speculate about.

As I walked into caucus, Senator Mark Bishop, a right-winger from Western Australia, said he wanted to get me to expand on my position on refugees and asylum seekers. I said I was happy to. So when it was time for caucus members to ask questions of the executive he asked whether reports of my comments in *The Australian* of last week were accurate. He was referring to reports of the answer I gave to a meeting of NGOs on human rights convened by DFAT. I told him the reports in *The Australian* were definitely accurate (after all, I had given them to Greg Sheridan because I wanted them to be seen).

I said three things stood out about what was happening with irregular arrivals in Australia. First, all the irregular arrivals were now being brought by people smugglers. The boats weren't full of people who, as a result of persecution, had bundled themselves together and seized a fishing trawler. They were brought here by streamlined syndicates who charge $10,000 a person. Second, the irregular arrivals were economic migrants, not refugees. There has been a big spike, for example, in Iranians. They are members of the majority religious and ethnic group in Iran, who have had their living standards squeezed and so give money to a people smuggler who gets them to Indonesia and then to a boat leaving an Indonesian port. Third, there is a big increase in numbers with 3000 irregular arrivals a month hitting our shores. And that's without a war in the region. It can be 3000 a month, it can be 5000 a month (I don't think I went quite this far in talking to the caucus but it's what I believe). And this supplants our big regular publicly supported immigration program, with its 20,000-a-year humanitarian intake.

I then offered the quote – I said from George Orwell – that 'when the facts change, I change my mind'. Graham Perrett, the Queensland member, interjected that it was in fact Lord Keynes. I responded that it was the widely held view that it was Lord Keynes but the people overlooked the fact he made the remark after a conversation with George Orwell three days earlier at a dinner party in South Kensington. Much laughter, good-natured.

Later, one of the members said it was the line on people smugglers that they'd been waiting to hear from the government for a long time. I said – somewhat cheekily – it's a line I would have implemented had I been running the bloody government. Someone told me – it may have been mischief-making – that the Prime Minister had allowed her jaw to drop at the emphatic nature of my answers. This just confirms it was the right policy and she and her predecessor should have cleaved to it.

Back to the events of the day.

Flat out all afternoon. After an early lunch with a Chinese Assistant Minister for State Security Huang Dianzhong, I hurl myself into the parliament gym, then Question Time, then meet the Deputy Foreign Affairs Minister of Belarus (I work hard at trying to identify common interests; even draw a blank at mining – they don't have commercial quantities of anything); a call from Marty about the fire crisis in Sumatra and whether we have fire-bombing aircraft (no, we rented ours from Russia); a visit from an old acquaintance who presses a case for us opening an embassy in Ukraine (our budget will never allow it); a call to Radoslaw Sikorski, the Polish Foreign Minister, about an announcement I plan tomorrow on regular ministerial consultations with Poland; a visit from Chris Hayes MP to be photographed presenting me with a petition on Vietnam human rights; an interview with ABC *Newsline* that covers Indonesian Papua and Myanmar; an interview with an online News Limited site about my views on asylum seekers.

My eyes are burning with a violent fatigue: I must see an ophthalmologist. I can't give up my cables and reports.

I leave parliament to attend a reception at DFAT for the tenth anniversary of the Council for Australian–Arab Relations. Then to the home of the Argentine Ambassador for dinner with ten

Latin American heads of mission. I dispensed charm everywhere. Told our host his home with its Argentine art reminded me of the Buenos Aires Jockey Club; the Cuban Ambassador that US attitudes to his country were a pathology; the Colombian about Márquez; the Uruguayan that Montevideo's heritage-building stock was a treasure; the Mexican Ambassador that we were both pivotal powers; the Brazilian Ambassador that I wanted to read a good translation of *The Lusiads*; and so on ...

I planned to head off to Indonesia tomorrow but the Rudd challenge looks like it's coming to a head.

WEDNESDAY, JUNE 26, 2013
Canberra

I wake up in the Realm Hotel and ring Richard Marles, the Victorian Rudd supporter, and tell him I need the Rudd camp to say something definite by midday or I am out of Canberra on my way to Jakarta. 'Sorry, you've got until about five o'clock,' I told him, 'when my plane will leave Sydney.'

I arrive at Parliament House for a meeting of the Senate caucus where artificial jollity still prevails and people discuss the business of the last two sitting days of the year of the grumpy parliament. Kim Carr, another Rudd supporter, growls conspiratorially about how I've got to stick around (same as he did in March) but I tell him unless there's an announcement I have no alternative but to take off. He seems, grudgingly, to accept this. I add, 'Rudd's numbers men, they've got to get it together.' He says, 'That's the problem – there aren't numbers men. If there were, this would have been resolved. There are just big egos.'

Martin Ferguson came into the office and said he'd heard that in focus groups conducted by the party adman, the mob said they'd voted Labor last time but would not under Gillard, yet would return to the fold under Rudd. I told him I'm headed for Indonesia this afternoon so he needed to get something firm about a challenge running on the wires if he wanted me to stay behind.

At 11 am I go downstairs to meet the Prime Minister to talk about the messaging for my trip to Indonesia today, where I am to soften them up for her meeting with the President on July 5. We sit in her office with advisers. She says the Indonesians must be clear she absolutely intends to raise with the President our desire to send back by plane failed asylum seekers. In other words I should not allow the Indonesians to think they can tell me the President won't want to discuss this. We also talk about the other component: persuading the Indonesians to tighten up their VOA system that allows Iranians into their country even if they haven't a return fare and thus transit on their way to Australia. And we talk about the support package we will offer them on infrastructure if they cooperate with our pressing concern on these IMAs. The key message is this issue will hurt the Indonesia–Australia relationship if not solved and will be worse if the government changes in September.

When we finish after about twenty minutes I ask for a moment alone with her. What I say is unrehearsed and untested and has not been sought by anyone in the Rudd camp. I say, 'I'm happy to accept everything you want to say about Kevin … but let's talk about it from your perspective … you want to face the Sunday after the next election like Kristina Keneally or Anna Bligh … if our vote's at twenty-nine per cent now, then a burst of bad luck in the campaign could see it fall to twenty-five … more boats for example … on the other hand, you can give a speech today that will produce a surge of goodwill … you could be sitting in your former Prime Minister's office in a few months taking phone calls offering you a job as Vice Chancellor or Chancellor, positions on boards ... you'd get a phone call from the UN given the positive impact you made with your speech of last year ... it's only ninety days left as Prime Minister ... it's not worth fighting about ... and if you fight to the end there's no surge of goodwill with all that can bring.'

She just replied that she can't hand over the leadership in these circumstances because it's not about any issue of party principle or policy. It's not like other party ruptures where there's an issue like state aid. That was basically all of her argument and, of course, it's entirely irrelevant to my proposition.

So I leave to furiously sign documents before I go to the National Press Club.

At the National Press Club I deliver what I consider a satisfactory speech, a tour of my foreign-policy exertions over the past fourteen months, without reference to what I call 'a solemn and weighty tome' that they could collect on the way out. Then when it came to question time the chairman announced he had just heard that there was a petition circulating to call a special caucus meeting on the leadership. So the first half-dozen questions were all about this. My instincts were to say *absolutely nothing* about the leadership so I brushed it all away with a joke that foreign ministers according to convention – one I invented this week – don't talk about domestic politics.

When we left we entered the cars full of our luggage and headed to the airport. Parked outside the terminal I took a call from Kevin Rudd who confirmed it was on, a petition of caucus members was being collected. 'They'd easily get thirty-five votes and the caucus meeting could be as early as this afternoon.' We waited in the lounge and watched House of Representatives Question Time, then cancelled our flights and I parked myself in the DFAT office, not Parliament House, because I didn't want to be caught up in the petition or approaches to the Prime Minister.

At 4.20 pm we hear the news that Gillard has called the ballot for seven o'clock tonight.

At the caucus meeting we voted to replace Gillard with Rudd by fifty-seven votes to forty-five, a bloodless exercise driven by the imperative of minimising Labor's loss and ensuring the very existence of a social democratic party. I didn't feel great sympathy even when the result was announced. And Julia – feisty professional – was not looking for any. The premature removal of Rudd in 2010 was a step into the unknown that produced the hung parliament and his nagging fightback. Three years of instability. No chance of the conservative, cautious, canny Labor government that could have set us up for a long stretch in power.

Play the game: you win.

Play the game: you lose.

Play the game.

I did a flat, mediocre *Lateline* interview but at least intruded the argument that in the end loyalty to the party subsumes loyalty to any individual. And so to bed.

FRIDAY, JUNE 28, 2013
Jakarta

Took off last night on a Singapore Airlines flight from Sydney. On my BBC iPlayer I watched two more episodes of the 1994 version of *Martin Chuzzlewit*, with lavish production values for its time (i.e. somewhat short of the 2008 *Little Dorrit*) but with high comic acting; episode one of the dramatisation of Alan Clark's diaries capturing the isolation and ignominy of being a junior minister; and Alan Bennett's *An Englishman Abroad* with Alan Bates understatedly playing Guy Burgess, expatriated in Moscow in 1958, pining for the niceness of English life, the luxury of Jermyn Street tailoring and the richness of London gossip.

Arrived at 1 am local time in Singapore and got a few hours' sleep at an airport hotel. Up at 5 am and just landing now in Jakarta.

SATURDAY, JUNE 29, 2013
Jakarta

I continue to be uneasily amazed by what one can do with virtually no sleep. On Friday I went into a meeting with the Indonesian Coordinating Minister for Legal, Political and Security Affairs, Djoko Suyanto. I knew my task was difficult. I had to persuade the Indonesians to start thinking about two things.

First, suspending or ending the Visa on Arrival that they extend to all Islamic countries in respect of Iranian arrivals. If we can stop Iranians who've bought a place on a boat to Australia, arriving by air in Jakarta, then we curb this recent spike in people-trade activity. It's running at 3000 a month and this is plainly unsustainable. Second, to take back the Iranians we reject, have them processed (at our expense) in Indonesia and to send them back to Iran. This is clearly the bigger ask.

I've never actually had a diplomatic mission of this sort; that is, a mission to go in and persuade a government to do something this specific (as opposed to vote us on to the Security Council). My visit is one week in advance of the Prime Minister's visit. I've got to pave the way for Rudd to get progress on this front. The only preparation has been from a visit by Nick Warner talking to his counterparts and I think something of his representations have massaged their way through the Indonesian system. Therefore I didn't take Minister Suyanto by surprise. He receives me politely and does not raise objections to what we put to him.

We then call on my old friend Marty Natalegawa, familiar now with me and I very relaxed with him. In the Foreign Ministry we have a tête-à-tête and I tell him these are extremely high-priority goals for Australia. Again, he's received a briefing from Indonesian security following Nick's visit. Marty makes the point, an altogether reasonable one, that Indonesia can't be seen to be doing anything like this at the request of any other country. They've got to do it responding to their own dynamics. We then sit down with advisers at the long table and tick off our now very familiar bilateral agenda. How familiar with all this stuff I have become! We then go to join our wives at a restaurant at a Dutch colonial building.

SUNDAY, JUNE 30, 2013
Jakarta

Last night a small dinner at our Ambassador's residence with Sabam Siagian, the former Indonesian Ambassador to Australia (1991–1995) and a former editor of the *Jakarta Post*. Just H, James Larsen and Greg Moriarty, our Ambassador.

I decided to steer the conversation on to that curious conclusion in the Luttwak book: that after 2009 and China's assertive behaviour it was Australia that took the lead in assembling the resistance.

Greg found it hard to believe we had been that strategic and focused and consistent. James thought Rudd had definitely been strong on Chinese behaviour.

As shown by the 2009 Defence White Paper with the blood-curdling chapter inserted at his insistence?

Yes, said James.

And, I thought, as confirmed by his remarkable comments to Hillary Clinton in 2009 that the US should be prepared for a military response to China 'if everything goes wrong', as revealed in a WikiLeaks cable.

Sabam expressed his Southeast Asian curiosity about why Australia wants to be so close to America. It was a curiosity I picked up in Malaysia, meeting think-tankers and former diplomats, and in Thailand meeting a similar group. Not hostile or critical, just curious about our choice. Why would we want to be so attached to the stars and stripes?

Especially, he said, as a strong Indonesia straddles our northern approaches.

'Not just Indonesia,' I said. 'But it's in our interest to have the ten ASEAN states all strong and resilient. To have the fragile ones like Myanmar, Cambodia and Laos (and, speaking prophetically, Timor Leste) catch up with the rest. Then who knows? Maybe the instinct to be so close to the US would count for less.'

Nobody knows at what rate the US will decline or China rise. Or whether Indonesia will crumple under the weight of political Islam and corruption.

Nobody writing in 1913 came close to predicting the dramas of the twentieth century.

At home Rudd out-polls Abbott as preferred Prime Minister and lifts us to forty-nine per cent. Fine, as it goes. Fine, as it goes.

Letter to Henry Kissinger

Sunday, June 30, 2013

Dear Henry,

… I've been caught up in travel and the tense political
competition within the government which resulted in Kevin
Rudd being voted back as party leader last Thursday. The
vote in the party room was 57 to 45 and reflected an appalling
position in the polls and the feeling the party could at least
minimise its losses under a more popular figure.

Rudd has kept me foreign minister. I am in Brunei at the
moment for what is a pretty non-contentious East Asia
Summit. John Kerry will attend it which is good because, as
the performance of Hillary Clinton and President Obama
confirmed, America is judged to be successful in Southeast
Asia simply by turning up at these gatherings. Sadly Secretary
of State Kerry cancelled visits to Indonesia and Vietnam, but
who can blame him for giving priority to the Middle East
peace process if he and the President judge that there is some
chance of an Israel–Palestinian convergence. Middle Eastern
peace won't happen without American leadership. And as
you told me nine months ago, you suspect Obama will want a
Palestinian state as one of his legacies.

Have you dipped into Edward Luttwak's new book, *The Rise
of China vs. the Logic of Strategy*? I've heard you mention the
author in a couple of our conversations and, despite some
reservations about his judgement and style, I find enough in
the book to keep me absorbed. He has a chapter on Australia
and gives us credit for being the first to organise resistance to

increased Chinese assertiveness or aggrandisement. This has a lot of truth in it. Certainly Rudd as Prime Minister in his first manifestation (2007–2010) vigorously hedged (or over-hedged) in his position on China.

As for Rudd's prospects now (and mine) the elections are scheduled for September 14 and Rudd's return has lifted our stocks in the polls so we now stand at 49 per cent to 51 per cent for the conservative coalition and Rudd's personal popularity is 51 per cent to Tony Abbott's 34 per cent. He has personal peculiarities as a leader – of which I think you are aware – which we expect to see demonstrated once again.

I did vote for him in the party room because the defeat we were staring at under Julia Gillard would have been so catastrophic the party might have been crippled for all time, especially given the structural decline of social democracy.

All my best to Nancy and we trust the birthday celebrations were as buoyant as they deserve to be.

Bob Carr

SATURDAY, JULY 6, 2013
Sydney

A relief to sleep in one's own bed. Eat one's own food. Go to Pilates at Bondi and stretch for two hours and go to Fitness First and try to reclaim some muscle tone and to have a night at home watching the DVD of the *Martin Chuzzlewit* I saw on the BBC iPlayer so Helena can savour the cunning acting of Paul Scofield, Tom Wilkinson and Philip Franks.

This is what I'd been doing ...

After Indonesia, to Brunei for a cluster of meetings around the East Asia Summit. In such gatherings I always remind myself of Australia's interest in having ten prosperous, resilient societies in the band of ASEAN states to our north, on a trajectory of economic growth and social enhancement. In particular, I like the notion of a zone of prosperity from Assam to Yunan and the notion that every part of this ASEAN world be well disposed to us.

There was the familiar dramatis personae assembled, all members like me of the exclusive but perhaps overrated Foreign Ministers' Club. Pre-eminently John Kerry, who I one hundred per cent approve of because he's shuffling between Oman, Jerusalem and Ramallah on his fifth visit to the Middle East, trying to restart the peace process. 'Two states for two people' as President Obama said. A last effort at achieving this great global good even when the two parties seem to lack the determination to make it work. And when all of us were giving boring, drab set-piece contributions at the table, Kerry spoke with animation about climate change and later, at a Friends of the Lower Mekong meeting, spoke about how America was actually dismantling dams as he warned the Asians about building them. He wears his own personal uniform: a tailored grey or navy suit hanging on his lanky frame (I felt his arms when we embraced for the cameras and they were as lean as mine), a white shirt and the simple elegance of a Hermès tie.

I was chosen out of the twenty-eight foreign ministers to be seated on his left-hand side at the big official dinner where we were all wearing batik shirts in the ASEAN style; His Royal Highness, the Sultan of Brunei, our host, was on his other side. I reminded myself that Kerry had been in the navy in the Vietnam War, a volunteer. He'd sailed with a gunboat on the Mekong and slept on its banks. He'd been his party's unsuccessful candidate for President and now sits in the ranks of the also-ran but as one of the honourable also-rans, who would have been better for the country than the man who defeated him.

Yet it was hard to engage. After all, you've got to be cautious when you are in his position. I praised him for his efforts at Middle East peace and said, 'It's got to work, hasn't it? There's no Plan B.' But he replied, 'Oh, I've got a Plan B!' Yes? Interesting. I tried to engage him further. 'Provisional state and interim boundaries? Or if the Palestinians don't get a state, you urge they have citizenship rights in a greater Israel?' His response: 'Oh look, the dancers are coming on!'

Well, who can blame him?

During a break in the conference, I wandered into the casual lunch, joining the rest of the club. There was Sergey Lavrov, the Russian Foreign Minister, somewhat non-communicative right now, sitting with no charm or energy to waste on the likes of me. Foreign Minister Luvsanvandan Bold of Mongolia gives me a big welcome grin, as does Dipu Moni, the Bangladeshi Foreign Minister who took over from me as Chair of the Commonwealth Ministerial Action Group; and there is the hyperactive, beaming Turkish Foreign Minister Professor Ahmet Davutoğlu, with his reputation for plans and theories and diplomatic architecture. Of course, all the ASEAN Foreign Ministers were there, who I've gotten to know: Anifah from Malaysia, whose wife Helena gets on with so well, who gets down to Australia for the Melbourne Cup and other race events; I joke with him about his elections and our approaching ones. There's Shanmugam, the intelligent, astute Indian lawyer from Singapore, with whom I've had those conversations about the character of Chinese power; there's the charming, American-accented Albert del Rosario, a seventy-something Filipino businessman who did a five-year stint for his country in Washington before emerging as a hard-line, anti-China Foreign

Minister. There's the short, round-cheeked U Wunna Maung Lwin, the Foreign Minister of Myanmar, who I think regards me and Australia as special friends; and the small, sharp-faced Vietnamese Foreign Minister, Pham Binh Minh, with the floppy Beatles-style haircut – a son of a Foreign Minister – who allows me to press some human-rights cases without taking objection or storming out, a diplomatic professional.

I enter the conference on the first day with Wang Yi, the relatively new Chinese Foreign Minister who I spent time with in Beijing in April and who has been mounting a charm offensive in Asia to restore China's image after the assertiveness phase. He held my hand as we walked along the carpet – communicating trusted intimacy, I guess – and made reference to the Rudd return. 'You know, in China … some people love him … and some people … hate him!' I told him I understood that to be true.

Meetings were somewhat ritualistic, all the work having been done by officials beforehand and the communiqués and press statements barely worth taking note of. But ASEAN unity was restored after the debacle of April when they couldn't even agree on a minimal statement on the South China Sea.

In the second day at Brunei, my stomach kept emptying: my first travel sickness. The dehydration felled me. I could not stand up. It must have been a mussel eaten at the Sicilian restaurant on the first night. I had said to our High Commissioner as we had left the hotel, 'Local delicacies? Chilli crab?' And he looked at me blankly. Brunei is not known for its food. But I didn't expect it to give me my first experience of stomach convulsions since the Bekaa Valley in Lebanon in 1997. Whenever I tried to walk around the room, I felt faint. We flew out, overnight in Manila. By the time we got to Korea for the 2+2, I was living on a new level of exhaustion. But Stephen Smith and I got through those meetings with our counterparts and a meeting with the diminutive, charming President Park. 'Our relationship with her is a success for Australian diplomacy,' said Smith as we left the Blue House. 'She came to Australia under a special visitors program a few years ago. I saw her. Kevin made a fuss of her. When I came up here she was a mere backbencher but the embassy insisted on taking me to see her. She sees us as friends.' The old story: you keep in touch with people when they are in disgrace or opposition or obscurity and they remember you fondly.

Flew home overnight, a mere one hour's sleep while my mind roamed over the controversy I'd unleashed by telling the truth about the people-smuggling rackets and the fake asylum-seeker claims that were pouring through our status-determination process. It's irritating that the monolithic political orthodoxy rears up against you when you dare to assert the home truths: 1) it's now all people-smuggling, 2) it's now growing as a share of the migrant intake.

As soon as I was home and showered I had to go off and speak at the funeral of Paddy Bastic, a 96-year-old veteran branch member and embodiment of Irish-Catholic, inner-city-born, Labor supporter. I put notes together in the pew and even approximated this quote from Proust: 'People do not die for us immediately ... they continue to occupy our thoughts in the same way as when they were alive. It is as though they were travelling abroad.' I said, 'That's Paddy, too vivid to be lost to us. It's as if he were away on one of his trips, meeting relatives in Ireland or New Jersey.'

Then I went to the University of New South Wales and gave a speech on China at their Confucius Institute. By this time, sleep deprived, my voice was shrinking. Went to the physio for my shoulder; met our UN Ambassador, Gary Quinlan; got a haircut at Double Bay; met a Macedonian delegation and went off to a Macedonian dinner at Lilyfield where I gave the third speech of the day, entirely unruffled by a clumsy Liberal backbencher who tried to get the crowd motivated against me by working up some chauvinism. Unfortunately for him, the chairman of the gathering was thinking strategically. Sure, he was disappointed in me not meeting their demands for us dropping the official term 'Former Yugoslav Republic of Macedonia'. But he spoke diplomatically in thanking me for my attendance.

Going into One Bligh – the new ministerial office – today I had bumped into Tony Abbott, walking out in casual clothes, his suit over his shoulder … and, interestingly, he had chosen to stop and talk. He was pensive. He said, 'Well, you never know where it goes in this business. The people seem to like Kevin.' He said he thought Julia was impressive but the people obviously didn't. He said you never can tell what will happen. I said I'd been an opposition leader myself and watched John Fahey replace Greiner and score a great hit with the public. But I had agreed that you never can tell where this business takes you. I told Abbott if he won he'd have to take drastic action on people-smuggling or the numbers would keep rising and crowd out our regular immigration program. 'If you choose to do something tough with the tribunals or go to a referendum to see that courts are stopped overruling executive government on status determination, I'll back you.' He had said he didn't think limiting judicial oversight was even possible under our system. I told him again to think about a referendum because we'd lost control of our borders.

MONDAY, JULY 8, 2013
Sydney to Singapore

Last night, my first conversation with the Prime Minister, on the phone. Told him my contribution would be: (1) ethnic campaigning; (2) fundraising. Told him he should let his mind play on what we could do post-election, like work on the agenda of middle or pivotal powers (he said he had ideas on that and I said that was good because I had none, nor did South Korea or Turkey; and Indonesia seemed resistant to the notion anyway). Said I agreed with what he had told Gary Quinlan about the subject we sponsor in 'our month' in the Security Council presidency, September.

Gillard had wanted something with a gender theme, women in peace-building. But Rudd grasps this is worthy but not relevant to the Security Council's mission, which is security. I settled the route by which he would get to see proposed ambassadorial appointments.

He asked my view on an election date. 'You've actually been through the madness of federal campaigns,' I said. 'But I would think … what with the surge … earlier.' He said he hadn't made up his mind.

My op-ed on people-smuggling appeared in all News Limited papers on Sunday. I made the following points: (1) just about all the boats are coming from people-smuggling; (2) the numbers are spiking – at 3000 a month they represent twenty per cent of the migrant intake (a point nobody has made before); and (3) they appear to be increasingly economic migrants. Peter Crawford said this is the most serious assault on our sovereignty since the war. James said you can at least say we've witnessed a serious compromise of territorial integrity.

My political antennae twitching, I rang Tony Burke from the airport this morning to say don't stop at pledging that people who burn their passports will be put at the end of the queue (his weekend announcements running with my op-ed); say they'll be knocked out of the queue altogether. He said he'd thought of that and is discussing it. It's what the opposition is urging; we should just adopt it. And I suggested any asylum seekers who attempt to blackmail us into taking them with threats of suicide should be denied asylum forthwith.

Five more boats this weekend. People smugglers running our immigration program for us, determined to saddle us with an underclass.

I will be in Singapore and Myanmar till Friday night, with the extra authority that comes with representing a government now ahead in the polls. My old mate Peter Crawford says his Unitarian Church congregation had gone from being reluctantly pro-Abbott to enthusiastically pro-Rudd. 'He'll crush Abbott. Look, he's a baby face ... a motor mouth ... with a full head of hair ... and a will to power.'

As my little encounter with the Opposition Leader confirmed, Abbott is sounding pensive.

WEDNESDAY, JULY 10, 2013
Singapore

Delicious that Liberals are staring at polls that put us 50:50 and Rudd ahead as preferred Prime Minister. Their snouts were poised, but the trough, with its flavoursome offerings, has been withdrawn. My default expectation is that I'll be in the job after the election.

Continuity is the thing. This has been the third time since December I've dropped off in Singapore and sat down for a curry with Foreign Minister Shanmugam, this time at breakfast in a tiny South Indian café. Fine flavours; astute choice by him. I told him about the disaster Australia faces with people-smuggling. He, a lawyer, recognised straight away the trouble has been served up by our courts, which have taken it on themselves to render it impossible to send anyone back.

We talked about our common view of the US and China. In my view we and Singapore are moving to something of a strategic partnership. We talked Indonesia – he's a pessimist. Also met the Deputy Prime Minister. Gave the Fullerton Lecture on Australia and Asia, did local and Australian media.

Up at 4.30 am and now bouncing through cloud on a chartered jet, above the Gulf of Tonkin, in the direction of Myanmar.

SATURDAY, JULY 13, 2013
Sydney

In the Orwellian, entirely artificial capital Nay Pyi Taw I saw everyone: three ministers, President Thein Sein, Aung San Suu Kyi and Shwe Mann, the Speaker of the Parliament. I made sure I raised the Rohingya with each of them. Then in our chartered plane – Australian pilots – we flew the half-hour journey from Nay Pyi Taw to Yangon in the afternoon.

Had to find time in Yangon for a teleconference at the embassy for a meeting of the National Security Committee. When Rudd, in the chair, heard I was in Myanmar, he joked that all of China would be following our meeting.

'No, it's all safe,' I said. 'I *am* in Yangon. But they've got me in a sort of shipping container inside our embassy.' This morning I'd met the Yangon Heritage Trust, a group of Australian businesspeople, representatives of the Rohingya and representatives of their enemies, the Burmese from Arakan. But I had cancelled two other meetings to be hooked into this cabinet committee devoted to the issue of our times – the blow-out in people-smuggling – and to Rudd's hydrogen-bomb response.

He's going to take those Iranian queue jumpers and resettle them; not just process them, but *resettle* them in Papua New Guinea. In a masterstroke he's got Peter O'Neill signed up for it and will shoot up there on Sunday to seal it.

It was my first cabinet meeting with him in the chair.

He was efficient, not wordy. He had electric authenticity, that of an authentic prime minister, as opposed to Gillard's mechanised efficiency, which I had found admirable enough in its own way.

And – this is the key – he was saying what I have been yearning to hear about the asylum-seeker racket that is undermining the country's sovereignty. He knows it's got to be solved. He said what's happening now will give rise to xenophobia in Australia. He asked officials what the monthly intake now was. Around 3000 was the answer. He asked for views on what the annual intake could become. One adviser said 50,000, which is around a quarter of the annual migrant intake – a quarter! Delivered by smugglers! Outsourced to them!

I leapt in to say that this was the biggest threat to Australian territorial integrity since WWII and that I agreed with the Prime Minister's view that we needed to quickly demonstrate that people-smuggling would be defeated – that they couldn't get settled in Australia. I said we needed a decisive intervention and this minute proposing settlement in Papua New Guinea was it. I was the one minister to back him on principle. He emphasised the matter had to be kept secret until the weekend when he was flying to Papua New Guinea to talk to O'Neill. Full marks to him, by the way, for pushing it this far with the PNG government.

SUNDAY, JULY 14, 2013
Sydney

Cabinet meeting. This time I reached it through video conference from the new Bligh Street parliamentary offices. Jason Clare, Tony Burke and Anthony Albanese were with me in Sydney; Prime Minister Rudd in Brisbane; other ministers and officials in Canberra; Ministers Penny Wong from Adelaide and Alan Griffin from Melbourne. We were bedding down the Prime Minister's package for Papua New Guinea. His command of it – this sounds slavish – was extremely thorough. He wrapped it up with this summary at the end: we've got to talk about 'adjusting policy on border security … to take account of changing external circumstances'.

He went on to say that we were doing this not just because it was 'a political pain in the bum' (which was clearly the Gillard motivation) but because it's 'about Australia's territorial integrity' (which is the view I've formed – and which I'm glad to hear he's formed as well). He's off to Papua New Guinea tomorrow.

SUNDAY, JULY 21, 2013
Sydney

'Believe me,' says Crawford. 'Rudd is beating Abbott hands down.' We'll win seats in Queensland; could even pick up Macquarie (held by the Libs by 1.3 per cent), the seat that stretches over the Blue Mountains, in this state.

On Friday I entertained a boardroom lunch raising funds for

Susan Templeman, our candidate in Macquarie. She's energetic, presentable. I then met members of the LGBTI community to talk about rights as a goal in foreign policy, met a delegation of Vietnamese leaders on human rights in Vietnam, and met two representatives of the Australian Tamil Congress to assure them that our relations with Sri Lanka did not prevent us focusing on reconciliation and human rights. And it doesn't.

The Prime Minister roars over the political landscape. I, and other ministers, follow in his wake. On Monday Marty was in town to be conferred an honorary degree from Macquarie University in company with me (I generally consider honorary degrees – this is my second – a nuisance: the conferral wastes half a day and requires a speech and you can't include them in your CV because they mean nothing). That evening we took Marty and his wife, Sranya, to dinner at Kingsleys steakhouse on the Woolloomooloo Finger Wharf, interrupted by agitated text messages from Kevin about Marty's comments in a Sky interview that seemed to relax official Indonesian attitudes towards Abbott's policy of sending back the boats:

> Bob, I gather Marty was not helpful with his public
> statements on Opposition policy today, a bob each way. What
> happened? Also when are we getting the Iranian decision?
> Tks KR

I replied that Marty meant he was prepared to talk to the opposition about *what they meant* by 'turn back' but hadn't softened on their policy. Kevin responded:

> That is diplomatic nonsense Bob and Marty knows it. It is
> clear as day. Please lean hard on timing re Iran and cattle
> quotes announcement. Tks KR

I replied:

> With him now. Very good on Iran. Not even matter of weeks.
> Paper with Min of Justice, process well underway ...

That is, the Indonesians withdrawing Visas on Arrival for Iranians.

As we left the restaurant I suggested Marty join me for the Channel 10 news interview that was to take place at the end of the wharf. He was willing to appear before the cameras and this gave him a chance to restate opposition to Abbott's policy of unilateral action on the boats. I later texted Rudd:

> I put spin on what he was saying but like you I think he
> (backed by the President) is using deliberately soft language
> so as not to be seen as taking sides. I will ring morning radio
> now to say they (the Indonesians) still won't accept Abbott's
> policy. Bob

And I did but I woke up the next morning to turn on the phone and get a text from a clearly irritated Prime Minister:

> See today's Australian headline. I rest my case. Can you
> please call. KR

Nothing to do, though. The Indonesian President and Foreign Minister are not going to join our pre-election campaign. From their perspective, why should they? But two days later Indonesia delivered its decision on visas for Iranians. They will no longer grant Iranian visitors a Visa on Arrival ($25 when they hit Jakarta Airport). Exactly what we want. It's what I asked them to do on my visit a few weeks ago without any real expectations that they would see an advantage in it. This is good. Mission accomplished.

It's a blow to the people-smuggling rackets.

This week at long meetings of the National Security Committee of cabinet we tick off our new policy, big and bold. It says simply – as I dictate this I appreciate again the boldness of it – if asylum seekers come here and win a claim, they'll be resettled in Papua New Guinea. Not in Australia. None in Australia. All in PNG. It is a masterstroke by Rudd and it emerged from Rudd's administration, the PMO. I had not seen the minute till last week and assume it was an idea he had brought with him, although it may have been gestating somewhere under Gillard.

I watched Rudd in the National Security Committee with admiration. Rather scary. He was ferocious, ploughing down the agenda, knowledgeable about every item, totally in charge of his public servants and ministers. He announced it on Friday, with PNG Prime Minister Peter O'Neill.

On Saturday the headlines proclaimed:

Rudd moves to banish the boats (*Sydney Morning Herald*)

Rudd's hardline PNG solution (*The Australian*)

Hellhole solution: Rudd sends boat people to lawless PNG (*Daily Telegraph*)

I did morning TV today speaking in its defence.

It is exactly what the country needs: a simple declarative statement that if you pay a people smuggler to bring you into Australian waters you will not be processed on Australian soil and not be resettled here, even if you are found to be a refugee. The refugee advocates simply repeat their incantations and mantras as if the numbers were running at a few hundred a year instead of 40,000 to 50,000 (based on latest monthly arrivals) representing over twenty per cent of the country's migrant intake.

On our way home from a Sikh dinner in Castle Hill last night I rang Dastyari. He said he now believed, 'We can win this thing.' He spoke of a plan to endorse Peter Beattie for a Liberal-held seat in northern Brisbane and stated he will be our Minister for Northern Australia. He believed Kevin would go to an election early, depending on the next batch of polling. Meanwhile, Jason Li, a brilliant, young, Chinese-background Australian, was off and running as our candidate in Bennelong with its big Chinese voting bloc. I had discovered him at the 1999 republican convention and introduced him to the party.

A busy day tomorrow with the National Security Committee to consider reforms to refugee-status determination. I am emphatic on this because I have heard of the soft-headedness and special pleading that has corrupted this whole process and given us the highest rate of settlement approvals of any of the countries that receive refugees.

All of a sudden, after sixteen months in the job, I'm back to normal. I sleep. My weight is steady at twelve-and-a-half stone. On weekends I sit down and read a book, currently Christopher Clark's *The Sleepwalkers* about the causes and origins of WWI. Yes, really back to normal. I can even listen to classical music (Bellini's *I Puritani*, a Metropolitan Opera production on DVD or Rachmaninoff's Symphony No. 3). I have bought a 16-kilogram kettlebell for my home workouts. I never reach for a sleeping tablet. I fall asleep in a flash, generally before Phillip Adam's program ends at 11 pm and when I wake up during the night I go back to sleep.

SUNDAY, JULY 28, 2013
Hong Kong

Last week in the Solomons again the chief satisfaction of this privileged job: getting to know the leadership of 'the nations of the world', and of interesting nations at that. None, I say again, more of a discovery than this country: about 550,000 people, almost 1000 islands, the big ones strung out in two lines facing one another across 'the slot', a passageway of water, 'a small island developing state' – according to one categorisation – or 'a failed state' until rescued from civil disorder by ten years of effort invested by Australia and the others in the South Pacific, donating defence personnel and police to maintain order. It was to mark the tenth anniversary of the Regional Assistance Mission to the Solomon Islands (RAMSI) that I came, flying up in a VIP with Melissa Parke and David Feeney, talking with them on the three-hour Sydney to Honiara flight about the remarkable Labor resurgence under Rudd.

After our bilateral the Prime Minister of the Solomons, Gordon Darcy Lilo, said the right thing at our joint media conference. There was no immediate plan, he said, but sometime in the future the Solomons could sign up to regional resettlement as PNG had done. Since asylum seekers and Kevin's bold plan are still the *only* question for Australian media and we had Simon Benson of the *Daily Telegraph* travelling with us, this was very helpful. Certainly anything to the contrary would have stung like a malaria-laden mosquito bite as the boats keep arriving unhelpfully at Christmas Island, and News Limited – in a frenzy of Rupert-driven hatred of Rudd and Labor – keeps raging that the PNG arrangement is doomed.

I work out in the gym of the Heritage Park Hotel and recruit their only staffer as a personal trainer. He puts me through a routine. He tells me he lives with his in-laws in Honiara – the capital, where we are – but the house is packed with family. 'There is not much privacy,' he reflects. And there in a flash one is reminded of the compromises of poverty, family members packed tight. A married couple having a room of their own is something that happens only when a nation reaches middle-income status.

Flew home Wednesday night and to Hong Kong the next morning, watching *Haute Cuisine*, a movie about a woman recruited as Mitterrand's chef, steeped in rural French cuisine, and to her life in his private kitchen in the Élysée Palace. Also read the July–August *Foreign Affairs* magazine and worked at memorising, slowly, the first of *Hamlet*'s seven soliloquies. 'O, that this too too solid flesh …' My aim is to know everything about this play.

In 1972 when I was National President of Young Labor observing the US presidential election campaign, I watched Senator Chuck Percy, the liberal Republican – a breed now extinct – speak to a university audience in Chicago. I was struck by how he stood and spoke about foreign policy without notes, looking his audience in the eye. It's what I now do here at the Australian Chamber of Commerce lunch and the Asia Society in Hong Kong. I speak about the economic revolution of the last thirty or forty years in East Asia and the social gains – like women's attendance at university or longer life spans or a reduction in maternal deaths – that accompany higher income levels. I speak about how Australia can help the Chinese secure energy and resource and food security. I explain our attachment to the US based on Australia's sense of our strategic security. I talk about territorial conflicts in the South China Sea and how we don't take sides but favour a settlement based on suspending disputes over sovereignty and agreeing to jointly develop resources.

From the Solomons to China.

'The nations of the world.'

SUNDAY, AUGUST 4, 2013
China to Sydney

Nothing has prepared me for the striking modernity of these Chinese cities. Chengdu, the capital of Sichuan, western China, I had expected to find poor and struggling; Chongqing (we reached it by train) I had expected to find grimy and polluted. But, as I said to Helena, they are not that far behind Singapore, these cities with their towers, parks and shopping malls. In my formal sessions with mayors and party secretaries I was able to praise the good planning and design and pedestrian amenity, with universal tree planting in the streets. I super-praised historic-building protection … in order to nudge them to do more.

Then we flew to Fujian, where Helena's grandmother and grandfather had originated, and we made a lightning tour of three coastal cities, Fuzhou, Quanzhou and Xiamen. H loved it, though her Hokkien – her grandmother's dialect – is different from most versions we encounter. Quanzhou's history is a case study in the overlap of cultures, like the civilisation of the Moors in Andalusia, but exemplifying the core Chinese virtue: harmony. During the Yuan and Ming dynasties, for roughly 370 years, it was a thriving port bursting with merchants and missionaries. As a result, the museum now displays decorative stonework from old churches no longer standing, showing angels with Chinese characteristics and hints of Nestorian and Armenian cultures; the remains of Hindu temples; and rich material from Islamic buildings. Indeed, one of the oldest mosques in China, built in 1009, still functions and I greeted the imam. Quanzhou is described as the start of the Maritime Silk Road. What a port it must have been, what a dizzying mix of peoples and cultures, what a place for a traveller from Persia or the Caucasus in which to disembark and explore.

Further south, Xiamen was a treaty port, one of the five that

China was forced to open to the world after its defeat in the first Opium War that ended with the Treaty of Nanjing 1842. Our visit was no more than one overnight stay and less than twenty-four hours. But we did have lunch in a hotel overlooking a formidable harbour and Gulangyu Island, which has buildings from the nineteenth century – churches and consulates, it being the centre for Western activity.

This trip was to be a happy sojourn, generating pre-election publicity in the Chinese press back in Australia, promoting Aussie businesses, building on the April Beijing visit and giving me another study of China before our defeat. I was interrupted by calls from the Prime Minister and his adviser, and my former chief of staff, Bruce Hawker, agitated about the increasingly bitter Murdoch press campaign against us. Col Allan, former editor of the *Daily Telegraph* and now editor of the *New York Post* was back from New York whipping up the editors into a fury against Labor. They wanted me to check out things with him. As a result, I made a call to Col, friendly enough but it confirmed that he had no reason to be back in Australia but to fling a fury of propaganda at us. When the Prime Minister received this news, back came a message: return to Australia immediately.

I reconnected with Bruce and talked him through things calmly. I assured him I'd give him a Murdoch-newspaper strategy within days but I wouldn't come back early to do it.

Returned overnight on Friday and, without any sleep, went into the office on Saturday morning and dictated the following statement for Rudd to consider using if he wants to take head-on the ferocious News campaign:

Murdoch and the Federal Elections

It's clear the News Limited or Murdoch papers have committed themselves to a campaign of unprecedented intensity against the Rudd Labor Government.

The Prime Minister should refer to this head-on. The party should respond to the most outrageous bias seen in a lifetime …

Here is a rough and ready first draft of what the Prime Minister might say at an appropriate time in the campaign:

I wish to speak about a matter that has to do with the fairness of these elections.

It is about media coverage …

This deliberate top-level decision at News Limited – for that's what I believe it to be – is a distortion of the Australian democratic process and the Australian values of fair play …

This is not a political leader griping about bad coverage.

It is about a fair go for Australians so they can hear both sides, and be able to make up their own minds …

I am releasing today a batch of examples of front-page beat-ups, stories without substance and completely distorted coverage of important political issues …

But we'll fight back in the spirit of cheerful Australian defiance, without personal rancour.

Accordingly, from today, my party will issue a day-to-day rebuttal of the Murdoch-owned media and publish it on a website to be called 'A Fair Go – You Decide'.

My deputy Anthony Albanese or another minister will be up each day and provide the rebuttal to the latest bias.

It will be a big job.

We are not dealing here simply with traditional press bias. The Australian Labor Party has lived with that for more than a century. We are dealing with a motivated campaign to control the electoral process ...

No other Australian Government has been so upfront with the people about the challenges we face as a nation in the years ahead.

No other Australian Prime Minister has chosen to announce the necessary tough measures before an impending election.

I have taken this course because I trust and honour the intelligence of an informed electorate.

All the more essential, therefore, that we should respond urgently to the deliberate misinformation from one section of the media.

Later

A quiet Sunday recovering from China. I did a walk around Maroubra and then read *Heaven Cracks, Earth Shakes*, a book by James Palmer on the death of Mao and the Tangshan earthquake. I lay in the backyard in the sun, tried to soak up some Vitamin D after all those hours in air-conditioned hotels and on planes leaching my stock of antioxidants. Helena cooked some crab ravioli and we came into town so I could do some work in the office. Then I went down to the gym. While I was warming up on the cross-trainer I saw the Prime Minister appear on TV announcing a September 7 election.

How will we go?

We are 50:50 in Sydney marginals. What we could do to lift the vote any further I just don't know, after a financial statement in which we increased the tax on cigarettes and the elimination of concessions on leased motor vehicles. Nasty budgetary measures hurting ordinary folk: this is counterintuitive when your marginal seats are balanced on a knife-edge. Sam Dastyari, who's privy to the party polling, says our chances of winning may be one in three; earlier he had told me, 'I might be drinking the Kool-Aid but I think we can win this thing.'

I guess our chances have faded, are fading.

Rudd said something in the media conference about me possibly representing Australia at the G20 in St Petersburg in the last week of the campaign. I should be wildly excited about this but I can only think of the acute jetlag and the stuffy formalities and of missing out on my friends at the Pacific Island Forum meeting in the Marshall Islands at the same time.

It would be sweet to have some more time in the job but every part of our life fades behind us like an illusion, until we can barely believe we did those things and lived that way. In the end, I suppose, little matters and nothing matters very much.

THURSDAY, AUGUST 8, 2013
Sydney

I have been around politics for a long time, a seasoned politician – a description that would have thrilled me as a youngster if a clairvoyant had told me that was what I would become, when I was infatuated with the idea of being a career politician.

This morning the party had me hit Wyong on the Central Coast to campaign for thirty-something hospital pharmacist Emma McBride, candidate for the seat of Dobell. I had campaigned for her father in the State election of 1991 and then, very happily, the by-election that followed a court challenge to the close result, in 1992. This was twenty years back. Here I was, in a dusty rented shop about to become her campaign headquarters, telling her – Grant's daughter – how to sell herself to the locals. All campaigns start this way: in a dusty rented shop.

And today at 7.30 am I was on the steps of Lakemba mosque, celebrating the end of Ramadan, with a mainly Lebanese congregation. I'm here determined to shake a thousand hands. They all know me. It's like greeting old friends. They all know my position on Palestine.

Here, in front of the mosque, when it was time for the politicians to speak from the top of the steps, Treasurer Chris Bowen made some commitment to support their retirement or nursing-home venture. Joe Hockey told them he had a Palestinian heritage and would be the first Arabic-background minister. All matter-of-fact. My turn came. I walked up to the microphone without notes and told them that I'd been coming here every year since 1988 when I had showed up as a new Leader of the Opposition. Instant connection. Loud applause. I told them I'd keep turning up, whatever happens. Loud applause. I told them that we supported the rights of the Palestinians and believed in a Palestinian state 'in the context of a Middle Eastern peace' and, later, 'with security guarantees for Israel' (the important qualifiers). Then I told them we opposed Israeli settlements on Arab land and held to the position that *all* settlements were illegal. Loud applause. And then I repeated: I was proud to have been here every year since 1988 and I would keep coming whatever happened on September 7. Loud applause.

That's all. Look them in the eye. Fling the words out in an energised voice. Make connection. Personalise. I know this community, I know this crowd; it's confidence that lends resonance. Fling the ideas out like an athlete throwing a discus; don't mumble apologetically. In the end, psychology shapes the message – do you like your audience, like your story, like yourself in the role? Sometimes the medium *is* the message.

You *want* to be a politician? And you deliver in banalities in a dull monotone? Or shrink before a crowd? Miss opportunities to fire an audience with your ideas? It's a profession. It's a craft. Learn it.

Love it.

SATURDAY, AUGUST 10, 2013
Sydney

I bowl over several speeches, a 'nightcap' speech on the presidency of Franklin Roosevelt to the Australian American Leadership Dialogue, a speech on security in Asia to the same Dialogue and, representing Rudd, I share a platform with Tony Abbott. This was at the Australian American Leadership Dialogue's gala dinner in the cavernous Eveleigh Railway Workshops, now baptised

Carriageworks, which as Premier I had conserved as a performance venue. I told the crowd of perhaps 500 that our alliance with the US was not the only international personality Australia had. I said that in Southeast Asia – I was thinking of my exchanges in Kuala Lumpur or Bangkok or Jakarta – Australia's alliance with the US is seen as redundant and puzzling (actually I did not put it as candidly as that, but it is the case). We're seen in the Pacific as a good friend and partner and our US alliance is irrelevant there. We have engagement with Africa in which context we're seen as different and fresher than America or Europe. The alliance is not the only garb we wear in the world, I told them. And yet ... I went on to quote how I once explained to a Chinese minister that our support for a treaty alliance with America runs deeps for historic reasons: small population over a large continent, the 1942 fall of Singapore, a deep desire to be linked with a dominant maritime power etc. So much for Australia's long-term *interest*. But I also spoke about common values and how impressed I was by the President's defence of freedom of expression to the UN in September last year.

I was happy with this. The best I could do anyway. The audience would have to accept it, whether it leaves them happy or not.

During the evening, Colin Rubenstein of the Melbourne-based Israel lobby came up to me with his wife and said, 'You've been getting around a lot ... lost your balance a bit at the Lakemba Mosque ...' The rudeness was characteristic, the arrogant tone commonplace; the ire at me repeating the government's views on illegality of Israeli settlements was inevitable. I said, 'It has always been our view that those settlements are illegal – all of them. And it's the view of the rest of the world apart from America, which uses the word "illegitimate". And it was repeated by me and William Hague in our communiqué in Perth in January.'

Abbott cruises, buoyed up by polling and media support. We were pleasant.

SUNDAY, AUGUST 11, 2013
Sydney to Melbourne to Sydney

A sour note creeps into the election. Kevin was unconvincing at a media conference responding to an *Australian Financial Review* story suggesting the Coalition was prepared to examine an increase in the GST. His eyes avoided the camera. He lamely played with a jar of Vegemite. He didn't sound as if he believed the threat he was making. A bit of Keating or Carr assertiveness was surely mandated. Juggle a loaf of bread, a bottle of milk and a jar of Vegemite. Declare boldly that the bad budgeting on the other side made a GST increase inevitable. Look the camera and the public in the eye while you do it. I said to Helena, 'You either play this card and run hard with it or you don't touch it.' A bad poll (us slipping back to forty-eight per cent) on the front page of the Fairfax papers on Friday completed the image that despite the recruitment of Peter Beattie, we're going backwards. And the hammering from the Murdoch tabloids is relentless, manic, cruel.

Today we caught a lunch at the Museum of Sydney Café with Beazley, who's out here for the Australian American Leadership Dialogue. He thinks Kevin's personality holds everything back. Graeme rings in search of good lines to feed to Rudd. Rudd's now rehearsing with Faulkner for his debate tonight at the National Press Club with Abbott.

Beazley tells me that the US administration has high hopes on Iran. If the sanctions coalition can hold for another eighteen months they think the new President is capable of selling a deal to the Supreme Leader. I am sceptical. 'This is the same mob who told us the Russians were going to support a Geneva II agreement on Syria?' I asked. Kim replies, 'Well, you asked me what they think and this is what they think.' He rocks with the hearty Beazley laugh.

I then asked him about the Middle East peace process. He said there's a view that while the Israelis want to force the Palestinians into two enclaves, they really know this will condemn them to endless fighting. Some Americans think that Syria's so bad it will push both Israel and Palestine to a settlement. Americans believe there is an opportunity in the next six months and the fact that Martin Indyk, a realist and a pessimist, has been recruited for the talks as US special envoy and is optimistic suggests the possibility of some movement. Again, I am sceptical. But Beazley says the mood of optimism about this is 'infectious … miracles do happen. There is a stock of saints in the Catholic Church to prove it and they've all been through verification.' More big-bellied Beazley laughter.

Well, I think again of how our American friends had such a mistaken line – even I sensed it was mistaken – on the readiness of the Russians to move on Syria.

On the US budget, Beazley says a catastrophe is still possible. A catastrophe instead of more muddling through. And Barry Jackson, formerly Speaker John Boehner's chief of staff, told me on Friday during the Dialogue that he was deeply depressed by the uncompromising stand of hard-line Republicans and an aloof President when it comes to getting a compromise.

I tease Kim that if he'd stayed in the House of Representatives he'd have become Prime Minister. He agrees but says the Rudd forces made him leave. They were threatening to wipe out Beazley supporters Swan and Smith if he didn't go.

A sunny day in Sydney.

I leave the Beazleys and Helena at the Museum of Sydney Café and head to the airport to fly to Melbourne to do a dinner in support of the Islamic Museum of Australia. Fortunately, I get to fly back tonight for that sanest thing in the world: a night in one's own bed.

MONDAY AUGUST 12, 2013
Sydney

Tonight a respite from the campaign. An evening devoted to archaeology and ancient civilisations, focusing on religious tolerance in the cultures of Asia Minor, or modern Turkey. With H, a three-professor, one-ambassador private dinner, marking the visit to Sydney, as a guest of Alexander Cambitoglou, Professor Emeritus of Archaeology at Sydney University, of Professor Angelos Chaniotis, from the Institute of Advanced Study at Princeton. Theme of the evening – the overlap of cultures, with Ambassador Ross Burns speaking about the Taurus Mountains, the historical medieval border between the Graeco-Roman and Muslim worlds; Chianiotis about the Meander Valley, where Greeks, Muslims and Jews lived side by side for hundreds of years; and Vrasidas Karalis, Professor of Modern Greek and Byzantine Studies at Sydney University about the Digenes Akrites epic, the Taurus Mountains ballads on a Twyborn Border Lord, which describes a world where the Graeco-Romans and the Muslims lived together and fough occasionally. No hatred, but gallantry and respect for each other. An enlightening four hours, with a lesson for today.

THURSDAY, AUGUST 15, 2013
Sydney to Launceston to Sydney

My instincts are to keep my head down. This is a sour campaign for us. Abbott is 'sleepwalking' to his win. Rudd appears a tone-deaf campaigner who relies on notes, seems to expect to lose. Surely, though, he can hold the primary vote at thirty-five per cent where it was lodged in the last poll. Surely.

I fly to Launceston to campaign for Geoff Lyons in Bass, doing interviews from home and at the airport on the killing of Muslim Brotherhood demonstrators in Egypt. Here the task is to vigorously condemn the slaughter (which the Sunni community in Australia expects, or demands, rightly) and restate the importance of protecting minorities (which the Coptic Christians in Australia expect). I know this landscape. The Grand Mufti told me at Tony Burke's Iftar dinner he had urged Muslims to adhere to democratic practice only to see their government overthrown and leader arrested. Of course the best course would have been a Muslim Brotherhood government continuing to the next elections and being judged by the voters – that is, a democratic evolution and the maturing of the Arab Spring. Not to be, for in the Arab world everything gets worse. Again, as it was said in *Lear*: 'The worst is not/So long as we can say, "This is the worst."'

I perform my duty for the stumbling, wounded party, read cables and Chinese history, and contemplate a life of more bushwalks.

SATURDAY, AUGUST 17, 2013
Sydney

Last night did a fundraiser for John Murphy, the Labor Member for Reid. It was at the Sydney Rowing Club and the food – mixed seafood entrée and a big lamb chop – wasn't repellent. The big tables of building-industry types were paying $1500 a head. I had conversations with a couple with Lebanese backgrounds about Thursday's bomb in South Beirut that has forced us to increase our travel warnings. Two migrants from China who've set up their own businesses made me marvel again at the liberation of talent and energy that the fall of Mao unleashed. These people would have been slaves on collective farms if the system had not reformed. Well, I entertained them with my stump speech – conversational, given sitting down: Australia is a good global citizen … examples of our overseas development assistance like saving the people of Kiribati or training midwives in Cambodia … the opportunities of our China relationship … gossip about America and its politics.

Murphy saw us off at about 9.45 pm. Like everyone, he is puzzled about the failures of the Rudd campaign. There'd been a mad dash by the Prime Minister to the Northern Territory to release a two-page policy based on reduced company taxes for investors. Is this the best that eighteen months of reflection on the backbench could produce? Why hadn't he been beating up a policy with visits to the Northern Territory and roundtables and town-hall forums in Darwin over the last eighteen months instead of travelling the world to deliver unremarkable papers on foreign policy? There is a deathly unanimity in all the polls. One predicts that Peter Beattie will fail to win Forde sixty to forty per cent. Today's newspapers pick up stories of tension between the ALP's Melbourne office and the hurtling Rudd team with its dizzying itinerary changes. He seems happy with the crowd scenes in shopping centres. We've got three weeks of this to go.

I wake up today to get a message from Bruce Hawker that Rudd wants me to go public and insist Abbott disown his candidate for McMahon, who's been revealed by the *Sydney Morning Herald* to have been picked over (but not condemned) by the Police Royal Commission and accused of having an association with Roger Rogerson. But won't media ask why this guy went on to serve as a police officer during my years as Premier? Won't they at least quibble that there were no adverse findings made by the Royal Commission? And won't Abbott slap it down with a reference to the Obeid stench in New South Wales? I point this out. 'Thanks for your help,' says Bruce Hawker sarcastically.

Well, I know how hard running a campaign is and I give it a shot, delivering 2GB a grab and, later in the day, forcing it into a Sky interview that is mainly about Egypt, Lebanon and Schapelle Corby. It just doesn't take off. The story was too small in the Herald to start with and there are too many other things happening in politics. The momentum is all Abbott's way. But they can't criticise me; I did try. All the publicity about Labor's campaign is negative. We are trapped in a nightmare, seeing Rudd's tide ebb and the vote fall – oh my God, this cannot be happening – to where it was under Gillard.

SUNDAY, AUGUST 18, 2013
Sydney

Other ministers and I are asked to turn out.

It's a rally in a pocket-handkerchief-sized park in Parramatta and I watch from the edge of the crowd. There are a few hundred activists summoned by ALP Head Office – in Labor T-shirts, holding placards for local candidates – as Kevin rallies them, or 'revs them up' as Anthony Albanese promised. He hits wrong notes: 'Tony Abbott will tear the country down.' There are shades of Hewson with his rallies in 1993, and the risk that on TV news, everything will sound strident and desperate.

In the biting spring sunshine, behind my aviator sunglasses and under my Panama, I feel a wave of sympathy for Kevin and Thérèse, who is up there by his side, as the tide runs out. He couldn't be banging away harder; and his instincts shown in those recent cabinet meetings were those of a decent Australian Prime Minister in charge of the country. But the pro-Labor surge was illusory and he is watching it fade.

Abbott is sure-footed and who wouldn't be, buoyed up by the daily Murdoch sponsorship? Kevin can't complain, of course; he's a career politician and our breed adheres to Disraeli's dictum: never complain and never explain.

Play the game: you win.

Play the game: you lose.

Play the game.

MONDAY, AUGUST 19, 2013
Sydney to Jakarta

Off to Jakarta for the Special Conference on Irregular Movement of Persons, the Indonesian response to our agitation over people-smuggling. I started the day with an 8 am interview on ABC Radio National with Fran Kelly. Dealt with two issues: the violence in Egypt and the flotilla of protesters headed for Indonesian Papua. 'This activity by a fringe group of Australians offers a cruel hope to the people of the two Indonesian Papuan provinces,' I tell her, talking about the flotilla. It's true, of course: this tiny group holds out the illusion of independence from Indonesia and armed with this false hope a few Papuans will go out and risk their lives, while these online activists who promote their cause sit safely at their computers in Leichhardt. Except for this group that threatens to steer three little boats into Indonesian waters. If they get convicted of an immigration offence or subversion they can't expect Australian diplomats to troop into jail to visit them for the next five or twenty years and to make painful representations on their behalf. That's my position anyway. I'll pull the rug on their consular support.

I'm booked on a 1.45 pm flight so at home I do twenty minutes of intense body weight exercises and then lie in the sun in the backyard to immunise myself against the toxicity of sitting in a fuselage for eight hours breathing fried air. Still, for the flight I've got my iPad with its BBC iPlayer application so I revel in the acting of Alan Bates and Coral Browne in Alan Bennett's short play *An Englishman Abroad*. It's about a meeting in Moscow in 1958 between exiled spy Guy Burgess and touring actress Coral Browne. Must be seeing it for the tenth time. I draft a letter to the playwright:

Dear Mr Bennett,

I don't know whether you know that the BBC has *An Englishman Abroad* on their iPad application and with all the flying I do I've found it the best entertainment I've ever had on a plane. My wife Helena and I saw it years ago in the National Theatre but that of course didn't include many of the delights in this gem of a TV play, such as the close-up of

Bates' fleshy, handsome face as he shifts tone and asks the question he deeply wants answered: 'What do people say about me in England?' Understatement unites his and Ms Browne's precise, masterful acting and understatement is the flavour of your writing.

Later, when Coral Browne asks him why he spied, you have him pause momentarily and say, 'It seemed like the right thing to do.' Here I think you capture the infantile nature of his politics, his Cambridge Marxism. You also capture this political naivety when Ms Browne reminds him of all the shortcomings of 'the comrades' and asks him what he sees in the Soviet Union. He pauses and pronounces, 'The system.' For her part Browne really captured her own character – a curious challenge to play oneself – when she says she's just a silly actress and talks about how readily she fell for his charm. Nice to have him throw out the line, playing the pianola, 'I'll think of a 100 things to ask you when you're gone.'

Damn it! The two of them were so thoroughly excellent and there are so many little touches to lurk in one's memory. Again, let me savour it – you have him say of England, 'Little art, little music ... timid, tactful ... nice.' He longs for the Reform Club and 'the streets of London' and 'sometimes, the English countryside'.

Another observation: how well your play and Schlesinger's production stand up across this gap of years. Finally, juxtaposing the poster portraits of Marx, Engels, Lenin with the words of Jack Buchanan's song was a nice touch:
Who stole my heart away? (picture of Marx)
Who makes me dream all day? (picture of Engels)
Dreams I know can never come true. (picture of Lenin)

With best wishes,
Bob Carr
Foreign Minister

Letter from Alan Bennett

Thursday, September 12, 2013

Dear Mr Carr

Many thanks for your lovely letter and I'm so glad *An Englishman Abroad* stands up after 30 years. We had such a good time doing it – Coral B particularly heroic as she was ill for much of the time and John Schlesinger was always on a pretty short fuse, so that sometimes made it quite tense. I miss Alan Bates so much – he was always laughing and with him it never seemed like work.

It is so good of you to write at such length and great detail. I'll put your letter into my copy of the script!

All good wishes
Alan B

TUESDAY, AUGUST 20, 2013
Jakarta

Arrived here late last night.

With the time difference I got up at 4 am and lay on the floor of my room at the Four Seasons Hotel doing an hour of Pilates while letting the global trivia from BBC and CNN wash over me. I rang H back in Sydney and she said Hockey was struggling on *Q&A* last night over costings. She said that under pressure his mannerisms and verbal tics reminded her of Obeid. Then I went to the gym to do some cardio.

Ambassador Greg Moriarty briefs me that we've got several problems with the Indonesians. First, this dumb flotilla arouses all their paranoia about Australia. I'll deal with that. I'll make it clear the protestors can get no support from us. I think this will make them desist. I tell the Ambassador that at the first press conference I will slam the flotilla and say that if they get into trouble its crew will have no Australian consular support whatsoever. I'm not going to allow some hippies to fracture this relationship.

Then Greg told me the Indonesian foreign ministry thinks that Australia keeps mounting demands for *them* to solve *our* people-smuggling problems. I'll deal with that, too. I think there's a way though. And there's a media story suggesting we read material on them collected by British intelligence at the second G20 in 2009 in London. This comes from the Manning or Snowden leaks. Do we take our strategic partnership with the UK more seriously than with Indonesia? This is the Indonesian response. And who could blame them? I have no advice on whether this is true or, like so much of this stuff, a beat-up. But the appeal of intelligence – for its own sake, without compelling urgency – should never have been allowed to get in the way of our friendship with Indonesia, if in fact it did. Better (again, *if* it happened) to have said to the

Brits, 'No thanks, don't want to see it …we're comfortable with Indonesia whatever stand they take here.'

The pursuit of intelligence of questionable value has got to be *weighed*. Weighed against the harm if the intelligence gathering is exposed.

We've got the half-day conference on irregular immigration, people-smuggling and human trafficking hosted by the Indonesians – efficiently organised by Marty – and a reasonable communiqué already agreed on, and tonight the Ambassador and I have dinner with General Prabowo, one of the several candidates for the presidency next year who I met on my last visit. It was my idea that we build the relationship with him and the other likely contenders.

Not that I will have the time to do anything with it.

Yesterday, August 19, the *Australian Financial Review* ran an interview with the former US Deputy Secretary of State Richard Armitage – he worked under Colin Powell – criticising Australia for appeasing China in our latest Defence White Paper. I know Rich from the Australian American Leadership Dialogue. He's a very decent man who has adopted six children, three of them African-American. And generally a realist on foreign policy. A friend of Australia's and Australians. But on China he's an unabashed hawk. I recall him at a meeting of the Dialogue in 1999 or 2000 – before Bush's administration – declaring that Australia had to choose between the US and China, that there was a high likelihood of a conflict over the Taiwan Straits (!) and if China attempted to take over democratic Taiwan, Australia would be expected to play its part (!). 'What side will you take, Australia?' he was asking. Now, again, Armitage isn't a swivel-eyed neo-con nutcase. In fact, when he returned to politics he opposed the ultra-nationalists Rumsfeld and Cheney, siding with his own boss, Powell. In 2004 when, as Premier, I delivered a speech in Sydney savaging the Bush administration on climate change and Iraq, he was tipped off by the Sydney Consul General and rang me at home the next morning to assure me that there were some good people battling inside the Bush administration to turn things around. 'Don't give up, mate,' he'd said. That is, don't give up on the Americans ... just because of George W.

Here he is, however, deploring that Australia's national-security approach relied on the US maximising cooperation with China and minimising competition. This is very likely drawn from some of my recent speeches; I've said precisely that, have spelt out that Australia's interests lie in a sound bilateral relationship between the US and China. He then talks up 'the possibility of violence' as a result of the Chinese position on the South China Sea and the East China Sea. He told the *Australian Financial Review* that military conflicts in Asia over the next fifteen to thirty years are 'quite likely'.

Well, here we cut to the chase.

I think of Alexander Downer who told me that if you *want* a Cold War with China, you will *get* a Cold War with China. I recall Malcolm Fraser when he called on me early in my time as Foreign Minister telling me that America was capable of fighting a land war in Asia against China, losing it and then retreating from the region. He told me that Bob Menzies had told the Eisenhower administration that Australia would not side with the US against China over Taiwan (although I did not succeed in finding anything to confirm this). I think of Dennis Richardson saying, when we discussed the work in the lead-up to AUSMIN last year, that 'our interests are different from a great power's'.

Then there are the voices from Southeast Asia who use language identical to mine, who all see a good US–China relationship as their dream, a bad US–China relationship as their nightmare. Singapore is in this category. Why would it be remotely in Australia's interest to be nagging America to regard conflict in our region as inevitable? Or insisting the US view China as an emerging competitor or antagonist? Further, why would we do this when both the US and China tell us their relationship is in good working order?

Rich, pal, butt out of the China business.

Reflecting the consensus of people in my department and Gillard's instincts, Australia's got this right. In my short time in the job, and to the extent I can say I've steered things, I've got this one right. Unruffled. Appropriate. Or as right as things can be in the improvised world of international relations.

Of course, I'm still left with the mystery of how those fire-breathing references in the 2009 White Paper got there and whether the theory in the book by Luttwak is correct, namely, that Australia led in organising a resistance to Chinese assertiveness post-2009.

Before I'm out of the job I must talk to Dennis Richardson. And when I am out of a job I must talk to Rudd. Nail down this mystery, for the sake of history.

SATURDAY, AUGUST 24, 2013
Sydney

Flew from Jakarta via Singapore into Brisbane, arriving late on Wednesday night. The next morning I visited Jim Chalmers in the seat of Rankin (Craig Emerson's former seat) and, with the queasy abattoir smell of barbequing sausages wafting around us, I addressed a group of old ALP branch members – sometimes I think all branch members are old – and recent African migrants. I spoke about the links with Africa built up by the Labor government. One seven-foot South Sudanese man asked me about discrimination. He said eggs had been thrown at him. I told him all this had been faced by the Indo-Chinese in the '80s and the Middle Eastern arrivals in the '90s and, like those groups, the recent African arrivals would end up being accepted and celebrated.

Then I went to a Chinese fundraising lunch with Graham Perrett in the seat of Moreton. One walks into crowds at fundraisers rather like Federico Fellini in *Eight and a Half*, the director in a black felt hat with people looming up on each side and then fading:

'We've got big problems with our visas!'

'You need to assure the Muslims ...'

'I can't get any progress on air links with Taiwan ...'

I reply:

'I'll read your submission ...'

'Thanks – we're doing that!'

'Give Graham the details ... let's sit down after the election.'

Interesting, as always, that with a growing Chinese population, Australia's Chinese cuisine remains as bad as it was forty years ago: ceramic lumps of material purporting to be food, lolling arrogantly in laboratory sauces.

Outside I do TV interviews on the allegations of chemical-gas use in Syria and then we drive down to see Beattie in the electorate of Forde (he needs a swing of 1.6 per cent). Given the recent speculation he's not going to win, he and his wife, Heather, are comfortable and relaxed. Fatalistic, I guess. With a flat in New York, why not? We do a publicity event at a local chocolatier for TV and local press. There'll be a negative story in the *Courier Mail*, of course.

I scheduled a one-hour workout at Fitness First in the Brisbane CBD and while in my gym gear the manager lets me do four radio interviews about Syria from his office. It's a part of the job I love, explaining things to big audiences through live radio or on

Lateline. Some of the interviews better than others, only the one with Richard Glover on ABC 702 Sydney was first class. Then I open a Yangon Heritage presentation but take over the running order of events and speak quickly, so that my staffer and I can get an earlier flight, which means I'll be in Maroubra in time for a home-cooked meal.

The next day I campaign on the South Coast in an old court-house at Milton, talking to a group, organised by the lively Labor candidate Neil Reilly, concerned about aid policy – Australia at its best. Then to Year 11 and 12 students at St Joseph's Catholic High School for Stephen Jones, the Member for Throsby. I talk about our foreign policy in terms of anecdotes and stories. Then home to Maroubra where I go to bed to nurse a low-level flu before heading out to Bankstown Sports Club to speak for Jason Clare.

Today – Saturday – Sam Dastyari tells me we'll lose something like twelve seats and we've still got two weeks in which things could get worse. He says Rudd's campaigning very poorly, doesn't take advice and with Hawker seems to inhabit an alternate universe.

I get a call that Rudd has summoned a meeting of the National Security Committee of cabinet to talk about Syria. In this frame of mind, I ponder, what is he planning to do … on Syria? I have to fly to Canberra at 5 pm. Groan. The City of the Dead. I thought I was done with it.

SUNDAY, AUGUST 25, 2013
Sydney

Flying into Canberra on a Saturday or Sunday night and, even worse, arriving at the Mughal mausoleum that poses as the parliament of a democracy – this is dismal, like feeling an episode of melancholia take hold, and I half-resented the Prime Minister for summoning a National Security Committee meeting for six-thirty last night. A *Saturday* night, summoned to parliament! He entered the National Security Committee room somewhat late: slightly red-eyed, pallid and pudgy but, once again, getting the meeting underway, he demonstrates ease and competence as Prime Minister. What's the threshold diplomatic question? What was the evidence of chemical weapons use? Is this *assessment* as opposed to *raw intelligence?* Why would the Assad regime do this when they are winning on the ground and a UN inspection team has just entered? All the surgically precise questions to put. He's seeking a telephone conversation with Obama and has secured one with Hollande. 'You've been in touch with missions?' he asks me. 'Yes,' I said. Which is not strictly true. In fact, not true at all. But I don't see what this would have added; the momentum is carrying us along.

I tell him I'll be speaking with Hague from the UK and Fabius from France.

The only other minister there is Mike Kelly, who's fighting for his seat of Eden-Monaro – with a possibility, he thinks, he could break the pattern of history and hold that 'bellwether' seat even as we slide out of government. As the meeting breaks up and I contemplate sitting in a car for three hours, struggling with a flu-like virus, for the drive back to Sydney, the Prime Minister asks if I could stifle my dislike of Canberra – is it that obvious? – and be at the media conference on Syria in the morning? And so I face what I never thought I'd face again – a night in Canberra, at the Realm Hotel.

Before I go and check in I get a call from Jamie Clements, the new General Secretary of the New South Wales ALP, asking me whether I want to catch up with him. He says he's got a big donor who will be meeting Kevin later in the night, an Australian-Chinese who intends to be generous to the party. I've got nothing else to do so I go over to the Park Hyatt Hotel and join them in the suite. A donation, apparently of $100,000. We chat and then, as planned, the Prime Minister arrives. Sitting on the couch next to me, he seeks permission to talk in Mandarin because our new friend doesn't speak English although his son does. I suggest Kevin tell him about his conversations with President Xi on a free trade agreement. Later I suggest he mention the opening of our Consulate General in Chengdu. Levitated into this space – out of the campaign hubbub – the Prime Minister is briefly inhabiting a placid space, momentarily forgetting that the *Sunday Telegraph* is going to savage him with a front page saying in the middle of the crisis over Syria he darted off to record an ABC cooking show, forgetting stubbornly forlorn polls, forgetting the lousy fortnight that lies ahead.

After the Prime Minister and our Australian–Chinese friend leave I stay on to have a grilled salmon and broccoli on room service while Jamie shares with me the general campaign gloom.

This annoying virus that I picked up either in Indonesia or shaking hands all day in Brisbane on Thursday (without a hand sanitiser in the car – damn! Staff should see this as a requirement) has me sleeping only in patches. But I'm present at Kevin's media conference in the Prime Minister's courtyard at 10 am. Afterwards, he and I sit down in his office. He drinks tea, I hot water. He talks about the sour tone of the election. Sour, largely because of the relentless hammering from the Murdoch press.

He reflects on what a sad country it'll become if Abbott wins, with Murdoch being given the right to buy Channel 10 – the current cross-media laws prevent that happening but Abbott will change them out of gratitude – and ABC funding being hacked and the Fairfax media fading away. He reflects on how few people run the country: the Murdoch media, the heads of Rio and BHP, probably the heads of the big banks, and 'that mob', by which he means the hard-line, Likud-aligned pro-Israel lobby in Melbourne. This follows a reference I had made to Middle East policy. I told him that 'that mob' doesn't belong on the list of who runs Australia, considering how support for their one and only cause had evaporated in the cabinet and the caucus rooms, as shown by last year's controversy over Palestinian status. And evaporated in the community, including in the boardrooms. He talked about ideas of elevating and making public the Murdoch bias in the campaign. I didn't tell him he'd missed that opportunity. I had supplied a script. He hadn't used it at the start of the campaign. It was now too late. 'Let us sit upon the ground and tell sad stories of the deaths of kings.' Kevin's Richard II moment.

Then he's off and I limp back to Sydney on the 11.20 am flight.

A cloudless day. I had planned a bushwalk in the Royal National Park. I was relieved that this crisis meeting in Canberra had stopped it. Hot sun and a bubbling fever don't go well together. Anyway, while I was in Canberra I managed to clean out most odds and ends from my desk and bathroom. I retrieved all the books that I wanted to keep; the rest I've left for the Coalition minister who moves in. Spent the rest of the day in bed and watched the Channel 10 news to see Tony Abbott's policy speech. Slick, damn it. But disgracefully crammed with new public spending, especially the sprawling paid parental-leave scheme.

Abbott doesn't have to promise anything.

MONDAY, AUGUST 26, 2013
Sydney

I'm serious about pinning down the unanswered question in our China policy, going back to 2009 and the White Paper. There was Luttwak's book saying Australia had initiated the regional reaction to China's assertiveness, there was Paul O'Sullivan's comment that Rudd himself had insisted on the inflammatory chapter being planted in the White Paper, there was my conversation with Pezzullo on 'hedging' against China going beyond merely being assertive, and acting aggressively.

Today I had lunch with Pezzullo, these days the CEO of Australian Customs and former Defence Deputy Secretary and adviser to former Foreign Minister Evans. We started on options on Syria. He sees great difficulties in America dealing with the surface-to-air power that the Syrian regime enjoys. But my real purpose was to get him talking on the story of China and us, those 2009 and 2013 Defence White Papers in particular. What had motivated our now-reinstated leader when it came to those somewhat fearful statements about the Chinese in the 2009 document? Is he, in fact, the 'original Cold Warrior on these things'? (I had heard him jocularly refer to himself as this.) Pezzullo thinks that the first White Paper reflected an approach to containment that drew on early Cold War attitudes to the Soviet Union: a statement, in effect, to a large Marxist-Leninist power that we expect you to be around in your present form for some time, we will engage with you comprehensively, but we have apprehension about your political values, and we need to send a message that your rise will need to be balanced, and potentially countered, by the actions of others. This lunch was at the Chophouse across the road from my Sydney office (where I can get well-done grass-fed steak with broccoli). As I left I resolved – especially given my conversation with him yesterday – to go to Kevin himself and tease it out. Which must await the election outcome and my return from Russia.

THURSDAY, AUGUST 29, 2013
Sydney

At Sutherland District Trade Union Club on Monday night I join a big gathering of Labor loyalists, the happy mob who had stood by me during my various State campaigns. I give them value for their money: a wide-ranging speech with a nice defence of what we did for them as a State government – rebuilding Sutherland Hospital, Liverpool Hospital and building the Woronora Bridge and the Bangor Bypass. Hospitals and roads: yes, infrastructure. I tell some funny campaign stories. I give them the stump speech on achievements in foreign policy and overseas development assistance, without notes, with eye contact and, I hope, good humour. And in return they serve up my perfect meal – some succulent grilled barramundi in a bowl of carrots, onions and broccoli. I tell the club president: 'The best meal I've had in a licensed club in memory.'

Like being Premier again.

Then I spent a day and a half campaigning in Perth.

On the Qantas flight across the continent when I got up to go to the toilet I caught a glimpse of me on TV, in the opposite aisle, being interviewed in the recent ABC Whitlam documentary, *Whitlam: the Power and the Passion*. I looked like a gargoyle, a carved stone grotesque in a cornice, from Vézelay Cathedral.

In Perth I sat down with our seven heads of mission from Africa, in town for the Africa Down Under Conference, a mining-industry gathering we sponsor, a useful point of contact between the continent and us. This meeting with Australian ambassadors (Pretoria, Accra, Addis Ababa, Nairobi, Harare, Abuja, Port Louis) is like sinking into a luxurious warm bath: while the campaign rages outside, an hour of the purest tranquillity; while we slide to defeat, with only a week or so left in government, I act the role of minister. And these heads of mission, good public servants, are decent enough to let me indulge myself. A leisurely briefing. 'So … what about Mali?' I ask. Well, it turns out the Sahel used to suffer drought every ten years and it now suffers drought every three. Yes, climate change at work. The extra drought is caused by the heating of the Indian Ocean. As for its politics, Mali now has an elected government. Niger has included its Tuareg minority in its government and it's keeping al-Qaeda out. We talk about the Democratic Republic of the Congo, which rivals Syria as a humanitarian catastrophe, and talk especially about the Rwandan generals engaged in M23, one of the many militia picking the country to pieces.

In Zimbabwe the only hope now lies in moderates asserting themselves in Zanu-PF as the era of 89-year-old Mugabe winds down. We talk about Kenya, where the President and Vice-President are being accused before the International Criminal Court in The Hague of culpability for killings – deaths generated by post-election violence. South Africa will be at the G20 with me; we talk about their priorities. As I depart this meeting and head for the fundraiser with Alannah MacTiernan, Labor candidate for Perth and a former State minister, at Silks Restaurant in the local casino, I feel a momentary ache for the world of cables and global trivia and the opportunity to gently assert an Australian interest – the world that I will lose shortly.

But instead of flying back into Sydney from Perth, I am summoned by the Prime Minister to Canberra. Oh God, I thought I'd never spend a night in a Canberra hotel, never walk again in the Mughal mausoleum. This, for a 7.30 am meeting on Syria. Without a change of shirt, I'm having to face the catastrophe of wearing the same Bulgari tie two days in a row. What a collapse in standards. The end can only be ruin and decay. Canberra *again*! How weary, stale, flat and unprofitable seem to me all the uses of this world.

FRIDAY, AUGUST 30, 2013
Sydney

There's a gap, Mark Latham writes in the *Australian Financial Review*, between Abbott's fire-breathing declaration in May of a budget emergency and his commitment on Sunday to a surplus of a mere one per cent of GDP in ten years' time, four elections off.

Abbott, writes Latham, is determined to create extra middle-class welfare entitlements: a paid parental leave scheme, a policy of 'compo-for-nothing carbon-tax payments', abolition of means-testing of the private health insurance rebate and cheaper medicine for self-funded retirees. He is, argues Latham, 'an old-fashioned state paternalist'.

Here is the underlying challenge of government: how does our political system restrain this remorseless pressure to increase the size of public spending? The conservative side hasn't a clue any more than Labor.

Today I attended an assembly at Tyndale Christian School in Blacktown with Ed Husic, Member for Chifley, just a bit distracted by the fact Tony Abbott had appeared this morning in his electorate. Jeepers, what's the polling telling him? Then to York Street for lunch with half-a-dozen liberal Jews, supporters of the

New Israel Fund. They are irritated by the Melbourne-based Israel lobby. They can live with our position on Palestinian status at the UN but would enter an argument against our position that all settlements are illegal. I told them we need to keep in touch after the election, win or lose. I said social democratic parties were moving away from their romantic attachment to Israeli kibbutzim and Ben-Gurion's values as Israel becomes more religious and chauvinist and the Palestinians on the West Bank have their houses bulldozed.

I suggested, however, there may be a new alliance we could forge with the Jewish community: Labor will oppose the BDS movement (boycott, divestment and sanctions directed at isolating Israel) as we have been doing but, on the other hand, be explicitly opposed to settlements and engage with moderate Palestinians, emphatic on an authentic two-state solution. That is, with a viable, contiguous Palestinian state. Blocking the BDS is vital to Israel because the analogy of apartheid will be pushed strongly by churches and unions around the world if there's no progress on two states.

Then I get in the car and it's off to talk to the Shi'a community at the Al Zahra Mosque in Arncliffe. Their imam is a moderate. We sit down over Lebanese pastry and he talks about the threat of Wahhabi Islam driven out of Saudi Arabia. I outline our record of opposing discrimination against minorities – the Alawite, the Christians and Shi'a in Syria and the Shi'a in Pakistan. I outline our position on the Middle East.

SATURDAY, AUGUST 31, 2013
Sydney

Tonight, Saturday, I fly out to represent Australia at the G20, expecting America to take limited strikes against Syria, probably while I'm in the air.

I wake up and turn on my phone to get hit with a request to go on *AM* and talk about Syria. About ten minutes' notice. *AM* to me is the touchstone, the perfect vehicle, living history. A message to the country's opinion elite. I read my briefing notes in five minutes and go live to enunciate the Australian position on Syria. I say the evidence points 'overwhelmingly' to regime use of chemical weapons. Australia recognises the need for 'an appropriate robust response' to the breach of 'an international norm'. In supporting America I didn't invoke ANZUS or the normal clichés. Instead I spoke about Australia's history of leading work against chemical weapons. I said the vote in the British parliament against their military involvement with Obama is a continuing reaction to the deceit about the Iraq War in 2003. I also said the US was not seeking war. It was not doing things to seek access to oil or strategic advantage. In the absence of UN action it felt obliged 'to enforce a norm' against chemical weapons use. I was proud of these formulations. Easily up to the gold standard of a Gareth Evans at his best.

I rang Beazley in Washington. He said the Secretary of State was only able to quote the support of France and Australia in his overnight statement. So there would be a keen interest in these comments. He would get them to the White House. I told him to pay careful attention, when he gets the transcript, to the way it was pitched: I was accommodating the people who were let down by the WMD deceit of 2002–03. And we had to talk about international norms, not international law.

Today *The Australian* is a carnival of anti-Labor beat-ups and Rudd hate, page after page. One of their polls shows us losing badly in Victoria.

Late in the day I go for a walk around Maroubra before heading for the Commonwealth Parliamentary Offices. At 7 pm there'll be a video-conference cabinet meeting on Syria. While I'm beating a path along Malabar Road I get a phone call from Bruce Hawker. He relays a message from the Prime Minister that I should stay back in Australia so I can be here for the commencement of the airstrikes against Syria. I tell him to go back to the Prime Minister and explain that I'm packed, ready to fly out tonight and I've done media all day on this subject and it's up to him to carry it tomorrow. Indeed, the media would only be interested in the views of the Prime Minister tomorrow, not the views of the Foreign Minister. He says he'll go back to Rudd. He does and the Prime Minister accepts my proposition.

Helena and I leave the house with our bags to drop into the Commonwealth Parliamentary Office. The meeting of the National Security Committee starts with ministers plugged in from around Australia. It is as serious a discussion as I've ever had at cabinet level: what is the legal basis for a military strike in the absence of a Security Council decision? That's the theme. But one week before polling day, with the polls and the media unanimous that we are to be badly routed, the meeting has more than a touch of Admiral Doenitz about it.

At last, I get away. To the airport as Foreign Minister for one last time and the Etihad flight to Abu Dhabi.

Then – with five hours or so of good, natural sleep – I get off the plane to get the message that the American President has said there will be *no* military action until he gets the support of Congress. Whaaat? I've gone public supporting the principle of American military action. Ahead of most of the allies. Will this leave us high and dry? I get Patrick to put out a statement back home saying:

Restraint becomes a great power. As allies of America, we're more comfortable with an ally that shows due judgement than one that attempts to define its greatness by lunging into adventurous wars ... It enhances America's status and enhances our trust in the President's judgement. And again, it's a contrast with the decision on Iraq in 2002–03...

That'll work.

In the first-class lounge I get a quick neck-and-shoulder massage and a fresh vegetable juice. Then it's off, in daylight, on a four-hour flight to Moscow.

To Moscow.

Moscow! Moscow!

What words!

MONDAY, SEPTEMBER 2, 2013
Moscow

Arrived yesterday. The Ambassador, Paul Myler, took us straight to a late lunch in a Georgian restaurant, then on a long walk to clear our heads. Wonderful revelation, for once a win for urban heritage and encouragement for my campaign to save Yangon's old buildings; Moscow is protecting and restoring its historic-building stock – everywhere. Just thrilling to have this confirmed. New building is concentrated in a new city centre; the old Moscow – the city of Gogol, Herzen, Tolstoy, Chekhov – is intact. Happy at this. I slept without a Normison but with nutty dreams that included Bronwyn Bishop as a circus dwarf.

Obama's decision on Syria apparently stunned his staff. He

told them America has a 'war weary public'. Beazley told me Obama would get the sixty votes to bring it on in the Senate. He could lose the house.

TUESDAY, SEPTEMBER 3, 2013
Moscow

A cable from Washington says:

> Australia's stance, previously useful, had now become vital. The strong countries are not a long list. Both Sherman and Medeiros were effusive in their gratitude for statements by Australia's Prime Minister and Foreign Minister.

Paul O'Sullivan's notion of Australia as 'a different kind of ally' (to the US), one always to be counted on, is perhaps being fleshed out here. Except … our friends better not get the notion we will lend even tokenistic military support. Five hundred to 1000 deaths a month in Iraq. The Australian public (the American too, of course) does not look favourably on the prospect of more wars in the Middle East, even if people like Daniel Pipes of Washington's Middle East Forum adhere to the neo-con theology that the capacity and willingness to wage wars in the Middle East is the true test of America's greatness (his article in *The Australian* on August 26 says just this).

The whole neo-con tribe and ultras like Rumsfeld should have been put on trial.

WEDNESDAY, SEPTEMBER 4 –
THURSDAY, SEPTEMBER 5, 2013
Moscow, St Petersburg

In the lead-up to the G20, after a 6 am start to get the train to St Petersburg, I have an exhausted, jetlagged day of meetings. Former Finance Minister Alexei Kudrin resigned from Putin's government over big increases in military spending. We sat down with him in a rooftop restaurant with a view to St Isaac's. He talked about the role of the G20 in developing a package of standards for stock exchanges and financial regulation. Then on Russia, he says Russia has more migrants coming in to work than the USA. He says he cannot see how Italy can service its debt. He says there are various 'risk zones' that still exist around the world and with these long-term risks there can be no credit expansion. Russian growth, now at 3.2 per cent, is being revised downwards. This year it'll be under 1.8 per cent. He says he's seeing populist policies … no structural reform … and no investment growth. The country's headed for low growth. Despite his criticisms he stays close to Putin and may get back into government.

Ambassador Myler then takes us down to meet the LGBTI network in their office at Ligovsky Prospekt. They talk about the impact of two laws: one against propaganda on behalf of sexual diversity and the other banning 'foreign agents' working in Russia. In their routine NGO work they are potentially vulnerable under both prohibitions. Then, dead with jetlag, I meet Sharan Burrow, the Australian trade-union official who now leads the International Trade Union Confederation. She talks about the international trends against labour. When talking to Prime Minister Singh of India she'd told him that sixty-eight per cent of jobs in his country had no rules. No, Singh said, the informal sector is actually ninety-two per cent. She claims that President Yudhoyono told her that the days of wealth being driven by low-wage jobs are over. She wants labour's concerns threaded into the G20 discussions, particularly the key argument that if you grow jobs, you deliver growth. Jobs drive growth, not the other way around.

And so the G20 starts.

On Thursday at 4 pm, leaping out of my vehicle in St Petersburg, I'm greeted in front of a wall of photographers and journalists by President Putin himself. A quick exchange and I enter the West Entrance of the Konstantinovsky Palace.

I climb the steps into an anteroom to be greeted by Ban Ki-moon. Then I manage brief exchanges with Prime Minister Lee of Singapore, President Park of South Korea and the Sultan of Brunei. I've met each this year. Then President Yudhoyono and President Xi Jinping: I tell them if there's a change of government, I would not expect policies affecting Indonesia and China to change. Then we walk into the meeting room. Momentary panic – maybe as the only Foreign Minister here I might have been overlooked, maybe there will be no seat with 'Australia' in front. But in fact, at the circular table … I'm seated between Putin, who's going to chair the meeting, and Yudhoyono. And seated on the other side of Yudhoyono is America – that is, President Obama.

We take our seats and it falls to Putin to open with remarks about both the need for fiscal consolidation and the need for economic growth. When he finishes he hands to Christine Lagarde, whose autograph I secured on *TIME* magazine back in the Bo'ao Forum. She says 'a better mix of policies is required'. Xi Jinping talks about the need to improve the 'quality' of growth and the need for 'interconnected' growth and tells us that China is integrated with the world economy. Prime Minister Singh tells us the world economy is not in a good shape, Japanese Prime Minister Abe that Abenomics and similar measures are working, Canadian Prime Minister Harper – opening in French and switching to English – that we shouldn't attribute slow growth to fiscal policies in some countries and there are structural reforms needed.

So it goes. I look around. Twenty leaders here. Parliamentary careerists, technocrats, political buccaneers, clan chieftains, dynastic heirs.

As Gore Vidal remarked looking down on the US Senate, 'I cannot feel humble.' Interested, curious, of course. Just not humble.

Back to the contributions.

Herman Van Rompuy from the European Council says that its policies have restored stability in the Eurozone and the existential threat is gone. The Prime Minister of Italy says the G20 needs a strong growth narrative as opposed to a narrative about surviving crisis but that we've got to avoid a jobless recovery. Then comes the longest intervention of this session – that from President Kirchner of Argentina, who produces an old-fashioned bit of stump oratory attacking ratings agencies for their treatment of Argentina. 'And we pay off our debt!' She speaks as if she's addressing a Peronist rally in the barrios. Hints here of her trademark nationalism and protectionism. I've been briefed Argentina's contribution to the G20 will be 'meagre' and Kirchner will 'avoid any commitments to structural reform or extension of the "standstill" on trade protectionism'.

Drawing a refreshing contrast, Prime Minister Lee of Singapore talks about the challenges of new technology such as artificial intelligence and new industries. He says we must not penalise countries with lean public sectors (this, I thought, the most original contribution so far). He refers to old dogmas, like the dogma that laissez-faire means prosperity and the dogma that safety nets mean security. He says these have got to give way: they don't work. President Obama says we can't be satisfied with where we are and talks about the need for structural reforms. For the US that means paying attention to technical education and confusion in the tax code.

I'm not scheduled to speak in this section. Jetlagged and starving (it's now 8.30 pm) I listen to the Brazilian President, Dilma Rousseff. She was elevated to succeed President Lula for whom she had worked as chief of staff and Energy Minister. I wonder what the kitchens have prepared for dinner at the nearby Peterhof and keep thinking of the 1939 song 'Watercolor of Brazil' which never fails to lift my spirits:

Braz…illll.

Braz…illll.

Slightly delirious, I indulge a fantasy of the world leaders moving from behind these tables, linking one another in a conga line and led by Putin – with Obama clutching his hips and being held on to, in turn, by Kirchner or Rousseff – doing a round of the room.

Bra…zillll.

Bra…zillll.

How disrespectful. But there's little to inspire respect in the contributions I had just heard. Having privatised three big enterprises and fought excessive union claims and struggled with State budgets I didn't feel that any here – amiable democrats though many of them are – could teach me much. A rousing performance of samba might have swept things along better – certainly more than another speech seeking to balance fiscal stimulus and structural reform; growth and jobs and fiscal consolidation. We all struggle with these contradictions.

I think of Kissinger's caution at Bohemian Grove that governments can't demand sacrifices from their peoples. Italy confirms that governments can cut budgets but the electorate can then elect a different government that has pledged to reverse the cuts.

As I'm looking at these twenty nations I also think every one of them has trouble selling reform to its own community. We're fighting an election in Australia where both sides are committing to expand the public sector. And there are no slashing economic reformers here. Think of India, think of the US and the division between Congress and President over budget. Germany and France, and my conversation yesterday with former Finance

Minister Kudrin. Yet the communiqué– already agreed on – has a commitment to structural reform as its centrepiece. Unrealisable, especially in the form of courageous coordinated action like the commitment to stimulus and avoiding recession that justified the G20 in the first place.

This G20's a summit in need of leadership and a concrete agenda.

Again, I think about the challenge of making our existing international architecture work better, rather than adding to it. And it'll be a challenge when it's Australia's responsibility to make this G20 function in a serious way. This meeting is a gathering of leaders looking for a task.

Again, I look around the table. It's fronted by glittering career-ists. Nothing wrong with that. Building a career in public service is no bad thing. Christine Lagarde is managing director of the International Monetary Fund; she's got a quasi-divine status in this sitting. But the status was won by political slog, and was not that hard. She was a member of a centre-right political party and served as Trade Minister; and then as Finance Minister. In essence, she was a career politician (as far as I'm concerned, a noble title) who rose through the ranks of the French UMP, a small outfit with a membership of 300,000, and was elevated into the IMF after Dominique Strauss-Kahn was set up with rape charges in New York in 2011. The job was always going to go to a European and a French Finance Minister is sitting pretty.

Rousseff was endorsed by her predecessor and Kirchner took the presidency from her husband. As for Obama, whose steward-ship of foreign policy I wholeheartedly endorse, for him … what? Just the instincts of a Chicago politician – again, nothing ignoble in that – who saw an opening and went for it. His Democratic opponents for the 1996 primary election to the Illinois State Senate fell out of the race and in his 2004 Senate bid his Republican challenger withdrew after the release of child-custody records.

Credit where it's due. Deification not required.

It's not that hard to get here, to this table. A bit of application, a bit of luck, some patience. Every election that's ever been held, someone loses. But someone wins. There's always a vacancy and it's got to be filled. With competence you can keep on rising. None of this warrants deference.

On one occasion my advisers and I were being bustled through the VIP section of Singapore Airport and I saw two blue-collar staff – may have been cleaners, may have worked with ground transport – bundle themselves out of the way of this VVIP party. For a split second I saw the dark eyes of one of the staffers – an Indian, maybe a migrant worker from the subcontinent – flash with trepidation and deference. I wished there had been a way to get a message to him. It would read: no one in this little delegation being escorted to their first-class seats deserves your deference. The Australian Foreign Minister in his navy-blue tailored suit and his Hermès tie – he grew up in a fibro house on a sandhill where bare feet wore out old lino and fried eggs on fried bread would pass as Sunday-night dinner. The Minister for Foreign Affairs of the Commonwealth of Australia is like all his ilk: making it up as he goes along, improvising and thinking out loud and hoping it all hangs together.

Just like the other representatives of the twenty biggest economies around this table, just like the heads of international organisations like the IMF and the European Union.

In these settings we've got to be able to find space for the sentiment of the American radical Eugene V. Debs in 1918 being convicted for opposing the war (I came across it in a new biography of Woodrow Wilson the *Sydney Morning Herald* has asked me to review and which I'm carrying in my luggage):

[W]hile there is a lower class, I am in it, and while there is
a criminal element, I am of it, and while there is a soul in
prison, I am not free.

We get bused to the Peterhof Grand Palace, 'the Russian Versailles', for dinner. I stride in with Prime Minister Lee and tell him I liked his comment that countries with lean public sectors should not be penalised even as we strive for fiscal stimulus. We chuckle about the Argentine intervention. He tells a joke that I recognise about Eva Peron.

Obama has insisted on bringing the issue of Syria to the G20 table. One might ask why. The world knows he is not carrying his own Congress. The world knows his proposition to punish Syria is opposed by a majority of the American people. The British parliament has just rebuffed its own Prime Minister on the same question. But he's bringing it here and it becomes the subject of our discussion at dinner. And this fits into a picture of American vulnerability. We all overlook that the crisis on North Korea has come and gone without nuclear disarmament being enforced. On Iran, America is required to live in hope. It has beaten a retreat from all the indifferent effects of the Iraq adventure and glumly accepts that Afghanistan – which looked retrievable even at that Brussels conference I attended in April – is going to be disastrous, sad at least. The US, broke, economising and war-weary, can only get its way through alliances and through persuasion.

We sit down without officials at a big roundtable and Ban Ki-moon is called to outline the history of UN inspections to date; then Erdogan of Turkey sails in with a vigorous response supporting action as quickly as possible, which I count as support for a punishing US strike. Obama summarises the US position. He says candidly that he's struggled to find solutions for this problem without dragging the US into a war in the Middle East. He said Americans don't want war, his supporters don't want it even more than other Americans, but there's a need for what he calls 'a limited, proportionate action that sends a message'. He speaks of high confidence that chemical weapons were used and that the Syrian government was responsible. He says a violation of international law must have consequences. 'My overwhelming preference would be to deal with this multilaterally through a UNSC resolution.' And just as candidly he admits that he has a lot of work to do at home. But, this is the guts of it:

> But I believe that if we, as the international community
> and especially the G20, find ourselves paralysed then
> this international norm will unravel and with it other
> international norms and people will look back with regret
> that it had been inconvenient to deal with this issue at this
> time. And it will force us to tougher decisions down the line.
> And people ask what's in it for al-Assad. Let me remind them
> this is the person who, in the face of civil protest, arrested
> and killed enough people that he started a civil war. Is this
> a regime capable of miscalculation? I think the evidence on
> that is clear. I hope we can all work together. I am committed
> to a political solution. But if we can't take a limited
> proportional action sending a message that we won't stand by
> then this will be a blot on all our legacies.

Then there are contributions from the others. But there is not much new to be said about Syria. The only test is whether the participants are prepared to support the US President in his bid to punish Syria without a Chapter VII resolution from the Security Council. Hollande, Harper and Cameron say things that represent support for what Obama is seeking. At 11.22 pm it comes to Germany, and Chancellor Merkel makes a somewhat rambling intervention. She says, unhelpfully, that this has been a failure of international organisations and we can't turn a blind eye to chemical weapons but, on the bottom line, she is simply urging we exchange intelligence. She says it is a matter of violation of international law, not a matter of regime change. Her bottom-line position seems only to be, 'We need to use our contacts to persuade all actors to take part in discussions.'

Prime Minister Letta of Italy is just as disappointing to the US. He refers to the letter from Pope Francis to President Putin calling for restraint. 'This is a big factor for me domestically,' he says. Effectively, he is saying, 'We must insist that we need to find a way to sanction any intervention ... if everyone is convinced it was Assad then we need UNSC sanction.' And then Rousseff of Brazil, Singh of India, Yudhoyono of Indonesia and Zuma of South Africa all made their contributions. They all defer to the notion of a UN mandate. They say no to Obama.

Kirchner of Argentina again speaks longer than anyone else. She diverts, to say she's opposed to *any* intervention in the Middle East. Everyone was mistaken on Egypt, she says. At this point, Merkel, Cameron and Park look distinctly restless.

President Xi says it's not appropriate to discuss this at the G20. The UNSC is the most 'authoritative and credible body in the world; no other body is more legitimate and perfect. Any action in Syria should abide by the UN charter.' Hard to get more definitive than that.

This goes on while dinner is served, course by delicious course. Out of exhaustion I veer towards eating everything but notice the steely resolve of President Obama, Leader of the Free World and Leader of the Slim People of America: anything with sugar, carbs or fat in it he pushed to one side. On the other hand, he may have done what I would have liked to, that is, eaten an entirely healthy meal before heading here.

I scribbled a note to Obama telling him that Australia supports him. He nodded curtly and said he appreciated it. Thus, in the dying days of my time as Aussie Foreign Minister, I fulfil a traditional function of my ilk. And I think of those various admonitions in the last eighteen months that have touched on our alliance relationship with the Yanks. I think of Paul O'Sullivan's challenge that we should aspire to be 'a different kind of ally', one that America can count on through thick and thin – as they can at this instance. Of Nicholas Moore saying, 'Australians will always prefer American values.' And yet of Dennis Richardson's cautionary warning in the lead-up to the AUSMIN talks, that 'our interests are different from a great power's'. And of my own contempt for the record of the neo-cons and ultra-conservatives who produced Iraq and (I now think) Afghanistan. Even of the brutal summation of Malcolm Fraser in his conversation with me early in my time as Foreign Minister that America loses wars. Hence the implication: we've got to be careful with them. And yet the pulling power – the charm – of US values at their best, of liberal internationalism.

In the middle of the last set of contributions, after Rousseff and before Yudhonoyo, I make my contribution. Here's what the notes record:

> We are a strong supporter of action. Our intelligence has looked
> at the raw material and agreed that this attack originated with
> the Assad regime with the highest likelihood. It is inconceivable
> that the opposition would act against an area they held
> especially as they did not have the capacity to deliver an attack
> of such magnitude. We acknowledge Obama's restraint. But an
> international norm has been astonishingly violated. We need
> to mobilise all our friends, all our contacts, to progress Geneva
> II. But while we work to ceasefire and political settlement, can
> we at least agree that doctors and nurses should not be targeted,
> that hospitals should not be used as bases, that medical convoys
> should be able to move between crews and between sides.
> Everyone on the ground should at least be able to enter a
> functional hospital and get treatment.

And then it's Putin's turn. He's made himself the last speaker. It's a brilliant intervention and tough, defiant. He declares that

Russia does not protect Assad. He says video materials do not prove anything. He says chemical weapons that had been detected in Aleppo were 'makeshift', implying that those ones came from the opposition, not from the government. We should get belligerent parties to Geneva II. He offers to get Assad.

Gazing at him, from his other side, President Kirchner looks enthralled. She bats her eyelids. I recall my briefing notes said she was 'flirtatious'. If my wild notion of a big samba dance to the tune 'Brazil' had taken off she would have grabbed the Russian President by the hand and had him on the dance floor before any other celebrants.

Putin goes on, declaring actions outside the UNSC are illegitimate and that they 'cause chaos'. And then he concludes with two very cunning debating points. He quotes what an unnamed US leader said on one occasion about the prospect of another intervention in the Middle East. He's barely into it when I recognise the words as being those of Obama himself, campaigning for the US Senate and making a bid for the anti-war vote: 'I am against this hasty war …' Then President Putin suggests we might listen to the Pope and he quotes the letter from the Holy Father about the need to avoid force. Bang! Cop that!

A tough intervention and at about 1 am we adjourn and all of us stagger out into the summer night and car transport to our villas.

Bob Carr

FRIDAY, SEPTEMBER 6, 2013
St Petersburg

In 1953 America overthrew an elected government in Iran, a classic CIA coup. The US then supported the authoritarian regime of the Shah for a quarter of a century, torture chambers and all. In 1981 it supported Iraq's war of aggression against the country. More recently, it secured a two-year freeze on uranium enrichment from the Iranian government as a trust-building measure then appeared to threaten regime change by talking up 'colour revolution' like the one in Georgia, a clear provocation to Tehran.

It brands Iran part of an axis of evil, ignores the help it has provided in beating the Taliban in Afghanistan. Then America in 2011 opted to remove Gaddafi even though he gave up his nuclear weapons. Again, what message of consistency does this send to Tehran?

Akbar Ganji covers this terrain in the September–October edition of *Foreign Affairs*. You read it and think, yes – from Tehran's perspective – America's a stumbling giant, inept and unsubtle in diplomacy, inconsistent in policy. Anatol Lieven wrote in the *International Herald Tribune* on the need for Iranian and Russian participation with the US in laying the diplomatic basis for an eventual settlement in Syria. It was headed 'Attack Syria, talk to Iran'.

Talk to Iran.

The charm of America at its liberal internationalist best cannot blind us to the Great Republic's capacity to get things gloriously wrong.

SATURDAY, SEPTEMBER 7, 2013
St Petersburg

Woke up around 3 am, here in the villa, thinking of polling day at home, the posters and how-to-votes, the flurries and last-minute panics; the period after lunch when the flow of voters dwindles; the candidates suddenly arriving – local celebrities for a day, their pictures everywhere – to greet their volunteers; this whole sacramental exercise in democracy always in baking sunshine, at least in my imagination; and this, the only election since 1963 where I haven't worked on a booth or toured them (although 2010 was difficult, my attendance was shame-faced and fleeting). It felt weird to be out of the country. Pulled my airline sleep mask on and fell back into a sleep till around 8 am.

In beautiful summery weather – not a cloud, hot in the sunlight – Helena, the Ambassador, my two staff, James Larsen and Patrick Low, and I drove to the Piskaryovskoye Memorial Cemetery. Arrived at 10.30 am. There are mass graves here, half a million citizens of Leningrad buried. Think on that: half a million. A siege that lasted 900 days; a city bombed daily. The daily ration was a single lump of bread and the people swelled up with malnutrition and died; epidemics sweeping through the city claimed more. I think of Kissinger's observation on the Russians when we were at Bohemian Grove: 'The greatest quality of their people is endurance.' I was accompanied by a big, uniformed Russian army officer and a stout, classically Russian lady, her blonde hair in a bun. With them I followed the four wreath-bearing, goose-stepping soldiers along the path between the grassed-over mounds – half a million buried beneath them. As I stood before the memorial I thought how trivial my own position, to be part of an Australian government to be voted out of power in an hour, in a peacetime election, with the rest of my life ahead of me. How trivial, compared to this site and what it represents.

A little museum presents the photos. A recording of Shostakovich's Leningrad Symphony plays. There's a photo of an 11-year-old girl, Tanya Savicheva, who saw her grandparents die, then her parents; then, paralysed, survived on a stretcher to be evacuated to a children's home in a village, to die herself in summer 1943.

I thought of my parents or grandparents in Botany and Milsons Point reading of the battle of Leningrad in the Australian papers, mere words on paper to represent this mighty drama.

I told the Russian party that in fifteen minutes the polls would close in Australia. I said that laying a wreath here was very likely my final official duty as the Foreign Minister of my country, here in this cemetery of the Hero City. Our eyes met. I could feel no greater honour, I told them. Their faces suggested they understood this to be true and that I meant it.

Then I went over to greet three Australian journalists. I spoke of my honour in being here for what could be my final official duty. In response to questions, I ruled out standing as leader and pledged to stay in the Senate, sort of.

The first results should come through any minute. What would happen to the grand, battered old party I joined at age fifteen? A wipeout? Or a more manageable defeat?

We had time to fill, before the train to Moscow. We drove to the Smolny Institute, a Tsarist school for girls of the nobility taken over by Lenin in 1917 and later the centre of city government. This is somewhat exotic: it's election night back home and to see out the day I'm touring a Lenin museum site when all my life I opposed Lenin; when, for a time, I defined my Labor Party activism as stopping a Leninist takeover of a social democratic party. That's what I described the commies as – the Leninists.

In this context, this is indeed a strange day. We looked at the bedroom of Lenin and his wife, Nadezhda Krupskaya. As we did, in came the news Matt Thistlethwaite was holding Kingsford Smith. Thank God, the safe Labor seat where I joined the party in 1963 and which I spent a quarter of a century aspiring to represent. Here was Lenin's office, with a view to the Neva; and Patrick tells me Michelle Rowland is fighting off her hapless Liberal opponent in Greenway – delicious triumph – but we were losing three seats in Tasmania. Down a long red-carpeted corridor to the office where Kirov was assassinated in 1934, the murder that initiated the Great Terror; and we get news Jason Clare, Tony Burke and Chris Bowen have got back – in other words, in western Sydney the party lives; a defeat, but not that existential one that had haunted us.

I talk to Jamie Clements, the New South Wales ALP General Secretary, who says my efforts campaigning in ethnic communities had paid off in three seats. The truth is we were losing *marginal* seats in western Sydney but not *heartland* ones. This is what Rudd promised if we took him back, and credit should be paid. It's a setback for those opportunist Liberal candidates I had seen appearing at Islamic functions and who I had sent slinking off when I spoke about our respective party records.

We leave the Smolny. It's a stunningly beautiful day and I look back on the classic façade, yellow walls and white columns in the Russian style; a bronze statue of a gesticulating Lenin. The gardens of the city spill over with flowers. We speed past the Tauride Palace where the First Duma convened in 1906, beyond the spire of the cathedral in the Peter and Paul Fortress where the Romanov emperors are entombed and where Dostoevsky was imprisoned. The sky is perfect. Too hot for a jacket.

Our party has a snack in a café on the Moika Canal, around the corner from the Hermitage. We see three Aussie tourists as we go in. They know the result. We get photographed with them. I ring Richard Marles and send congratulatory text messages to Bowen, Burke, Clare, Thistlethwaite. And I hear Rudd got back; another defeat for his local Liberal opponent, another of those big-spending smart-alec Libs buoyed up by News Limited. At the end of lunch we gather on the pavement, next to the canal. I farewell and thank James Larsen, the professional diplomat who was my principal adviser, and Patrick Low, my media adviser. They fly back to Australia tonight. We keep Patrick for another month but James must be released back into the department to be elevated next year as Ambassador to Turkey. My offices have already been cleared out, photos, personal files, books in packing cases.

So, in the middle of Leninist memorabilia and the grand buildings of Peter the Great, we've just experienced a majesty superior to the claims of tsarist autocracy and proletarian dictatorship: a free election where the people get to determine their rulers and, in doing so, replace one set of politicians with another. And the Australian people have been doing it without resorting to revolution or coup or putsch since they first got to pick the Lower House in a colonial legislature in 1856. Part of the miracle is that the losers accept a defeat, clear out their offices and go off to plan for another day. The magisterial workings of a parliamentary democracy, and a confirmation that every political career in a democracy ends with packing cases, not the gallows or a detention camp.

That evening, with the Ambassador, but no longer with the standing of Foreign Minister, H and I do what Chekhov's *Three Sisters* never pulled off – we board the train to Moscow, in our case, the 7.25 pm from Moskovsky Station. We and our four big bags have been helped on the train by embassy staff, concentrated here in St Petersburg to support our representation at the G20. When we disembark in Moscow we'll have our own arrangements: effectively I'm no longer Minister.

I look out the window at little dachas, meandering rivers, fields and fir forests. This is the journey made by my friends from Russian short stories, plays and novels. This is the view they gazed at. I had persuaded Helena, sitting opposite me, to read Bulgakov's *The Master and Margarita*, the novel all Russians seem to know, set in Moscow in 1937. She's starting it now.

The eighteen months are up, ending as it was always going to end, although I would never have guessed in St Petersburg.

Had this been history? Seeing President Thein Sein's face lighten when I told him Australia was lifting, not just suspending, sanctions on Myanmar because we believed in him and his reform program. Meeting Syrian refugees in Zaatari camp in Jordan and resolving there should be a pact to get medicine into the country they had escaped.

And there is the US–China question.

On the steps of the Konstantinovsky Palace after our G20 gathering, Wang Yi, the Chinese Foreign Minister, had farewelled me, knowing I was about to be replaced and pronounced: 'You ... are ... a ... friend.' The same day I receive a farewell text from Jeff Bleich, the US Ambassador in Canberra, thanking me for my support of the President's position on Syrian chemical weapons. I thought of Kurt Campbell's observation that when it comes to the America and China relationship, Australia can simply be 'the most desired girl on the block'. We *don't* have to choose: I had tilted things a little, helped a correction or two, settled on a formulation and it seemed to be holding and to reflect a national interest. And I thought of Kurt Campbell's other observation: that Australian foreign policy is a successful one (securing Australian interests and reflecting Australian values) although it always seems to make Australians uncomfortable to hear this said. Since April there's been no complaint from Australian business or Hugh White or former Prime Ministers Fraser, Hawke and Keating that our China relationship was being sacrificed by our relationship with the US. But I never did get to talk to Kevin about the mysteries of the 2009 White Paper or his 'Cold Warrior' instincts on the Chinese at that time, about hedging versus over-hedging versus containment.

Was it all history? The accommodation of Indonesian sensitivities? The closer alignment of Australian policy with ASEAN?

Planting the notion of resource-sharing in the contested territory of the South China Sea? The meeting with President Morsi where I pressed the Copts? And the patient reaffirmation of ties with old friends, Japan and South Korea?

Last year at a dinner in the apartment of Isi Leibler in Jerusalem I had raised settlements and their role in undermining a two-state solution. A Likud government minister, Dan Meridor, had courteously etched for me the Israeli government position, a humane voice in the Likud. Later, our host Isi Leibler had shown me his collection of Judaica, which occupies another floor of the apartment building – the stories of every aspect of Jewish life. Within months, Meridor would be dropped from his party's ticket for the Israeli elections. I think of the delegation of conservative Christians in my office and the member of the Salvation Army who told me of their tour of Palestine and – houses demolished and farms locked off – the *grace* of the Palestinians. I recall the debate in our government about Palestinian status at the UN, the imperative of giving hope to Palestinians and sending a message to the Israelis about settlements, then advising the Palestinians – after their win – not to overplay their hand.

I think of the nations in the South Pacific, right now wrapping up the Pacific Islands Forum in the Marshall Islands.

Few more vulnerable than tiny Kiribati, the island state – no, the atoll state – out there in the Pacific. I thought of the prospect of rising sea levels taking out its fresh drinking water in twenty years' time and the prospect of over 100,000 people having to evacuate their sand and palm trees as desperate environmental refugees. But I also think of Australia's role as friend, delivering on a commitment to see that their youngsters speak English and have trade qualifications so if they have to leave their fragile island home, they do so as skilled, sought-after migrants.

And Australia can be liked here – warmly, even naïvely.

I think of the villager who stepped forward from the crowd up in Wapenamanda, Papua New Guinea, and said in Enga, 'All you educated people have spoken. I'm an ordinary man and I want to say something. I want to thank Australia. I want to thank Australia for being here to see our local member sworn in. I want to thank Australia for its friendship and support …' In the Solomons we stopped the descent into clan warfare.

That glorious spray of islands – that continent of islands – across the entire southwest Pacific. When, if at all, will I get to visit them again? And how can I, how can Australia, lend a helping hand?

'Yes, the Caribbean nations – all fourteen of us – will vote for Australia,' said Dessima Williams, the Ambassador of Grenada at the United Nations. She said the nations of the Caribbean liked Australia's stance on climate change, on tighter control for small weapons and on the marine environment. I had told them that we supported their bid for a small monument to the transatlantic slave trade. 'We expected no less from Australia,' she said. 'A country with an ethical basis for its policy … as shown by The Apology.'

All the way off, they liked our international character.

I stole Kevin Rudd's words to say at my meetings with African nations, 'We are not Europe, we are not America; we are Australia, and we look across the Indian Ocean to the African world.'

Yes, I had stepped into this narrative, though only briefly.

Outside there were more clusters of derelict dachas, clumps of pine and birch and marshes – country that had been occupied by the Germans when the city was besieged and those mass graves were being slowly filled with the brave, broken bodies of its hero citizens.

Yes, it was history.

It was history. But speeding past, and already fading like an illusion.

ACRONYMS

ACTU	Australian Council of Trade Unions
AIPAC	American Israel Public Affairs Committee
ALP	Australian Labor Party
ANSF	Afghan National Security Forces
ANU	Australian National University
ANZUS	Australia, New Zealand, United States Security Treaty
APEC	Asia–Pacific Economic Cooperation
ASEAN	Association of Southeast Asian Nations
ASIO	Australian Security Intelligence Organisation
ASIS	Australian Secret Intelligence Service
ATT	Arms Trade Treaty
AUKMIN	Australia-United Kingdom Ministerial Consultations
AUSMIN	Australia-United States Ministerial Consultations
AWU	Australian Workers Union
CARICOM	Caribbean Community
CHOGM	Commonwealth Heads of Government Meeting
CMC	Central Military Commission
COAG	Council of Australian Governments
COIN	Counter-insurgency
CSIS	Center for Strategic and International Studies
DFAT	Department of Foreign Affairs and Trade
DLP	Democratic Labour Party
DMZ	Demilitarised Zone
EAS	East Asia Summit
FDR	Franklin Delano Roosevelt
FSA	Free Syrian Army

FTA	Free Trade Agreement
HRC	Human Rights Council
ICAC	Independent Commission Against Corruption
ICC	International Criminal Court
ICRC	International Committee of the Red Cross
ILO	International Labour Organization
IMA	Irregular Maritime Arrival
IMF	International Monetary Fund
IRA	Irish Republican Army
ISAF	International Security Assistance Force
ISI	Inter-Services Intelligence
JFK	John F. Kennedy Airport
KPMG	Klynveld Peat Marwick Goerdeler
LDC	Least Developed Country
LGBTI	Lesbian, Gay, Bisexual, Transgender and Intersex
LLRC	Lessons Learnt and Reconciliation Commission
LSE	London School of Economics
MFA	Ministry of Foreign Affairs
MP	Member of Parliament
MSG	Monosodium glutamate
NAM	Non-Aligned Movement
NATO	North Atlantic Treaty Organization
NBN	National Broadband Network
NGO	Non-Governmental Organisation
NSW	New South Wales
OCHA	Office for the Coordination of Humanitarian Affairs
ONA	Office of National Assessments
PAP	People's Action Party
PLA	People's Liberation Army
PMO	Prime Minister's Office

POW	Prisoner of War
RAMSI	Regional Assistance Mission to Solomon Islands
RSL	Returned and Services League
SBY	Susilo Bambang Yudhoyono
SEAL	Sea, Air and Land
SIDS	Small Island Developing States
SLOC	Sea Lines Of Communication
TAB	Totalisator Agency Board
TGV	Train á Grand Vitesse
TPP	Trans-Pacific Partnership
UAE	United Arab Emirates
UMP	Union pour un Mouvement Populaire (Union for a Popular Movement)
UNESCO	United Nations Educational, Scientific and Cultural Organization
UNHCR	United Nations High Commissioner for Refugees
VOA	Visa on Arrival
WA	Western Australia
WHO	World Health Organization
WMD	Weapons of Mass Destruction

ACKNOWLEDGMENTS

First, my acknowledgment to Elena Collinson, who transcribed and fact-checked and researched and recast and challenged and negotiated. She helped get some scrappy, disordered, on-the-run notes into this relative coherence while retaining the quotidian immediacy and messiness of the diary form and leaving all responsibility for judgment and accuracy with me. She never lost sight of the fact that proceeds will help poor youngsters in developing countries get plastic surgery through Interplast Australia and New Zealand. Elena is generous enough to acknowledge that her reward is the experience itself, a unique addition to her already first-rate education and well-read intelligence.

Acknowledgment is due as well to Phillipa McGuinness, who encouraged me in the task of sharing with the Australian people just what a foreign minister does, and to Jo Butler for her careful editing, dextrously accomplished within a short space of time.

I'd also like to acknowledge the very small number who read the diary and offered responses, especially Lyle Chan, who enjoys a ferocious capacity for detecting the wrong note in quotes and historical references.

Finally, my thanks to the following for permitting me to quote from their material:

Alan Bennett – letter to Bob Carr, September 12, 2013.

Troy Bramston – 'The day Carr won the Mid-East conflict', *The Australian*, November 29, 2012.

Andrew Clennell – 'Barry O'Farrell a mystery man to many – voters don't know who he is', *Daily Telegraph*, September 19, 2012.

Bill Clinton – letter to Bob Carr, June 20, 2012.

David Crowe and Dennis Shanahan – 'Julia Gillard facing rebellion in the ranks over foreign policy and media reform', *The Australian*, November 12, 2012.

Phillip Coorey – 'Backbench revolt forces PM to drop Israel support', *Sydney Morning Herald*, November 28, 2012.

Fairfax Syndication – 'My Sydney' by Bob Carr, *Sydney Morning Herald*, January 2, 2013; 'A loss for the Jewish lobby' by Andrew Clark, *Australian Financial Review*, December 1, 2012.

Global Times, 'Australia needs to learn to take Chinese goals more seriously' by Loong Wong, April 9, 2013.

HarperCollins USA – *Game Change: Obama and the Clintons, McCain and Palin, and the Race of a Lifetime* (2010) by Mark Halperin and John Heilemann; *The Making of the President 1968* (2010) by Theodore White.

Michael Gordon – 'Gillard plans Jakarta talks on boat people', *Sydney Morning Herald*, June 20, 2013.

David Hare – *The Absence of War* (1993), Faber. All rights whatsoever in this play are strictly reserved and application for performance etc., must be made before rehearsal to Casarotto Ramsay & Associates Ltd., 7-12 Noel Street, London W1F 8GQ (<rights@casarotto.co.uk>). No performance may be given unless a licence has been obtained.

Peter Hartcher – 'Humiliating defeat forces Gillard to back down over Palestinian vote', *Sydney Morning Herald*, November 28, 2012; 'China's bullying tactics backfire', *Sydney Morning Herald*, June 25, 2013.

Harvard University Press – *The Rise of China vs The Logic of Strategy* (2012) by Edward Luttwak.

International Creative Management – *All That Is* (2013), by James Salter, Picador.

Paul Keating – 'Asia in the new order: Australia's diminishing sphere of influence', Keith Murdoch Oration, State Library of Victoria, November 14, 2012.

Peter Leahy – 'We must not get too close to the US', *The Australian*, April 12, 2012.

Samantha Maiden – 'How some cannibals, a throne and a hairy pig won over Foreign Minister Bob Carr', *Sunday Herald Sun*, December 9, 2012.

Subhas Menon – letter to Bob Carr, July 31, 2012.

MIT Press – *Lee Kuan Yew: The Grand Master's Insights on China, the United States, and the World* (2013) edited by Graham Allison, Robert D. Blackwill and Ali Wyne.

Paul Monk – 'China's dragon culture obscures lack of strategy', *The Australian*, October 1, 2012.

New York Review of Books – 'How Millions Have Been Dying in the Congo', a review of Jason Stearns's book *Dancing in the Glory of Monsters: The Collapse of the Congo and the Great War of Africa* by Neal Ascherson, April 5, 2012.

Oxford University Press USA – *China Goes Global: The Partial Power* (2013) by David Shambaugh.

Random House USA – 'The Lowboy' in *The Stories of John Cheever* (1978) by John Cheever; *Monsoon: The Indian Ocean and the Future of American Power* (2010) by Robert Kaplan.

Greg Sheridan – 'Carr's co-operation recipe for a calmer sea', *The Australian*, August 23, 2012; 'Carr playing honest broker in Burma', *The Australian*, June 28, 2012.

Singapore Press Holdings – 'To S'pore – for bright ideas and a good curry' by David McMahon, *The Straits Times*, April 17, 2013.

Cameron Stewart – 'We're all friends here', *The Australian*, November 16, 2012.

Laura Tingle – 'Through the hurly-burly to a last hurrah', *Australian Financial Review*, November 30, 2012.

Ariana van der Heyden White – *The Making of the President 1968* (2010) by Theodore White.

Peter van Onselen – 'Diplomat Carr a blocking agent to Rudd comeback', *Sunday Telegraph*, October 20, 2012.

Tony Walker – 'Status quo prolongs the misery', *Australian Financial Review*, November 29, 2012.

Hugh White – *The China Choice* (2013), Black Inc.

The Wylie Agency, Inc. – *Game Change: Obama and the Clintons, McCain and Palin, and the Race of a Lifetime* (2010) by Mark Halperin and John Heilemann

INDEX